CULTURAL HERITAGE LAW AND POLICY

Series Editors

PROFESSOR FRANCESCO FRANCIONI

Professor of International Law and Human Rights and Co-Director of the Academy of European Law at the European University Institute in Florence

PROFESSOR ANA VRDOLJAK

Professor of Law at the University of Technology, Sydney

Enforcing International Cultural Heritage Law

CULTURAL HERITAGE LAW AND POLICY

The aim of this series is to publish significant and original research on and scholarly analysis of all aspects of cultural heritage law through the lens of international law, private international law, and comparative law. The series is wide in scope, traversing disciplines, regions, and viewpoints. Topics given particular prominence are those which, while of interest to academic lawyers, have significant bearing on policymaking and current public discourse on the interaction between art, heritage, and the law.

Enforcing International Cultural Heritage Law

Edited by

FRANCESCO FRANCIONI

JAMES GORDLEY

OXFORD
UNIVERSITY PRESS

OXFORD
UNIVERSITY PRESS

Great Clarendon Street, Oxford, OX2 6DP,
United Kingdom

Oxford University Press is a department of the University of Oxford.
It furthers the University's objective of excellence in research, scholarship,
and education by publishing worldwide. Oxford is a registered trade mark of
Oxford University Press in the UK and in certain other countries

First Edition published in 2013

Impression: 1

British Library Cataloguing in Publication Data
Data available

ISBN 978–0–19–968024–5

Printed and bound in Great Britain by
CPI Group (UK) Ltd, Croydon, CR0 4YY

Contents

List of Contributors ix
Table of Cases xiii
Table of Legislation xvii

Introduction 1

I. THE INTERNATIONAL LEGAL FRAMEWORK

1. **Plurality and Interaction of Legal Orders in the Enforcement of Cultural Heritage Law** 9
   I. Introduction 9
   II. Plurality of Perspectives 10
   III. Plurality and Interaction of Legal Regimes 12
   IV. Plurality and Interplay of Enforcement Mechanisms 17
   V. Interaction between Domestic Adjudication and International Enforcement 20
   VI. Conclusion 20

2. **Enforcement of Restitution of Cultural Heritage through Peace Agreements** 22
   I. Introduction 22
   II. Peace through Reparations 23
   III. Peace through Unity 27
   IV. Peace through Division 31
   V. Conclusion 38

3. **The Role of International and Mixed Criminal Courts in the Enforcement of International Norms Concerning the Protection of Cultural Heritage** 40
   I. Introduction: The Enforcement of Crimes against Cultural Heritage 40

II. Enforcement of International Law on Cultural Heritage in Practice: The Case Law of the International Criminal Tribunal for the Former Yugoslavia 44
III. The Contemporary Significance of Cultural Heritage: Beyond State Property and Exterior Worth 55
IV. Conclusion: Taking a Lesson for the Future from the Balkan Wars 58
V. Postscript 59

4. Illicit Trade in Antiquities: A View 'From the Ground' 65
I. Introduction 65
II. This Way to the Mummy 66
III. Local Impacts at Home in the United States 66
IV. Looting in Conflict Zones 68
V. Proactive Approaches for Site Protection in Conflict Zones 70
VI. The Market for Illicit Antiquities 73
VII. Conclusion 76

II. ENFORCEMENT BY DOMESTIC COURTS

5. Sovereign Immunity and the Enforcement of International Cultural Property Law 79
I. Introduction 79
II. Should Sovereign Immunity from Jurisdiction be Granted in Art-Recovery Suits? 81
III. Immunity of Cultural Property from Execution: An Absolute Rule? 92
IV. Conclusion 108

6. The Enforcement of Foreign Law: Reclaiming One Nation's Cultural Heritage in Another Nation's Courts 110
I. Introduction 110
II. The Enforcement of the Export Laws of One Nation in the Courts of Another 110
III. The Repatriation of Cultural Heritage 119
IV. Conclusion 124

7. **The Enforcement of Underwater Cultural Heritage by Courts** 125
I. Introduction 125
II. Claimants to Rights over Cultural Objects at Sea 126
III. Domestic Courts' Arguments: A Critical Analysis 136
IV. Some Unanswered Questions 144

8. **Enforcement by Domestic Courts: Criminal Law and Forfeiture in the Recovery of Cultural Objects** 150
I. Introduction 150
II. Types of Illegal Conduct in the Movement of Antiquities 152
III. Legal Actions 160
IV. Shifts in Recovery Methods and Deterrent Effect: Unintended Consequences 167

III. ALTERNATIVE METHODS OF ENFORCEMENT

9. **Plurality and Coordination of Dispute Settlement Methods in the Field of Cultural Heritage** 177
I. Introduction 177
II. The Legal Framework for Cultural Heritage Protection 178
III. A Critical Appraisal of the Legal Parameters 183
IV. The Enforcement of Cultural Heritage Law through Dispute Settlement Means 186
V. Critical Appraisal of the Dispute Resolution Methods 194
VI. Disclosing the Judicial's Ongoing Penchant for Culture-Sensitive Rulings 196
VII. International Public Policy and Coordination in Dispute Settlement for the Enforcement of Cultural Heritage Law 203

10. **Social Norms and Illicit Cultural Heritage** 206
I. Introduction 206
II. Antiquities Appearing on the Market Since 1970 are Presumed Illicit 214
III. The Return of Illicitly Excavated Objects 216
IV. The Culture of Antiquities Looting in the American Four Corners Region 222
V. Conclusions 226

11. The Quest for the Masterpiece: Traditional Practices of Collecting in American Museums 228

I. Introduction 228

II. Recently Revised Ethical Standards and Acquisition Policies 230

III. From Ethics to Action: What Else Can Museums Do? 237

12. Enforcing Import Restrictions of China's Cultural Objects: The Sino–US Memorandum of Understanding 240

I. Introduction 240

II. Legal Basis for the MOU 241

III. The Signing of the MOU and Its Main Contents 244

IV. Positive Impact on Protection of Chinese Cultural Heritage by the MOU 247

V. Conclusion 254

Index 257

List of Contributors

Alessandro Chechi is currently a researcher and assistant at the Art-Law Centre in the Law Faculty of the University of Geneva. He is lecturer in international law at the University of Lille, France. He holds law degrees from the University of Siena (JD, 2001), University College London (LLM, 2003), and the European University Institute (PhD, 2011). He is also reporter for Italy on the *International Law in Domestic Courts* – an Oxford University Press project running since 2007.

Derek Fincham is an Assistant Professor at South Texas College of Law. Since 2008 he has served as a trustee of the Association for Research into Crimes Against Art (ARCA). He earned his PhD in law from the University of Aberdeen, Scotland examining the response of the United States and the United Kingdom to the illicit trade in cultural heritage. He also holds a JD from Wake Forest University, and a BA from the University of Kansas.

Holly Flora is Associate Professor of Art History at Tulane University, and formerly an Andrew Mellon Curatorial Fellow at The Frick Collection and Curator at the Museum of Biblical Art in New York. She is the author of *The Devout Belief of the Imagination: the Paris Meditationes Vitae Christi and Female Franciscan Spirituality in Trecento Italy* (Turnhout: Brepols, 2009) as well as numerous articles and exhibition catalogues. She has received fellowships from the American Association of University Women, the Metropolitan Museum of Art, the Scuola Normale Superiore in Pisa, Italy, the International Center of Medieval Art, and the American Academy in Rome.

Francesco Francioni, Juris Dr. (Florence), LL.M (Harvard) is professor of international law and co-director of the Academy of European Law of the European University Institute. He is a member of the Institute de droit international and of the Board of Editors of the European Journal of International Law, as well as general editor of the Italian Yearbook of International Law. He has participated in the negotiations for the main international legal instruments for the protection of cultural property in the past twenty years and served as President of the UNESCO World Heritage Committee in the years 1997–1998.

Patty Gerstenblith is Distinguished Research Professor of Law at DePaul University and director of its Center for Art, Museum and Cultural Heritage Law. She is a Director of the US Committee of the Blue Shield and Co-Chair of the American Bar Association's Art and Cultural Heritage Law Committee. In 2011 President Obama appointed her to chair the Cultural Property Advisory Committee in the US Department of State, to which she had also been appointed by President Clinton. Her most recent work is the third edition of her casebook, *Art, Cultural Heritage and the Law* (Carolina Academic Press, 2012). Gerstenblith received her AB from Bryn Mawr College, PhD in Art History and Anthropology from Harvard University, and JD from Northwestern University.

James Gordley is W. R. Irby Professor of Law at Tulane Law School and Shannon Cecil Turner Professor of Jurisprudence Emeritus at the School of Law of the University of California Berkeley. He is a Fellow of the American Academy of Arts and Sciences, a Corresponding Fellow of the British Academy, and a *membre titulaire* of the International

Society of Comparative Law. His published works include *Foundations of Private Law* (Oxford University Press, 2006), *An Introduction to the Comparative Study of Private Law* (Cambridge University Press, 2006) (with Arthur von Mehren), and *The Philosophical Origins of Modern Contract Doctrine* (Oxford University Press, 1991).

Federico Lenzerini is Professor of International Law and European Union Law at the University of Siena (Italy). He is also Professor at the LLM.Program in Intercultural Human Rights of the St. Thomas University School of Law, Miami (FL), USA. He occasionally provides consultancies to UNESCO and, on several occasions, has been Counsel to the Italian Ministry of Foreign Affairs for international negotiations related to cultural heritage. He is a member of the Committee on 'Cultural Heritage Law' of the International Law Association.

Riccardo Pavoni is Associate Professor of International and European law at the Department of Law of the University of Siena. He is the associate editor of the *Italian Yearbook of International Law* and a member of the editorial board of the *Oxford Reports on International Law in Domestic Courts* (<http://www.oxfordlawreports.com>). He is co-director of the Tulane-Siena Institute for International Law, Cultural Heritage, and the Arts. He has been a visiting professor at various institutions, including at Tulane University School of Law (2010), Charles University in Prague (2008), and the University of Amsterdam (2006). Currently, his main research areas cover international and European environmental law, the law of international immunities, the relationship between international and domestic law, and international cultural heritage law.

Dr Laurie W. Rush has served as the Installation Archaeologist and Cultural Resources Manager, United States Army Installation Management Command, Fort Drum, New York since 1998. Since 2006, she has also been directing the US Department of Defense In Theater Heritage Training Project funded by the Office of the Secretary of Defense.

Patrizia Vigni is Researcher 'Ricercatore' of International Law at the Law Faculty of the University of Siena (Italy) since 2001. She obtained her degree in Law at the University of Siena in 1992 and a Magister Juris at the University of Oxford (UK) in 1996, and completed her doctorate in International Law at the University of Siena in 1998. She is Lecturer of the courses of International Dispute Settlement and Legal Research at the Law Faculty of the University of Siena, and legal advisor to the Italian Ministry of Foreign Affairs with regard to the negotiations concerning the Antarctic Treaty. Her main research fields are the Antarctic Treaty system, the interaction between treaty regimes, State compliance with international treaties on human rights, international dispute settlement, the law of the sea, diplomatic and consular protection, EU citizenship, and the conservation of underwater cultural heritage

Ana Filipa Vrdoljak is Professor of International Law, Faculty of Law, University of Technology, Sydney, and Visiting Professor, Legal Studies Department, Central European University, Budapest. She has previously been Marie Curie Fellow (2006–2008) and Jean Monnet Fellow (2004–2005) at the Law Department, European University Institute, Florence.

Wang Yunxia is a Professor of Legal History and Cultural Heritage Law, and Director of the Institute of Cultural Heritage Law at Renmin University of China. She holds an

LLB degree from East China University of Political Science and Law (1984), and a PhD degree from Renmin University of China (1996). She has previously been a co-researcher on cultural property law at the Kyoto Retzimacan University of Japan (1997) and a visiting scholar on international human rights at Nottingham University in the UK (1999). Her research areas include Oriental Law, Comparative Legal Culture, and Cultural Heritage Law. She recently edited a *Textbook on Cultural Heritage Law* (Commercial Press, 2012) and a thesis collection named *Cultural Heritage Law: Notions, System and Methods* (Renmin University Press, 2012).

Table of Cases

Agudas Chasidei Chabad v. Russian Fed'n, 466 F. Supp. 2d 6 (D.D.C. 2006, per Lamberth CJ), 528 F.3d 934 (D.C. Cir. 2008, per Williams SCJ) 87, 89, 90, 105, 106, 108

Agudas Chasidei Chabad v. Russian Fed'n, 729 F. Supp. 2d 141 (D.D.C. 2010, per Lamberth CJ) 105

Agudas Chasidei Chabad v. Russian Fed'n, 798 F. Supp. 2d 260 (D.D.C. 2011, per Lamberth CJ) 108

Alfred Dunhill of London, Inc. v. Republic of Cuba, 425 U.S. 682 (S. Ct. 1976) 87

Allred v. Biegel, 240 Mo. App. 818 (Ct. App. 1949) 155

Andrew Orkin v. The Swiss Confederation, et al., 2011 U.S. Dist. Lexis 4357 (13 Jan. 2011) . . . 199

Andrew Orkin v. The Swiss Confederation, et al., 770 F. Supp. 2d 612, 2011 U.S. Lexis 24507 (S.D.N.Y. 11 Mar. 2011), *aff'd*, Andrew Orkin v. The Swiss Confederation, et al., 2011 U.S. App. (12 Oct. 2011) 91, 199

Aqua Log, Inc. v. State of Georgia, 594 F.3d 1330 (11th Cir. 2010) 138

Atocha Case, 569 F 2d. 330, 337 (1978) 136

Attorney General of New Zealand v. Ortiz [1982] 3 QB 432, *rev'd*, [1984] A.C. 1, *add'd*, [1983] 2 All E.R. 93 . . . . 111, 112, 113, 120, 195

Autocephalous Greek Orthodox Church in Cyprus v. Willem O.A. Lans (District Court, Rb Rotterdam, 4 Feb. 1999; confirmed in Appeal, Hof Den Haag, 7 Mar. 2002, 99/693) 184

Autocephalous Greek-Orthodox Church of Cyprus & the Republic of Cyprus v. Goldberg & Feldman Fine Arts, Inc., 717 F. Supp. 1374 (S.D. Ind. 1989), *aff'd*, 917 F.2d 278 (7th Cir. 1990) 153, 161, 167, 187, 201, 202, 209

Bakalar v. Vavra, 619 F.3d 136 (2d Cir. 2010) 153

Bakalar v. Vavra, 819 F. Supp. 2d 298 (S.D.N.Y. 2011), *aff'd*, 2012 U.S. App. LEXIS 21042 (2d Cir. 2012) 153, 161

Bennis v. Michigan, 516 U.S. 442, 116 S. Ct. 994, 134 L. Ed. 2d 68 (1996), 167

Beyeler v. Italy, Application No. 33202/96, European Court of Human Rights, Judgment of 5 Jan. 2000 18

Campuzano v. Iran, 281 F. Supp. 2d 258 (D.D.C. 2003) 101

Case No. 002/19-09-2007, Extraordinary Chambers in the Courts of Cambodia, Closing Order against Ieng Sary, Khieu Samphan, Nuon Chea and Ieng Thirith 59

Case Concerning the Temple of Preah Vihear (Cambodia v. Thailand), International Court of Justice, Judgment of 15 June 1962, ICJ Reports, 1962 . . . . 6, 17, 187

Claude Cassirer v. the Kingdom of Spain and the Thyssen-Bornemisza Collection Foundation, 461 F.Supp. 2d 1157 (C.D. Cal. 2006), 580 F.3d 1048 (9th Cir. 2009), 590 F.3d 981 (9th Cir. 2009), 616 F.3d 1019 (9th Cir. 2009), 2010 WL316970 (9th Cir. 12 August 2010) 84, 87, 88, 89, 90, 91, 92, 198

Certain Property (Liechtenstein v. Germany) (Preliminary Objections), International Court of Justice, Judgment of 10 Feb. 2005, ICJ Reports, 2005 . . . . 6, 17, 104, 187

De Csepel v. Republic of Hungary, 808 F. Supp. 2d 113 (D.D.C. 2011, per Huvelle DJ) 84, 85, 87, 88, 89

De Préval v. Adrian Alan Ltd. (1997) (unreported) 202

Demartini c. Williams, Tribunal Correctionnel, 18th Chamber, 6 July 2001 201

Diag Human v. Czech Republic, Case No 72 E 1855/11 z-20 (District Court of Vienna, 21 June 2011) 99

Dole Food Co. v. Patrickson, 538 U.S. 468 (2003) 92

Entscheidungen des Bundeserichtshofs in Zivilsachen, BGH, 22 June 1972, BGHZ 59 No.14, 82 203

Erie R.R. v. Tompkins, 304 U.S. 64 (1938) 115
Federal Republic of Germany v. Autonomous Prefecture of Vojotia, Court of Cassation, 20 May 2011, No. 11163. 92
Ferrini v. Germany, Court of Cassation, 11 Mar. 2004, No. 5044 . . . . 3, 100
Garb v. Republic of Poland, 440 F.3d 579 (2d Cir. 2006, per Cabranes CJ) 92
Case Concerning the Application of the Convention on the Prevention and Punishment of the Crime of Genocide (Bosnia and Herzegovina v. Serbia and Montenegro), International Court of Justice, Judgment of 26 February 2007 (Genocide case) 17, 45, 55
Government of Peru v. Johnson, 720 F. Supp. 810 (C.D. Calif. 1989), *aff'd*, 933 F.2d 1013 (9th Cir. 1991) 119, 161
Government of the Islamic Republic of Iran v. Barakat Galleries Ltd. [2007] EWHC 705 QB, *rev'd*, [2007] EWCA Civ.1374. . . . . 86, 102, 103, 152, 156, 162, 200, 203, 209
Greek Orthodox Patriarchate v. Christies, Inc., 1999 U.S. Dist. LEXIS 13257 (S.D.N.Y. 1999). 153, 167
In re Flamenbaum, 945 N.Y.S.2d 183 (App. Div. 2012) 168
In re Peters, 821 N.Y.S.2d 61 (App. Div. 2006) 153
In re: Islamic Republic of Iran Terrorism Litig., 659 F. Supp. 2d 31 (D.D.C. 2009, per Lamberth CJ) 103
Insurance X v. A.M., ATF 122 III 1, 5 Mar. 1996 202
Italian State v. X & Court of Appeal of the Canton of the City of Basle, 82 I.L.R. 24, Swiss Federal Tribunal, 6 Feb. 1985. . . . . 85, 86
Jeannerette v. Vichy, 693 F.2d 259 (2d Cir. 1982) 110, 111, 112
Jurisdictional Immunities of the State (Germany v. Italy: Greece Intervening), International Court of Justice, Judgment of 3 Feb. 2012 . . . . .80, 90, 92, 93, 100
Kalogeropoulou & Others v. Greece & Germany, Application No. 59021/00, European Court of Human Rights, Decision of 12 Dec. 2002. 93
King of Italy v. Marquis Cosimo de Medici Tornaquinci, (1918) 34 T.L.R. 623 . . . . 112, 113
Kunstsammlungen zu Weimar v. Elicofon, 478 F.2d 231 (1973), 536 F. Supp. 829 (E.D.N.Y. 1981), *aff'd*, 678 F.2d 1150 (2d Cir.1982) 187, 188
L. v. Chambre d'accusation du Canton de Genève, ATF 123 II 134, 1 Apr. 1997, SJ 1997, 529. 203
Magness v. Russian Fed'n, 54 F. Supp. 2d 700 (S.D. Tex. 1999, per Hittner DJ). 83
Magness v. Russian Fed'n, 84 F. Supp. 2d 1357 (S.D. Ala. 2000, per Butler CJ) 107
Malewicz et al. v. City of Amsterdam, 362 F.Supp.2d 298 (D.D.C. 2005); 517 F.Supp.2d 322 (D.D.C. 27 June 2007). 83, 84, 87, 88, 89, 90, 92, 97, 105, 109, 198
Maria Altmann v. Republic of Austria, 142 F. Supp. 2d 1187 (C.D. Cal. 1999), *aff'd*, 317 F.3d 954 (9th Cir. 2002), as amended, 327 F.3d 1246 (9th Cir. 2003), 541 U.S. 677 (2004). 82, 87, 89, 91, 92, 107, 109, 193, 194, 195, 197, 198
Matthews v. Bay Head Improvement Ass'n, 471 A.2d 355 (N.J. 1984), *cert. denied*, 469 U.S. 821 (1984). 122
Mazzoni c. Finanze dello Stato, Tribunale di Venezia, 8 Jan. 1927 197
Menzel v. List, 267 N.Y.S.2d 804, 809 (Sup.Ct. N.Y. 1966), *rev'd*, 246 N.E.2d 742 (N.Y. 1969) 197, 209
Naftzger v. Am. Numismatic Soc'y, 42 Cal. App. 4th 421 (1996). 202
Navigational and Related Rights (Costa Rica v. Nicaragua), International Court of Justice, Judgment of 13 July 2009 17
O'Keeffe v. Snyder, 416 A.2d 862 (N.J. 1980). 161
Odyssey Marine Exploration Inc. v. The Unidentified Shipwreck Vessel & the Kingdom of Spain, the Republic of Peru, United States District Court, Middle District of Florida, Tampa Division, 3 June 2009. . . . . 128, 129
Odyssey Marine Exploration v. The Unidentified Shipwrecked Vessel, 657 F.3d 1159 (11th Cir. 2011, per Black CJ) 94

Odyssey Marine Exploration, Inc. (Keith Bray, Intervenor Plaintiff) v. Spain, Docket n. 10-14396, 31 Mar. 2011 140
Odyssey Marine Exploration, Inc. v. Kingdom of Spain, Docket n. 10-10269, 21 Sept. 2011 . . . . . 130, 138, 139, 143
Odyssey Marine Exploration, Inc. v. The Unidentified Shipwrecked Vessel, No. 8:07-cv00614-SDM-MAP, 21 Sept. 2011 201
Odyssey Marine Exploration, Inc., Applicant v. Kingdom of Spain, et al., Decision No. 11A745, 9 Feb. 2012 141
Office des poursuites et faillites du district de Martigny v. Compagnie Noga d'importation et d'exportation SA, No 5A.334/2007/frs (Swiss Federal Tribunal, 29 Jan. 2008) 98
Penn Central Transportation Co. v. City of New York, 438 U.S. 104 (1978) 122
Porter v. Wertz, 416 N.Y.S.2d 254, 259 (App. Div. 1979) 201
Prince Hans-Adam II of Liechtenstein v. Germany, Application No. 42527/98, European Court of Human Rights, Decision of 12 July 2001 . . . . . 104, 105
Prince of Liechtenstein v. Municipality of Cologne (Cologne Regional Ct., 11 Nov. 1991) 104
Prosecutor v. Blaskić, Case IT-95–14-T, Trial Chamber, Judgment of 3 Mar. 2000 . . . . . 48, 50, 51
Prosecutor v. Brđanin, Case IT-99–36-T, Trial Chamber II, Judgment of 1 Sept. 2004 . . . . . 45, 47, 49, 50, 51
Prosecutor v. Gotovina, Čermak, Markač, Case IT-06–90-T, Trial Chamber I, Judgment of 15 Apr. 2011 51
Prosecutor v. Jokić, Case IT-01–42/1-S, Trial Chamber I, Judgment of 18 Mar. 2004 52
Prosecutor v. Karadžić & Mladić, Cases IT-95–5-R61 and IT-95–18-R61, Trial Chamber, Review of the Indictment Pursuant to Rule 61 of the Rules of Procedure and Evidence, 11 July 1996 45
Prosecutor v. Kordić & Cerkez, Case IT-95–14/2-T, Trial Chamber, Judgment of 26 Feb. 2001 . . . . . 47, 50, 51, 57
Prosecutor v. Krajišnik, Case IT-00–39-T, Trial Chamber, Judgment of 27 Sept. 2006 50
Prosecutor v. Krstić, Case IT-98–33-A, Appeals Chamber, Judgment of 19 Apr. 2004 . . . . . 53, 54, 55
Prosecutor v. Martić, Case IT-95–11-T, Judgment of 12 June 2007 . . . . . 49, 50
Prosecutor v. Milutinović, Šainović, Ojdanić, Pavković, Lazarević, Lukić, Case IT-05–87-T, Judgment of 26 Feb. 2009 . . . . . 49, 50, 51
Prosecutor v. Naletilić, Case IT-98–34-T, Trial Chamber, Judgment of 31 Mar. 2003 48
Prosecutor v. Strugar, Case IT-01–42-T, Trial Chamber II, Judgment of 31 Jan. 2005 . . . . . 47, 48, 49, 52, 53
Prosecutor v. Tadić, Case IT-94–1-T, Trial Chamber, Judgment of 7 May 1997 . . . . . 45, 47, 48
Prosecutor v. Tadić, Decision on the Defence Motion for Interlocutory Appeal on Jurisdiction, Appeals Chamber, Decision of 2 Oct. 1995 . . . . . 47, 48
R.M.S.Titanic, Inc. v. RMS Titanic, *in rem*, U.S. Court of Appeals, No 04–1933, 31 Jan. 2006 . . . . . 133, 141
Republic of Croatia v. Tr. of the Marquess of Northampton 1987 Settlement, 610 N.Y.S.2d 263 (1st Dep't 1994), *appeal denied*, 642 N.E.2d 325 (N.Y. 1994) 161, 211
Republic of Lebanon v. Sotheby's, 167 A.D.2d 142 (N.Y. App. Div. 1990) 211
Republic of Peru v. Yale Univ., Compl. filed 5 Dec. 2008, Case 1:08-cv-02109-HHK (D.D.C. 2008) 20, 168, 190, 221
Republic of Turkey v. Metro. Museum, 762 F. Supp. 44 (S.D.N.Y. 1990) 160, 167
Republic of Turkey v. OKS Partners, 1994 U.S. Dist. LEXIS 17032 (D. Mass. 1994) 150, 160, 167
République fédérale du Nigeria c. Montbrison (Court of Cassation, 2006, JCP 2006, IV, 3005, 1917) 184
Rubin v. Iran, 349 F. Supp. 2d 1108 (N.D. Ill. 2004) 102
Rubin v. Iran, 456 F. Supp. 2d 228 (D. Mass. 2006) 102
Rubin v. Iran, 637 F.3d 783 (7th Cir. 2011, per Sykes CJ) 103

Rubin v. Iran, 810 F. Supp. 2d 402 (D. Mass. 2011, per O'Toole, Jr. DJ) 102
Rubin v. Iran, *aff'd*, 541 F. Supp. 2d 416 (D. Mass. 2008) 102
Solomon R. Guggenheim Found. v. Lubell, 567 N.Y.S.2d 623 (Ct. App. 1991). 161, 202
Sud Fondi Srl v. Italia, Application No. 75909/01, European Court of Human Rights, Decision of 20 Jan. 2009. 18
Swift v. Tyson, 41 U.S. 1 (1842) 115
The Apollon, 22 U.S. 362 (1824) 113, 212
The Art Museum Subdistrict of the Metro. Zoological Park and Museum Dist. of the City of Saint Louis & the County of Saint Louis v. United States of Am., Case 4:11-cv-00291, Complaint filed 15 Feb. 2011 (E.D. Mo. 2011) 169
Trib. Torino, 25 Mar. 1982 123
United States v. Aleman, 728 F.2d 492 (11th Cir. 1984) 171
United States v. An Antique Platter of Gold, Known as a Gold Phiale Mesomphalos c. 400 B.C., 184 F.3d 131 (2d Cir. 1999) 157, 165
United States v. An Archaic Etruscan Pottery Ceremonial Vase c. Late 7th Century, B.C. and a Set of Rare Villanovan and Archaic Etruscan Blackware with Bucchero and Impasto Ware, c. 8th-7th Century, B.C., Located at Antiquarium, Ltd., 948 Madison Avenue, New York, New York 10021, 96 Civ. 9437, verified complaint dated 12 Dec. 1996 . . . . 165, 200
United States v. Austin, 902 F.2d 743 (9th Cir. 1990) 224
United States v. Caliendo, 910 F.2d 429 (7th Cir. 1990) 170
United States v. Davis, 648 F.2d 84 (2d Cir. 2011), *aff'g*, United States v. Painting Known as 'Le Marché', 2010 U.S. Dist. LEXIS 53420 (S.D.N.Y. 2010) 166
United States v. Diaz, 499 F.2d 113 (9th Cir. 1974). 155
United States v. Eighteenth Century Peruvian Oil on Canvas Painting, 597 F. Supp. 2d 618 (E.D. Va. 2009) 173
United States v. Gerber, 999 F.2d 1112 (7th Cir. 1993) 156, 162
United States v. Hall, 104 F. A'ppx 475 (6th Cir. 2004) 164
United States v. Hollinshead, 495 F.2d 1154 (9th Cir. 1974) 162, 199
United States v. Hooshmand, 931 F.2d 725 (11th Cir. 1991). 170
United States v. La Jeune Eugenie, 26 F. Cas. 832 (1822). 116, 117, 118
United States v. Ligon, 440 F.3d 1182 (9th Cir. 2006). 224
United States v. Mask of Ka-Nefer-Nefer, Complaint filed 16 Mar. 2011, Case 4:11-cv-00504-HEA; 2012 U.S. Dist. LEXIS 47012 (E.D. Mo. 2012) 166, 169
United States v. McClain, 545 F.2d 988 (5th Cir. 1977); 593 F.2d 658 (5th Cir. 1979) 111, 112, 113, 119, 120, 156, 162, 170, 199
United States v. Melnikas, 929 F. Supp. 276 (S.D. Ohio 1996) 161
United States v. One Ancient Egyptian, Yellow Background, Wooden Sarcophagus, Dating to the Third Intermediate Period, Complaint filed 8 Oct. 2009, Case 09–23020 (S.D. Fla. 2009) 166
United States v. Portrait of Wally, A Painting by Egon Schiele, 2009 U.S. Dist. LEXIS 91464 (S.D.N.Y. 2009). 109, 166, 188, 212
United States v. Pre-Columbian Artifacts and the Republic of Guatemala, 845 F. Supp. 544 (N.D. Ill. 1993) 120, 199
United States v. Schultz, 178 F. Supp. 2d 445 (S.D.N.Y. 2002), *aff'd*, 333 F.3d 393 (2d Cir. 2003) 152, 156, 161, 162, 170, 171, 199, 200, 201, 208, 209
United States v. Shumway, 112 F.3d 1413 (9th Cir. 1997). 223
United States v. The Schooner Amistad, 40 U.S. 51 (1841) 116
United States v. Tidwell, 191 F.3d 5–20 (1999) 224
Vineberg et al. v. Maria-Louise Bissonnette et al., 529 F. Supp. 2d 300 (27 Dec. 2007). 198
Vineberg v. Bissonnette, 548 F.3d 50 (1st Cir. 2008) 153
Whiteman v. Dorotheum GMBH & Co. KG, 431 F.3d 57 (2d Cir. 2005, per Cabranes CJ) . . . 107
Winkworth v. Christie, Manson & Woods Ltd., [1980] 1 Ch. 496, [1980] 1 All E.R. 1121 153

Table of Legislation

International

Agreement between the United Nations and the Royal Government of Cambodia Concerning the Prosecution under Cambodian Law of Crimes Committed during the Period of Democratic Kampuchea, Phnom Penh, 6 June 2003 43

Agreement on Succession Issues of the Former Socialist Federal Republic of Yugoslavia, Annexes A to G, Vienna, 29 June 2001 32

American Convention on Human Rights, San José, 22 Nov. 1969 18

Convention (IX) Concerning Bombardment by Naval Forces in Time of War, The Hague, 18 Oct. 1907 41

Convention Concerning the Protection of the World Cultural and Natural Heritage, Paris, 16 Nov. 1972 . . . . . . 15, 52, 135, 144

Convention (I) for the Amelioration of the Condition of the Wounded and Sick in Armed Forces in the Field, Geneva, 12 Aug. 1949 13

Convention (II) for the Amelioration of the Condition of Wounded, Sick and Shipwrecked Members of Armed Forces at Sea, Geneva, 12 Aug. 1949 13

Convention (I) for the Peaceful Settlement of International Disputes, The Hague, 18 Oct. 1907 38

Convention for the Safeguarding of the Intangible Cultural Heritage, Paris, 17 Oct. 2003 . . . . 1, 12, 16

Convention on Jurisdictional Immunities of States and Their Property, New York, 2 Dec. 2004 . . . . 81, 82, 83, 95–97, 98, 99, 100

Convention on Stolen or Illegally Exported Cultural Objects, Rome, 24 June 1995 . . . . 1, 14, 80, 81,131, 132, 146, 147, 152, 157, 182, 185, 201, 210, 242

Convention on Succession of States in respect of State Property, Archives and Debts, Vienna, 7 Apr. 1983 32

Convention on the High Seas, Geneva, 29 Apr. 1958 . . . . 94, 130, 139

Convention on the Means of Prohibiting and Preventing the Illicit Import, Export and Transfer of Ownership of Cultural Property, Paris, 17 Nov. 1970 . . . . 1, 5, 13, 17, 26, 32, 38, 66, 80, 81, 117, 126, 131, 132, 152, 156, 158, 181, 182, 185, 189, 192, 200, 203, 204, 210, 212, 214, 234, 240, 242, 243, 244, 246, 248, 246, 252

Convention on the Prevention and Punishment of the Crime of Genocide, Paris, 9 Dec. 1948 54

Convention on the Protection and Promotion of the Diversity of Cultural Expressions, Paris, 20 Oct. 2005 57

Convention on the Protection of Cultural Property in the Event of Armed Conflict, The Hague, 14 May 1954 . . . . 1, 12, 13, 20, 24, 38, 41, 42, 43, 47, 104, 181, 184, 185, 04

Convention on the Protection of the Underwater Cultural Heritage, Paris, 2 Nov. 2001 . . . . 1, 16, 130, 134, 135, 142, 143, 144, 145, 147, 148, 149, 183

Convention on the Recognition and Enforcement of Foreign Arbitral Awards, New York, 10 June 1958 195

Convention on the Settlement of Matters Arising out of the War and the Occupation, Bonn, 26 May 1952 104

Convention (III) relative to the Treatment of Prisoners of War, Geneva, 12 Aug. 1949 13

Convention (IV) relative to the Protection of Civilian Persons in Time of War, Geneva, 12 Aug. 1949 13

Convention (IV) respecting the Laws and Customs of War on Land and Its Annex, The Hague, 18 Oct. 1907 . . . . 24, 41, 47, 184
Convention (II) with respect to the Laws and Customs of War on Land and Its Annex, The Hague, 29 July 1899 . . . . 24, 184
European Convention for the Protection of Human Rights and Fundamental Freedoms, Rome, 4 June 1950 . . . . 18, 94, 170
European Convention on State Immunity, Basel, 16 May 1972 . . . . 81, 82
European Convention on the Protection of the Archaeological Heritage, London, 6 May 1969 148
European Landscape Convention, Florence, 20 Oct. 2000 11
Declaration Concerning the Intentional Destruction of Cultural Heritage, Paris, 17 Oct. 2003 . . . . 1, 13, 42
Declaration on the Rights of Indigenous Peoples, New York, 13 Sept. 2007 . . . . 1, 12, 20
International Convention for the Unification of Certain Rules Relating to the Immunity of State-Owned Ships, Brussels, 10 Apr. 1926 94
International Convention on Salvage, 28 Apr. 1989 . . . . 129, 134
Memorandum of Understanding between the Government of the People's Republic of China and the Government of the United States of America on Implementation of Import Restrictions of Categorized Archaeological Objects between the Paleolithic Era to Tang Dynasty and Historic-Site Sculptures and Mural Art Works of over 250 Years Old, Washington, 14 Jan. 2009 . . . 5, 240–255
Protocol Additional to the Geneva Conventions of 12 August 1949, and relating to the Protection of Victims of International Armed Conflicts (Protocol I), 8 June 1977 . . . . 13, 18, 41
Protocol Additional to the Geneva Conventions of 12 August 1949, and relating to the Protection of Victims of Non-International Armed Conflicts (Protocol II), 8 June 1977 . . . . 13, 41
Protocol to the Convention for the Protection of Cultural Property in the Event of Armed Conflict 1954, The Hague, 14 May 1954 . . . . 24, 38, 181
Second Protocol to the Hague Convention of 1954 for the Protection of Cultural Property in the Event of Armed Conflict, The Hague, 26 Mar. 1999 . . . . 1, 13, 38, 41, 42, 181, 185
Statute of the International Criminal Court, Rome, 17 July 1998 . . . . . 13, 41, 56, 59, 62, 63
Statute of the International Criminal Tribunal for Yugoslavia, 25 May 1993 . . . . 13, 41, 47,48, 49, 53, 54, 56, 59
Treaty of Peace between the Allied and Associated Powers and Austria, Saint-Germain-en-Laye, 10 Sept. 1919 (Treaty of Saint-Germain) 33, 34, 35, 36
Treaty of Peace between the Allied and Associated Powers and Germany, Versailles, 28 June 1919 (Treaty of Versailles) 24, 25, 26, 27, 33
Treaty of Peace between the Allied and Associated Powers and Hungary, Trianon, 4 June 1920 (Treaty of Trianon) 33, 36
Treaty of Peace between the Holy Roman Emperor and the King of France and their respective Allies, Munster (Westphalia), 24 Oct. 1648 (Treaty of Westphalia) 23
Treaty of Peace with Turkey, Sèvres, 10 Aug. 1920 (Treaty of Sèvres) 29, 36, 37
Treaty of Peace with Turkey, Lausanne, 24 July 1923 (Treaty of Lausanne) 29, 30, 31
Treaty of Rapallo between the Kingdom of Italy and the Kingdom of Serbs, Croats and Slovenes, 12 Nov. 1920 (Italo-Austrian Treaty) 36
United Nations Convention on the Law of the Sea, 10 Dec. 1982 . . . . . . 3, 16, 94, 129, 133, 134, 135, 142, 143, 144, 183, 185, 201

Canada

First Nations Sacred Ceremonial Objects Repatriation Act, 2000 186
Justice for Victims of Terrorism Act (Bill C-10), 2012 96
State Immunity Act, 1985 96

China

Law for Protection of Cultural Relics, 2002 248
Regulation for Protection of the Great Wall, 2006 247

Germany

Gesetz zum Schutzdeutschen Kulturgutesgegen Abwanderung (Act on the Protection of German Cultural Property), 1999 . . . 105

Japan

Act No. 24 on the Civil Jurisdiction with Respect to a Foreign State, 2009 96

Italy

Code on Cultural Properties and Landscape, 2004, 126 132

Russia

Law on Cultural Valuables Displaced to the USSR as a Result of the Second World War and Located on the Territory of the Russian Federation, Federal Law No 64-FZ, 1998 90

Switzerland

Loi federale sur le transfert international des biens culturels, 2003 98
Ordonnance sur le transfert international des biens culturels, 2005 98

United Kingdom

Customs and Excise Management Act, 1979 159
Dealing in Cultural Objects (Offences) Act, 2003 . . . . 156, 157, 159, 179
Tribunals, Courts and Enforcement Act, 2007 94

United States

Antiquities Act, 1906 155
Archaeological Resources Protection Act (ARPA), 1979 . . . . 67, 155, 162, 163, 165, 199, 200, 206, 223, 224
Civil Asset Forfeiture Reform Act, 2000 . . . . 157, 166
Convention on Cultural Property Implementation Act (CPIA), 1983 . . . . 158, 159, 165, 166, 206, 243, 244
Foreign Sovereign Immunities Act (FSIA), 1976 . . . . 3, 82, 83, 84, 86–92, 100, 101, 102, 103, 105, 106, 107, 108, 139, 140, 198, 199
Immunity from Seizure Act (IFSA), 1965 . . . . 88, 89, 95, 101, 105, 106, 107
International Emergency Economic Powers Act, 1977 158
Native American Graves Protection and Repatriation Act (NAGPRA), 1990 . . . . 155, 221, 224
National Stolen Property Act (NSPA), 1934 . . . . 157, 162, 167, 170, 179, 199, 224
Payne-Aldrich Tariff Act, 1909 157
Terrorism Risk Insurance Act (TRIA), 2002 102

Introduction

Francesco Francioni and James Gordley

Over the past two decades, international law has seen a remarkable intensification of interest in cultural property and a significant expansion of the legal tools for its protection. New multilateral conventions have been negotiated and soft-law instruments adopted to address new types of cultural heritage, such as the 2001 Underwater Cultural Heritage Convention, the 2003 Convention on the Safeguarding of Intangible Cultural Heritage, the 2003 Declaration on the Intentional Destruction of Cultural Heritage, and the 2007 Declaration on the Rights of Indigenous Peoples. Intense work has been undertaken in the same period for updating and completing older regimes on cultural property protection. This is the case with the 1999 Second Protocol to the Hague Convention for the Protection of Cultural Property in the Event of Armed Conflict (1954), and with the adoption of the 1995 UNIDROIT Convention, which has filled some private law gaps of the 1970 UNESCO Convention on the Means of Prohibiting and Preventing the Illicit Import, Export and Transfer of Ownership of Cultural Property. This law-making activity has stimulated the development of a vast body of academic writings spanning different disciplines and aspects of cultural heritage, from the material to the intangible.[1]

At the same time, cultural heritage concerns have started to pervade other areas of international law and international adjudication. It is common today to find references to cultural heritage protection in the adjudication of investment disputes, in WTO law, in the jurisprudence of human rights courts, and even in the work of WIPO, which has been striving for the accommodation of intellectual property rights (IPRs) with manifestation of cultural heritage commonly identified as 'traditional knowledge'. Today, it is safe to say that cultural heritage law is a discrete branch of international law, and at the same time it constitutes an evolving dimension of many other areas of international law.

But as in other areas of international law—especially the law of environmental protection—rule making at the level of treaty law and of other international law instruments has not been matched by a corresponding development of

[1] For an overview of law making in the area of cultural heritage, see the UNESCO publication *Standard Setting in UNESCO: Normative Action in Education, Science and Culture* (UNESCO Publishing and Martinus Nijhoff: Leiden/Boston, 2007).

enforcement procedures and mechanisms. No general court exists or is being considered in the field of cultural heritage. Even in the critical area of illicit trade in cultural property—the breeding ground for the greatest number of cultural heritage disputes—the UNESCO Intergovernmental Committee on Restitutions shows a dismal record of under-utilization and remains inaccessible to private parties. To this 'weakness' of international cultural heritage law corresponds a gap in the relevant legal literature, which has addressed so far the issue of the implementation of cultural heritage law almost exclusively within the perspective of private international law and the role of courts in deciding the issues of applicable law and the competent forum.

This book aims to fill this gap by providing a multilevel analysis of the possible approaches to the enforcement of international cultural heritage law. The first part examines the opportunities for enforcement offered by international mechanisms and methods. The second part focuses on the role of domestic adjudication, including limits posed by international law, such as jurisdictional immunities. The third part is devoted to the analysis of alternative means of implementation and dispute settlement such as arbitration, diplomatic negotiations, practices of museums, and the development of social norms.

The first chapter by Francesco Francioni connects the idea of pluralism in the variety of cultural expressions with the plurality of legal orders that may come into play in the enforcement of norms in the protection of cultural heritage. The chapter shows how different legal orders (domestic and international) and different systems of norms (wartime and peacetime, public and private) interact one with another at various levels of regulation of cultural property and in the process of enforcement. The chapter emphasizes the importance of cultural property as an international public good, and the role that public and private actors have in contributing to the enforcement of international rules in the protection of art and heritage as a common good of humanity.

Chapter 2 by Ana Vrdoljak provides innovative insights on the role of peace treaties by focusing on a set of important treaties following the First World War and dealing with restitution, reparation in kind, and reconstitution of national cultural patrimony. The chapter examines also important aspects of state succession in relation to the dissolution of multinational states such as Austria and the Ottoman Empire. These early examples of cultural heritage enforcement by peace treaties provide in the opinion of the writer an important legacy to build on in view of the contemporary settlement of disputes in post-conflict situations.

Chapter 3 by Federico Lenzerini examines the recent jurisprudence of the International Criminal Tribunal for Former Yugoslavia and, more in general, the practice of international and mixed criminal courts and tribunals in the enforcement of the principle of individual criminal responsibility for offences against cultural heritage. He focuses on the role of international criminal law as a tool for the enforcement of cultural heritage law, because of the human dimension of cultural property, and its importance to peoples and communities as part of their cultural and spiritual identity. The examination of the case law, especially that arising from the Balkan wars, shows that destruction of cultural heritage was neither the result of military necessity nor the unfortunate collateral damage of the conduct of hostility, but an intentional attack on an essential element of the life and identity of the targeted people, thus a continuation of ethnic cleansing by different means.

Chapter 4 by Laurie Rush provides a 'view from the ground' on the variety of methods for preventing and combating looting of archaeological sites and illicit traffic in antiquities and examines models of legislation, physical protection, and the setting up of specialized agencies, such as the Italian Corps of the Carabinieri for the protection of cultural patrimony. The chapter provides original information about the direct experience of the writer in peacetime looting, and the suppression of illicit traffic in conflict situations such as Iraq.

The second part of this book examines the enforcement of cultural heritage and cultural property law in domestic courts. In this area, an issue of concern is the prerogative of states either to raise a defence or to assert a right on the basis of their sovereignty.

Chapter 5 by Riccardo Pavoni deals with the extent to which states can raise the defence of sovereign immunity from suit and execution. He describes three exceptions to immunity from suit that may apply in cases involving cultural property. One is the 'commercial exception' to state immunity, such as that provided by article 10 of the United Nations Convention on State Immunity (UNCSI), or § 1605(a)(2) of the Foreign Sovereign Immunities Act (FSIA) in the United States. A second is the 'ownership, possession and use of property' exception and its limitations (as per article 13 UNCSI, or § 1605(a)(4) FSIA). A third is the 'expropriation' exception of § 1605(a)(3) of the FSIA. Pavoni discusses the difficulties that result from the recognition of these limited exceptions. In the area of immunity from execution, he considers to what extent a 'cultural heritage' exemption from measures of constraint is legitimate when claims for the recovery of art based on customary or treaty obligations or for the return of cultural objects taken away in times of war or peace are brought before the courts. He also discusses the contours and feasibility of a 'cultural human rights' exception to sovereign and sovereign-property immunity along the lines of the Italian *Ferrini* jurisprudence.

Chapter 6 by PatriziaVigni concerns one of the most problematic claims that a state can raise on the basis of its sovereignty: a claim over cultural property found under the sea. The claim may be based on the state of origin; that is, the state where a historic object had been produced and used before it disappeared into the sea. Alternatively, such a claim may be based on the sovereign right of a flag state over its vessels, as recognized by customary international law, the 1982 United Nations Law of the Sea Convention, and admiralty law. In addition, coastal states have sovereign rights over their territorial sea and the natural resources of their continental shelf and powers of control over activities in contiguous areas such as salvage operations. Vigni notes that domestic courts have allowed the sovereign rights of states asserted on these grounds to prevail over other interests. These other interests include those of private persons and those arising from the special status of cultural objects as part of the heritage of humankind, as recognized, in particular, by the 2001 UNESCO Convention. She argues that these interests are entitled to a greater degree of protection.

The following chapters examine the protection that domestic courts afford cultural heritage and cultural property when a sovereign state asserts a claim or a defence.

Patricia Gerstenblith describes in Chapter 7 how three types of illegal activity are dealt with in civil and criminal cases: the looting of cultural objects from sites in which they are buried or concealed, the theft of such objects from their owners, and the smuggling of such objects across international boundaries in violation of export laws. She discusses the extent to which domestic courts can provide protection, given the complexities of international and domestic law. She concludes that civil suits for the recovery of cultural objects are playing a declining role due to the difficulties of bringing such actions. Criminal suits have been ineffective because of the insufficient effort of law enforcement due in part to a lack of resources, and in part to the relatively low priority that governments have assigned to cultural objects.

The first of these problems, the obstacles to civil suits, is addressed in Chapter 8 by James Gordley. One obstacle is a rule that art objects smuggled out of a country in violation of its export laws cannot be reclaimed on the grounds that one country will not enforce the export control laws of another. Gordley argues that this rule should not be applied to objects that are important to a nation's cultural heritage even under existing law. Another obstacle is a rule that a state cannot claim the return of cultural property on the ground of ownership unless it has the normal rights of an owner to use, possess, and dispose of the objects. Gordley argues for the recognition of a different sort of property right in the state, a right to guard and preserve cultural objects, which would allow it to reclaim objects smuggled abroad just as it can protect these objects while they are still within its borders.

The third part of the book is devoted to alternative methods of enforcement of norms for the protection of cultural property and cultural heritage.

Alessandro Chechi acknowledges in Chapter 9 the difficulties of bringing suits in domestic courts. They may be barred for a number of technical reasons, such as the expiration of limitation periods or the application of anti-seizure legislation or the rules on state immunity. Litigation entails zero-sum solutions that often force a judge to assign a financial loss either to the dispossessed owner or the current good faith possessor. Moreover, litigation is expensive. According to Chechi, despite these difficulties, there has not been a widespread use of alternatives such as negotiation, mediation, and arbitration. Negotiation and mediation cannot ensure that a suit will be settled or that the settlement will be enforceable.

Arbitration may be as costly and time-consuming as conventional litigation. Chechi sees a more hopeful alternative in an increasing willingness of domestic courts to recognize the special features of suits over cultural objects, the unique features of the art market, and to reach solutions that reconcile the historical, moral, cultural, financial, and legal issues involved. This willingness is illustrated by cases in which judges have ordered the restitution of cultural objects seized in times of war, cases in which they have given effect to the laws of source countries despite the rule against extraterritorial enforcement of export laws, cases in which they have tightened the obligation of purchasers to investigate the provenance of art, and cases in which they have found ways to allow claimants to sue even many years after the wrongdoing.

Derek Fincham focuses in Chapter 10 on the implementation potential arising from the spontaneous observance of international standards by museums and cultural heritage institutions. He describes a positive change in the social norms observed by museums and galleries. Museums are increasingly hesitant to acquire objects without a documented pre-1970 provenance. When objects are shown to have been illicitly excavated, nations are asking for their return, and in several notable cases, museums have been willing to return them. The next logical step, according to Fincham, should be an increasing acceptance of these norms by individuals.

Holly Flora describes in detail in Chapter 11 the change in the formal ethical standards adopted by leading American museums. She concludes that although these new standards reflect a long-needed awareness by museums of the problem of looting, museums like the Metropolitan Museum in New York have a great deal of latitude in acquiring an object without full provenance, provided it is not proven to be illegal and if there is a strong enough case for its importance. She doubts that the new standards will prevent looters from doing what they now do. Indeed, the stakes are effectively higher, which might encourage a different, and perhaps even more dangerous, kind of trafficking via new networks that will establish false provenances for looted objects. Moreover, even in this era of stricter standards, museums continue to buy objects from the same dealers, albeit with a stricter eye towards provenance.

The final chapter, Chapter 12, by Wang Yunxia provides an analytical study of the recent Memorandum of Understanding (MoU) between China and the United States on import restriction of cultural objects from China. The MoU is presented as a diplomatic model of enforcement of international cultural heritage law through cooperation between importing countries and source countries. This model, based on the specific provision of Article 9 of the 1970 UNESCO Convention, in the opinion of the author, could be extended also to cover other lines of illicit traffic in antiquities and cultural objects, particularly those linking China to Japan and South Korea.

PART I

THE INTERNATIONAL LEGAL FRAMEWORK

1

Plurality and Interaction of Legal Orders in the Enforcement of Cultural Heritage Law

Francesco Francioni *

I. Introduction

In introducing this book on the enforcement of cultural heritage law, an explanation is due for the meaning of the title chosen for this chapter. 'Plurality and interaction of legal orders' seeks to convey the idea that enforcement of the law in the area of cultural property entails a continuous interaction and hybridization of different legal orders, private and public, domestic and international, national and regional, and soft and mandatory law. These different legal orders coexist, interact, and collide especially when their driving agents—courts and tribunals—are called to enforce standards on the protection of cultural property and heritage. It is at this stage that legal pluralism may be used to elude the effective protection of cultural heritage—for example, by the skilful use of conflicts of laws in order to validate title over objects of dubious provenance (stolen art or illegally exported antiquities) or, vice versa, to enhance the protection of cultural heritage, as when we use legal pluralism as a tool for multi-level regulation and international cooperation.

But what is the meaning of 'legal order' in the context of this discussion? It may be useful to recall that the idea of 'legal order' (*ordinamento giuridico, ordonnoncement juridique, Rechtsordnung*) emerged at the beginning of the 20th century largely as a reaction to the dominant theories of legal positivism. A sophisticated conceptualization of it can be found in the work of a Sicilian jurist, Santi Romano, whose ground-breaking book *L'Ordinamento giuridico*, published in 1907, is premised on the idea that law as a *legal order* is not the sum total of binding norms, as assumed by legal positivism, but is rather the underlying social structure made up of the individual and collective beliefs, practices, and shared inclinations of members of the society, and the material organization that is the

* Professor of International Law, European University Institute, Florence.

reflection of such practices and inclinations. This is what has been called the 'institutional' theory of the law, a theory that is easier to comprehend when using a language, like Italian, which has different words for law as a legal order (*diritto*) and law as binding enactment of a recognized legislative authority (*legge*).

But the main reason for connecting Santi Romano's work to the theme of this book is his idea of law as a 'plurality of legal orders', law beyond the state, and as a product of the social organization of any given society within, outside, and above the state. This idea is incredibly modern in today's globalized world. But, more importantly, it fits the context of this book on cultural heritage and the law. Pluralism and diversity are the distinguishing features of cultural expressions. Art itself, as a medium essentially devoted to giving form to cultural expression, always transcends its economic value as a mere object and reflects the pluralism and diversity of tastes and inclinations of the societies that have produced it. In this respect it corresponds well with the idea of law as a plurality of legal orders. This is evident to anyone who visits this very small part of the world that we call Europe. Exploring its territory, the visitor will find traces of almost 3,000 years of human history in the archaeological site of Stonehenge, in the Etruscan cities of the dead, in the magnificent vestiges of Greek colonization and of Imperial Rome, in the amazing variety of styles in architecture and urban landscape, ranging from the severe Romanesque parish churches that punctuate the pilgrims' roads of the Middle Ages, to the imposing gothic cathedrals and the ornate drama of the Baroque. This variety is not only due to the succession of different periods of history; it is also due to different interpretations and renditions of the spirit of the same epoch. This is evident when we compare the luminous elegance of the Renaissance buildings in the Florence of Leon Battista Alberti with the monumental grandeur of papal Rome, and with the richly ornate Venetian style of the same epoch, so clearly contaminated by its oriental influences.

In the infinite variety of its expressions, art and heritage reflect the variety of collective inclinations and social organizations of the communities that have produced and maintained them. To paraphrase the old adage used by Santi Romano, *ubi societas ibi jus,* we could say *ubi societas ibi ars et jus.*

With this in mind, in the following parts this chapter will examine 1) the plurality and interaction of different legal perspectives of cultural heritage; 2) the plurality and interaction of different legal regimes on the protection of cultural heritage; and 3) the plurality and interaction between different mechanisms of enforcement at the international and domestic level.

II. Plurality of Perspectives

On the notion and significance of cultural heritage, international and comparative law scholars, as well as experts in cultural heritage diplomacy, have been divided until recently between two conceptions of cultural property: those who viewed it as part of the nation and those who looked at it as part of the heritage of humankind. The first epistemological perspective would justify the retention of cultural objects within the territory of the state and the imposition of export controls and limitations on private ownership over cultural goods in the name of public interest. The second perspective, on the contrary, would underplay the role of cultural heritage as an element of national identity and would emphasize its significance as part of the heritage of humanity, thus supporting the broadest access to it and its international circulation to facilitate exchange and cultural understanding among different peoples of the world. It is a commonplace that this latter view is not favoured by 'source countries', which have suffered the loss of their cultural patrimony in the past, and may continue to suffer today as a result of illicit traffic. On the contrary, it is preferred by policy-makers, collectors, and museums in art-importing countries for its capacity to contribute to a cosmopolitan order in which cultural exchange can support the intellectual and moral progress of humanity.

One may wonder whether this dual perspective has ever accurately reflected the spirit of the law and policy attitudes toward the conservation and management of cultural heritage. Certainly, this black and white view of the role and significance of cultural heritage is today being replaced by a more sophisticated and pluralistic conception of cultural expressions that transcends the raw distinction between national and international attitudes.

Today, cultural property may be seen as part of national identity, especially in the post-colonial and post-communist contexts, where cultural heritage plays an important role in 'transitional justice', both in the form of restitution of art looted or damaged or the reinstatement of monuments charged with political meanings.[1] At the same time, cultural objects can be seen as part of the physical public space that conditions our world view and which is part of what we normally call 'the environment' or the 'landscape'. This role of cultural heritage as part of public space opens the way to a holistic approach to heritage; that is an approach that brings together cultural and natural heritage and takes into account the interactive link of such heritage with the real life of people inhabiting it. It is this holistic conception of heritage that underlies the very international efforts at developing normative instruments for the protection of landscape.[2]

Cultural objects may be seen as moveable artefacts susceptible to economic evaluation, and for this reason subject to exchange in domestic and international

[1] See the removal of the monument to the resistance to Nazism in Estonia—which saw it as a monument to the Soviet occupation—and the bitter Russian reaction, which saw the removal as a provocative act of historical revisionism.

[2] See the European Landscape Convention, Florence 2000, Council of Europe Treaty Series note 176; the UNESCO Proposal Concerning the Desirability of a Standard Setting Instrument on Historical Urban Landscapes, 18 Aug. 2011, General Conference 36 C/23, as well as the legal opinion provided by this author on the feasibility of a global landscape convention in view of the decision of the Executive Board of UNESCO of 11 May 2011 (on file with author).

commerce; but they may also be seen as objects endowed with intrinsic value as expressions of human creativity and as part of a unique or very special tradition of human skills and craftwork, which today we call 'intangible cultural heritage'.[3] Masterpieces of painting, sculpture, mosaics, inlaid wood, musical instruments, and oral heritage displayed today in museums, exhibitions, and shops owe their existence to social structures and traditions that have nurtured and maintained the human knowledge and skills necessary to produce them.

Cultural property today can be seen as the object of individual rights, property rights, but also as 'communal property' or public patrimony, which is essential to the sentiment of belonging to a collective social body and to the transmission of this sentiment to future generations. In this sense, cultural heritage becomes an important dimension of human rights, in as much as it reflects the spiritual, religious, and cultural specificity of minorities and groups. This specificity, which is antagonistic to the dominant idea of heritage as part of the nation, finds its most pregnant expression in the cultural rights of indigenous peoples in the 2007 UN Declaration.[4]

III. Plurality and Interaction of Legal Regimes

This diversification in the way of thinking about cultural property has been accompanied by a growing complexity of the law and by increasing interaction between different regimes of international regulation. Since the creation of the United Nations Educational, Scientific and Cultural Organization (UNESCO),[5] numerous multilateral treaties have been adopted that have contributed to giving a precise definition to the concept of 'cultural property', as an autonomous category of goods previously considered elusive and fragmented.[6] At the same time, international practice and treaty law has seen a dynamic evolution from the concept of 'cultural property' as an object to the broader concept of 'cultural

[3] *See* UNESCO Convention for the Safeguarding of the Intangible Cultural Heritage, adopted in Paris on 17 Oct. 2003, *available at* <http://portal.unesco.org/en/ev.php-URL_ID=17716& URL_DO=DO_TOPIC&URL_SECTION=201.html> (last accessed 4 February 2013).

[4] United Nations Declaration on the Rights of Indigenous Peoples, General Assembly Resolution, 13 Sept. 2007, Sixty-First Session, Supp. No. 53 (A/61/53), especially arts. 11–16.

[5] UNESCO was created on 16 November 1945 by the representatives of 37 countries which signed the Constitutive Act (entry into force 4 Nov. 1946), *available at* <www.unesco.org/new/en/unesco/about-us/who-we-are/history/constitution/>.

[6] The synthetic expression 'cultural property' was used for the first time in the Hague Convention on the Protection of Cultural Property in the Event of Armed Conflict of 1954, *available at* <http://portal.unesco.org/en/ev.php-URL_ID=13637&URL_DO=DO_TOPIC&URL_ SECTION=201.html> (last accessed 4 February 2013). In the preceding international instruments there was no unitary notion of cultural property, but rather an empirical indication of objects of historical, monumental, or humanitarian interest that should be spared from acts of war. *See* Articles 27 and 56 of the Annexed Regulation of the IV Hague Convention of 1907, as well as Article 5 of the IX Hague Convention.

heritage'. This has been made possible thanks to the interaction of cultural property law with human rights law, which has permitted an expansion of the scope of protection from material cultural goods to the 'associative' social value of these goods as significant elements of a cultural community and as expression of its creative spirit and identity.

Plurality and interaction of legal orders also underlie the reciprocal influence between international humanitarian law and the specific rules on the protection of cultural property in the event of armed conflict, both international and internal.[7] Further, international law of armed conflict has converged with international criminal law and has become an element for innovation and progressive development of international cultural heritage law in three distinct directions: 1) the elevation of attacks against cultural property to the legal status of international crimes, especially war crimes and crimes against humanity;[8] 2) the consolidation of the law of individual criminal responsibility *under international law*, not only under domestic law, for serious offences against cultural objects;[9] 3) the progressive development of the law of state responsibility for the intentional destruction of cultural heritage.[10]

In the field of peacetime international law, public law and private law have converged toward the development of obligations to prevent and repress the illicit traffic of moveable cultural property.[11] At the level of public law, a growing number of importing and exporting states have ratified the 1970 UNESCO Convention on Illicit Traffic of Cultural Property—now in force in all major art market countries.[12] At the level of private international law, the adoption of the 1995

[7] *See* 1949 Geneva Conventions (Convention (I) for the Amelioration of the Condition of the Wounded and Sick in Armed Forces in the Field; Convention (II) for the Amelioration of the Condition of Wounded, Sick and Shipwrecked Members of Armed Forces at Sea; Convention (III) Relative to the Treatment of Prisoners of War; and Convention (IV) Relative to the Protection of Civilian Persons in Time of War) as well as their Additional Protocols of 1977, particularly Articles 52(1), 53 and 86 of Protocol I and 16 of Protocol II.

[8] *See* Article 3 d of the Statute of the International Criminal Tribunal for Yugoslavia and Article 8 b ix and 8 e iv of the Statute of the International Criminal Court.

[9] Second Protocol to the Hague Convention of 1954 for the Protection of Cultural Property in the Event of Armed Conflict, adopted 26 Mar. 1999, published in 38 ILM (1999) at 769–82, especially arts. 15–18; Article 3d of the Statute of the International Criminal Tribunal for Yugoslavia, 32 ILM (1993) at 1192–5; Article 8 of the Statute of the International Criminal Court, 37 ILM (1998) at 999–1019.

[10] *See* UNESCO Declaration Concerning the Intentional Destruction of Cultural Heritage adopted by the General Conference of UNESCO at its 33rd Session, Paris, 19 Oct. 2005, *reprinted in Standard Setting in UNESCO*, Volume II (2007), at 733; *see also* Francioni and Lenzerini, 'The Destruction of the Buddhas of Bamiyan and International Law', 14 *Eur. J. Int'l L.* (2003) at 619.

[11] Convention on the Means of Prohibiting and Preventing the Illicit Import, Export and Transfer of Ownership of Cultural Property, adopted in Paris on 14 Nov. 1970, *available at* <http://portal.unesco.org/en/ev.php-URL_ID=13039&URL_DO=DO_TOPIC&URL_SECTION=201.html> (last accessed 4 February 2013).

[12] *See* <http://portal.unesco.org/la/convention.asp?KO=13039&language=E&order=alpha>. This Convention has been ratified by 120 states, among which are the largest importers and exporters of cultural objects, such as the United States, the United Kingdom, Switzerland, Japan, Italy, and France.

UNIDROIT Convention[13] has laid down innovative rules on acquisition of title over stolen or illegally exported cultural goods, on restitution and compensation of *due diligence* purchasers, on time limits for the presentation of claims, and on the relevance of foreign public law in restitution disputes. With regard to these two instruments, one can appreciate the interaction between public international law and private law with the goal of preventing and suppressing the illicit traffic in cultural objects. The UNIDROIT Convention incorporates the international public policy principle that legal acquisition of a stolen cultural object must never be allowed and provides that the possessor of a stolen cultural object shall be bound to return it.[14] In this sense, principles of public international law become the instrument to bridge the gap between incompatible domestic legal orders, establishing on the one side (civil law) that the *bona fide* purchaser of a stolen moveable shall acquire the legal title, and on the other side (*common law* systems) that the purchase *a non domino* of a stolen cultural object will never entail the acquisition of the legal title.

The UNIDROIT Convention offers other examples of a fruitful interaction of different legal orders with a view to advancing the objective of a more effective protection of cultural property against the danger of clandestine traffic and of consequent loss and dispersion. One such example is provided by Article 3 para. 2 which permits the qualification as 'stolen object'—thus subject to mandatory return—of 'a cultural object which has been unlawfully excavated or lawfully excavated but unlawfully retained', when such qualification is consistent with the law of the state in which the excavation took place (that is, with national laws that characterize underground archaeological objects as patrimony of the state). It is evident that this provision makes it possible to overcome the obstacle posed by the plurality and autonomy of different domestic legal orders, which on the one side consider the underground archaeological heritage as public property, and those which, on the other side, permit private ownership of archaeological objects by the owner of the land and by private parties. The solution offered by the UNIDROIT Convention reflects the awareness of a conflicting relationship between a plurality of domestic legal orders and a progressive accommodation between them in support of a policy of legal cooperation in the fight against illicit traffic of antiquities.

In a more nuanced mode, interaction between private law and public law can be discerned in certain restitution disputes when the act of returning the cultural object not only involves the restoration of ownership to the original title holder (as in the case of theft or illegal export), but also the acknowledgement of historical injustice or international crimes. This is the case in the many recent

[13] UNIDROIT Convention on Stolen or Illegally Exported Cultural Objects, adopted 24 June 1995, *available at* <http://www.unidroit.org/english/conventions/1995culturalproperty/1995culturalproperty-e.pdf> (last accessed 4 February 2013).

[14] UNIDROIT Convention art. 3.

disputes involving Holocaust-looted art,[15] war plunder, and acts of cultural dispossession during periods of colonial domination. In these cases, the principle of non-retroactivity of international treaties can be a formidable obstacle to the return of cultural objects to their lawful owners. Yet, the rigidity of the non-retroactivity principle can be tempered by principles of transitional justice and more precisely by the principle of 'non-legitimation' of past wrongs, such as that which may be found in Article 10(3) of the UNIDROIT Convention.[16]

Interaction between international law and domestic law is at the heart of the innovative regime of 'world heritage' protection as provided by the 1972 UNESCO Convention Concerning the Protection of the World Cultural and Natural Heritage. This Convention, with its 190 contracting parties coinciding with the near totality of the international community of states, has established and developed a system of international cooperation for the conservation and valorization of certain cultural and natural properties of outstanding universal value.[17] The secret of its success lies in the careful combination of national legal orders, based on the principle of territorial sovereignty, with the international law concept of 'world heritage' attached to properties of such exceptional value so as to entail becoming the object of a general interest of humanity to their conservation and transmission to future generations. The interaction between national law and international law follows a creative pattern of division of labour between national and international law. At the national level, the territorial state maintains the exclusive right to identify and propose the nomination of a property located in its territory for inscription in the World Heritage List. At the international level, the competent body of the Convention—the World Heritage Committee—has the power to evaluate the proposed property, to approve or reject its inscription in the List, and to monitor its state of conservation for the purpose of maintaining its world heritage status, or deciding its demotion in the List of World Heritage in Danger or even its deletion from the List.[18] The World Heritage regime is a good example of how even the fundamental principle of territorial sovereignty can interact with international law. World heritage properties, unlike

[15] On this, see O'Donnell, 'The Restitution of Holocaust Looted Art and Transitional Justice: The Perfect Storm or the Raft of the Medusa?', 22 *Eur. J. Int'l L.* (2011) at 49.

[16] Article 10(3) reads as follows: 'This Convention does not in any way legitimize any illegal transaction of whatever nature which has taken place before the entry into force of this convention … nor limit any right of a State or other person to make a claim under remedies available outside the framework of this Convention for the restitution or return of a cultural object stolen or illegally exported before the entry into force of this Convention'. The same concept is affirmed in the sixth paragraph of the Preamble of the UNIDROIT Convention.

[17] Convention Concerning the Protection of the World Cultural and Natural Heritage, adopted in Paris on 16 Nov. 1972, *available at* <http://portal.unesco.org/en/ev.php-URL_ID=13055& URL_DO=DO_TOPIC&URL_SECTION=201.html> (last accessed 4 February 2013).

[18] This has occurred twice, in relation to a natural site of Oman, and in relation to the cultural site of the city of Dresden, Germany.

common heritage resources,[19] remain subject to the sovereignty of the territorial state; at the same time such sovereignty must be exercised in such a way as to serve the international law objective of conserving and protecting a property in the general interest of the international community.

More recently, at the threshold of the 21st century, other manifestations of the plurality and interaction of legal orders in the regulation of cultural heritage have emerged in connection with the development of treaty regimes for the protection of underwater cultural heritage[20] and for the safeguarding of intangible cultural heritage.[21] The first was the result of the gaps in, and unsatisfactory application of, the international legal order of the oceans, as codified in the 1982 UN Convention on the Law of the Sea. This Convention did not provide an adequate answer to the problem of the protection of underwater cultural heritage from the risk of unauthorized and unregulated retrieval of such heritage for purely commercial purposes. The 2001 UNESCO Convention, with its technical annex on 'rules concerning activities directed to underwater cultural heritage', in spite of its still limited number of ratifications and the criticism raised regarding its cumbersome system of inter-state cooperation, represents a commendable effort at integrating cultural heritage concerns in the legal order of the oceans, which since time immemorial had developed under the impulse of prevailing commercial and security interests.

The 2003 Convention for the Safeguarding of Intangible Cultural Heritage, as well as the 2005 Convention on cultural diversity, are themselves the product of the growing concern with the preservation of cultural pluralism and diversity in the age of globalization. But in a deeper sense they are also the result of an interaction between two different sets of international norms, cultural heritage norms and human rights norms. The novelty of the intangible heritage regime is in the protection of cultural heritage not as a *res* endowed with its own intrinsic value—aesthetic, historical, archaeological—but rather because of its association with a social structure of a cultural community which sees the safeguarding of its living culture as part of its human rights claim to maintain and develop its identity as a social body beyond the biological life of its members. According to this perspective, the 2003 Convention denotes a confluence of international cultural heritage law with human rights law, the protection of minorities, and the emerging law on the protection of the rights of indigenous peoples.

[19] That is, the mineral resources of the international seabed area under Part XI of the UN Convention on the Law of the Sea.

[20] Convention on the Protection of the Underwater Cultural Heritage, adopted in Paris on 2 Nov. 2001, *available at* <http://portal.unesco.org/en/ev.php-URL_ID=13520&URL_DO=DO_TOPIC& URL_SECTION=201.html> (last accessed 4 February 2013).

[21] Convention for the Safeguarding of the Intangible Cultural Heritage, *see earlier* note 3.

IV. Plurality and Interplay of Enforcement Mechanisms

Unlike other fields of international law, such as foreign investment, trade, and human rights, international cultural heritage law does not have an ad hoc mechanism of norms enforcement and dispute settlement. No general court exists nor is envisaged in this respect, and even the UNESCO Committee on Restitutions, which is the result of an internal decision of the Organisation rather than an institutional organ of the 1970 Convention, is severely under-utilized and remains unavailable to private parties. The International Court of Justice (ICJ), as the principal organ of the United Nations, has rarely had an opportunity to address questions of cultural property and cultural heritage. In the old case of the *Temple of PrehaVihear,* now revived before the Court in matters of interpretation,[22] although the cultural property in question was not the subject matter of the dispute *in se et* per se—it was only the point of reference for the establishment of a controversial boundary—the Court ruled that Thailand was under an international obligation to return parts of the cultural property that had been removed from the site of the temple. Another case brought by Liechtenstein against Germany in 2004 for the return of certain works of art confiscated after the Second World War in a third country never moved beyond the preliminary objection phase when the Court declined to exercise jurisdiction.[23] More recently, the ICJ has had the opportunity of elaborating on the relevance of cultural heritage in the context of genocide,[24] and in the 2009 case of *Navigational and Related Rights* (*Costa Rica v Nicaragua*) upheld the cultural traditions of the local indigenous population (fishing) as a component of their right to the preservation of a form of subsistence economy.[25]

The absence of a specialized forum for the enforcement of cultural heritage norms and the scarcity of cases brought before the ICJ is somewhat compensated by the use of 'borrowed fora'; that is, of dispute settlement mechanisms established for the enforcement of other categories of international norms. This is the case with human rights courts and with international criminal jurisdictions whose jurisprudence shows a growing number of cases involving a close interaction, and sometimes a conflict, between human rights standards and cultural

[22] *Case Concerning the Temple of Preha Vihear* (Cambodia v Thailand), Judgment of 15 June 1965, ICJ Reports (1962), at 6 ff.

[23] Certain Property (Liechtenstein v Germany), Judgment of 10 Feb. 2005.

[24] *Genocide* Case *(Bosnia-Herzegovina v Serbia),* Judgment of 26 Feb. 2007. Here the Court was presented with the applicant's argument that the documented systematic destruction of religious buildings, libraries, and other cultural properties was evidence of the respondent's plan to accomplish a deliberate act of obliteration of all traces of life and culture of the Muslim population in the targeted territory, so as to amount to genocide. The Court, although recognizing the character of international crimes of such acts, declined to consider them as evidence of the special intent to commit genocide. *See* paras. 335–344.

[25] Judgment of 13 July 2009, paras. 134–144.

heritage norms. This occurs especially when an individual or a private entity invokes international law in order to protect property rights. The European Court of Human Rights has adjudicated several cases involving the difficult accommodation of the individual right to private property and the public interest in the conservation of cultural goods. In these cases[26] the Court has not gone beyond a strict application of the provision of Protocol I on the protection of the individual right of 'every natural or legal person to the peaceful enjoyment of his possessions'.[27] Thus, the public interest in the conservation of a collective cultural patrimony or of the public value of a cultural landscape has been left in the shadow of the law or, at best, assessed as an element capable of affecting the market value of the property in dispute. A more progressive balancing between individual rights and public interest in cultural property has been achieved by the American Court of Human Rights. Its jurisprudence broke new grounds in the interpretation of Article 21 of the American Convention on Human Rights. This article, originally meant to protect property as an individual right, has been construed in light of the collective interest of cultural communities, local groups, and indigenous peoples to enjoy and develop their special relationship with cultural sites and ancestral lands as part of a communal cultural right. The American Court inaugurated this bold hybridization of the individual right to property with a communal notion of cultural property with the 2001 judgment in the *AwasTingni* case, and confirmed this approach in subsequent case law, notably, in *Moiwana Community v Suriname* and *YakyeAxa v Paraguay* (2005).

Another area of international dispute settlement that reveals a potential for cross-fertilization between cultural heritage norms and other branches of international law is that of international arbitration, to which other chapters (Chechi) in this book are dedicated. Here it is sufficient to point out that a distinct practice in the field of investment arbitration is emerging in which cultural heritage norms, even if technically they are not part of the law applicable to the dispute, influence the way in which the applicable treaty norms are interpreted and implemented by the arbitrators, thus ultimately conditioning the outcome of the decision. A pertinent example is provided by the *Parkering* arbitration concerning a dispute arising from a public tender launched by the city of Vilnius, Lithuania, for the construction of a modern carpark in the historical city centre, a site inscribed in the UNESCO World Heritage List. The claimant, a Norwegian company, complained that the Lithuanian authorities had breached the most-favoured nation clause contained in the applicable Bilateral Investment Treaty by awarding the

[26] *See* particularly *Beyeler v Italy*, Application note 33202/96, Decision of 5 Jan. 2000, concerning the compatibility of Italy's pre-emption and export control law on art works with Protocol 1 to the European Convention on Human Rights, and *Sud Fondi Srl c Italia,* Application No. 75909/01, Decision of 20 Jan. 2009, where the Court found that the Italian decision to demolish a large building erected in a protected coastal area in violation of national landscape regulation amounted to a breach of the principle *nullumcrimen sine lege* (Article 7 of the Convention) and of the right to property.

[27] Article 1 of Protocol I.

contract to a Dutch company. In rejecting the claim, the ICSID arbitral tribunal gave considerable weight to the cultural heritage impact of the claimant's project as compared to the less intrusive project of the Dutch bidder and concluded that the two investors were not in 'like circumstances' for the purpose of the applicable investment treaty:

> The difference in size of [the] ... project, as well as the significant extension of the [claimant's project] ... into the Old Town near the cathedral area, are important enough to determine that the two investors were not in *like circumstances*. Furthermore, the Municipality of Vilnius was faced with numerous and solid oppositions from various bodies that relied on archaeological and environmental concerns. In the record, nothing convincing would show that such concerns were not determinant or were built upon to reject [the claimant's project]. Thus, the city of Vilnius did have legitimate grounds to distinguish between the two projects.[28]

This award breaks new ground in introducing cultural heritage concerns as legitimate aims that the host state may pursue in adopting regulation or taking measures that have an impact on the economic interests of an investor and may constitute a *prima facie* violation of its obligations under international investment law. It builds upon earlier precedents, such as *SSP v Egypt*, in which the ICSID tribunal had even recognized international cultural heritage norms—also in this case the World Heritage Convention—as relevant applicable law in an investment dispute. This trend has been confirmed in more recent practice. In *Glamis Gold* (2009) and *Grand River* (2011), both involving investors' claims against the United States, under NAFTA Chapter 11, the arbitral tribunals based their decision on the assumption that cultural heritage standards may be relevant in the assessment of the legality of the host state's regulatory action affecting the economic interests of the investor. In the first case, the ICSID tribunal rejected the claim of a Canadian company that the stringent regulations adopted at the federal and state levels on the conduct of mining operations in California would amount to indirect expropriation and breach of legitimate expectations of the foreign investor. The cultural value of the mining site as ancestral land of a tribal community of Native Americans, together with compelling environmental considerations, was a factor in support of the legitimacy of the regulatory measures imposed by the United States' authorities in view of protecting the environment and landscape value of the relevant territory.

The second case, decided in January 2011, concerned a complaint by a Canadian indigenous community that the federal compensation scheme imposed in the United States on the tobacco industry to redress the victims of smoking amounted to a breach of their investors' rights under NAFTA. The award rejected the complaint on its merits, but at the same time made express reference to relevant international standards on cultural heritage, notably the 2007 UN Declaration on

[28] ICSID Case No.AR/05/08, Sept. 2007.

the Rights of Indigenous Peoples, as potentially applicable law also in economic disputes.

V. Interaction between Domestic Adjudication and International Enforcement

So far, this chapter has examined the interaction among mechanisms of law enforcement in a 'horizontal' dimension; that is, in the relation between different bodies of international adjudication. But today an intense interaction occurs also in a 'vertical' dimension; that is, between national courts and international mechanisms of dispute settlement. National courts can be catalysts in accelerating the settlement of a cultural property dispute at the international or transnational level. One may recall the *Altman* case, in which the Supreme Court of the United States held that the Government of Austria could not enjoy sovereign immunity in relation to a civil action brought before American courts for the restitution of a series of valuable paintings (Klimt) that Austria had obtained as a consequence of Nazi persecution of Austrian Jews. This decision was followed by consent to arbitration by the disputing parties and eventually by an arbitral award that required Austria to return the disputed art to the claimant. In criminal matters, the high-profile prosecution in Italy of Marion True, former curator of the Getty Museum, for her alleged implication in the Medici (from the name of the person responsible for the organized looting) connection in illicit traffic of antiquities from Italy to the United States, paved the way and set new patterns for the negotiation and conclusion of innovative agreements between the Italian Government and several major United States Museums, among them the Getty, Metropolitan of New York, Boston, and Cleveland museums. Similarly, the 2009 suit brought by Peru in the United States against Yale University for the return of the treasures of Macchu Picchu influenced the negotiation of a 2010 accord between Peru and Yale and the subsequent conclusion of a memorandum of understanding in February 2011 between Yale and Cuzco University for the development of a joint centre for the study of Inca culture and the shared management of the disputed antiquities.

VI. Conclusion

The idea of cultural heritage as a 'common heritage of humanity' can be traced back to the 1954 Hague Convention for the Protection of Cultural Property in the Event of Armed Conflict, according to which 'damage to cultural property belonging to any people whatsoever means damage to the cultural heritage of all mankind, since each people makes its contribution to the culture of the world'.

This universalist idea must be reconciled with the infinite variety of cultural expressions and with the role of art as a medium essentially devoted to giving form to the plurality and diversity of tastes, beliefs, and inclinations of the different societies in which it is produced. This contribution has tried to show how different legal orders and different sets of norms—public and private, domestic and international, wartime and peacetime—interact one with another at different levels of regulation and protection of cultural property. This interaction is all the more significant at the level of enforcement of international standards where the absence of a centralized system of dispute settlement shifts the responsibility for the effective implementation of the law to the initiative of national courts and tribunals, governmental agents, and private actors, such as museums and art collectors. All of them, with different roles and different normative perspectives contribute to the enforcement of international standards on the conservation and management of cultural property as part of the 'cultural heritage of humankind'.

2

Enforcement of Restitution of Cultural Heritage through Peace Agreements

Ana Vrdoljak[*]

I. Introduction

Peace agreements consolidated in modern times provide an important source of international law. They have been especially significant in the formulation of the international and regional protection of cultural heritage from the early 20th century onwards.[1] There has been a marked escalation in the number, and a transformation in the nature, of armed conflicts since the end of the Cold War.[2] Most are intra-state conflicts, with many driven by ethnic and religious differences,[3] with minorities and indigenous peoples 'often the targets, rather than the perpetrators of violence'.[4] This period has also witnessed a concomitant proliferation in peace agreements.[5] Although peace agreements covering intra-state conflicts had increased, a significant proportion of conflicts resumed, particularly those with an 'ethnic' element.[6] The UN Secretary-General noted, '[N]urturing ethnic cultures and traditions lay[s] the foundations for lasting stability'.[7] There is an urgent need to examine the role of culture and cultural

* Professor, Faculty of Law, The University of Technology, Sydney, and Visiting Professor, Legal Studies Department, Central European University.

[1] C. de Visscher, 'International Protection of Works of Art and Historic Monuments', *Documents and State Papers* (1949) 821.

[2] L. Harbom and P. Wallensteem, 'Armed Conflicts 1946–2009', 47(4) *J. Peace Research* (2010) 501; Human Sec. Report Project, *Human Security Report 2009/2010* (Vancouver: HSRP, 2010) [hereinafter HSRP].

[3] Kreutz, 'How and When Armed Conflicts End', 47(2) *J. Peace Research* (2010) 243.

[4] United Nations, Report of the Independent Expert on Minority Issues, UN Doc.A/65/287 (2010), 5.

[5] L. Harbom et al., 'Armed Conflict and Peace Agreements', 43(5) *J. Peace Research* (2006) 617.

[6] Harbom and Wallensteem, *see earlier* note 2; HSRP, *see earlier* note 2; Kreutz, *see earlier* note 3; G. Stewart et al., 'Major Findings and Conclusions on the Relationship between Horizontal Inequalities and Conflict', in F. Steward (ed.), *Horizontal Inequalities and Conflict* (New York: Palgrave Macmillan, 2010) 285–300.

[7] UN Doc.SG/SM/12833 (2010).

heritage in the implementation of relevant international norms and maximizing successful, sustainable peace agreements.

I would suggest that how cultural heritage is historically dealt with in peace agreements falls broadly into three discernible categories:

(1) restitution and restoration of cultural heritage as reparations *between* existing states, post-conflict;
(2) cultural rights guarantees and restitution and protection of cultural heritage *within* existing states; and
(3) cultural rights guarantees and restitution and protection of cultural heritage in *new* states, being the latest iteration.

This classification is vital because as each distinct category transitions from violent conflict to peace, it brings with it its own dangers for cultural heritage and differing responses to such threats.

In this chapter, I explore the implications of this three-tiered typology for the implementation of cultural heritage law—with particular reference to restitution—using the relevant peace treaties arising from the Paris Peace Conferences of 1919 as case studies. These treaties not only typify the 'old wine in new bottles' adage but laid down foundational principles for contemporary international cultural heritage law, and their implementation schema may provide potential solutions for the resolution of disputes today. Whilst remaining cognizant of their limitations, these post-First World War peace treaties deserve to be reassessed in respect of their contribution to the development and implementation of cultural heritage law.

II. Peace through Reparations

Until the 1990s, the preponderance of peace agreements concerned international armed conflicts; that is, *between* existing states. Treaties from the 1648 Treaty of Westphalia to the post-1945 peace agreements moved beyond the immediate inter-state conflict and endeavoured to attain lasting peace through the establishment of a new international order. From provisions covering religious tolerance, to minority guarantees, to early human rights protections, each of these peace settlements addressed the 'cultural' to varying, but limited, degrees.[8] They in part defined and were defined by these treaties which frame the new international order.

From 1815 onwards, these peace agreements often also contained detailed provision for restorative reparations covering cultural heritage. In response to violations of the laws of war and international humanitarian law, they sanctioned external restitution between states of movable cultural heritage (for example,

[8] P. Thornberry, *International Law and the Rights of Minorities* (Oxford: Clarendon Press, 1991); A. F. Vrdoljak, *International Law, Museums and the Return of Cultural Objects*, (Cambridge: Cambridge University Press, 2006).

artworks, archives, etc.) and reconstruction of immovable heritage (for example, libraries, places of worship, etc.).[9] These peace treaty provisions and subsequent practice arising from their implementation reinforced the emergence of a specialized field of international law for the protection of cultural heritage[10] and codification in the 1954 Hague Convention for the Protection of Cultural Property during Armed Conflict and its two protocols.[11]

Until the mid-20th century, these two strands in inter-state peace agreements ran parallel. It was only with the Allied governments' response to the atrocities of the 1930s and 1940s that they combined.[12] This merging reflected the design of the post-1945 international order and ensuing codification of human rights and cultural heritage protections.

A. Post-First World War Treaty Framework Sanctioning Reparations

The restitution provisions contained in the Treaty of Peace between the Allied and Associated Powers and Germany (Treaty of Versailles) of 1919 set a precedent for the return of cultural objects as a remedy for significant and deliberate cultural loss inflicted in contravention of international law, particularly international humanitarian law, even if the object being 'returned' was legally acquired by the holding state.[13] US delegate David Hunter Miller noted that there was an entitlement to damage for violations of international law, which included obligations arising in respect of cultural property protected by the 1899 and 1907 Hague Regulations.[14] The peace conference delegates were motivated by a broader desire

[9] W. W. Kowalski, in T. Schadla-Hall (ed.), *Art Treasures and War* (London: Institute of Art & Law, 1998); Vrdoljak, *see earlier* note 8, at 77–87; A. F. Vrdoljak, 'Cultural Heritage in Human Rights and Humanitarian Law', in O. Ben-Naftali (ed), *International Human Rights and Humanitarian Law* (Oxford: Oxford University Press, 2011), at 250–302.

[10] De Visscher, *see earlier* note 1; Vrdoljak, *see earlier* note 9.

[11] Convention for the Protection of Cultural Property in the Event of Armed Conflict, 14 May 1954, in force 7 Aug. 1956, 249 UNTS 240; Protocol for the Protection of Cultural Property in the Event of Armed Conflict, 14 May 1954, in force 7 Aug. 1956, 249 UNTS 358; Second Protocol to the Hague Convention for the Protection of Cultural Property in the Event of Armed Conflict, 26 Mar. 1999, in force 9 Mar. 2004, (1999) 38 ILM 769; *see* G. Berlia, 'International Protection of Cultural Property by Penal Measures in the Event of Armed Conflict', UNESCO Doc.5C/PRG/6 (1950); R. O'Keefe, *The Protection of Cultural Property in Armed Conflict* (Cambridge: Cambridge University Press, 2006).

[12] Berlia, *see earlier* note 11, at 2; Vrdoljak, *see earlier* note 9, at 266 ff.

[13] Arts. 245–247, Treaty of Peace between the Allied and Associated Powers and Germany, Versailles, 28 June 1919, in force 10 Jan. 1920, Cmd 516 (1920); *British and Foreign State Papers*, vol.112, at 1; (1919) 225 Parry's CTS 189; (1919) 13(supp.) *Am. J. Int'l L.* 151 at 276.

[14] D. H. Miller, Memorandum, 'The American Program and International Law', (31 July 1918), in P. M. Burnett, *Reparation at the Paris Peace Conference from the Standpoint of the American Delegation* (2 vols, New York: Columbia Univ. Press, 1940), vol. 2, at 170. *See* arts. 27 and 56 of the Convention (II) with Respect to the Laws and Customs of War on Land and Its Annex: Regulations Concerning the Laws and Customs of War on Land, 29 July 1899, in force 4 Sept. 1900, 187 *Parry's CTS* (1898–99), 4291(supp.), *Am. J. Int'l L.* (1907) 129; Convention (IV) Respecting the Laws and Customs of War on Land, and Annex, The Hague, 18 Oct. 1907, in force 26 Jan. 1910, 208 *Parry's CTS* (1907), 77 2(supp.), *Am. J. Int'l L.* (1908) 90.

to secure peace and stability by restoring communities, territories, and cultural objects and archives. US President Woodrow Wilson stated that liberated territories must be 'restored', adding, 'Without this healing act the whole structure and validity of International Law is forever impaired'.[15] Elaborating upon Wilson's words, D. H. Miller noted that restoration was not limited to physical reconstruction but would extend to psychological restoration, including the reconstitution of national cultural patrimonies.[16]

Article 247 of the Treaty of Versailles concerning restitutions to be made to the University of Louvain and Belgium were to be mediated through the Inter-Allied Commission (Reparations Commission) established under the Treaty.[17] The Commission was to consider reparation claims and provide Germany (and its allies) with 'a just opportunity to be heard'.[18] Five delegates from the nominated Powers would take part and vote on proceedings which were held in private.[19] The Commission was not bound by any particular rules of law, evidence, or procedure but was to be guided by 'justice, equity and good faith' and its decisions were to 'follow the same principles and rules in all cases where they were applicable'.[20]

B. Rationale for the Versailles Reparations Provisions

There was little agreement amongst legal commentators of the class of the return sanctioned by Article 247 of the Treaty of Versailles. Such returns proscribed by the provision were described as reparations, restitution-in-kind, or reconstitution of works of art. Indeed, usage of these terms in this context bears little resemblance to the terminology of reparations in state responsibility with which we are familiar today.

1. Reparations

There was great resistance among the Allied peace negotiators to the broadening of the 'reparations' element of the peace agreements to cultural heritage. Allied governments were particularly reluctant to sanction the plunder by a victor of another state's cultural heritage. The works of art returned pursuant to Article

[15] Burnett, *see earlier* note 14, vol.2, at 303, doc. 454

[16] Burnett, *see earlier* note 14, vol.1, at 423, doc. 47.

[17] Articles 233 and Annex II, Treaty of Versailles. Articles 245 and 246 make no specific referenceto the application of the Reparation Commission. Indeed, Article 245 states that the transfers were to take place 'in accordance with a list which will be communicated ... by the French Government'. Article 246 provided that 'delivery of the articles ... will be effected in such a place and in such conditions as may be laid down by the Governments to which they are restored'.

[18] Pt. VIII Reparations, Section I: General Provisions, Art. 233, Treaty of Versailles.

[19] Including the United States, Great Britain, France, Italy, Japan, Belgium, and the Serb-Croat-Slovene State: Pt. VIII Reparations, Section I: General Provisions, Annex II, para. 2, Treaty of Versailles.

[20] Pt. VIII Reparations, Section I: General Provisions, Annex II, para. 11, Treaty of Versailles.

247 had been acquired by the German holding institutions legitimately and had not been confiscated during the First World War.[21] Therefore, Charles de Visscher argued this was neither a case of restitution nor recovery but was acknowledgement of Belgium's 'right to compensation' for cultural losses caused by German infringement of the rules of war.[22] This interpretation was augmented by the location of the provision within the Treaty and its enforcement by the Reparation Commission, whose mandate covered the full range of war reparations.[23]

2. *Restitution-in-Kind*

The Treaty of Versailles provision arose initially from an acceptance of restitution-in-kind in recognition of the massive cultural losses suffered by France and Belgium.[24] Unlike the French, Belgium successfully introduced a provision, Article 247, that reduced its claims for restitution from the general to the specific.[25] It permitted the return of objects of equivalent number and value to the University of Louvain and the reconstitution of specific art works to Belgium generally that had been legally acquired by the returning states prior to the armed conflict. Even though the peace negotiators were at pains to diminish the appearance of promoting such relief, Article 247 became an important, early example of restitution-in-kind.[26] The British delegate expressed concern about the draft provision sanctioning this remedy because '[t]he bartering about of objects of art caused very bitter feeling in 1814'.[27] Indeed, German commentators feared that the draft article would lead to a repetition of the Napoleonic confiscations which had occurred one hundred years before, undertaken under the legal 'fig leaf' of peace treaties.[28]

[21] T. Bodkin, *Dismembered Masterpieces: A Plea for their Reconstruction by International Action* (London: Collins, 1945) at 12–15; De Visscher, *see earlier* note 1, at 829–830; D. Rigby, Cultural Reparations and a New Western Tradition, 13 *Am. Scholar* (1943–44) 273, at 279.

[22] Bodkin, *see earlier* note 21, at 13; De Visscher, *see earlier* note 1, at 830; UNESCO 1969, Means of Prohibiting and Preventing the Illicit Import, Export and Transfer of Ownership of Cultural Property, Preliminary Report, 8 Aug. 1969, UNESCO Doc.SHC/MD/3 (1969), 11; *cf.* Burnett, *see earlier* note 14, at 127–128; B. Hollander, *The International Law of Art for Lawyers, Collectors and Artists* (London: Bowes & Bowes, 1959) 32; US Dep't of State, *Treaty of Versailles and After* (Wash., DC: USPO, 1947) 443.

[23] Pt. VIII Reparations, Section II: Special Provisions, Treaty of Versailles.

[24] J. W. Garner, *International Law and the World War*, 2 vols. (London: Longman, Green & Co., 1920), vol.1, at 434; C. Phillipson, *International Law and the Great War* (London: T. Fisher Unwin Ltd, 1915), at 159–174.

[25] Burnett, *see earlier* note 14, vol. 1, at 981–982, 1009, docs. 284 and 286.

[26] Kowalski, *see earlier* note 9, at 35; Martin, 'Private Property, Rights and Interests in the Paris Peace Treaties', 24 *British Y.B. Int'l L.* (1947) 277; I. Vásárhelyi, *Restitution in International Law*, revised by Gy. Haraszti and translated by I. Szaśzy (Budapest: Publishing House of the Hungarian Academy of Sciences, 1964) 34.

[27] Burnett, *see earlier* note 14, vol. 1, at 876, doc. 254.

[28] Grautoff, 'Foreign Judgments on the Preservation of Monuments of Art', in P. Clemen (ed.), *Protection of Art During the War: Reports Concerning the Condition of Monuments of Art at the Different Theatres of War and the German and Austrian Measures Taken for Their Preservation, Rescue and Research* (Leipzig: E. A. Secmann, 1919) 129; W. Treue, *Art Plunder: The Fate of Art in War and Unrest*, translated by B. Creighton, (New York: Methuen, 1961), at 222–223.

3. *Reconstitution of Works of Art*

The majority of commentators concurred that this provision facilitated the reconstitution of the works of art but could not agree whether the rationale was the promotion of Belgian national patrimony or the heritage of humanity.[29] Thomas Bodkin, whilst advocating the reconstitution of dismembered works of art, questioned the legitimacy of its application in this case. He argued that the lack of security and poor conditions under which the works were kept on their return to Belgium threatened cultural objects that were part of the common heritage of all mankind.[30] On the other hand, de Visscher maintained the provision facilitated the reconstitution of national cultural patrimony, a purpose which rendered it consistent with the restitution provisions contained in other Paris peace treaties.[31]

4. *Reconstitution of National Cultural Patrimony*

The notion of the reconstitution of national cultural patrimony also informed Article 245 of the Treaty of Versailles. This provision provided for the restitution from Germany to France of 'trophies, archives, historical souvenirs or works of art' taken from France during 'the War of 1870–71 and the World War'.[32] With the territorial restoration of Alsace-Lorraine to France, there was a similar restoration of cultural heritage with a special link to this territory.[33] Further, there was a belief that the restoration of the cultural objects would secure a great measure of stability within Europe. Significantly, the provision endeavoured to correct a historic wrong by redistributing cultural objects which had been removed well prior to the First World War. This rationale also underpinned peace agreements finalised between successor states following the dissolution of the Austro-Hungarian Empire discussed in the following section.

III. Peace through Unity

Peace agreements covering *intra-state* conflicts represent the dominant core of contemporary international law-making and scholarship in this area. The period after 1989 has been defined by a sharp escalation in armed conflicts *within* existing states, which were invariably characterized by ethnic and religious divisions.[34]

[29] Bodkin, *see earlier* note 21, at 13–15; De Visscher, *see earlier* note 1, at 830; D. Rigby, 'Cultural Reparations and a New Western Tradition', 13 *Am. Scholar* (1943–44) 273, at 279–280.

[30] Bodkin, *see earlier* note 21, at 14; De Visscher, *see earlier* note 1, at 830.

[31] De Visscher, *see earlier* note 1, at 829.

[32] The requirements of Article 245 were fulfilled. *See* Hollander, *see earlier* note 22, at 32.

[33] Burnett, *see earlier* note 14, vol. 2, at 303–304, doc. 454.

[34] Harbom and Wallensteen, *see earlier* note 2.

In contrast to prior historical periods, a significant proportion of intra-state conflicts were terminated by peace agreements.[35] The two decades after 1989 also witnessed an exponential rise in peace agreements, with a majority covering intra-state conflicts.[36] These peace agreements have proved diverse and innovative in redefining state institutional structures and processes to defuse divisions and stave off renewed violence. Provisions covering cultural heritage have figured prominently in several of these peace agreements.

The sheer volume and creative nature of these post-Cold War peace agreements has led to responses from legal scholars and international organisations, focused predominantly on civil and political aspects of peace (and transition) processes. The United Nations has adopted various guidelines and recommendations which redefine and reinforce rule of law principles, human rights, combating impunity, and democratic governance.[37] Likewise, legal and social science scholarship has focused on this growing body of legal practice to theorize anew on rule of law, constitutionalism, and governance. Indeed, one leading scholar has argued that these agreements have given rise to a specialized body of law governing peacemaking.[38]

These conflicts and related peace processes intensified multilateral law-making and scholarship on cultural heritage and related human rights norms, particularly cultural rights.[39] The last two decades have seen the adoption of seven multilateral instruments on cultural heritage. These have broadened the types of cultural heritage recognized and protected by the international community to include intangible heritage and promoted the importance of cultural diversity and the effective realization of human rights. Likewise, there has been a reiteration and elaboration of existing human rights norms and adoption of specialist international and regional minority instruments which has led to a resurgence in cultural rights and culminated in the appointment of the first UN Independent Expert on Cultural Rights in 2009.[40] Yet, reference to peace agreements and their implementation is largely *tangential* to these efforts.

[35] C. Bell, *On the Law of Peace: Peace Agreements and the Lex Pacificatoria* (Oxford: Oxford University Press, 2008) 305–37; Kreutz, *see earlier* note 3.

[36] Bell, *see earlier* note 35, at 5.

[37] United Nations, Secretary-General Comments on Guidelines Given to Envoys, UN Press Release SG/SM/7257 (1999) 10; United Nations, The Rule of Law and Transitional Justice in Conflict and Post-Conflict Societies, UN Doc.S/2004/616 (2004), 21–23; United Nations, Updated Set of Principles for the Protection and Promotion of Human Rights Through Action to Combat Impunity, UN Doc.E/CN.4/2005/102/Add.1 (2005).

[38] Bell, *see earlier* note 35.

[39] J. Toman, *Cultural Property in War: Improvement in Protection* (Paris: UNESCO Pub'g, 2010); E. Stamatopoulou, *Cultural Rights in International Law* (Leiden: Martinus Nijhoff Publishers, 2007); M. Weller (ed.), *Universal Minority Rights* (Oxford: Oxford University Press, 2007); A. F. Vrdoljak, 'Genocide and Restitution: Ensuring Each Group's Contribution to Humanity', 22(1) *Eur. J. Int'l L.* (2011) 17.

[40] Human Rights Council Resolution 10/23 (2009); *see, eg,* Declaration on the Rights of Persons Belonging to National or Ethnic, Religious and Linguistic Minorities, UNGA Res. 47/135, 18 Dec.

A. Post-First World War Peace Agreements and Remedies

The first peace treaty with Turkey and the Allied Powers (Treaty of Sèvres (1920)) represented an early intersection in international law between restitution of cultural property and nascent human rights protections through formulation of protection for minorities and denunciation of crimes against humanity.[41] The unratified Treaty of Sèvres was of limited immediate impact, being replaced by the Treaty of Lausanne in 1923.[42] Nonetheless, principles contained in this peace treaty served as a significant precursor to the international community's response to the subsequent formulation of specialist cultural heritage instruments after 1945.

The first efforts to define what constitutes crimes against humanity occurred after the First World War in response to the persecution of minorities by a state within its own territory. The Preliminary Peace Conference established the Commission on the Responsibilities (1919 Commission),[43] to investigate violations by Germany and its allies of the laws and customs of war and 'the principles of the laws of nations as they result[ed] from the usages established among civilized peoples, from the laws of humanity and from the dictates of public conscience'.[44] It recommended the peace treaties include provisions for the establishment of a tribunal to investigate and prosecute persons on charges including murders and massacres, deportation of civilians, denationalization of the inhabitants of occupied territory, pillage, confiscation of property, wanton devastation and destruction of property, and wanton destruction of religious, charitable, educational, and historic buildings and monuments.[45] The commission found that these acts were prohibited by the Hague Regulations and those not specifically enumerated fell within the Martens clause.[46]

The Treaty of Sèvres accommodated the 1919 Commission's recommendation.[47] Under Article 230, Turkey was obliged to recognize and cooperate with any tribunal appointed by the Allies to prosecute alleged perpetrators responsible for

1992, UN Doc.A/Res/47/135; (1993) 32 ILM 911; Council of Europe, Framework Convention for the Protection of National Minorities, 1 Feb. 1995, in force 1 Feb. 1998, CETS No.157.

[41] Treaty of Peace between the Allied and Associated Powers and Turkey, 10 Aug. 1920, not ratified, 15(supp.) *Am. J. Int'l L.* (1921) 179; Vrdoljak, *see earlier* note 38.

[42] Treaty of Peace with Turkey, 24 July 1923, in force 5 Sept. 1924, 28 LNTS 12.

[43] Commission on the Responsibilities of the Authors of War and on Enforcement of Penalties for Violations of the Laws and Customs of War, Majority and Dissenting Reports, Conference of Paris, 14 *Am. J. Int'l L.* (1920) 95, at 122 (hereinafter 1919 Commission).

[44] Eighth recital, preamble, 1907 Hague IV Convention ('Martens clause').

[45] 1919 Commission, *see earlier* note 43, at 114–115.

[46] Arts. 42–46, Section III, 1907 Hague IV Convention; 1919 Commission, *see earlier* note 43, at 19.

[47] *See* Art. 228, Treaty of Sèvres. As a consequence of the United States' dissenting report, no provision for the prosecution of crimes against 'the laws of humanity' was included in the peace treaties with Germany, Austria, Hungary, or Bulgaria. 1919 Commission, *see earlier* note 43, at 14; Memorandum of Reservations Presented by the U.S. Representatives, Annex II, 4 Apr. 1919, 14 *Am. J. Int'l L.* (1920) 127, at 134.

massacres during the war on 'territories which formed part of the Turkish Empire on 1st August 1914'. The later Treaty of Lausanne contained no such provision. Instead, it incorporated a Declaration of Amnesty which was 'desirous to cause the events which have troubled the peace in the East to be forgotten'.[48] These thwarted prosecution efforts were an extension of a lengthy history of minority protection in international law aimed at preventing such policies and acts.

While the Treaty of Sèvres reflected the schema of minority protections contained in other Paris peace treaties, it was markedly different from them.[49] Its provisions reinforced Allied efforts to hold persons accountable and 'to repair so far as possible the wrongs inflicted on individuals in the course of the massacres perpetrated *in Turkey* during the war'.[50] Accordingly, the Treaty sanctioned the reversal of forced assimilation and restitution of confiscated property. It provided that because of the nature of the regime in Turkey from 1 November 1914, conversions to Islam by non-Muslims were not recognized unless such persons voluntarily adhered to the Islamic faith after 'regaining their liberty'. Turkey was to assist searches for and return of individuals 'of whatever race or religion, who [had] disappeared, been carried off, interned or placed in captivity'.[51] It established an arbitral commission composed of representatives nominated by Turkey, the claimant community and the League's Council, with power to detain any person who took part in or incited massacres or deportations and make orders concerning their property.[52] It was required to facilitate the work of mixed commissions appointed by the League's Council to receive and investigate complaints from victims or their families and order the release and restoration of the 'full enjoyment' of the rights of such people.

The Treaty of Sèvres also provided for the internal restitution of property to victims of the massacres or deportations perpetrated within Turkish territory during the war.[53] An arbitral commission composed of representatives nominated by Turkey, the claimant community and League's Council had power to detain persons who took part in or incited massacres or deportations and make orders concerning their property. Turkey was required to recognise the 'injustice of the law of 1915 relating to Abandoned Properties' declaring it and related legislation 'null and void, in the past as in the future'. Property was to be restored free of any encumbrances or compensation to the present occupier or owner. Current owners or occupiers could bring an action against those from whom they had acquired title. The commission could dispose of the property of individual

48 Arts. II, IV, and V, Declaration of Amnesty, 24 July 1923, annexed to Treaty of Lausanne.

49 C.A. Macartney, *National States and National Minorities* (Oxford: Oxford University Press, 1934), at 255; H. W. V. Temperley, *History of the Peace Conference of Paris* (1920–24), reprint, 6 vols. (New York: Oxford University Press, 1969), at 102.

50 Art. 142, Treaty of Sèvres (emphasis added).

51 Art. 142, Treaty of Sèvres.

52 Art. 144, Treaty of Sèvres.

53 Art. 144, Treaty of Sèvres.

members to the community if they had died or disappeared without heirs. Interest in immovable property was voided, with the government indemnifying the present owner. Turkey was required to provide labour for any necessary reconstruction or restoration work.

None of the reported decisions of proceedings brought pursuant to this provision dealt specifically with cultural property.[54] Nor was a similar provision inserted in the subsequent Treaty of Lausanne. Nevertheless, the basic principles contained in the Treaty of Sèvres became an important precedent for Allied governments after the Second World War when they addressed the restitution of cultural property removed from groups persecuted by the Axis forces.

IV. Peace through Division

Most recently, peace agreements have facilitated the establishment of *new* states. By loosening prior staunch resistance by the international community to the emergence of states outside the colonial context, this development permits comparison with models in international law-making sanctioned during the inter-war period. Examples sanctioned by peace processes include the Kosovar declaration of independence in 2008 and the southern Sudan referendum and subsequent secession in 2011. Whilst it is too early to assess the full implications of these processes and events for the international community and international law, it appears that notionally they may broaden the discourses arising in respect of peace agreements covering intra-state conflicts concerning rule of law, governance, constitutionalism, and human rights within states, and outward to states as units within the international community—potentially recalibrating the international legal order beyond purely statist approaches.

This shift is exemplified in provisions covering cultural heritage in peace agreements concerning new states. The international community's response to the ethnic and religious conflict and its legacy in Kosovo is an important contemporary example. As a negotiated settlement between Serbia and Kosovo was not possible, the UN Special Envoy endorsed Kosovar independence subject to the new state's acceptance of various obligations. These obligations covered cultural rights and cultural heritage of various communities, to be overseen by an international monitor, while Serbia was to undertake to return cultural objects removed from Kosovar territory.[55] The substance and rationale for these provisions is strikingly similar to those in peace agreements establishing new states after the First World War.[56] The UN Comprehensive Proposal states they are to promote 'a spirit of tolerance, dialogue and support reconciliation between the Communities'.[57]

[54] Hollander, *see earlier* note 22, at 32–34.

[55] Hollander, *see earlier* note 22, at 32–34.

[56] Vrdoljak, *see earlier* note 8, at 73.

[57] United Nations, Comprehensive Proposal for the Kosovo Status Settlement, UN Doc.S/2007/168/Add.1 (2007), Annex II, 2.6.

Many of the principles now being demanded by the international community in the context of new states have their roots in the post-1919 peace treaties and requirements for membership of new states into the League of Nations.

A. Post-First World War Peace Treaties with Austria and State Succession

Post-First World War peace treaties covering Central and Eastern Europe dealt with restitution of cultural property on the basis of state succession and the principles of territoriality and reciprocity and in the context of the creation of new states. The treaty arrangements regulated the relations between predecessor and successor states following the dismantling of the Austro-Hungarian Empire and the dissolution of the Hapsburg monarchy. The provisions were fuelled by the ambitions of new states to recreate, or more often create anew, a national culture to bolster the legitimacy of these states as nations and the integration of ceded territories.[58] The treaty provisions seemed to signal the ascendancy of the idea of national cultural patrimony and the claims of successor states. However, in practice during the inter-war period, these claims were sacrificed for the 'higher' interests of science and art. This privileging, of these museums and their collections, had been foreshadowed with the earlier codification of international law covering the rules of war and the protection of cultural property.

1. Competing Arguments of Predecessor and Successor States

Austria, as the de facto predecessor state, resisted the dismantling of Viennese collections arguing that its claims should not be restricted to only cultural objects of Austrian origin. Furthermore, it maintained that such cultural objects were an integral part of historic (imperial) collections forming part of its national cultural heritage.[59] It argued that the integrity of existing collections should not be disturbed because they were of immense scientific and artistic value. They were, it maintained, 'the spiritual possession of all those untold thousands who lay claim ... to culture, and ... transcending all national boundaries'.[60]

This universalizing (cultural heritage of humanity) and objectifying (arts and sciences) of the role of Austrian collections strove to depoliticize the place of these cultural materials in its own national patrimony and devalue rival claims to

[58] The elliptical nature of 'country of origin' as the basis of restitution claims troubled some jurists. Visscher, *see earlier* note 1, at 836–837. These principles, and their contestation, were reiterated in subsequent treaties including the Vienna Convention on Succession of States in Respect of State Property, Archives and Debts, Vienna, 7 Apr. 1983, not in force, UN Doc.A./CONF.117/4, and (1983) 22 ILM 306; Agreement on Succession Issues between the Former Yugoslav States and Annexes A to G, 29 June 2001, (2002) 41 ILM 3.

[59] Treue, *see earlier* note 28, at 223–224.

[60] E. Leisching, *cited in* Treue, *see earlier* note 28, at 223–4; see Burnett, *see earlier* note 14, vol. 1, at 332, doc. 705.

the cultural objects. This predecessor state maintained that the collections must remain in the imperial capital for two reasons:(1) the more 'advanced' predecessor state was the natural guardian of this legacy for all peoples, and (2) the superior economic and technical strength of this state meant that it was better able to care for the objects.

The successor states of the former Austro-Hungarian Empire argued that the same objects formed an essential part of their national cultural patrimony. For them, the peace treaty provisions facilitated the reconstitution of the national cultural heritage of communities affected by territorial changes following the dissolution of the empire.[61] Successor states refuted the suggestion that universal collections would be dismantled, noting their claims were modest and necessary for the administration of ceded territories.[62] These states maintained the measures were a small step in righting a historic wrong; that is, the reversing of the past centralizing policies that had transported their cultural treasures to imperial Viennese collections.

2. *Enforcement Framework and Guiding Principles*

The Treaty of Peace between the Allied and Associated Powers and Austria of 1919 (Treaty of Saint-Germain) governed the redistribution of cultural property and archives between various successor states following the dissolution of the Austro-Hungarian empire.[63] Like the Treaty of Versailles' reparations provisions, it too provided for the creation of a Reparation Commission. Its structure was modelled on the Versailles Treaty template.[64] The Hapsburg monarchs had pursued an aggressive policy of centralizing cultural treasures and archives from all corners of their realm in institutions in the imperial capital, Vienna. These post-war 'peace' efforts to return equitably cultural materials to ceding states following the collapse of the empire are important early precedents for restitution claims in peace agreements sanctioning new states—or peace through division. With rival national narratives to sustain, there was inevitable disputation between the predecessor state and successor states over the same cultural objects and archives. The Treaty provided that the dispute would be resolved by an arbitral commission.

[61] De Visscher, *see earlier* note 1, at 830; W. W. Kowalski, 'Repatriation of Cultural Property Following a Cession of Territory or Dissolution of Multinational States', 6 *Art Antiquity & L.* (2001) 139, at 143.

[62] Burnett, *see earlier* note 14, vol.1, at 336, doc.716; Temperley, *see earlier* note 49, vol.5, at 10–11.

[63] Arts. 191–196 and Annex I–VI, Treaty of Peace between the Allied and Associated Powers and Austria Together with Protocol and Declarations, St Germain-en-Laye, 10 Sept. 1919, in force 8 Nov. 1921, UKTS No.11 (1919); Cmd 400 (1919); *British and Foreign State Papers*, vol. 112, at 317, 14(supp.) *Am. J. Int'l L.* (1920) 1, at 77.

[64] Pt. VIII: Reparation, Section I: General Provisions, Article 179 and Annex II, Treaty of Saint-Germain. The provision also permitted delegates from Greece, Poland, Romania, and Czechoslovakia.

The scheme for the redistribution of archival and historical material between predecessor and successor states under the Treaty of Saint-Germain favoured the principle of territoriality (Articles 192 and 193). Under the oversight of the Reparations Commission, Austria was to return 'all records, documents, objects of antiquity and of art, and all scientific and bibliographical material taken away from the invaded territories, whether they belong to the State or to provincial, communal, charitable or ecclesiastical administrations or other public ... institutions' since 1914.[65] The relevant period was extended to ten years prior for records, documents, and historical materials in the possession of public institutions which have 'direct bearing on the history' of the ceded territory and from 1861 in the case of Italy.[66] The new states or existing states which had acquired territory from the former monarchy were required to return materials reciprocally in their territory dating back no more than twenty years which had a 'direct bearing on the history or administration of Austria'. The territorial link possibly related to a portion of or one group of people in the successor state, yet, the right of restitution to the cultural object was afforded to the relevant state, not to that group. Similar and more specific provision was made in respect of cultural objects forming part of the royal collections by Article 196, discussed on p. 35.

The symbolic significance of the possession of these cultural objects for both national identities rendered their return to ceded territories from the imperial collection particularly problematic. The Treaty of Saint-Germain addressed the restitution of cultural objects, in respect of specific objects (Article 195) and by a general right to negotiate (Article 196).

Article 195 (and Annexes II–IV) provided an adjudication and enforcement procedure to resolve claims by various successor states to specific manuscripts and objects. Within a year of the Treaty of Saint Germain's coming into force, the Reparation Commission would appoint a Committee of three jurists to examine how objects in Austria's possession were removed by the relevant ruler in Italy, Belgium, Poland, or Czechoslovakia. If the Committee found that objects were removed contrary to the rights of these territories, the Reparation Commission would order restitution and the parties would abide by its decision. Only Belgium and Czechoslovakia utilized this procedure which in effect amounted to an international arbitration.

The main issue raised in the claims brought before the Committee of Three Jurists, pursuant to Article 195, was whether cultural objects purchased by a reigning Hapsburg monarch became their personal property absolutely and could therefore be removed permanently from their place of origin. The claimant states

[65] Article 192 also provided that the Commission would apply Article 208 where applicable, which provided that 'any building or other property situated in the respective territories transferred to the States referred to in the first paragraph whose principal value lies in its historic interest and associations, and which formerly belonged to [certain territories], may, subject to the approval of the Reparation Commission, be transferred to the Government entitled thereto without payment'.

[66] Art.193, Treaty of Saint Germain.

argued that the objects formed part of their public domain and should revert to them upon the dissolution of the empire. Austria argued that the ceding states had no legal claim to recovery because the objects formed part of the personal property of the Hapsburg monarch.

The Committee in all three cases found for Austria and refused to pass 'the verdict of history' on the government of the Hapsburgs. Even though the dispute was between two states, the Committee resolved the claims by reviving internal constitutional arrangements between a sovereign and its subjects.[67] Accordingly Austria, as the designated 'predecessor' state, obtained various accoutrements of the empire, including imperial collections without the possession of any corresponding territories.[68] The Committee categorically rejected the Czechoslovak argument that it should 'right a historic wrong' by reversing the centralizing policies of the Hapsburg monarchy which for centuries had removed cultural heritage from all corners of its empire.[69] It also refused to 'be guided by justice, equity and good faith', maintaining it had no authority to deviate from established juridical methods.[70] By adopting this strategy, the Committee ignored the unequal relations between the parties that had enabled the transaction to occur at all. This inequality was reaffirmed with its privileging of the law of the predecessor state.

The Treaty of Saint-Germain also granted successor states a general right to negotiate the restitution of cultural objects from imperial collections, which they claim as part of their national cultural patrimony, guided by the principles of territoriality and reciprocity. Article 196 recognized that 'object[s] of artistic, archaeological, scientific or historic character forming part of the [imperial] collections' could 'form part of the intellectual patrimony of the ceded districts', and 'may be returned to their districts of origin'. It also placed a freeze on the disposal of former imperial collections by the predecessor state for a period of twenty years after the dissolution of the empire. This ensured accessibility and preservation of these objects and archives for nationals of the successor states.

Despite the potentially far-reaching consequences of Article 196 for the re-allocation of archives and cultural property, it is generally agreed that its

[67] Allied Powers (1919–), Reparation Commission, 1921, 'Belgian Claims to the Triptych of Saint Ildephonse and the Treasure of the Order of the Golden Fleece, Report of the Committee of Three Jurists', 25 Oct. 1921, Annex no.1141 at 14, 19–21, 51; De Visscher, *see earlier* note 1, at 834; Kowalski, *see earlier* note 9, at 30; Kowalski, *see earlier* note 61, at 144; O., 'International Arbitrations under the Treaty of St Germain', 4 *British Y.B. Int'l L.* (1923–24) 124, at 129.

[68] *Cf.* Art.11, Peace Treaty between Poland, Russia and the Ukraine, 18 Mar. 1921, in force upon signature, 6 LNTS 123; see De Visscher, *see earlier* note 1, at 836; J. Chrzaszczewska, 'Un exemple de restitution. Le traité de Riga de 1921 et la patrimoine artistique de la Pologne', 17–18 *Mouseion* (1932) 205; Kowalski, *see earlier* note 9, at 32–33; Kowalski, *see earlier* note 61, at 151; L. V. Prott and P. J. O'Keefe, *Law and the Cultural Heritage, Volume 3: Movement* (London: Professional Books, 1989) 829.

[69] It found that the principle that 'a country which is an integral part of a composite State has a right, in case the State should be partitioned, to claim the property acquired with the aid of the local revenues of the said country' was not recognized in international law nor could it be implied from the peace treaties. De Visscher, *see earlier* note 1, at 832; O., *see earlier* note 67, at 127.

[70] De Visscher, *see earlier* note 1, at 832; O., *see earlier* note 67, at 126.

application had little practical effect on the integrity of Viennese collections.[71] For example, the Italo-Austrian Treaty of 1920 amicably resolved Italian claims under Article 196 by recognizing that the 'juridical and historic status of those objects was of special character' and distinguishable from the claims of other states.[72] Furthermore, Italy 'recognised the advisability of preventing, in the higher, general interest of civilisation, the dispersion of the historic, artistic, and archaeological collections of Austria which in their entirety constitute an esthetic and historic entity, indivisible and celebrated'.[73] Yet, Austria obtained an unfettered title with no restrictions preventing it from dispersing the collections if it so wished.

The Treaty of Peace between the Allied and Associated Powers and Hungary of 1920 (Treaty of Trianon) confronted issues raised by restitution claims made by two (or more) successor states on former imperial collections.[74] Article 177 reaffirmed Hungary's right to negotiate the division of these collections on the same terms as other successor states under Article 196 of the Treaty of Saint-Germain.[75] Hungary persistently challenged the notion of territorial link as the trigger for selecting and returning public records and cultural objects to ceded territories. It advocated the application of the principle of nationality so that objects and archives relevant to the Hungarian people should be returned regardless of the territory of post-war Hungary.[76] In the end, the territoriality principle long contested by Hungary survived.[77] It also ceded to Austrian demands for an acceptance of the inviolability of the Viennese collections.[78]

B. Post-First World War Peace Treaty with Turkey and State Succession

As explained earlier, the first Treaty of Peace with Turkey of 1920 provided for protection of minorities and restitution of their property. The Treaty also redefined relations between Turkey, successor states, and mandating powers following

[71] De Visscher, *see earlier* note 1, at 834; Treue, *see earlier* note 28, at 231.

[72] Art. 4, Italo-Austrian Treaty, in Visscher, *see earlier* note 1, at 834–835. The treaty finalized Italian claims pursuant to Articles 191–196 of the Treaty of Saint-Germain, without recourse to adjudication.

[73] Italy also agreed to 'energetically oppose' the claims of other states which if accepted would 'prejudice ... the integrity of the Austrian collections, which must be preserved in the interests of science' (art. 9).

[74] Burnett, *see earlier* note 14, vol.1, at 333, 345–7, 349; Kowalski, *see earlier* note 9, at 146.

[75] Article 193 of the Treaty of Saint Germain mirrored Articles 177 and 178 of the Treaty of Trianon. *See* Burnett, *see earlier* note 14, vol. 1, at 346–347, docs. 740–744; De Visscher, *see earlier* note 1, at 835–836; Kowalski, *see earlier* note 61, at 146; Treue, *see earlier* note 28, at 228–229.

[76] Burnett, *see earlier* note 14, vol.1, at 345–346, doc. 739.

[77] With the exception of objects specifically of Hungarian origin or character, Austria agreed to the relinquishment of a limited number of works of art to improve existing Hungarian collections of historic or artistic interest. Agreement between Austria and Hungary, Venice, 27 Nov. 1932, 162 LNTS 396; *see* H. Tietze, 'L'accord Austro-Hongrois sur la réparatition des collections de la maison des Habsbourg', 23–24 *Mouseion* (1933) 92–97.

[78] De Visscher, *see earlier* note 1, at 836–7. Hungary was granted 'privileged rights' of access to collections of 'common cultural interest' (art. 4). Kowalski, *see earlier* note 9, at 148.

the dismantling of the Ottoman empire.[79] The restitution provisions in this peace treaty varied from those contained in the treaties covering the dismantling of the Austro-Hungarian empire. These variations arose because the treaty arrangements did not strictly involve state succession but 'colonial' secession—the transfer of authority from one colonial occupier to another.[80] For example, Article 420 of the Treaty of Sèvres addressed restitution of archives and cultural property which belonged not only to the Allied Powers and their nationals but included 'companies and associations of every description controlled by such nationals'.[81] The place and conditions of return were not to be resolved by the Reparation Commission, but were 'laid down by the Governments to which they are to be restored'.[82] In addition, under Article 422, the Turkish government was required to return relevant objects to ceded territories and if they had passed into private ownership 'it would take the necessary steps by expropriation or otherwise to enable it to fulfill [this] obligation'.

The Treaty of Sèvres most starkly departed from other Paris peace treaties by requiring that mandated territories pass domestic legislation controlling archaeological sites and the export of archaeological materials (Article 421 and Annex).[83] The role of the mandating power and its relations with other powers came to the fore in the proposed scheme which regulated access and control of excavation sites, and the 'equitable' division of archaeological finds.[84] Article 421, and Annex, exposed the competing interests concerning the protection of cultural objects and sites in the mandated territories. On the one hand, the mandating power had a duty to the international community to ensure free and equal access to archaeological 'resources' which would feed the universal collections of the metropolitan capitals. On the other hand, it also had a duty to the peoples of the mandated territories to protect their cultural objects and sites. While the Treaty of Sèvres was never ratified, its proposed legislative model covering archaeological sites and finds was incorporated into the domestic laws of several states in the Middle East, including, for example, Palestine.[85]

[79] Arts. 420–425, Treaty of Sèvres.

[80] Arts. 424 through 425 of the Treaty of Sèvres provided for the transfer of archives and records based on the principle of territoriality, with reciprocity applying only to the provision covering Wakfs, localized religious communities in areas ceded from Turkey. This class of property rights has long been recognized in Muslim countries. C. Phillipson, *Termination of War and Treaties of Peace* (London: E. P. Dutton & Co., 1916) 319.

[81] Treaty of Sèvres.

[82] *See* Art. 184, Treaty of St Germain; Art.168, Treaty of Trianon.

[83] There was a lengthy legal history of attempting to regulate the export of archaeological finds in the Ottoman territories. E. R. Chamberlin, *Preserving the Past* (London: Dent, 1979), at 109–112; P. J. O'Keefe and L. V. Prott, *Law and the Cultural Heritage, Vol.1: Discovery and Excavation* (London: Professional Books, 1983) 43,§§ 228–237.

[84] Art. 421 Treaty of Sèvres, Annex, points 6 to 8. Points 1 to 5 provided the framework for the regulation of transactions of antiquities by the Department of Antiquities.

[85] Section 7, Palestine Antiquities Ordinance 1921. *See* Art. 21 of the British Mandate for Palestine, LNOJ (Aug. 1922) 3rd Year, No.8, Pt.II, at 1007ff; O'Keefe and Prott, *see earlier* note 83, at 49, § 234.

V. Conclusion

An abiding legacy of the post-First World War peace treaties is that they formulated and implemented principles which remain current in contemporary international law for the protection of cultural property. These obligations and the remedies consequent on their breach covered the law of armed conflict and international humanitarian law, human rights and minorities, and state succession and recognition of new states. In addition, these peace treaties bolstered such obligations through the articulation of mechanisms for enforcement and the resolution of disputes including reparations commissions, arbitral commissions, and judicial tribunals. This fostered an environment which promoted the nascent efforts toward the formulation of specialist multilateral instruments for the restitution of cultural objects which were illicitly removed from their country of origin which would be realized half a century later with the 1970 UNESCO Convention, and the protection of cultural property during armed conflict and belligerent occupation contained in the 1954 Hague Convention and its Protocols.[86] However unlike these latter day conventions, the earlier inter-war draft instruments prepared by the League of Nations on repatriation of cultural objects contained provisions concerning arbitration and referral to the Permanent Court of International Justice, the precursor to the International Court of Justice.[87]

It is also important to recall that these inter-war initiatives were contained in peace agreements. At a time when the international community, through organisations like the United Nations and regional organizations like the European Union and

[86] Convention on the Means of Prohibiting and Preventing the Illicit Import, Export and Transfer of Ownership of Cultural Property, 14 Nov. 1970, in force 24 Apr. 1972, 823 UNTS 231; 1954 Hague Convention; 1954 Hague Protocol; 1999 Hague Protocol.

[87] Art. 7 of the Draft International Convention on the Repatriation of Objects of Artistic, Historical or Scientific Interest Which Have Been Lost or Stolen or Unlawfully Alienated or Exported (First draft, 1933) provided:

> Should any dispute arise between the High Contracting Party as to the interpretation or application of the present Convention, and should it be impossible to reach a satisfactory solution of such dispute through diplomacy, it should be settled in accordance with the provision in force between the Parties with reference to the settlement of International disputes.
>
> Should no such provisions exist between the Parties to the dispute, the latter shall be submitted to an arbitral or judicial procedure. Failing agreement upon the choice of some other tribunal, the Parties shall, at the request of any one of them, submit the dispute to the Permanent Court of International Justice if they are all parties to the Protocol ... or if they are not all Parties to the Protocol, they shall submit the dispute to a Court of Arbitration constituted in accordance with the Hague Convention of 1907 for the Peaceful Settlement of International Disputes.

Replicated in the 1936 draft in Art. 18 and Art. 14 in the 1939 Draft but not adopted because of the outbreak of war. Drafts reproduced in De Visscher, *see earlier* note 1, Annexes.

Organization of American States, is devoting increased resources to ensuring sustainable and long-lasting peace in regions scarred by conflict, it is timely that the role of culture and cultural heritage toward the attainment of this aim be properly examined. A re-assessment of the provisions covering cultural heritage (and cultural rights) contained in the extensive network of post-First World War peace agreements is a vital step along this path.

3

The Role of International and Mixed Criminal Courts in the Enforcement of International Norms Concerning the Protection of Cultural Heritage

Federico Lenzerini *

I. Introduction: The Enforcement of Crimes against Cultural Heritage

> [H]e who becomes master of a city accustomed to freedom and does not destroy it, may expect to be destroyed by it, for in rebellion it has always the watchword of liberty and its ancient privileges as a rallying point, which neither time nor benefits will ever cause it to forget.[1]

Throughout the centuries, devastation of cities and destruction of cultural heritage have constantly been perceived as necessary side-effects of armed conflicts in order to defeat the enemy and to extinguish definitively all ashes of its resistance, through eliminating the tangible memory and the self-pride of its identity reflected in the products of its culture. From the demolition of the Temple of Serapis in Alexandria, ordered by the Roman Emperor Theodosius in 391 AD to eliminate the last refuge of non-Christians, to the blatant destruction of the two ancient giant Buddha statues in the Afghan valley of Bamiyan by the Taliban regime in March 2001[2]—as part of a wider plan to eradicate all memories of non-Muslim culture—many cases have occurred in which humanity has shown ferocious determination in eliminating the traces of the groups perceived as hostile at a given time.

* Ph.D., International Law. Professor of International Law and European Union Law, University of Siena (Italy). The author occasionally provides consultancies to UNESCO.

[1] N. Machiavelli, *De Principatibus* (The Prince) (1532), 51.

[2] *See*, on this case, F. Francioni and F. Lenzerini, 'The Destruction of the Buddhas of Bamiyan in International Law', in 14 *Eur. J. of Int'l L.* (2003), 619 ff.

In order to react to such an unfortunate tendency, by the beginning of the 20th century the international community started to produce legal norms aimed at preventing belligerent acts against cultural property and enforcing their punishment, with the specific purpose of protecting the interest of the territorial state in the preservation of its own cultural items. From the old-fashioned Article 27 of the Regulations annexed to Convention IV on the Laws and Customs of War of 1907,[3] through, inter alia, the 1954 Hague Convention on the Protection of Cultural Property in the Event of Armed Conflict,[4] the two 1977 Protocols to the Geneva Conventions on Humanitarian Law of 1949,[5] the statutes of the International Criminal Tribunal for the Former Yugoslavia (ICTY)[6] and the International Criminal Court (ICC),[7] the Second Protocol to the 1954 Hague

[3] *See* Convention (IV) Respecting the Laws and Customs of War on Land and Its Annex: Regulations Concerning the Laws and Customs of War on Land, The Hague, 18 Oct. 1907, *available at* <http://www.icrc.org/ihl.nsf> (last accessed 25 July 2012). Article 27 states, 'In sieges and bombardments all necessary steps must be taken to spare, as far as possible, buildings dedicated to religion, art, science, or charitable purposes, historic monuments, hospitals, and places where the sick and wounded are collected, provided they are not being used at the time for military purposes'. The same principle is also expressed by Article 5 of the Convention (IX) Concerning Bombardment by Naval Forces in Time of War, *available at* <http://www.icrc.org/ihl.nsf> (last accessed 4 February 2013).

[4] 249 UNTS 240.

[5] *See* Protocol Additional to the Geneva Conventions of 12 August 1949, and Relating to the Protection of Victims of International Armed Conflicts (Protocol I), 1125 UNTS 5. According to Article 53:

> Without prejudice to the provisions of the Hague Convention for the Protection of Cultural Property in the Event of Armed Conflict of 14 May 1954, and of other relevant international instruments, it is prohibited: (a) to commit any acts of hostility directed against the historic monuments, works of art or places of worship which constitute the cultural or spiritual heritage of peoples; (b) to use such objects in support of the military effort; (c) to make such objects the object of reprisals.

In addition, Article 85 considers the act of 'making the clearly-recognized historic monuments, works of art or places of worship which constitute the cultural or spiritual heritage of peoples and to which special protection has been given by special arrangement, for example, within the framework of a competent international organization, the object of attack, causing as a result extensive destruction thereof, where there is no evidence of the violation by the adverse Party of Article 53, subparagraph (b), and when such historic monuments, works of art and places of worship are not located in the immediate proximity of military objectives' as a grave breach of the Protocol, amounting to a war crime. Protocol Additional to the Geneva Conventions of 12 August 1949, and Relating to the Protection of Victims of Non-International Armed Conflicts (Protocol II), 1125 UNTS 609, affirms at Article 16 that '[w]ithout prejudice to the provisions of the Hague Convention for the Protection of Cultural Property in the Event of Armed Conflict of 14 May 1954, it is prohibited to commit any acts of hostility directed against historic monuments, works of art or places of worship which constitute the cultural or spiritual heritage of peoples, and to use them in support of the military effort'.

[6] *See later* text accompanying note 26.

[7] *See* Rome Statute of the International Criminal Court (1998), *available at* <http://untreaty.un.org/cod/icc/statute/romefra.htm> (last accessed 16 January 2013). Article 8(2)(a)(iv) includes in the category of war crimes the '[e]xtensive destruction and appropriation of property, not justified by military necessity and carried out unlawfully and wantonly'. Similarly, Articles 8(2)(b)(ix) and 8(2)(e)(iv) classify as a war crime the act of '[i]ntentionally directing attacks against buildings dedicated to religion, education, art, science or charitable purposes, historic monuments, hospitals and places where the sick and wounded are collected, provided they are not military objectives' with regard to, respectively, international and non-international armed conflicts.

Convention,[8] to the 2003 UNESCO Declaration on the Intentional Destruction of Cultural Heritage,[9] international law in the field has significantly evolved to incorporate the perception of cultural *heritage* as a common interest of humanity as a whole.[10] This process has also led to developing the characterization of crimes against cultural heritage as *war crimes*, implying that *individual* criminal responsibility of perpetrators may directly arise from the relevant rules of international law.

The latter characterization of international law on cultural heritage has opened new perspectives with respect to the enforcement of crimes against cultural heritage, allowing extension beyond the usual dynamics of international responsibility as limited to interstate relations. In particular, in principle prosecution and punishment of individual perpetrators of crimes against cultural heritage are possible not only at the domestic judiciary level, but also before competent international bodies. Of course, the inherent limit of international judicial enforcement of international crimes in general, and crimes against cultural heritage in particular, rests in the fact that it is practicable only whether and to the extent that specific tribunals exist having the competence to adjudicate the crimes in point. At present, however, several tribunals actually exist which are attributed such a competence.

[8] Second Protocol to the Hague Convention of 1954 for the Protection of Cultural Property in the Event of Armed Conflict, 1999, 2253 UNTS 172. The whole Chapter 4 of the Protocol deals with the issue of criminal responsibility and jurisdiction. Article 15, in particular, in listing the acts which are considered as serious violations of the Protocol, states:

> 1. Any person commits an offence within the meaning of this Protocol if that person intentionally and in violation of the Convention or this Protocol commits any of the following acts: a. making cultural property under enhanced protection the object of attack; b. using cultural property under enhanced protection or its immediate surroundings in support of military action; c. extensive destruction or appropriation of cultural property protected under the Convention and this Protocol; d. making cultural property protected under the Convention and this Protocol the object of attack; e. theft, pillage or misappropriation of, or acts of vandalism directed against cultural property protected under the Convention. 2. Each Party shall adopt such measures as may be necessary to establish as criminal offences under its domestic law the offences set forth in this Article and to make such offences punishable by appropriate penalties. When doing so, Parties shall comply with general principles of law and international law, including the rules extending individual criminal responsibility to persons other than those who directly commit the act.

[9] *See* <http://portal.unesco.org/en/ev.php-URL_ID=17718&URL_DO=DO_TOPIC&URL_SECTION=201.html> (last accessed 25 July 2012). Article VII, in proclaiming the principle of individual criminal responsibility for acts of destruction of cultural heritage, affirms:

> States should take all appropriate measures, in accordance with international law, to establish jurisdiction over, and provide effective criminal sanctions against, those persons who commit, or order to be committed, acts of intentional destruction of cultural heritage of great importance for humanity, whether or not it is inscribed on a list maintained by UNESCO or another international organization.

[10] This idea is already present in the Preamble of the 1954 Hague Convention, paragraphs 2 and 3 of which, respectively, express the view that 'damage to cultural property belonging to any people whatsoever means damage to the cultural heritage of all mankind, since each people makes its contribution to the culture of the world', and consider that 'the preservation of the cultural heritage is of great importance for all peoples of the world and that it is important that this heritage should receive international protection'.

First, we have ad hoc international criminal tribunals—like the ICTY—established in order to judge international crimes perpetrated in a specific territory during a predetermined time span; these tribunals are of exclusive international character in all their elements, including administration and judge membership, as well as applicable law.

In addition to international tribunals, 'mixed courts' also exist, which are nationally located tribunals with some degree of 'internalization' in terms of administration, membership, applicable law or support. Mixed courts may be defined as arrangements in the context of which 'national and international elements are embodied in the organization, structure and functioning of the Court systems, in the criminal procedures employed, and in the application of laws'.[11] Therefore, they usually have both national and international judges and may usually apply both domestic and international law. Among mixed courts, to the purpose of this chapter, the Extraordinary Chambers in the Courts of Cambodia—commonly known as the 'Khmer Rouge Tribunal'—are of special significance. They consist of a national Court—established by means of an agreement between the Royal government of Cambodia and the United Nations on 6 June 2003[12] and composed of both national and international judges—which has the competence to prosecute members of the Khmer Rouge for serious violations of Cambodian criminal law and international law (including international treaties ratified by Cambodia) perpetrated during the period between 17 April 1975 and 6 January 1979. Indeed, according to Article 6 of the 2004 Amended Cambodian Law on the Establishment of the Extraordinary Chambers in the Courts of Cambodia for the Prosecution of Crimes Committed During the Period of Democratic Kampuchea,[13] the Extraordinary Chambers have the power to bring to trial all suspects who committed or ordered the commission—during the above period—of, inter alia, 'destruction and serious damage to property, not justified by military necessity and carried out unlawfully and wantonly'. In addition, according to Article 7 of the same Law, the Chambers 'have the power to bring to trial all Suspects most responsible [in the same period] for the destruction of cultural property during armed conflict pursuant to the 1954 Hague Convention for Protection of Cultural Property in the Event of Armed Conflict'.

Finally, also the ICC—as a Court of permanent character and with potentially unlimited territorial jurisdiction—has the competence to prosecute the persons responsible for war crimes, including destruction or intentional attacks against

[11] *See* K. Ambos and M. Othman, 'Introduction', in K. Ambos and M. Othman (eds), *New Approaches in International Criminal Justice: Kosovo, East Timor, Sierra Leone and Cambodia* (Freiburg 2003), 2.

[12] *See* Agreement between the United Nations and the Royal Government of Cambodia Concerning the Prosecution under Cambodian Law of Crimes Committed during the Period of Democratic Kampuchea, 6 June 2003, *available at* <http://www.unhcr.org/refworld/docid/4ba8e2ea9dc.html> (last accessed 25 July 2012).

[13] *See* <http://www.eccc.gov.kh/sites/default/files/legal-documents/KR_Law_as_amended_27_Oct_2004_Eng.pdf> (last accessed 25 July 2012).

cultural property[14] perpetrated after the entry into force of its Statute for the State of which the person accused of the crime is a national or in the territory of which the crime occurred.[15]

II. Enforcement of International Law on Cultural Heritage in Practice: The Case Law of the International Criminal Tribunal for the Former Yugoslavia

A. The Destruction of Cultural Heritage Perpetrated During the Balkan Wars

During the Balkan wars, which took place in the territories of the Former Yugoslavia from 1991 to 1995, an impressive rate of awful and systematic violations of the most elementary rules of humanity were perpetrated, leading the conflict to become one of the world's most dreadful tragedies of the 20th century. Pursuing the goal of eliminating the enemy ethnic groups, the warring factions involved in the conflict—although to a different extent and, consequently, with different responsibilities—committed the most atrocious infringements of human dignity, including mass killings, summary executions, starving, systematic rape, forced pregnancies, and imposition of living conditions intended to produce genocidal effects. Furthermore, a number of additional measures were taken in order to weaken the resistance of the enemies through the mortification of their culture and beliefs and humiliation of their pride and self-esteem.

Among the strategies adopted in this respect, systematic plans of destruction of religious and cultural heritage of special spiritual significance were carried out. For example, in December 1991, during the Croatian War of Independence (1991–95), the ancient city of Dubrovnik was heavily shelled by the forces of Montenegro, leading over half of the buildings of the old town to be damaged (including the archives of the Festival Palace—which were completely destroyed—St Blaise's Church, the Franciscan Cathedral and Convent, the Dominican Convent, St. Clair's Convent, and the Fountain of Onofrio).[16] However, episodes of hostility against cultural properties (particularly those dedicated to religion) mostly recurred in the course of the Bosnian war, which took place in Bosnia and Herzegovina between March 1992 and November 1995. A study conducted on 277 mosques located in the area of the conflict showed that 92 percent of them (255) were destroyed (136) or heavily damaged (119) by the Serb forces as a result of shelling. Similarly, 75 per cent of the 57 Catholic churches which were

[14] *See earlier* note 7.

[15] *See* Articles 11 and 12 of the Statute.

[16] *See* Final Report of the Commission of Experts Established Pursuant to Security Council Resolution 780 (1992), UN Doc. S/1994/674 of 27 May 1994, at IV.J.

the object of the same research were seriously injured (30) or destroyed (13).[17] In Mostar, '12 of 14 dzamija mosques ... were hit, and all 12 are in the upper damage classifications .... Five minarets were shot off at one level or another, and 4 others were hit'.[18] Serb forces also destroyed the 14 historic mosques located in the town of Foča and all the 16 mosques of Banja Luka, including the city's two most important ones (the Ferhadija Mosque, built in 1578, and the Arnaudija Mosque, built in 1587). Archives and libraries were also attacked during the conflict in Bosnia and Herzegovina, particularly in Sarajevo.[19] This, without mentioning the blatant destruction of the Stari Most—the well-known Mostar bridge—demolished on 9 November 1993 (4th anniversary of the fall of the Berlin Wall) because it was viewed as a connection uniting the Croat and Muslim communities living in town 'in spite of their religious differences and the circumstances of the present war'.[20]

These occurrences acquired a special shade of gravity exactly on account of the fact that—as already noted—they did not occur as 'side effects' of warring activities

[17] *See* A. J. Riedlmayer, 'Destruction of Cultural Heritage in Bosnia-Herzegovina, 1992–1996: A Post-War Survey of Selected Municipalities', (2002) 10, *available at* <http://hague.bard.edu/reports/BosHeritageReport-AR.pdf> (last accessed 25 July 2012).

[18] *See* Council of Europe, Parliamentary Assembly, 'The Destruction by War of the Cultural Heritage in Croatia and Bosnia-Herzegovina Presented by the Committee on Culture and Education', Information Report, Doc. 6756 of 2 Feb. 1993, Appendix C, 'War Damage to the Cultural Heritage in Croatia and Bosnia-Herzegovina', Report by Dr. Colin Kaiser, Consultant Expert, para. 155 (italics in original).

[19] *See* Int'l Court of Justice, Application of the Convention on the Prevention and Punishment of the Crime of Genocide (*Bosnia & Herzegovina v Serbia & Montenegro*), Judgment of 26 Feb. 2007, para. 341 f, *available at* <http://www.icj-cij.org> (last accessed 25 July 2012). Also the ICTY, in a number of cases, has reported evidence of aggressive acts perpetrated against cultural heritage during the Balkan wars. *See, eg, Prosecutor v Karadžić & Mladić*, Cases IT-95-5-R61 and IT-95–18-R61, Trial Chamber, Review of the Indictment Pursuant to Rule 61 of the Rules of Procedure and Evidence, 11 July 1996, para. 15 ('Throughout the territory of Bosnia and Herzegovina under their control, Bosnian Serb forces ... destroyed, quasi-systematically, the Muslim and Catholic cultural heritage, in particular, sacred sites. According to estimates provided at the hearing by an expert witness, ... a total of 1.123 mosques, 504 Catholic churches and five synagogues were destroyed or damaged, for the most part, in the absence of military activity or after the cessation thereof. This was the case in the destruction of the entire Islamic and Catholic heritage in the Banja Luka area, which had a Serbian majority and the nearest area of combat to which was several dozen kilometres away. All of the mosques and Catholic churches were destroyed. Some mosques were destroyed with explosives and the ruins were then levelled and the rubble thrown in the public dumps in order to eliminate any vestige of Muslim presence. Aside from churches and mosques, other religious and cultural symbols like cemeteries and monasteries were targets of the attacks.'); *Prosecutor v Tadić*, Case IT-94–1-T, Trial Chamber, Judgment of 7 May 1997, para. 149 ('[In the Banja Luka area] [n]on-Serb cultural and religious symbols throughout the region were targeted for destruction.'); *Prosecutor v Brđanin*, Case IT-99–36-T, Trial Chamber II, Judgment of 1 Sept. 2004 (in which the Tribunal ascertained that acts of wilful damage had been committed to the prejudice of both Muslim and Roman Catholic religious buildings and institutions in a number of municipalities by Bosnian Serb forces, with respect to which the Tribunal found that 'the devastation was targeted, controlled and deliberate' (*see* para. 642)). See also the cases quoted in the following Section. All ICTY judgments are *available at* <http://www.icty.org/sections/TheCases/JudgementList> (last accessed 25 July 2012).

[20] *See* Final Report of the Commission of Experts Established Pursuant to Security Council Resolution 780, *earlier* note 16, at IV.J.

aimed at pursuing different results, but were painstakingly and selectively planned in order to hit the sense of identity and self-worth of the communities which had a special spiritual and cultural connection with the heritage concerned. As emphasized in the Report resulting from the aforementioned study,

> [t]he damage to these monuments was clearly the result of attacks directed against them, rather than incidental to the fighting. Evidence of this includes signs of blast damage indicating explosives placed inside the mosques or inside the stairwells of minarets; many mosques are burnt out. In a number of towns ...the destruction of mosques took place while the area was under the control of Serb forces, at times when there was no military action in the immediate vicinity .... In many localities—especially in major population centers, but at times also in village settings—mosques were not only destroyed by burning and explosives, but the ruins were razed and the sites levelled with heavy equipment, and all building materials were removed from the site.[21]

This was also confirmed by the Special Rapporteur of the UN Security Council, who highlighted the fact that

> [t]he sacral edifices [shattered in Prijedor town] were allegedly not desecrated, damaged and destroyed for any military purpose nor as a side-effect of the military operations as such. Conversely, most of the destruction was due to later separate operations of dynamiting.... [Also] [t]he Catholic churches and religious buildings [destroyed and damaged] in Opstina Prijedor ...were allegedly desecrated, destroyed and damaged for no military purpose and not in connection with any military activity as such.[22]

In addition, in 1993 the Expert of the Council of Europe's Parliamentary Assembly noted that—with respect to the mosques destroyed by the Serb forces in Mostar—'[i]t may have been inevitable that mosques in a military "front" zone would be hit, but it is highly doubtful that a minaret can be brought down with a single large calibre shell, which implies a certain amount of deliberate targetting on these structures'.[23]

B. The ICTY Case Law on Cultural Heritage

The ICTY—established by the UN Security Council in 1993[24]—has the competence of dealing with hostile acts against cultural heritage, in respect to the

[21] *See* Riedlmayer, *earlier* note 17, at 11 f.

[22] *See* Final Report of the United Nations Commission of Experts Established Pursuant to Security Council Resolution 780 (1992), Annex V, 'The Prijedor Report', UN Doc. S/1994/674/Add.2 (Vol. I) of 28 Dec. 1994, at XI.A, *available at* <http://www.ess.uwe.ac.uk/comexpert/ANX/V.htm#II-XI> (last accessed 25 July 2012).

[23] *See* Council of Europe, Parliamentary Assembly, 'The Destruction by War of the Cultural Heritage in Croatia and Bosnia-Herzegovina Presented by the Committee on Culture and Education', *see earlier* note 18, Appendix C, 'War Damage to the Cultural Heritage in Croatia and Bosnia-Herzegovina', para. 155.

[24] *See* Resolution 827 of 25 May 1993.

Balkan wars, pursuant to paragraph (d) of Article 3 of its Statute.[25] This provision includes, in the list of violations of the laws and customs of war with respect to which the Tribunal may exercise its jurisdiction, 'seizure of, destruction or wilful damage done to institutions dedicated to religion, charity and education, the arts and sciences, historic monuments and works of art and sciences'.[26] The wording and structure of Article 3(d) is clearly influenced by Article 27 of the Regulations annexed to the Hague Convention IV on the laws and customs of war of 1907.[27] This is the reason why the provision in point does not include any explicit reference to the concept of 'cultural property' or 'cultural heritage'.[28] This notwithstanding, it actually encompasses its main manifestations, and in the practice of the ICTY, has proven effective in addressing hostile acts perpetrated against cultural heritage during the Balkan wars.

In order to verify the actual foundation of its mandate with respect to the acts of wilful damage to or destruction of cultural heritage, the ICTY has first addressed the issue of the scope and extension of international criminal law concerning such heritage. The fact that the crime in point 'has ...already been criminalised under customary international law' has been affirmed by the Tribunal since its very first (and leading) case, *Prosecutor v Tadić*, and has been later reiterated in *Kordić&Cerkez*,[29] *Brđanin*,[30] and *Strugar*.[31] As the Balkan wars—with respect to which the ICTY may exercise its jurisdiction—were of internal character, the Tribunal had also to ascertain that the customary status of the prohibition of wilful damage or destruction of cultural heritage extends to non-international armed conflicts. In this respect, in *Tadić* the Appeals Chamber affirmed that '[t]he emergence of international rules governing internal strife has occurred ... at the level of customary law ... some treaty rules have gradually become part of customary law. This holds true for ... Article 19 of the Hague Convention for the Protection of Cultural Property in the Event of Armed Conflict of 14 May 1954'.[32]

25 *See*, on this issue, M. Frulli, 'Advancing the Protection of Cultural Property through the Implementation of Individual Criminal Responsibility: The Case-Law of the International Criminal Tribunal for the Former Yugoslavia', in XV *Italian Y.B. Int'l L.* (2005), 195 ff.

26 The ICTY Statute is *available at* <http://www.icty.org/x/file/Legal%20Library/Statute/statute_sept09_En.pdf> (last accessed 25 July 2012).

27 *See earlier* note 3.

28 *See* Frulli, *see earlier* note 25, at 196 f.

29 *See Prosecutor v Kordić & Cerkez*, Case IT-95–14/2-T, Trial Chamber, Judgment of 26 Feb. 2001, para. 206.

30 *See Prosecutor v Brđanin*, Case IT-99–36-T, Trial Chamber II, Judgment of 1 Sept. 2004, para. 595.

31 *See Prosecutor v Strugar*, Case IT-01–42-T, Trial Chamber II, Judgment of 31 Jan. 2005, para. 229.

32 *See Prosecutor v Tadić*, Decision on the Defence Motion for Interlocutory Appeal on Jurisdiction, Appeals Chamber, Decision of 2 Oct. 1995, para. 98. Article 19 of the 1954 Hague Convention on the Protection of Cultural Property in the Event of Armed Conflict states:'1. In the event of an armed conflict not of an international character occurring within the territory of one of the High Contracting Parties, each party to the conflict shall be bound to apply, as a minimum, the provisions

The Chamber also added that 'customary rules have developed to govern internal strife ... cover[ing] such areas as ... protection of civilian objects, *in particular* cultural property'.[33] This position was confirmed by the Trial Chamber II in *Strugar*.[34]

The ICTY was offered the opportunity of scrutinizing cases falling within the scope of Article 3(d) in several instances, charging a number of perpetrators of voluntary acts of destruction of, or wilful damage to, cultural properties as responsible of grave breaches of the laws and customs of war. In chronological order, the first time that the ICTY extensively dealt with belligerent acts committed against cultural and religious properties was on the occasion of the *Blaskić* case, in which the Trial Chamber found the accused guilty of having violated the laws and customs of war under Article 3(d) of the ICTY Statute for ordering the acts of damage or destruction against institutions dedicated to religion or education belonging to the Muslim civilian population of Bosnia. The Chamber found that all objective conditions for considering such acts as unlawful were fully met,[35]

of the present Convention which relate to respect for cultural property. 2. The parties to the conflict shall endeavour to bring into force, by means of special agreements, all or part of the other provisions of the present Convention. 3. The United Nations Educational, Scientific and Cultural Organization may offer its services to the parties to the conflict. 4. The application of the preceding provisions shall not affect the legal status of the parties to the conflict'. The 'provisions of the present Convention which relate to respect for cultural property', to which para. 1 refers, are those contemplated by article 4 of the Convention, according to which: '1. The High Contracting Parties undertake to respect cultural property situated within their own territory as well as within the territory of other High Contracting Parties by refraining from any use of the property and its immediate surroundings or of the appliances in use for its protection for purposes which are likely to expose it to destruction or damage in the event of armed conflict; and by refraining from any act of hostility, directed against such property. 2. The obligations mentioned in paragraph 1 of the present Article may be waived only in cases where military necessity imperatively requires such a waiver. 3. The High Contracting Parties further undertake to prohibit, prevent and, if necessary, put a stop to any form of theft, pillage or misappropriation of, and any acts of vandalism directed against, cultural property. They shall refrain from requisitioning movable cultural property situated in the territory of another High Contracting Party. 4. They shall refrain from any act directed by way of reprisals against cultural property. 5. No High Contracting Party may evade the obligations incumbent upon it under the present Article, in respect of another High Contracting Party, by reason of the fact that the latter has not applied the measures of safeguard referred to in Article 3'.

[33] *See* Prosecutor v Tadić, Decision on the Defence Motion for Interlocutory Appeal on Jurisdiction, Appeals Chamber, Decision of 2 Oct. 1995, para. 27 (emphasis added).

[34] *Prosecutor v Strugar*, Case IT-01–42-T, Trial Chamber II, Judgment of 31 Jan. 2005, para. 230.

[35] According to the Trial Chamber, the conditions that must be satisfied in this respect are the following: 'The damage or destruction must have been committed intentionally to institutions which may clearly be identified as dedicated to religion or education and which were not being used for military purposes at the time of the acts. In addition, the institutions must not have been in the immediate vicinity of military objectives'. *See Prosecutor v Blaskić*, Case IT-95–14-T, Trial Chamber, Judgment of 3 Mar. 2000, para. 185. This position has been later (partially) corrected by the Tribunal. In *Naletilić*, the Trial Chamber 'respectfully reject[ed] that protected institutions "must not have been in the vicinity of military objectives". The Chamber does not concur with the view that the mere fact that an institution is in the "immediate vicinity of military objectives" justifies its destruction' (*see Prosecutor v Naletilić*, Case IT-98–34-T, Trial Chamber, Judgment of 31 Mar. 2003, para. 604). The Chamber thus considered that 'a crime under Article 3(d) of the Statute has been committed when: i) the general requirements of Article 3 of the Statute are fulfilled; ii) the destruction regards an institution dedicated to religion; iii) the property was not used for military purposes; iv) the perpetrator acted with the intent to destroy the property' (*Prosecutor v Naletilić*, para. 605). This position was

and rejected the argument of the Defence according to which the acts in point had become unavoidable due to the fact that the relevant religious or educational institutions had become locations of fighting. It was in fact 'barely plausible that soldiers would have taken refuge in the mosque [of Donji Ahmici] since it was impossible to defend';[36] in addition, the mosque 'was destroyed by explosives laid around the base of its minaret ...[making it] "an expert job" which could only have been carried out by persons who knew exactly where to place the explosives'.[37] As a consequence, the destruction of the institutions concerned 'was ... premeditated and could not be justified by any military purpose whatsoever. The only reasons to explain such an act were reasons of discrimination'.[38] Therefore, the Trial Chamber additionally qualified the plunder and wilful destruction of institutions dedicated to religion or education as a modality of perpetration of the crime against humanity of persecution—contemplated by Article 5(h) of the ICTY Statute—as this crime 'may take forms other than injury to the human person, in particular those acts rendered serious not by their apparent cruelty but by the discrimination they seek to instil within humankind .... [P]ersecution may thus take the form of confiscation or destruction of private dwellings or businesses, symbolic buildings or means of subsistence ....'[39]

confirmed by the Trial Chamber in *Strugar* (*Prosecutor v Strugar*, Case IT-01–42-T, Trial Chamber II, Judgment of 31 Jan. 2005, para. 301), stating that 'the special protection awarded to cultural property itself may not be lost simply because of military activities or military installations in the immediate vicinity of the cultural property' (*Prosecutor v Strugar*, para. 310). The Chamber also specified that 'Article 3(d) of the Statute explicitly criminalises only those acts which result in damage to, or destruction of, such property. Therefore, a requisite element of the crime charged in the Indictment is actual damage or destruction occurring as a result of an act directed against this property' (*Prosecutor v Strugar*, para. 308). The *Strugar* Chamber therefore concluded that 'reflect[ing] the position under customary international law ... an act will fulfil the elements of the crime of destruction or wilful damage of cultural property, within the meaning of Article 3(d) of the Statute and in so far as that provision relates to cultural property, if: (i) it has caused damage or destruction to property which constitutes the cultural or spiritual heritage of peoples; (ii) the damaged or destroyed property was not used for military purposes at the time when the acts of hostility directed against these objects took place; and (iii) the act was carried out with the intent to damage or destroy the property in question' (para. 312). This position was reiterated by the Trial Chamber I in *Prosecutor v Martić*, Case IT-95–11-T, Judgment of 12 June 2007, para. 96, affirmed by the Appeals Chamber on 8 October 2008. In *Brđanin* the Trial Chamber stated that 'destruction or wilful damage done to institutions dedicated to religion must have been either perpetrated intentionally, with the knowledge and will of the proscribed result or in reckless disregard of the substantial likelihood of the destruction or damage' (*see Prosecutor v Brđanin*, Case IT-99–36-T, Trial Chamber II, Judgment of 1 Sept. 2004, para. 599). Finally, in *Prosecutor v Milutinović, Šainović, Ojdanić, Pavković, Lazarević, Lukić*, Case IT-05–87-T, Judgment of 26 Feb. 2009, the Trial Chamber found that '[t]he *actus reus* of [the] offence [in point] is as follows: (a) the religious or cultural property must be destroyed or damaged extensively; (b) the religious or cultural property must not be used for a military purpose at the time of the act; and (c) the destruction or damage must be the result of an act directed against this property' (para. 206); according to Chamber, this applies also with respect to the offence of persecution as a crime against humanity (*see later* note 42).

36 *See Prosecutor v Blaskić*, Case IT-95–14-T, Trial Chamber, Judgment of 3 Mar. 2000, para. 421.

37 *Prosecutor v Blaskić*, para. 421 (footnotes omitted).

38 *Prosecutor v Blaskić*, para. 421.

39 *Prosecutor v Blaskić*, para. 227.

In this instance, the acts perpetrated against religious and educational institutions were clearly aimed at mortifying the local people's sense of belonging to the Muslim community, as it is demonstrated by the fact that the 'mosque had just been built [and] [t]he inhabitants of Ahmici had collected the money to build it and were extremely proud of its architecture'.[40]

One year later—in the case of *Kordić & Cerkez*—the Trial Chamber further elaborated this reasoning. In particular, the Chamber—also relying on the practice of the Nuremberg International Military Tribunal and of the International Law Commission[41]—found that the act in point,

> when perpetrated with the requisite discriminatory intent, amounts to an attack on the very religious identity of a people. As such, it manifests a nearly pure expression of the notion of 'crimes against humanity', for all of humanity is indeed injured by the destruction of a unique religious culture and its concomitant cultural objects. The Trial Chamber therefore finds that the destruction and wilful damage of institutions dedicated to Muslim religion or education, coupled with the requisite discriminatory intent, may amount to an act of persecution.[42]

[40] *Prosecutor v Blaskić*, para. 422.

[41] *See* Report of the International Law Commission on the Work of Its 43rd Session, 29 Apr.–19 July 1991, Supp. No. 10 (Doc. A/46/10), at 268 (according to which the 'systematic destruction of monuments or buildings representative of a particular social, religious, cultural or other group' amounts to persecution).

[42] *See Prosecutor v Kordić & Cerkez*, Case IT-95–14/2-T, Trial Chamber, Judgment of 26 Feb. 2001, para. 207; *see also Prosecutor v Brđanin*, Case IT-99–36-T, Trial Chamber II, Judgment of 1 Sept. 2004, para. 1050 ('[T]he Trial Chamber is satisfied that the persecutorial campaign against Bosnian Muslims and Bosnian Croats included killings, torture, physical violence, rapes and sexual assaults, constant humiliation and degradation, *destruction of properties, religious and cultural buildings*, deportation and forcible transfer, and the denial of fundamental rights. These acts were discriminatory in fact and were committed by the perpetrators with the requisite discriminatory intent on racial, religious and political grounds' (emphasis added)); *Prosecutor v Krajišnik*, Case IT-00–39-T, Trial Chamber, Judgment of 27 Sept. 2006, paras. 180–183; *Prosecutor v Martić*, Case IT-95–11-T, Judgment of 12 June 2007, para. 399 ('The Trial Chamber recalls that the church of the Assumption of the Virgin was destroyed and that it was not used for military purposes at the time of the destruction. The Trial Chamber recalls the manner in which the church was destroyed and concludes that this destruction was carried out with ... discriminatory intent .... The Trial Chamber therefore concludes that the elements of the crime of persecution ... have been met'.); *Prosecutor v Milutinović, Šainović, Ojdanić, Pavković, Lazarević, Lukić*, Case IT-05–87-T, Judgment of 26 Feb. 2009, para. 205; *Prosecutor v Đorđević*, Case IT-05–87/1-T, Trial Chamber II, Judgment of 23 Feb. 2011, para. 1771. In the latter case, the Trial Chamber also defined the elements necessary to qualify the destruction of religious sites 'as an underlying act of persecution', understood as 'the destruction or damage of an institution dedicated to religion, when the perpetrator acted with the intent to destroy or damage that property or in the reckless disregard of the substantial likelihood of the destruction or damage':

> In addition to the general elements of crimes against humanity and the specific elements of persecution, the Prosecution must prove the following elements of destruction of religious sites as an underlying offence: (a) The religious site must be destroyed or damaged extensively. (b) The destruction or damage must follow from an act directed against the property. (c) The destruction or damage must not be justified by military necessity, that is, the religious institution must not have been used for a military purpose or been in the immediate vicinity of military objectives. (d) The physical perpetrator, intermediary perpetrator, or accused acted with the intent to destroy or extensively damage the property, or in reckless disregard of the likelihood of destruction or damage.

This finding has been substantially confirmed by the Appeals Chamber, on the basis of the assumption that destruction of religious or cultural property would be subsumed under the broader category of 'destruction of property',[43] which, in turn, can be considered as a crime of persecution to the extent that, in light of the nature of such a destruction and its impact on the victims, all the elements of the crime in point are met.[44] However, some Trial Chambers have treated destruction of religious or cultural property as a category of persecution separate from the broader category of destruction of civilian property.[45] In particular, in *Kordić & Cerkez* the Trial Chamber stated that, while the offence of destruction of or wilful damage to institutions dedicated to religion or education 'overlaps to a certain extent with the offence of unlawful attacks on civilian objects',[46] a difference between the two offences is to be drawn on the basis of the greater *specificity* of the first one with respect to the second. Such a specificity rests on the fact that the *object* of the crime of destruction of or wilful damage to religious or educational institutions is *more specific*, these institutions being 'the *cultural heritage* of a certain population'.[47] As a consequence, the prohibition of the crime in point 'is the

Prosecutor v Đorđević, para. 1773. This statement is consistent with the position of the Trial Chamber in *Prosecutor v Milutinović, Šainović, Ojdanić, Pavković, Lazarević, Lukić*, Case IT-05–87-T, Judgment of 26 Feb. 2009, para. 207, according to which, with particular respect to the first of the listed requirements,

> [i]n order to rise to the level of equal gravity of ... crimes [against humanity], and therefore constitute persecution, Trial Chambers have held that the impact of the deprivation of destroyed property must be serious, such as where the property is indispensable, a vital asset to the owners, or the means of existence of a given population. For the same reasons, the Trial Chamber concludes that, if the property in question is not destroyed, the damage to it must be extensive in order to satisfy the equal gravity requirement. In this context, the terms 'destruction' and 'damage' are given their plain and common meanings, where the former term signifies demolition or reduction to a useless form, and the latter refers to physical injury or harm to an object that impairs its usefulness or value.

[43] *See Prosecutor v Milutinović, Šainović, Ojdanić, Pavković, Lazarević, Lukić*, Case IT-05–87-T, Judgment of 26 Feb. 2009, para. 204.

[44] *See Prosecutor v Blaskić*, Case IT-95–14-A, Appeals Chamber, Judgment of 29 July 2004, paras. 144–149. The essential condition for an act of destruction of property to be qualified as crime of persecution is that it is 'carried out on discriminatory grounds, and [that] the general elements of crimes against humanity are fulfilled'; when these two conditions are met, even '[a]n act of destruction of property which in itself does not have a severe impact on the victim, may still ... constitute the crime of persecution'. *See*, ultimately, *Prosecutor v Gotovina, Čermak, Markač*, Case IT-06–90-T, Trial Chamber I, Judgment of 15 Apr. 2011, para. 1830.

[45] *See Prosecutor v Milutinović, Šainović, Ojdanić, Pavković, Lazarević, Lukić*, Case IT-05-87-T, Judgment of 26 Feb. 2009, para. 204.

[46] *See Prosecutor v Kordić & Cerkez*, Case IT-95–14/2-T, Trial Chamber, Judgment of 26 Feb. 2001, para. 361.

[47] *Prosecutor v Kordić & Cerkez*, para. 361 (emphasis added); *see also Prosecutor v Brđanin*, Case IT-99–36-T, Trial Chamber II, Judgment of 1 Sept. 2004, para. 596 ('The offence of destruction or wilful damage to institutions dedicated to religion overlaps to a certain extent with the offence of unlawful attacks on civilian objects except that the object of the offence of destruction or wilful damage to institutions dedicated to religion is more specific').

lex specialis as far as acts against cultural heritage are concerned'.[48] This is to say that, when the target of an aggressive act committed against a property is part of the cultural heritage of a community, such an act acquires an *especially qualified degree of gravity*, which transcends the element of the physical and economic value of the property concerned and acquires a *spiritual* connotation. It is exactly the symbolic and spiritual significance of such a property which makes the act of destruction or wilful damage directed against it particularly serious, because it amounts to a mutilation of the very cultural and spiritual identity of the group that finds expression in that property.

This approach has been later expanded by the ICTY to the wider context of the interest of the international community as a whole. The Tribunal applied this line of reasoning with respect to the shelling of the old town of Dubrovnik, a property inscribed on the World Heritage List set up by the 1972 UNESCO Convention on the Protection of the World Cultural and Natural Heritage (World Heritage Convention).[49] In *Jokić*, the Trial Chamber I found that the shelling of the old town, resulting in the crime of destruction or wilful damage to institutions dedicated to religion, charity, education, and the arts and sciences, and to historic monuments, and works of art and science, 'represents a violation of values especially protected by the international community',[50] as '[t]he whole of the Old Town of Dubrovnik was considered, at the time of the events contained in the Indictment, an especially important part of the world cultural heritage … and the existence of its population was intimately intertwined with its ancient heritage'.[51] For this reason, '[t]he shelling attack on the Old Town was an attack not only against the history and heritage of the region, but *also against the cultural heritage of humankind*'.[52] The Trial Chamber also added that 'since it is a serious violation of international humanitarian law to attack civilian buildings, it is a crime of even greater seriousness to direct an attack on an especially protected site, such as the Old Town'.[53]

This reasoning was confirmed by the ICTY in another case concerning the shelling of the old town of Dubrovnik; that is, *Prosecutor v Strugar*. In this case, the Trial Chamber II—basing on the fact that 'the Old Town of Dubrovnik in its entirety was entered onto the World Heritage List in 1979'[54]—found that

> cultural … property is, by definition, of 'great importance to the cultural heritage of every people' … therefore …, even though the victim of the offence at issue is to be understood

[48] *See Prosecutor v Kordić & Cerkez*, Case IT-95–14/2-T, Trial Chamber, Judgment of 26 Feb. 2001, para. 361.

[49] 1037 UNTS 151.

[50] *See Prosecutor v Jokić*, Case IT-01–42/1-S, Trial Chamber I, Judgment of 18 Mar. 2004, para. 46.

[51] *Prosecutor v Jokić*, para. 51.

[52] *Prosecutor v Jokić*, para. 51 (emphasis added).

[53] *Prosecutor v Jokić*, para. 53.

[54] *See Prosecutor v Strugar*, Case IT-01–42-T, Trial Chamber II, Judgment of 31 Jan. 2005, para. 327 (footnotes omitted).

broadly as a 'people', rather than any particular individual, the offence can be said to involve grave consequences for the victim .... [Thus] the offences under Articles 3(b) and 3(d) of the Statute are serious violations of international humanitarian law.[55]

A very significant feature of this finding lays in the recognition of the *collective* character of the crime's victim; that is, a *people*. The Chamber thus transcends the traditional vision of human rights as enforceable and justiciable only when their breach affects one or more individuals specifically. In the case in point, any person belonging to the community prejudiced by the crime is victim of a wrong, which is suitable of materializing only to the extent that the individuals concerned are subsumed within the group of which they are part. No member of the community concerned is thus specially affected, and—at the same time—all such members are affected. In other words, the right to preserve and enjoy one's own culture normally takes a sense only whether and to the extent that it is exercised in community with the other members of the group. In the end, therefore, it is the collective right which is concretely safeguarded. In such a way, the ICTY translates into the scope of international humanitarian law a principle that had previously been accepted by international practice with respect to human rights law.[56]

Taking into account the multifaceted meanings and implications that the destruction of or wilful damage to cultural heritage may assume—depending on its degree of connection with specific communities and/or on the intention(s) lying behind such acts—the ICTY has also investigated one further issue; that is, whether the offence in point may be considered as a modality of perpetration of the crime of genocide. In this respect, the Tribunal has denied that this may actually occur:

[C]stomary international law limits the definition of genocide to those acts seeking the physical or biological destruction of all or part of the group. Hence, an enterprise attacking only the cultural or sociological characteristics of a human group in order to annihilate these elements which give to that group its own identity distinct from the rest of the community would not fall under the definition of genocide.[57]

Although quite debatable under an evolutionary perspective,[58] the position taken by the Trial Chamber is technically correct, as it is consistent with the

[55] *Prosecutor v Strugar*, para. 232.

[56] *See, eg,* Human Rights Comm., General Comment No. 23 of 6 April 1994, 'The Rights of Minorities (Art. 27)', paras. 6.2, 9, *available at* <http://www.unhchr.ch/tbs/doc.nsf/(Symbol)/fb7fb12c2fb8bb21c12563ed004df111?Opendocument> (last accessed 25 July 2012) ('Although the rights [of persons belonging to ethnic, religious or linguistic minorities to enjoy their own culture, to profess and practise their own religion, or to use their own language] are individual rights, *they depend in turn on the ability of the minority group to maintain its culture, language or religion.* Accordingly, *positive measures by States may also be necessary to protect the identity of a minority* and the rights of its members to enjoy and develop their culture and language and to practise their religion, *in community with the other members of the group* .... The protection of these rights is directed towards ensuring the survival and continued development of the cultural, religious and social identity of the minorities concerned'. (emphasis added)).

[57] *See Prosecutor v Krstić*, Case IT-98–33-T, Trial Chamber, Judgment of 2 Aug. 2001, para. 580.

[58] See, on this point, the discussion by this author in 'The Trail of Broken Dreams: The Status of Indigenous Peoples in International Law', in F. Lenzerini (ed.), *Reparations for Indigenous Peoples: International and Comparative Perspectives* (Oxford: Oxford University Press, 2008), 73, at 103 ff.

characterization of the crime of genocide endorsed by the 1948 UN Convention specific on the crime in point,[59] Article 2 of which—contemplating the acts that are suitable of qualifying genocide—has been reproduced by Article 4 para. 2 of the ICTY Statute.[60] During the *travaux préparatoires* to the 1948 Convention, the negotiators explicitly rejected—by twenty-five votes to six, with four abstentions—that the concept of 'cultural genocide' (as aimed at eliminating the cultural identity of a community or a group, without being accompanied by its physical destruction) could be considered as included within the scope of the notion of genocide.[61] Consequently, as noted by the International Law Commission in the Commentary to its Draft Code of Crimes against the Peace and Security of Mankind, the element of 'destruction' of a group included in the notion of genocide only refers to

> the material destruction of a group either by physical or by biological means, not the destruction of the national, linguistic, religious, cultural or other identity of a particular group. The national or religious element and the racial or ethnic element are not taken into consideration in the definition of the word 'destruction', which must be taken only in its material sense, its physical or biological sense.[62]

This notwithstanding, the ICTY has considered the destruction of cultural heritage as possible evidence of the element of *mens rea* of genocide.[63] In *Krstić*, the Trial Chamber pointed out that

> where there is physical or biological destruction there are often simultaneous attacks on the cultural and religious property and symbols of the targeted group as well, attacks which may legitimately be considered as evidence of an intent to physically destroy the group. In this case, the Trial Chamber will thus take into account as *evidence of intent to destroy the group* the deliberate destruction of mosques and houses belonging to members of the group.[64]

[59] *See* United Nations Convention on the Prevention and Punishment of the Crime of Genocide, 9 Dec. 1948, 78 UNTS 277.

[60] Article 2 of the Convention on Genocide (see previous note) states:

> [G]enocide means any of the following acts committed with intent to destroy, in whole or in part, a national, ethnical, racial or religious group, as such: (a) Killing members of the group; (b) Causing serious bodily or mental harm to members of the group; (c) Deliberately inflicting on the group conditions of life calculated to bring about its physical destruction in whole or in part; (d) Imposing measures intended to prevent births within the group; (e) Forcibly transferring children of the group to another group.

The text of article 4(2) of the ICTY Statute is identical to the provision just reproduced.

[61] *See Prosecutor v Krstić*, Case IT-98–33-T, Trial Chamber, Judgment of 2 Aug. 2001, at 202 note 1284.

[62] *See* 'Commentary on the International Law Commission Draft Code of Crimes against the Peace and Security of Mankind', Report of the International Law Commission on the Work of Its 48th Session, 6 May–26 July 1996, Official Documents of the United Nations General Assembly's 51st Session, Supp. No. 10 (Doc. A/51/10), at 90 f.

[63] *See*, on this point, Frulli, *earlier* note 25, at 209 ff.

[64] *See Prosecutor v Krstić*, Case IT-98–33-T, Trial Chamber, Judgment of 2 Aug. 2001, para. 580 (emphasis added). This position was further elaborated by Judge Shahabuddeen in his partial

It is to be noted that this position was subsequently endorsed by the International Court of Justice (ICJ). In particular, in its 2007 judgment concerning the case of the Application of the Convention on the Prevention and Punishment of the Crime of Genocide (*Bosnia and Herzegovina v Serbia and Montenegro*),[65] the ICJ—although stressing that 'the destruction of historical, cultural and religious heritage cannot be considered ...[as] fall[ing] within the categories of acts of genocide',[66]—recognized that 'such destruction may be highly significant inasmuch as it is directed to the elimination of all traces of the cultural or religious presence of a group ....'[67] The ICJ thus confirmed 'the observation made [by the ICTY] in the *Krstić* case that "where there is physical or biological destruction there are often simultaneous attacks on the cultural and religious property and symbols of the targeted group as well, attacks which may legitimately be considered as evidence of an intent to physically destroy the group"'.[68]

III. The Contemporary Significance of Cultural Heritage: Beyond State Property and Exterior Worth

The ICTY jurisprudence examined in the previous section epitomizes how—in most recent times—the perception by the international community of the significance of cultural heritage has evolved toward a markedly holistic perspective. This perspective transcends the traditional vision of cultural heritage—encompassed in particular in the 1907 Hague Conventions on the laws and customs of war—as a value worth safeguarding in the sovereign interest of the state in the territory of which it is located. It even transcends the approach of the World Heritage Convention, although this Convention greatly innovated the international legal perception of the significance of culture through moving from the idea of 'cultural *property*' to the more holistic view of 'cultural *heritage*' belonging

dissenting opinion to the judgment of the Appeals Chamber concerning the same case (*Prosecutor v Krstić*, Case IT-98-33-A, Appeals Chamber, Judgment of 19 Apr. 2004), in which he stated the following:

> Out of abundant caution, I would make two things clear. First, the question is whether there was the required intent, not whether the intent was in fact realised. Second, the foregoing is not an argument for the recognition of cultural genocide. It is established that the mere destruction of the culture of a group is not genocide: none of the methods listed in article 4(2) of the Statute need be employed. But there is also need for care. The destruction of culture may serve evidentially to confirm an intent, to be gathered from other circumstances, to destroy the group as such. In this case, the razing of the principal mosque confirms an intent to destroy the Srebrenica part of the Bosnian Muslim group.

See para. 53 of the opinion.

[65] *See earlier* note 19.

[66] *See* para. 344 of the judgment.

[67] Para. 344 of the judgment.

[68] Para. 344 of the judgment.

to humanity as a whole—as emphasized by the second sentence of its Preamble.[69] However, the scope of the World Heritage Convention is still limited in light of the complexity and width of the meaning of the term 'culture', because it considers that only those examples of material and immovable cultural heritage reaching the threshold of 'outstanding universal value' deserve protection in the interest of the international community. On the contrary, the new holistic perception of cultural heritage extends its attention to the *spiritual* significance of cultural properties, as an essential element of the identity of the human communities which reflect themselves on such heritage.

In more detail, the jurisprudence just examined shows, first of all, that acts of destruction and wilful damage against cultural heritage constitute a crime in themselves, resulting in a violation of the laws and customs of war. In stating this, Article 3(d) of the ICTY Statute (similarly to Article 8 of the ICC Statute) does not go beyond reiterating a rule that has been crystallized for a long time in the context of the international legal order. Thus, there is apparently nothing of an evolutionary character in this provision, as it derives from the traditional vision of cultural properties as nearly exclusive matters of state interest. On a closer look, however, one may note that the very fact of including the crime contemplated by Article 3(d) in the ICTY Statute implies that—when establishing the Tribunal—the members of the UN Security Council were aware that such a traditional vision was no longer adequate to express the reasons of the international community's concern to safeguard cultural heritage. In fact, it is evident that, once the prohibition of 'seizure of, destruction or wilful damage done to' such heritage is extended to *non-international* armed conflicts—as the Balkan wars actually were—its rationale *goes beyond* the 'mere' requirement of protecting an interest belonging to a sovereign State. The same reasoning may be extended to Article 8(2)(e)(iv) of the ICC Statute.[70] The object of protection has thus evolved toward a more mystical and intangible value; that is, the spiritual significance of cultural heritage for specific peoples, groups, or communities. It is exactly in light of this approach that, particularly since *Kordić & Cerkez*, the ICTY has emphasized that acts of destruction of or wilful damage to cultural properties—when 'the requisite discriminatory intent'[71] is present—may amount to persecution, that is, to a crime against humanity, which, by its own nature, reaches a higher threshold of seriousness than a 'simple' violation of the laws and customs of war.

In practical terms, this interpretation appears the most effective in consideration of the nature and rationale of most cases of destruction of cultural heritage, as reflected in the history of humanity. Since ancient times, the most aggressive acts against cultural properties have in fact been perpetrated with the specific purpose

[69] The second sentence of the Preamble of the World Heritage Convention affirms that 'deterioration or disappearance of any item of the cultural or natural heritage constitutes a harmful impoverishment of the heritage of all the nations of the world'.

[70] *See earlier* note 7.

[71] *See earlier* text accompanying note 42.

of annihilating the religious or cultural identity of the human communities especially interested in such properties. One formidable example of this reality is provided by the previously cited case of the Temple of Serapis in Alexandria, the destruction of which was ordered by the Roman emperor Theodosius in 391 AD with the purpose of defeating the last refuge of the pagan gods' faithful (who—on their part—preferred to lose their lives in the temple rather than surrender to the enemies).[72] This characterization of the intentional destruction of cultural heritage has not substantially changed after more than sixteen centuries, as demonstrated by the rationale inspiring the many occurrences of this crime during the Balkan wars or by the blatant destruction perpetrated in 2001 by the Taliban regime of the two giant Buddha statues located in the Afghan valley of Bamiyan, razed to the ground as part of a painstaking plan aimed at eliminating all 'idols [that] have been gods of the infidels'.[73]

The same rationale according to which destruction of, or wilful damage to, cultural heritage is to be qualified as a crime against humanity also underlies the finding of the ICTY (endorsed by the ICJ) that such an offence is suitable of constituting evidence to prove the mental element of the crime of genocide. This interpretation is certainly to be approved, as any action aimed at leading a community or a group to its physical destruction is suitable of maximizing its effectiveness when it is accompanied by measures—including the destruction of cultural heritage of special significance for the community concerned—which may produce the moral and psychological mortification of the group. Indeed, when a group is deprived of its spiritual points of reference—on which it projects its cultural and/or religious identity—its defensive strength and willingness to resist the enemies' attacks are contextually impaired, making its physical elimination easier.

One further element emerging from the ICTY case law on cultural heritage consists in the fact that the destruction of, or wilful damage done to, such heritage may result in an offence for the international community as a whole. While the Tribunal has raised this argument with respect to properties inscribed on the UNESCO World Heritage List only, it should be extended to all cases in which the crime in point is perpetrated with the purpose of destroying a specific culture. In all these instances, the value of cultural diversity—as 'common heritage of humanity [to] be cherished and preserved for the benefit of all'[74]—is in fact impaired, leading the whole humanity to be negatively affected by the acts in point.

[72] *See* <http://penelope.uchicago.edu/~grout/encyclopaedia_romana/greece/paganism/serapeum.html> (last accessed 25 July 2012).

[73] *See* Francioni and Lenzerini, *earlier* note 2, at 626.

[74] *See* UNESCO Convention on the Protection and Promotion of the Diversity of Cultural Expressions (2005) pmbl., second sentence, *available at* <http://portal.unesco.org/en/ev.php-URL_ID=31038&URL_DO=DO_TOPIC&URL_SECTION=201.html> (last accessed 25 July 2012).

IV. Conclusion: Taking a Lesson for the Future from the Balkan Wars

The evolutionary jurisprudence of the ICTY has provided a great contribution to opening the eyes of the international community and making it become aware that the significance of cultural heritage greatly transcends the sovereign interests of territorial states as well as the artistic, visual, and/or economic worth of such a heritage. In the various cases concerning situations of destruction of or wilful damage to cultural properties, the ICTY has carefully scrutinized the reasons which led perpetrators to commit such crimes and all the rationale inspiring—as well as the implications arising from—their behaviour. While no judicial action or legal interpretation will ever be capable of repairing the immense suffering caused by tragic conflicts like the Balkan wars, knowledge of how they have been conducted by the warring factions involved may provide a number of priceless lessons which may help reduce the risk that certain tragedies happen again in the future.

In the field of cultural heritage protection, the main lesson arising from the Balkan wars rests exactly in the consciousness that cultural properties are much more than a combination of stones or other building materials, and even much more than beautiful visual manifestations of the human genius. As seen in Part II, the very reason why during the Balkan wars cultural properties were systematically destroyed was that they were part of the deep distinctiveness of the members of the groups reflecting themselves in such heritage, feeding their sense of worth and of belonging to their own community. Thus, the ultimate target of these acts was not the destruction of the properties as such, but precisely the identity of the communities reflecting themselves on them, and, *a fortiori*, the physical integrity of those communities, which attained part of their defensive strength from the spiritual value of their own cultural heritage.

In summary, the Balkan armed conflicts have demonstrated that the most important feature of cultural heritage rests in the fact that it is perceived by people (as individuals) and peoples (as collectivities) as an essential part of their identity, it being an entity in which some of the most important values of their lives and of their way of being—if not the most important of all—are rooted. In light of this, it is important to be aware that, as its special significance makes cultural heritage one of the preferential targets of warring factions in non-international armed conflicts, it could also make it a reason triggering *ab initio* new internal conflicts, especially when disputes on its ownership and/or management or ethnicity-based problems exist.

The ICTY has paved a way that should be followed also by other international and mixed criminal courts having the competence of judging crimes against cultural heritage. This applies in particular to the Extraordinary Chambers in the Courts of Cambodia as well as to the ICC, which may use in this respect explicit provisions included in the legal instruments defining the law applicable by them. In this regard, the attitude of the Cambodian Extraordinary Chambers seems to be quite promising. In *Case 002*—concerning four high officials of the Democratic Kampuchea charged with crimes against humanity, grave breaches of the Geneva Conventions of 1949, and genocide[75]—the accused were allegedly responsible for, inter alia, persecution against Buddhists and Cham people; the mistreatment of these people translated into a wide number of acts, which included extensive destruction of pagodas, monasteries, mosques, and Buddhist statues, burning of Qurans, as well as conversion of the said religious edifices into meeting halls, detention centres, dining halls, pig farms, and warehouses.[76] In the part of the Indictment relating to the case in point concerning the applicable law, these acts are subsumed both within the category of grave breaches of the Geneva Conventions of 12 August 1949[77] and—most notably—within that of crimes against humanity, specifically religious persecution, determined by the 'country-wide suppression of Cham culture'[78] and the persecution against the Buddhists.[79] This is an encouraging symptom that the Khmer Rouge Tribunal is ready to follow the evolutionary interpretation developed by the ICTY in considering destruction of or wilful damage to cultural heritage—when perpetrated with a discriminatory intent—as a crime against humanity. The generalization of such an approach would ultimately allow other international or mixed courts to prosecute the persons responsible for crimes against cultural heritage even in the event that the legal instruments applicable by the judicial body concerned would not include any provision similar to Article 3(d) of the ICTY Statute, to Article 8 of the ICC Statute or to Article 7 of the Law on the Establishment of the Extraordinary Chambers in the Courts of Cambodia, allowing the extension of the scope of protection against the said crimes available under international law.

V. Postscript

At the time that this chapter was about to be sent to the publisher, the international community was shocked by the most heinous crime against cultural heritage perpetrated since the destruction of the Buddhas of Bamiyan in 2001.[80]

[75] *See* Case 002, <http://www.eccc.gov.kh/en/case/topic/2> (last accessed 25 July 2012). One of the accused, Ieng Thirith, sister-in-law of Pol Pot and former Social Action Minister in Democratic Kampuchea, was found unfit to stand trial for health reasons in 2011; in the second half of 2012 she was undergoing medical treatment, and her fitness to stand trial had to be re-evaluated before the end of 2012. On 14 December 2012 she was placed under supervision; see 'Supreme Court Chamber Places Ieng Thirith under Supervision', *available at* <http://www.eccc.gov.kh/en/articles/supreme-court-chamber-places-ieng-thirith-under-supervision> (last accessed 20 December 2012).

[76] *See* Indictment of Case 002, paras. 210, 321, 740, 743, 756, *available at* <http://www.eccc.gov.kh/sites/default/files/documents/courtdoc/D427Eng.pdf> (last accessed 25 July 2012).

[77] Indictment of Case 002, para. 1317.

[78] Indictment of Case 002, para. 1420.

[79] Indictment of Case 002, para. 1421.

[80] *See earlier* text accompanying note 2. It is to be emphasized that the time in which the present chapter is being written is particularly unfortunate for cultural heritage. Indeed, in addition to the

Following the Battle of Gao of 26–27 June 2012, the Al-Qaeda-related Islamic Group Ansar Dine (literally: 'Defenders of Faith') and its ally Islamist Movement for the Liberation of Azaward (MNLA) took control of the three main cities in the secessionist region of Azaward in Northern Mali: Gao, Timbuktu, and Kidal. The mythical Timbuktu, which was the spiritual capital of Islamism in Africa in the 15th and 16th centuries, is undoubtedly the best known among these three cities. It was inscribed on the UNESCO World Heritage List in 1988;[81] its three main mosques—Djingareyber, Sankore, and SidiYahia—represent(ed) some of the most extraordinary monuments of the heritage of humanity. On 28 June 2012, the World Heritage Committee, at its 36th Session in Saint Petersburg, decided to accept the request by the government of Mali to place Timbuktu—together with the Tomb of Askia, the other World Heritage property located in Northern Mali[82]—on the List of the World Heritage in Danger, in order 'to raise cooperation and support for the sites threatened by the armed conflict in the region'.[83] This decision was the spark triggering the iconoclastic fury of the leaders of Ansar Dine, who, on 29 June, started to deliberately destroy the cultural heritage of Timbuktu. The ancient monuments of the city were considered by the extremists to be idolatrous, on account of the conjecture that the mausoleums in Timbuktu being dedicated to saints (albeit Muslim saints) venerated human beings. For this reason, they asserted that those monuments were contrary to Islam because God is unique and only God may be the object of veneration. The destruction was considered as a 'divine order', to avoid that 'future generations … get confused, and start venerating the saints as if they are God'.[84]

Many 700-year-old irreplaceable monuments were systematically and painstakingly destroyed.[85] On 2 July the entrance door of the Sidi Yahia

case described in this Postscript, in the same days another irreplaceable heritage of humanity is being threatened by the blind rage of human beings. It is the case of Syria, where heavy fighting is taking place in Aleppo, which ancient city was inscribed on the World Heritage List in 1986 (*see* <http://whc.unesco.org/en/list/21>(last accessed 29 July 2012)). As reported by the UNESCO World Heritage Centre, at the moment of writing, due to the explosive security situation, it has not yet been possible to evaluate the possible damages produced by the fighting to the prejudice of the ancient city of Aleppo as well as of other World Heritage properties, including the Crac des Chevaliers, Palmyra, the Ancient Villages in Northern Syria and Damascus (*see* <http://whc.unesco.org/en/statesparties/sy> last accessed 4 February 2013). Furthermore, UNESCO is alarmed at the risks of looting and pillaging of movable cultural property. *See* 'The Director-General of UNESCO Appeals for the Protection of the World Heritage City of Aleppo', 27 July 2012, *available at* <http://whc.unesco.org/en/news/915> (all sources quoted in this footnote were last accessed 29 July 2012).

[81] *See*<http://whc.unesco.org/en/list/119> (last accessed 25 July 2012).

[82] The Tomb of Askia was inscribed on the World Heritage List in 2004. *See* <http://whc.unesco.org/en/list/1139> (last accessed 25 July 2012).

[83] *See* 'Heritage Sites in Northern Mali Placed on List of World Heritage in Danger', *available at* <http://whc.unesco.org/en/news/893> (last accessed 25 July 2012).

[84] *See* Callimachi, 'Islamist Fighters in Timbuktu Continue Destruction of City's Mausoleums, Heritage', *The Republic*, 3 July 2012, *available at* <http://www.therepublic.com/view/story/56d3cae1af864453b70c97849bb10a9a/AF – Travel-Mali-Timbuktu> (last accessed 25 July 2012).

[85] At the moment of writing, information concerning the destruction of monuments in Timbuktu is still fragmentary and possibly imprecise, because journalists are not allowed to reach the city.

mosque—which, according to the legend, was not to be opened until the 'end times'—was demolished in order to break down the mystery of that ancient building. Other monuments which were destroyed include the tombs of Sidi Mahmoud, Sidi Moctar, and Alpha Moya, the mausoleums of Cheikh el-Kebir, Alwalidji Baber Babeidje, and Alwalidji Ahamadoun Foulane, as well as the Djingareyber cemetery, including jars and other artefacts located around the tombs. After the demolitions, the perpetrators carried the clay obtained from the monuments outside the city on board a tractor, to prevent them from being rebuilt with the same clay in the future. According to witnesses residing in Timbuktu, the members of Ansar Dine have also threatened to destroy the mosques if there are saints inside them; several saints are actually buried in the three main mosques in the city.[86]

A few days after the beginning of the destruction of the buildings in Timbuktu, activists of Ansar Dine quartered in one of the city's libraries; there are reasons to suspect that an irreplaceable collection of medieval manuscripts (written in various African languages and Arabic) was the object of the same treatment suffered by the mausoleums and tombs.[87]

The whole international community was outraged by the destruction of Timbuktu's cultural heritage. To mention just a few of the countless official reactions condemning such a destruction, on 30 June UNESCO Director General Irina Bokova called on the people responsible 'to stop these terrible and irreversible acts, to exercise their responsibility and protect this invaluable cultural heritage for future generations'.[88] A few days later, the World Heritage Committee firmly

[86] The information provided in the text has been collected from news diffused by several sources. *See*, inter alia, A. Nossiter, 'Mali Islamists Exert Control, Attacking Door to a Mosque', *NY Times*, 2 July 2012, *available at* <http://www.nytimes.com/2012/07/03/world/africa/mali-islamists-exert-control-with-attacks-on-mosques.html>; 'Timbuktu Shrine Destruction a "War Crime": International Criminal Court', *Dilemma X*, 2 July 2012, *available at* <http://dilemma-x.net/2012/07/02/timbuktu-shrine-destruction-a-war-crime-international-criminal-court/>; 'Timbuktu's Sidi Yahia Mosque "Attacked by Mali Militants"', *BBC News*, 2 July 2012, *available at* <http://www.bbc.co.uk/news/world-africa-18675539>; 'Ansar Dine Breaks the Doors of Sidi Yahia Mosque in Timbuktu', *North Africa United*, 3 July 2012, *available at* <http://www.northafricaunited.com/Ansar-Dine-breaks-the-doors-of-Sidi-Yahia-mosque-in-Timbuktu_a1836.html>; 'U.N. Defers Decision on Military Intervention in Mali', *CNN*, 6 July 2012, *available at* <http://edition.cnn.com/2012/07/06/world/africa/mali-un-warning/index.html>; 'Mali: Islamists Continue Destruction of Religious Sites in Timbuktu', *AfriqueJet—Afrique Actualité Information*, 12 July 2012, *available at* <http://www.afriquejet.com/mali-islamists-continue-destruction-of-religious-sites-in-timbuktu-2012071241732.html>; Froelich, 'Mali: Islamists Destroy Historic City of Timbuktu', *Daily Beast*, 15 July 2012, *available at* <http://www.thedailybeast.com/articles/2012/07/15/mali-islamists-destroy-historic-city-of-timbuktu.html> (all sources quoted in this footnote were last accessed 25 July 2012).

[87] *See* 'After Tombs, Arabs Now Destroying Timbuktu's Manuscripts', *African Globe*, 11 July 2012, *available at* <http://www.africanglobe.net/africa/tombs-arabs-destroying-timbuktus-manuscripts/>; Hoebink, 'Mali Manuscripts at Risk', *Radio Netherlands Worldwide*, 20 July 2012, *available at* <http://www.rnw.nl/africa/article/mali-manuscripts-risk> (both sources were last accessed 25 July 2012).

[88] *See* 'UNESCO Director-General of UNESCO Calls for a Halt to Destruction of Cultural Heritage Site in Timbuktu', 30 June 2012, *available at* <http://whc.unesco.org/en/news/901> (last accessed 25 July 2012).

condemned and called for an end to the 'repugnant acts' of destruction.[89] The UN Security Council threatened sanctions against Ansar Dine, although it did not immediately approve a proposal by the Economic Community of West African States (ECOWAS) to establish a special force (including military personnel) for immediate intervention in Timbuktu.[90] On 10 July, the African Commission on Human and People's Rights expressed its

> utmost concern over the destruction and desecration of the mausoleums of Muslim saints and other ancient sites of the mythical city of Timbuktu ... undescor[ing] the fact that these sacred monuments classified by UNESCO as a world heritage are a symbol of the greatness of Africa ... join[ing] the international community in expressing its dismay and concern over such shameful and disgraceful acts ... and condemn[ing] in the strongest possible terms such barbaric and unspeakable acts which it considers as war crimes and crimes against humanity and which are inconsistent with the African Charter on Human and Peoples' Rights and other African and international legal instruments on human rights and international humanitarian law.[91]

The Organisation of the Islamic Conference issued a statement in which it declared that the destroyed monuments of Timbuktu were 'part of the rich Islamic heritage of Mali and should not be allowed to be destroyed and put in harm's way by bigoted extremist elements'.[92] Last but not least, the ICC Chief Prosecutor Fatou Bensouda referred to the criminal acts of destruction of religious buildings in Timbuktu as war crimes according to Article 8 of the ICC Statute,[93] which her office has authority to fully investigate in light of the fact that Mali is a party to the Statute.[94] On 18 July the Chief Prosecutor announced that she received a delegation from the government of Mali transmitting a request to investigate the situation in the country since January 2012 'to determine whether one or more persons should be charged for crimes committed'; the government declared that Malian courts are unable to prosecute or try the persons responsible for the alleged crimes. The Chief Prosecutor pointed out that she had been following 'the situation in Mali very closely since violence erupted there around 17 January 2012', as well as that, inter alia, she had previously stressed that 'the deliberate destruction of

[89] *See* 'World Heritage Committee Calls for End to Destruction of Mali's Heritage and Adopts Decision for Its Support', 3 July 2012, *available at* <http://whc.unesco.org/en/news/907> (last accessed 25 July 2012).

[90] *See* 'UN Threatens Sanctions on Mali's Shrine Vandals', *Arab News*, 6 July 2012, *available at* <http://www.arabnews.com/?q=world/un-threatens-sanctions-malis-shrine-vandals> (last accessed 25 July 2012).

[91] *See* African Comm'n on Human and People's Rights, 'Press Release on the Destruction of Cultural and Ancient Monuments in the Malian City of Timbuktu', 10 July 2012, *available at* <http://www.achpr.org/press/2012/07/d115/> (last accessed 25 July 2012).

[92] *See* 'Timbuktu's Sidi Yahia Mosque "Attacked by Mali Militants"', *see earlier* note 86.

[93] *See earlier* note 7.

[94] *See* 'Timbuktu Shrine Destruction a "War Crime": International Criminal Court', *earlier* note 86; 'ICC Threatens Mali Islamists with War Crimes', *Aljazeera*, 2 July 2012, *available at* <http://www.aljazeera.com/news/africa/2012/07/20127119538255768.html> (last accessed 25 July 2012).

the shrines of Muslim saints in the city of Timbuktu may constitute a war crime under Article 8 of the Rome Statute'. She concluded that she had instructed her Office 'to immediately proceed with a preliminary examination of the situation in order to assess whether the Rome Statute criteria … for opening an investigation are fulfilled', and that she was going to take a public decision 'in due course'.[95]

The way seems to be paved for the ICC to make a very important decision on the issue of destruction of cultural heritage. In legal terms, no doubts arise concerning the fact that the acts of destruction perpetrated by the members of Ansar Dine in Timbuktu constitute violations of international law. No reasonable doubts exist that such acts provide a 'reasonable basis to believe that a crime within the jurisdiction of the Court has been or is being committed', pursuant to Article 53.1 of the ICC Statute; indeed, the said acts have been/are being committed on the territory of a State which is party to the Statute[96] and consequently fall within one of the cases with respect to which the Court may exercise its jurisdiction according to Article 12.2. Another circumstance which cannot be reasonably denied is that the Malian region of Azaward is currently experiencing a situation of armed conflict, which started in March 2012 with the rebellion by the Tuareg and the consequent war of independence against the government of Mali. Indeed, the fact that the Battle of Gao has led Ansar Dine to take control of the main cities in the Azaward region does not imply that it also brought the ongoing armed conflict to an end, in light of the circumstance that the government of Mali has not yet surrendered to the loss of the said region (as demonstrated by the request recently addressed to the Chief Prosecutor of the ICC to investigate the situation in the country since January 2012).[97] Therefore, there are no obstacles to charge for war crimes the persons responsible for the acts in point. Consistently, on 16 January 2013 the ICC Prosecutor formally opened investigation into alleged crimes perpetrated in the territory of Mali since July 2012, including 'intentionally directing attacks against protected objects'.[98]

At this point, it would be appropriate that, once the case is in front of the Court, the judges will follow the example of the ICTY and consider the destruction of the ancient cultural heritage in the city as a crime against humanity in addition to being a war crime. In fact, 'all of humanity is … injured by the destruction of a

[95] *See* 'ICC Prosecutor Fatou Bensouda on the Malian State Referral of the Situation in Mali Since January 2012', ICC Press Release, 18 July 2012, *available at* <http://www.icc-cpi.int/NR/exeres/B8DAF5A7-DD53–43D2-A3A8–0BC30E6D00B9.htm> (last accessed 25 July 2012).

[96] Mali deposited its instrument of ratification of the ICC Statute on 16 August 2000; see <http://www.icc-cpi.int/Menus/ASP/states+parties/> (last accessed 25 July 2012).

[97] *See earlier* text accompanying note 95.

[98] See 'ICC Prosecutor opens investigation into war crimes in Mali: "The legal requirements have been met. We will investigate"', 16 January 2013, *available at* <http://www.icc-cpi.int/en_menus/icc/press%20and%20media/press%20releases/news%20and%20highlights/Pages/pr869.aspx> (last accessed 16 January 2013).

unique … culture and its concomitant cultural objects'[99] which made Timbuktu unique in the world. The Court should not even be too creative in order to identify the discriminatory intent[100] necessary for an attack against cultural heritage to be considered as an act of persecution. Such an intent is indeed inherent in the crime, and it was actually in the mind of the perpetrators when they intended to annihilate every trace of cultural goods which were not in line with their fanatic convictions. The persecution actually materialized into the prejudice of all people who do not share the extremist ideas of Islamism of the members of Ansar Dine and is particularly evident with respect to those living in Timbuktu, for whom—as emphasized by the UN Special Rapporteurs on cultural rights and on freedom of religion or belief—the destruction of their cultural heritage 'means the denial of their identity, their beliefs, their history, and their dignity'.[101]

99 *See earlier* text accompanying note 42.

100 *See earlier* text accompanying note 42.

101 *See* Office of the UN High Comm'r for Human Rights, '"A Very Dark Future for the Local Populations in Northern Mali," Warn UN Experts', 10 July 2012, *available at* <http://ohchr.org/en/NewsEvents/Pages/DisplayNews.aspx?NewsID=12337&LangID=E> (last accessed 25 July 2012).

4

Illicit Trade in Antiquities

A View 'From the Ground'

Laurie W. Rush[*]

I. Introduction

The market for illegal antiquities disrupts human society from the tiniest rural communities to the world stage of global politics. Individuals and institutions who purchase objects of questionable provenance knowingly contribute to illegal behaviour, not just theft and smuggling but also actions that endanger lives and encourage acts of criminal desperation. In other words, the collectors and enthusiasts who provide the market for illicit antiquities are playing more than a passive role in processes that encourage violence and conflict. From otherwise peaceful

* Dr Laurie Rush is an Anthropologist and Archaeologist who has served as a US Army civilian for fourteen years managing Cultural Resources at Fort Drum, NY. She has a BA from Indiana University Bloomington, an MA and PhD from Northwestern University, and is a Fellow of the National Science Foundation and of the American Academy in Rome. Under her leadership, the Fort Drum cultural resources program has won numerous Army and Department of Defense Awards including best program in the Army and Department of Defense in 2007 and best team in 2009. At the request of Major General Oates and the US State Department, Dr Rush was the military liaison for return of the Mesopotamian City of Ur to the Iraqi people in the spring of 2009. She also represented US Central Command at an Environmental Shura in Kabul, Afghanistan, in February of 2010. Dr Rush lectures widely in the US and overseas to both military and civilian audiences on the importance of identification of and respect for cultural property on the battlefield, including a series of State Department-sponsored lectures at Turkish Universities. Educational materials developed by her team in partnership with Colorado State University have reached over 125,000 US military personnel and are also being used by UNESCO, the Associated National Committees of the Blue Shield, and the Austrian Defence Academy. Dr Rush has been recognized by her peers with the Register of Professional Archaeologists Special Achievement Award, the Advisory Council for Historic Preservation Chairman's Award for Federal Achievement in Historic Preservation, and the Booth Family Rome Prize for Historic Preservation. She is the editor of the recent book, *Archaeology, Cultural Property, and the Military* (Newcastle Heritage Matters series 2, Suffolk: Boydell & Brewer, 2010), and author of numerous articles and book chapters concerning the importance of military education and planning for cultural property protection in crisis areas. The views expressed in this chapter are those of the author and do not necessarily reflect the official policy or position of the US Army, DoD, or the US Government.

communities to some of the most violent conflicts in the world, the presence of an antiquities market or, in some cases, even the perception of a market, is an extremely destructive force affecting multiple elements of local and international communities.

II. This Way to the Mummy

At the top of the stairs in the Swansea Museum stands a sign with an arrow, 'This Way to the Mummy ...' that leads to a door small enough for a child to open. Inside is a tiny room with a most impressive mummy that was given to the Royal Institution of South Wales in 1888 by Field-Marshal Lord Francis Grenfell, son of an important local family who had chosen the military for his career. Of course, in 1888, it was perfectly legal to purchase mummies in Egypt and export them to the United Kingdom. It is also true that it is still perfectly legal to keep and display objects of this nature, as long as the acquisition predates the 1970 UNESCO Convention on the Means of Prohibiting and Preventing the Illicit Import, Export and Transfer of Ownership of Cultural Property.[1] There is no question that museums with exotic collections have an extremely important role to play in education about other cultures and the past and in the preservation of antiquities. Many professionals who would be reading a paper like this one may well have been influenced in their career choice by an object or exhibition in a museum experienced as a child. However, no matter what the potential benefits might be, acquisition of collections and exhibitions needs to follow legal procedures. Failure to follow the law and engagement with the illicit antiquities market has serious negative effects all over the world.

III. Local Impacts at Home in the United States

In mid-June of 2011, the Archaeological Institute of America archaeology news picked up a story about a university summer field school being struck by vandals who dug looter holes into the test excavation units.[2] This summer field school was being held in a small town in southern Illinois, nearly adjacent to the university campus. It is difficult to imagine a more peaceful place on earth than a small town in southern Illinois during the early summer. Only an individual who has

[1] UNESCO 1970 Convention on the Means of Prohibiting and Preventing the Illicit Import, Export and Transfer of Ownership of Cultural Property, International Treaty, *available at* <http://portal.unesco.org/en/ev.php-URL_ID=13039&URL_DO=DO_TOPIC&URL_SECTION=201.html> (last accessed on 18 January 2013).

[2] Pawlaczyk, '"So Much Work and It Was Gone"; Vandals Hit SIUE Archaeology Dig', *News Democrat*, 16 June 2011, *available at* <http://www.bnd.com/2011/06/14/1748370/so-much-work-and-it-was-gone-vandals.html> (last accessed on 16 June 2011).

spent hours in the hot sun, painstakingly participating in a controlled excavation, centimetre by centimetre, screening all of the soil, and endeavoring to keep the walls perfectly straight and the unit floor perfectly level, can appreciate the anger, fury, and hurt of the experience of arriving at that same unit one morning only to discover that it had been destroyed in the night. The irony of this example is that the odds of an excavation of this nature ever yielding a marketable object are extremely low. The looting and vandalism at the Southern Illinois University Edwardsville campus field school was completely due to a perception. The perception was that there might be valuable objects in the soil and that these objects might be sold for cash in the illicit antiquities market. So even in this peaceful place, the social fabric of the community has been torn, and not even directly by the market in illicit antiquities but by a belief in that market. The incident in Edwardsville offers a manageable example and a useful baseline for considering the effects of far more dramatic cases on a much larger scale occurring in crisis and conflict areas around the globe.

Looting of archaeological property and Native American sacred places on public lands in the American West is a similar form of theft and has been a perpetual problem since settlement in the region by people of European descent. It is important to understand that in contrast to countries like Italy where all buried objects and features of archaeological significance belong to the state, in the US, objects excavated from private land become the property of the landholder. This distinction presents a challenge to law enforcement, because, once excavated, it is extremely difficult to determine whether an object came from public or private land. Adding to the confusion, when the Archaeological Resources Protection Act (ARPA)[3] was passed, a provision for the benefit of 'arrowhead' collectors was included that makes it legal to collect and keep intact stone projectile points from public land. Views of property rights in the American West further contribute to the complexity of challenges for enforcement of archaeological site protection and to extreme emotional responses when law enforcement responds to issues of looting on public lands. It is also critical to remember that many of the robberies damage and destroy Native American burials of human remains. As a result, there is completely understandable and justifiable anger in response to looting that comes from the Native American community members.

The recent Forest Service case in Utah illustrates the effects that a looting case can have on rural communities. In 2009, based in part from undercover operations and assisted by an informant, federal agents arrested and charged a series of prominent citizens for looting Native American archaeological sites on public land and selling the objects for profit using a series of dealers in the American Southwest. By 2011, as the cases were being resolved in court, threats against the

[3] Archaeological Resources Protection Act. Legislation of the United States Congress, 16 U.S.C. §§ 470aa–470mm; Public Law 96–95 and amendments, *available at* <http://www.nps.gov/archeology/tools/Laws/arpa.htm> (last accessed on 18 January 2013).

enforcement officials emerged. The informant committed suicide as did two of the defendants, one of whom was a prominent physician in the community who had been arrested previously for these same activities. These events were featured in US national news.[4] It is not difficult to imagine the strain on the small towns, where the accused as well as the enforcement officers live and work, when citizens begin to take sides and debate the issue. In some of these communities, private citizens do not believe that there is anything wrong with taking objects from public land. In fact some of these citizens think that is one of the purposes of public land, and they take pride in teaching their children these behaviours. In 2008, the cultural property officer at the United States Department of Justice provided federal cultural resources managers with links to YouTube videos of metal detector groups holding events at publicly owned Civil War battlefields where they picnicked after excavating and collecting Civil War memorabilia. The individuals and groups involved were so oblivious to the law that they posted the videos themselves, which were later used as evidence against them.

There also appears to be a relationship emerging between use of methamphetamines and theft of archaeological material from US public lands. Both activities thrive in remote rural places, and the artefacts can be sold to help purchase the drug ingredients and to set up laboratories. Again, the effects of these combined activities at the local community level are going to be complex and extremely negative.

IV. Looting in Conflict Zones

Stealing from archaeological sites is an activity that dates back thousands of years. One of the reasons that access to burial chambers in Egyptian pyramids involves complex mazes of pathways is that the architects had to take into consideration the presence of tomb raiders who would be keen to steal the wealth of goods buried with the important individuals for whom these monuments were built. In the recent past, the issue of large-scale looting on archaeological sites in conflict zones emerged, with the media attention paid to looting and damage at a series of major Mesopotamian archaeological sites throughout Iraq. The looting at the larger scale began during the sanctions against the Saddam Hussein government and escalated dramatically during the invasion in 2003. Looting of the Iraq National Museum in 2003 also brought the issue to the attention of the global media, and there was resounding criticism of the United States for failing to protect the

[4] Yardley, 'Utah Town Unsettled by Doctor's Suicide and an Inquiry on Indian Artifact Looting', *N.Y. Times*, 20 June 2009, *available at* <http://www.nytimes.com/2009/06/21/us/21blanding.html> (last accessed on 18 January 2013); Associated Press, 'Utah: Third Apparent Suicide in Indian Looting Investigation', *N.Y. Times*, 2 March 2010, *available at* <http://www.nytimes.com/2010/03/03/us/03brfs-THIRDAPPAREN_BRF.html> (last accessed on 18 January 2013).

cultural patrimony of Iraq. Not-for-profit organizations even emerged to address the problem, groups like Saving Antiquities for Everyone (SAFE).[5]

If the goal is to protect world heritage and archaeological properties over the long term, it is critical to remember that looting of archaeological properties occurs in the context of disruptions in the social order. When members of local communities pick up shovels and head for the nearest archaeological site, it is a symptom of complex factors at work, and no solutions will emerge unless those factors are identified and the behaviour is analysed from within that context. In the case of Iraq, clearly the motivation at the local level was economic desperation. Members of the Italian Carabinieri who were the only foreign force to successfully complete an interdiction mission against looters recognized the desperation of those individuals, some of whom expressed humiliation and shame given the fact that they knew that their behaviour was damaging and wrong. One of the factors was that years of economic sanctions levelled against the Hussein government and later conflict had disrupted the fragile economy based on the presence of foreign universities and institutes that came to Iraq for excavations season after season. When the foreign missions, some of whom were generously funded, were present, local labourers were on the payroll, and the missions contributed to the local economy in terms of paying for help with food, lodging, and supplies. As Dr Geoff Emberling, from the University of Chicago, pointed out in his comments during presentation of his paper given at the Society for American Archaeology meetings in 2007,[6] foreign archaeologists had actually trained many of the labourers who became looters when legitimate excavations ended.

One of the issues to be considered is that when looting does take place in conflict zones, it can be on an incredibly large scale with resultant massive destruction. Looting of ancient Mesopotamian city-sites like Umma and the necropolis at Larsa rendered the site areas into moonscapes of pits and broken objects. Looters discard and sometimes deliberately smash objects like pottery when they are disappointed with their find or when those objects do not appear to be of value. They show absolutely no respect for human remains, and it is not unusual to see bones strewn about a looted landscape. Looters may tunnel through archaeological ruins searching for tombs or cuneiform tablet libraries leaving sites vulnerable to collapse and making future systematic archaeological excavation compromised and dangerous. Looting in conflict zones can also spread to cultural institutions. The infamous example of the looting of the National Museum of Iraq in Baghdad illustrates how the entire cultural patrimony of a nation can become vulnerable to loss when unprotected. Since Baghdad, museum collections in Cairo and Libya were put at risk by revolutionary changes in government. In Cairo, there is the famous example of the Egyptian people establishing a human chain to protect

[5] *See* <http://www.savingantiquities.org/> (last accessed on 18 January 2013).

[6] Emberling, 'Archaeologists and the Military in Iraq, 2003–2008: Compromise or Contribution', *Archaeologies: J. World Archaeological Congress* (2008) 445–59.

their museum[7] while in Libya, careful curatorial storage at the museum in Tripoli as well as restraint on the part of the fighters and the general population protected collections during hostilities.[8] It is also important to recognize the fact that staff members at the National Museum of Afghanistan put their lives on the line to protect the most important objects and treasure in their collections on multiple occasions. They successfully hid and secured these artifacts in and around Kabul, preventing theft and destruction by both the Russians and the Taliban.[9]

Concern expressed about looting of antiquities by advocates from some of the new organizations like SAFE, and members of the public at large, is important and is certainly well intentioned. However, advocacy from outsiders for placing armed site guards in remote archaeological sites in situations where there is no community consensus for site protection is not the best solution, and at worst it is irresponsible. Arming a portion of a community to defend property from another portion of a community without the recognition that the looting is a symptom of greater challenges in society creates a situation that can easily lead to violence and death. The Italian Carabinieri offer the best training for archaeological site guards of any organization in the world. They have a systematic approach to teaching about mapping and documenting sites, construction of fencing and watchtowers, implementation of aerial surveillance, establishing communications and transportations systems for guards, and consideration for arming guards if necessary. However, even these measures are not enough if armed site guards are literally and figuratively standing alone against a local community that does not share the goal of protecting the site.

V. Proactive Approaches for Site Protection in Conflict Zones

However, there are examples where proactive approaches to protecting archaeological sites have made a difference even in cases of conflict, and nearly complete breakdown in social order. In two cases, when the foreign mission made the effort to ensure that the local families who had been living and working on these sites continued to be paid, not as excavators but as protectors, the sites were spared from damage.[10] In 2003, Dr Joris Kila, serving as a cultural property officer with

[7] Agence France-Presse, 'Egyptians Form Human Chain Around Cairo Museum', *AFP*, 29 January 2011, *available at* <http://www.zawya.com/story.cfm/sidANA20110129T131758ZPCI54> (last accessed on 30 January 2011).

[8] Lawler, 'Claims of Mass Libyan Looting Rejected by Archaeologists', *Science Insider*, 1 September 2011, *available at* <http://news.sciencemag.org/scienceinsider/2011/09/claims-of-mass-libyan-looting.html> (last accessed on 18 January 2013).

[9] Hebert and Cambon, 'Afghanistan; Hidden Treasures from the National Museum, Kabul', *Nat'l Geographic Society* (2008).

[10] Kila, 'Cultural Property Protection', Paper Presented at the Sustaining Military Readiness Conference, US Department of Defense, Phoenix, AZ (2009); Kathryn Hanson, Comments at the Association for Research into Crimes against Art (ARCA) Amelia, Italy (2011). Ms Hanson explained

the Netherlands Ministry of Defense, traveled with a US escort to Warka, the site of the ancient Mesopotamian City of Uruk. Once there, he was able to make contact with Sheik Altubi and his family. The Altubi family had been working with the German Institute of Archaeology for generations, and the site is also their home. Dr Kila insured that the payments from the Institute for continuing to protect the site were made to Sheik Altubi. As a result, when a combined delegation from the US State Department, the Archaeological Institute of America, and the United States Army checked on the site in the spring of 2009, it was found to be in excellent condition with respect to looting. The second example is the successful protection of the ancient site of Nippur where the University of Chicago Oriental Institute found a way to support the site guards in the midst of political turmoil and conflict.[11]

On rare occasions, fencing and interdiction can protect an archaeological site in an area where looting on a large scale is taking place. The ancient Mesopotamian City of Ur offers a case in point. Saddam Hussein had specifically located his airbase at Talil adjacent to the archaeological site of Ur with the hope that the presence of the ruins would protect it from aerial bombardment by Western forces. When US forces secured this base, they realized that the archaeological site of Ur could be vulnerable to the extensive looting taking place on archaeological sites throughout the south of Iraq. In response, they expanded the base perimeter to include the ancient city with its ziggurat that is known throughout the world. The fenced protection saved the site from looting and any form of major damage. However, because the site was within a US defensive perimeter, it was extremely difficult for the provincial archaeological site inspector to gain access.[12] In addition, members of the local community could look through the fence and see US forces visiting the site. They began to express their frustration and concerns through State Department channels and by late 2008, it became clear that it was time to rebuild the perimeter fence to separate the site from the base, putting stewardship for the site back in the hands of the Iraqis. After careful inspection by a combined military, state department, and academic team in April 2009,[13] on 13 May 2009, there was a ceremony for the formal return of the site with over 300 Iraqi community members in attendance. It is important to know that using the US presence to protect this site worked because of the immediate presence of overwhelming force. The Ur solution is rarely available in other situations.

that funds from the University of Chicago Oriental Institute have been supporting an extended family who have successfully protected the archaeological site of Nippur, Iraq.

[11] Hanson, Comments at the Association for Research into Crimes against Art, Annual Conference, Amelia, Italy (July 2011).

[12] Hamdani, 'The Damage Sustained to the Ancient City of Ur', in P. Stone and J. Farchack Bajjaly (eds), *In the Destruction of Cultural Heritage in Iraq* (Boydell, Woodbridge, UK, 2008), 151–156.

[13] Diane Siebrandt, Heritage Liaison for the US State Department, Baghdad, organized and funded the Ur site inspection. The team included Dr Laurie Rush, US Army Archaeologist, Dr Brian Rose, then-President of the Archaeological Institute of America, and Ms Siebrandt. They found the site to be in excellent condition.

Another example of a successful proactive approach for site protection was the use of Commander's Emergency Response Funds for reconstruction of tourist amenities at the site of Aqar Quf.[14] It is true that members of the local community had looted and vandalized the tourist café at the site. However, Agar Quf serves as an example of the principle that when overall social order improves within a community, archaeological site protection can become more realistic. In this case, site protection with the associated tourism potential is also contributing to additional future stability in the community. Once the café was repaired, visitors were able to return, spending money and supporting the associated jobs in the hospitality sector.

The situation that unfolded in Libya in 2011 illustrates a range of issues related to protection of heritage sites in conflict zones. In the spring of 2011, within 36 hours of the announcement of planned NATO intervention in Libya, a network composed of DoD archaeologists, State Department officials, academic subject matter experts, and representatives of non-governmental agencies like the US Committee of the Blue Shield (USCBS), the Associated National Committees of the Blue Shield (ANCBS), and the International Military Cultural Resources Working Group (IMCuRWG), all combined to develop archaeological coordinates for the Libya 'no strike' list and disseminated these coordinates to US Defense Intelligence Agency Air Combat Command, US Africa Command, and NATO planners. Within 36 hours of the announcement, information was in the hands of the appropriate military agencies. During the course of the NATO operations, Libyan archaeologists worked hard to release information about the status of Libyan archaeological sites and their Western archaeological colleagues, including US DoD archaeologists, worked to keep this information flowing to the military agencies. In July of 2011, UNESCO and the University of Naples II held a conference in Italy concerning the future of Libyan archaeological sites. As the conflict unfolded, differing reports concerning the status of Libyan antiquities emerged in the global media, illustrating the importance of having a responsible network of academic and military colleagues in place for evaluating and protecting cultural property in a conflict zone. The UNESCO/Naples II conference strengthened and enhanced the original 'no strike' list network, making it possible to link a Libyan archaeologist with representatives of IMCurWG and ANCBS for a cultural property fact-finding mission that took place in September of 2011.

The findings of this mission further illustrate the importance of proactive protection measures for cultural property at risk. Ironically, the negative attitude toward heritage and antiquities as espoused by the Gaddafi administration worked in favor of heritage protection as soon as rebel forces began to take responsibility.

[14] Roberts and Roberts, 'Cultural Heritage Preservation and Micro-Business: A Case Study in Successful Intervention by the United States Army in Iraq', *Southern J. of Entrepreneurship* (2009) 197–213.

As the IMCuRWG/ANCBS[15] mission reported, at Sabratha rebel forces refused to respond to provocation by Gaddafi forces that would have put features in the ancient Punic/Roman city at risk. At the National Museum and the Museum in Leptis Magna, museum staff members had put the most precious objects in secure and hidden storage areas, in some cases, even welding the access doors closed. At Leptis Magna, site managers permitted shepherds to bring their animals on site, and their presence effectively prevented hostile actions like booby trapping or mining the site area. In addition, Libyans explained to the inspection team members that military forces who wished to join the rebellion were offered the opportunity to guard at Leptis Magna as a form of rehabilitation. Heritage items that were deliberately damaged or destroyed included objects directly related to Gaddafi, such as his automobiles that were on exhibit in the National Museum.[16]

VI. The Market for Illicit Antiquities

A. Looting of Archaeological Sites and Thefts of Works of Art

Unfortunately, the market for illicitly excavated archaeological material encourages looting activity in stable but remotely located areas and archaeological sites. While the scale of looting in areas like these rarely approaches the massive destruction seen in lawless conflict areas, there is still significant damage and loss of cultural property. Looters in these areas also fail to show any respect for archaeological context, damaging the site as they go, and they also demonstrate complete disregard for human remains. Looting of archaeological sites is a global problem, and looting activities shift depending on the market for specific types of antiquities. Cultural institutions like art museums become complicit in this process directly and indirectly. The direct examples of complicity, such as the purchase and eventual repatriation of stolen objects by both the Getty and the Metropolitan Museum of Art, have been extensively documented by journalists and legal proceedings.

Perge, a Hellenistic and Roman city site in southern Turkey, has become victim to looters. In one particularly egregious example, the top half of a statue of Herakles was looted from Perge and sold to the Museum of Fine Arts, Boston. The bottom half was recovered by archaeologists and could be found on exhibit at the Antalya Archaeological Museum. Laser scanning analysis demonstrated

[15] Blue Shield and IMCuRWG, Mission Report: Civil-Military Assessment Mission for Libyan Heritage (2011), available at <http://www.blueshield.at/libya_2011/11–2011/mission_report_libya_11–2011.pdf> (last accessed on 18 January 2013).

[16] Smith, 'In Tripoli's Museum of Antiquity, Only Gaddafi Is Lost in Revolution', *Guardian*, 11 September 2011, *available at* <http://www.guardian.co.uk/culture/2011/sep/11/tripoli-museum-antiquity-shattered-gaddafi-image> (last accessed on 18 January 2013).

unequivocally that the two halves belonged together and that there was no possible legal pathway for the top half of the statue to be in Boston. Diplomatic efforts to convince the Museum to return their half of the Herakles eventually succeeded during the summer of 2011, and the reunification of the statue was celebrated in October of 2011.[17] For an American visiting the museum in Antalya prior to the agreement to return the object, it was humiliating to see the Herakles exhibition with the associated background information. A second example from Perge was a looted portion of the sarcophagus of Herakles. This object was repatriated by the Getty to Turkey in 1983. The good news is that Perge is now an important tourist destination near Antalya. Recognition that the site in good condition is more valuable to the local community than the potential profits from sale of looted objects from the site serves as a passive form of protection. Perge is also an important source of pride because Turkish archeologists and universities are responsible for its excavation and conservation program.

Hypothetical examples can illustrate the concept of indirect complicity. Imagine a blockbuster exhibition featuring Mayan ceramics traveling through a series of major US cities and European capitals featuring objects that may have recently been purchased for prices in the millions of dollars. This type of attention results in collector interest that drives up the market prices even further, encouraging individuals or even groups of organized criminals to initiate and/or ramp up illegal excavations at Mayan sites with the hope of finding more of these objects to smuggle out of the host country to sell for enormous profits. Illegally excavated objects also have the advantage of never having been documented, making it much more difficult for an owner or buyer to be accused of theft. Illicitly obtained objects can also take on additional value if they appear in museum exhibitions or if professionals identify them, translate text on them, or interpret them in any way.

B. Enforcement and the Carabinieri Command for the Protection of Cultural Property

Since 1969, the Carabinieri Command for the Protection of Cultural Property, in Italian, the Carabinieri Tutela Patrimonio Culturale or TPC, has emerged as the world's leading military and policing organization for the protection of cultural property. The Command is now a nucleus of over 200 officers distributed across a series of headquarters and twelve regional offices who have additional specialized training in various aspects of art crime and who also have deployment capabilities. The Italians have continued challenges with not just illegal excavations and theft of objects from archaeological sites and tombs but also with art fraud, art

[17] Dogan News Agency, 'Halves of Herakles Reunite in Southern Turkey', *Hurriyet Daily News*, 9 October 2011, *available at* <http://www.hurriyetdailynews.com/n.php?n=halves-of-herakles-reunite-2011-10-09> (last accessed on 18 January 2013).

theft, and related money laundering activities. The Carabinieri tracked down one of the major smuggling networks that handled archaeological objects leaving Italy for sale in major American museums, and the subsequent prosecutions and repatriations made headlines around the world. These accomplishments changed acquisitions practices at many US museums and have set precedents for repatriation of significant objects that are having rippling effects across the globe. The Carabinieri headquarters' capabilities, in addition to administrative leadership, include an archaeology unit based in Rome, an interactive inventory database of stolen works of art, a documentation programme for owners of art and archaeological objects, and support for nationwide educational initiatives. Their regional offices focus on law enforcement and protection of artwork and archaeological objects at the regional level. In Sicily, for example, illegal excavation is still a challenge, as is catching and prosecuting tombaroli, the Italian name for individuals who dig illegally in archaeological sites with the hope of finding objects that they can sell on the black market.

The Carabinieri are also the only military force in the world that can mobilize and deploy trained forces for the purposes of cultural property protection during full-spectrum military missions. In 2003, a multidisciplinary team of Carabinieri officers deployed to Nasiriyah province, Iraq, as part of a UNESCO peace-keeping mission. Several of the officers were members of the TPC, so they had experience with illegal excavations and protection of archaeological sites. These members organized the entire team to map and document the archaeological sites in the region, to initiate aerial surveillance, and to work with Iraqis in terms of training and equipping site guards. They even completed missions where they took looters by surprise, capturing them and recovering objects in the process of being removed from sites.[18] The officers' accounts of these experiences speak to the desperation of the looters, who in many cases were not career criminals. One, a former schoolteacher, even expressed recognition of and remorse for his role in the great damage to Iraq's heritage. When the Carabinieri officers discuss their memories of these experiences, great compassion for the Iraqi people is evident. There is no question that the extreme circumstances in Iraq combined with an art market completely lacking in ethical guidelines resulted in not just tremendous losses to Iraqi heritage but also tremendous costs to the integrity of communities and individuals at very local and personal levels. The Carabinieri also deployed a very experienced officer to the National Museum of Iraq in Baghdad after the looting. The Captain provided significant assistance not just in providing assistance for recovering lost items but also in terms of developing the database of missing items that is still available to law enforcement officials and the public and can be found linked to the Carabinieri data bank website, <http://tpcweb.

[18] Banerjee and Garen, 'Saving Iraq's Archaeological Past from Thieves Remains an Uphill Battle', *N.Y. Times*, 4 April 2004, *available at* <http://www.nytimes.com/2004/04/04/world/saving-iraq-s-archaeological-past-from-thieves-remains-an-uphill-battle.html?pagewanted=all&src=pm> (last accessed on 18 January 2013).

carabinieri.it/tpc_sito_pub/simplecerca.jsp> (last accessed on 18 January 2013) 'Reperti archeologici trafugatidall' Iraq.' It should also be mentioned that thirteen of these heroic Carabinieri lost their lives along with others as the result of a suicide bombing attack on their headquarters in Nasiriyah.

VII. Conclusion

Whether it is finding a meticulous test excavation destroyed in southern Illinois, or an entire Mesopotamian City looted to the point of looking like a moonscape with potentially millions of dollars' worth of artefacts headed for the global antiquities market, 'the view from the ground' reveals enormous costs in terms of pain and loss to individuals and society. The solutions will elude us until participants in this issue, from prosecutors to customers—and especially the customers—identify, appreciate, and take responsibility for the true impact of these crimes.

PART II

ENFORCEMENT BY DOMESTIC COURTS

5

Sovereign Immunity and the Enforcement of International Cultural Property Law

Riccardo Pavoni [*]

I. Introduction

There exists an ambivalent relationship between the law of state immunity and the enforcement of international cultural property law. On the one hand, immunity from *execution* generally fosters the special values associated with artworks belonging to the cultural heritage of states by shielding them from seizure, attachment, and similar measures of constraint when they are located in the territory of other states, especially when they are on loan to foreign museums and educational institutions. On the other hand, immunity from *jurisdiction* (understood *stricto sensu* as immunity from suit) may bar restitution claims brought by individuals who have been unlawfully dispossessed of cultural objects that are in the hands of foreign sovereigns. This is liable to occur when a court determines that proceedings against foreign states for the recovery of cultural property involve *jure imperii* activities, that is, activities which are a manifestation of sovereign authority, and as such, exempt from the jurisdiction of forum states. A comparable result may ensue from the application of the act of state doctrine so as to dismiss a restitution suit on the merits, by arguing that the adjudication of the case would require a review of the validity of foreign legislative, governmental or judicial acts. From this perspective, immunity rules may hamper, rather than promote, the effective enforcement of cultural property law as it pertains to the restitution of wrongfully taken art objects.

If these propositions appear rather straightforward, the vicissitudes of cultural goods and the dynamics of art markets are rarely so, with the consequent emergence of disparate legal situations which cannot easily be subsumed within the above scheme, and call instead for a balancing of the interests and values underlying the cases at hand and the applicable norms. Fortunately, a substantial practice concerning art-and-immunity disputes has blossomed, particularly in the United

* Associate Professor of International and European Law, University of Siena.

States of America (US), which offers several examples of the situations at stake and justifies a systematic appraisal of this area of the law, hitherto fairly undeveloped and largely theoretical. A key development now comes from the recent judgment of the International Court of Justice (ICJ) in *Jurisdictional Immunities of the State*.[1] This decision did not deal directly with the issues examined in this chapter, but it made important findings – for instance, on the maintenance of immunity despite the commission of grave crimes, and on the inapplicability of any balancing exercise in the field of state immunity – that will be discussed in the following parts.

Although judicial practice relating to art-and-immunity cases is growing, it appears necessary to test the indications emerging therefrom against the effective enforcement of international cultural heritage obligations. Indeed, it will be apparent that, in approaching such disputes, judicial bodies normally sidestep any discussion of the consistency of their findings with international norms aimed at the protection of cultural property. The usual approach is to focus exclusively on the relevant immunity rules, with no consideration of the special features which distinguish these cases.

It is useful, then, to recall that most significant in the context of the existing practice concerning art and immunity from *jurisdiction* are the prohibition of misappropriation of artworks by means of direct or indirect coercion (such as in armed conflicts), and the corresponding obligation to return such artworks to their rightful owners. These are well-entrenched norms of contemporary international cultural heritage law, embodied in customary and treaty rules.[2] However, several manifestations of practice remain problematic, for instance, because they refer to states which were not involved in the original unlawful takings or because they concern non-coercive peacetime transactions, where the applicable legal framework is only made up of treaties, essentially the 1970 UNESCO Convention[3] and the 1995 UNIDROIT Convention,[4] and thus reflects the latter's weaknesses and inherent limitations.

As for the cases about art and immunity from *execution*, the pertinent norm, arguably considered of a customary character,[5] has instead evolved within the law of state immunity, and prescribes that state cultural property is immune from enforcement proceedings, of whatever form and extent, instituted in another state.

[1] *Jurisdictional Immunities of the State (Germany v Italy: Greece intervening)* (3 Feb. 2012).

[2] The prohibition of misappropriations and looting is unquestionably of a customary nature, while the duty of restitution is at least arguably so. *See* Francioni, 'Au delà des traités: l'émergence d'un nouveau droit coutumier pour la protection du patrimoine culturel', 111 *Revue générale de droit international public* (2007) 19, at 27–30.

[3] Convention on the Means of Prohibiting and Preventing the Illicit Import, Export and Transfer of Ownership of Cultural Property, Paris, 14 Nov. 1970, in force 24 Apr. 1972.

[4] UNIDROIT Convention on Stolen or Illegally Exported Cultural Objects, Rome, 24 June 1995, in force 1 July 1998.

[5] Gattini, 'The International Customary Law Nature of Immunity from Measures of Constraint for State Cultural Property on Loan', in I. Buffard, J. Crawford, A. Pellet, and S. Wittich (eds), *International Law between Universalism and Fragmentation*. Festshrift *in Honour of Gerhard Hafner* (Leiden/Boston: Martinus Nijhoff, 2008) 421–39.

This norm serves the interest of the effective enforcement of cultural heritage law by recognizing the intrinsic value of cultural objects, ensuring respect for the integrity of the cultural patrimony of states, and sustaining the educational function of cultural property for humanity through the promotion of transnational exchanges and loans. Even here, however, it is appropriate to differentiate the various situations under which the principle of immunity from seizure of cultural property may be called into question. It seems, in other words, warranted to draw distinctions based on the claim upon which the judgment sought to be enforced against cultural property was obtained. There may be countervailing factors in the recognition of enforcement immunity for cultural objects, such as the existence of legitimate restitution claims or the violation of human rights by the foreign state owning or possessing the objects.

Part II discusses the law and practice about state immunity from jurisdiction in proceedings involving cultural objects, while Part III focuses on immunity from execution for state cultural property. Part IV offers some concluding remarks.

II. Should Sovereign Immunity from Jurisdiction be Granted in Art-Recovery Suits?

There are several ways of overcoming a defence based on sovereign immunity in suits brought against foreign states for the recovery of cultural property. Plaintiffs may either invoke treaties imposing a duty of restitution alleged to prevail over inconsistent customary immunity rules, or they may rely upon norms internal to the law of state immunity. In the former case, the most relevant treaty is certainly the 1995 UNIDROIT Convention which, unlike the 1970 UNESCO Convention,[6] foresees an unconditional duty of restitution of stolen cultural property[7] actionable by means of proceedings instituted by dispossessed individuals. However, the absence of a treaty clause subordinating the rules on state immunity to its obligations,[8] as well as the thin number

[6] As is well known, the restitution obligation envisaged by the 1970 UNESCO Convention only covers property stolen from museums and religious or public monuments and institutions. Crucially, such obligation is to be carried out pursuant to interstate/diplomatic requests (Art. 7). States parties are also bound 'to admit actions for recovery of lost or stolen items of cultural property brought by or on behalf of the rightful owners' (Art. 13(c)), but only to the extent this is 'consistent with the laws of each State' (Art. 13(c), first sentence). Such laws may well include immunity statutes or provisions governing the incorporation of customary rules on immunity in domestic legal systems.

[7] Art. 3(1).

[8] To the contrary, Art. 13(1) of the UNIDROIT Convention contains a savings clause granting precedence to any other legally binding international instrument 'which contains provisions on matters governed' by the Convention, 'unless a contrary declaration is made by the States bound by such instrument'. These instruments may well include the 1972 European Convention on State Immunity (ECSI), which however has been ratified by eight States only, and more importantly, the 2004 UN Convention on Jurisdictional Immunities of States and Their Property (UNCSI). Having been ratified by thirteen States only as of 1 October 2012, the UNCSI is not yet in force. It shall enter into force after ratification by thirty States.

of states parties,[9] make the UNIDROIT Convention an uncertain means for determining the state of the law in this area, also considering the shortage of pertinent practice.

A discourse centred on the rules internal to the law of state immunity is more interesting. In principle, suits for the recovery of artworks may be accommodated within certain generally recognized exceptions to state immunity.

A. The Property and Commercial Activity Exceptions

First of all, the exception relating to claims over 'ownership, possession or use of property' seems most relevant for our purposes. According to the UN Convention on Jurisdictional Immunities of States and Their Property (UNCSI),[10] it covers proceedings involving: (i) the rights or interests of states in, or their possession or use of, immovable property situated in the state of the forum; (ii) the rights or interests of states in movable or immovable property arising by way of succession, gift, or *bona vacantia*; and (iii) the rights or interests of states in the administration of property.

There is no doubt that, pursuant to this exception, 'property' includes 'cultural property', thereby making many art-related disputes amenable to its very broad formulation. It should be noted that the limitation consisting in the presence of the disputed property in the territory of the forum state is only foreseen for the first situation recalled in the previous paragraph, that is, proceedings generally involving rights or interests in immovable property that cannot be subsumed within the other two, more specific cases envisaged by the exception. Indeed, claims about purported successions or gifts may be brought against states even when cultural objects are abroad. For instance, Austria's assertion that the Klimt's paintings at issue in the *Altmann* case[11] were bequeathed to the Austrian Gallery (where they were still located at the time of the dispute), either by virtue of the will of the original owner or as a result of post-Second World War donations by the heirs, would potentially be covered by this exception.[12] While the classes of art-recovery disputes thus permitted may still appear narrow, the third sweeping clause in Article 13(c) UNCSI, namely, that relating to claims over the *administration* of property by states,[13] minimizes this concern.

[9] As of 1 October 2012, there are thirty-three states parties to the UNIDROIT Convention.

[10] Art. 13; *cf.* Arts. 9–10 ECSI.

[11] *Altmann v Republic of Austria*, 317 F.3d 954 (9th Cir. 2002, per Wardlaw CJ), 541 U.S. 677, 43 I.L.M. 1425 (S. Ct. 2004, per Stevens J).

[12] However, in the US, this exception is narrower than in the UNCSI, because the condition of the location of the property on US territory is stipulated for any kind of dispute amenable to its terms. *See* section 1605(a)(4) of the Foreign Sovereign Immunities Act (FSIA), 28 U.S.C. §§ 1330, 1602–1611.

[13] By way of *example*, Art. 13(c) singles out claims concerning trust property, the estate of a bankrupt or the property of a company in the event of its winding up.

Unfortunately, there is no court decision showing whether and why any distinction should be made in the application of the property exception to cultural objects. On the contrary, interesting indications emerge from the practice relating to the most classic exception to state immunity, that is, the commercial activity exception. Whenever art-recovery suits arise from commercial transactions entered into by foreign states, such as contracts for the sale, purchase, bailment, insurance, or loan of state cultural property, it may be argued that that exception applies. This seems correct especially in view of the widely accepted primary test for establishing 'commerciality', that is, the *nature* of the transaction at stake, as opposed to the subjective test of the *purpose* or *motive* behind the transaction.[14] Accordingly, for a foreign state's claim for immunity in art-recovery suits to succeed, it is not sufficient to rely upon the not-for-profit, scientific, cultural, educational, or otherwise public/*jure imperii* purposes sought to be realized when engaging in art-related commercial activities.

This line of argumentation has been canvassed by certain US courts, although essentially[15] in the context of the 'commercial activity' nexus required by the expropriation exception laid down in the 1976 Foreign Sovereign Immunities Act (FSIA).[16] Faced with a claim for the return of eighty-four paintings and drawings brought by the heirs of the Russian abstract artist Malewicz against the City of Amsterdam's Stedelijk Museum,[17] the Columbia District Court ruled that a sovereign's loan of artwork to foreign institutions for exhibition purposes had to be considered a commercial transaction. Judge Collyer significantly held: 'There is nothing "sovereign" about the act of lending art pieces, even though the pieces themselves might belong to a sovereign'.[18] This finding was greatly facilitated by the US court approach to the distinction between *jure imperii* and *jure privatorum* acts, pursuant to which the former are simply actions that only a state may perform. Therefore, insofar as art loans may also be executed by private museums and similar entities, they constitute commercial activity, with the obvious corollary that they are not in principle covered by sovereign immunity. The City of Amsterdam's argument that the loan at issue was intended for

[14] *See* section 1603(d) FSIA. Art. 2(2) UNCSI is instead rather inconclusive on the point.

[15] In a little-noticed—yet pioneering—case, a US district court unhesitatingly assumed jurisdiction on the basis of the commercial activity exception over a claim for damages arising from the expropriation of property, including cultural property, by *post*-Communist Russia in 1994, *Magness v Russian Fed'n*, 54 F. Supp. 2d 700 (S.D. Tex. 1999, per Hittner DJ). The Russian authorities had confiscated the property at issue, that is a historical piano factory containing a vast amount of antiquities and renamed the 'Red October Piano Factory', on the grounds that it constituted a national treasure. They had subsequently engaged in a host of commercial activities involving the property, such as—most strikingly—its lease for commercial purposes or sales of associated antiquities, as well as the solicitation of US tourism to Russian cultural sites or the organization in the US of exhibitions of antiquities of 'like kind and character' vis-à-vis the expropriated items, at 703–5. *See* further on this case, Part III.B.3.

[16] The expropriation exception is discussed below at Part II.B.

[17] *Malewicz v City of Amsterdam*, 362 F. Supp. 2d 298 (D.D.C. 2005, per Collyer DJ).

[18] *Malewicz v City of Amsterdam*, at 314.

eminently educational and cultural *purposes* was easily dismissed by recalling that, according to the FSIA, only the nature of the activity is relevant for establishing commerciality.[19]

Judge Collyer's perspective on transactions involving cultural property is confirmed by her further ruling in the *Malewicz* case, where she rejected the application of the act of state doctrine to the City of Amsterdam's allegedly fraudulent and bad faith acquisition of the disputed paintings in 1956. She found that no official/*jure imperii* act of state was accomplished by the City: '[A]ny private person or entity could have purchased the paintings for display in a public or private museum ... In other words, there was nothing *sovereign* about the City's acquisition of the Malewicz paintings, other than that it was performed by a sovereign entity'.[20] The *de Csepel* case[21] provides another example of this US jurisprudence. It involves an action seeking the return of at least forty works of art —namely, a portion of the so-called Herzog Collection —which were seized by Hungary and Nazi Germany during the Second World War and are currently housed by several agencies of Hungary, such as the Museum of Fine Arts in Budapest, the Hungarian National Gallery, and the Budapest University of Technology and Economics. One of the claims advanced by the heirs of Baron Herzog is a typical commercial claim: they assert breaches of a series of contracts for bailment of the disputed property allegedly concluded with the defendants in the aftermath of the Second World War and accordingly rely upon the FSIA's commercial activity exception.[22] While in the first decision on the case the import of these bailment contracts for the question of jurisdiction was not addressed on grounds of judicial economy,[23] their purported existence did have an impact on Judge Huvelle's analysis of the act of state doctrine:

Plaintiffs allege that they entered into a series of bailment agreements with defendants ... and that defendants have breached these bailments by refusing to return the property. The actions challenged by plaintiffs, therefore, are not 'sovereign acts', but rather *commercial*

[19] *Malewicz v City of Amsterdam*, at 314 (also discussing potential breach of loan agreement resulting from the transfer of lesser artworks than promised, as a situation that would not attract immunity); *see also Cassirer v Kingdom of Spain*, 616 F.3d 1019, 49 I.L.M. 1492 (9th Cir. 2010, per Rymer CJ): 'It is clear that activity need not be motivated by profit to be commercial for purposes of the FSIA ... [T]he commercial character of an activity depends on its nature rather than its purpose. Thus, it does not matter that the Foundation's activities are undertaken on behalf of a non-profit museum to further its cultural mission', at 1498.

[20] *Malewicz v City of Amsterdam*, 517 F. Supp. 2d 322, at 339 (D.D.C. 2007, per Collyer DJ) (emphasis in the original).

[21] *De Csepel v Republic of Hungary*, 808 F. Supp. 2d 113 (D.D.C. 2011, per Huvelle DJ).

[22] For background information, *see de Csepel v Republic of Hungary*, at 135–137; for details on the plaintiff's claim in question, *see* Plaintiffs' Memorandum of Points and Authorities in Opposition to Defendants' Motion to Dismiss the Complaint, at 38–42, *available at* <www.commartrecovery.org/sites/default/files/MemoLawOpp.pdf>.

[23] *De Csepel v Republic of Hungary*, at 133 note 4. The Court had already asserted jurisdiction pursuant to the FSIA's expropriation exception. *See* Part II.B.

acts that could be committed by any private university or museum. Such 'purely commercial' acts do not require deference under the act of state doctrine.[24]

These may be taken as rather straightforward applications of the commercial activity exception to sovereign immunity in the realm of cultural property disputes. From the perspective of cultural heritage law, there may be a host of objections to considering state transactions involving artistic treasures as just another 'purely commercial' matter. The substantive point, however, is that, under the appropriate circumstances, this classic exception may pave the way for legitimate claims for the restitution of property that has been wrongfully taken from their rightful owners by state actors.

This does not mean that any situation in which states currently possess property that at some point in time had been the subject of private transactions, either legal or illegal, would justify art-recovery claims to proceed and overcome pleas of sovereign immunity. In principle, immunity does not bar art-restitution suits brought on the basis of the commercial activity exception only when commercial transactions constitute the very subject-matter of the claim and relief sought. It does not suffice for such transactions to lie at the origins of the dispute. This is well illustrated by one of the few known (non-American) judicial decisions squarely involving immunity from jurisdiction in cultural property restitution proceedings.

In *Italian State v X*,[25] the Swiss Federal Tribunal granted immunity to Italy in respect of a restitution claim brought by an individual asserting ownership over a set of historic stone tablets that had been handed over to the Italian authorities to serve as evidence in criminal proceedings, pursuant to a request under the 1959 European Convention on Mutual Assistance in Criminal Matters (ECMACM). Italy had not fulfilled its duty to return such evidence to Switzerland 'as soon as possible', as prescribed by Article 6(2) ECMACM. However, it can be evinced from the decision that the disputed archaeological pieces had in the first place been unlawfully exported to Switzerland and eventually acquired by the plaintiff, contrary to Article 826(2) of the Italian Civil Code, which vests the Italian state with exclusive title over excavated cultural objects. Thus, the plaintiff could understandably speak of an 'astute manoeuvre'[26] set in motion by Italy in order to regain possession and title over the tablets without the inconvenience of bringing suit in Switzerland.

The Federal Tribunal afforded immunity because Italy was not relying on a property right arising from *jure privatorum* activities, but rather from 'its public law legislation protecting objects of historical and archaeological value';[27] hence,

[24] *De Csepel v Republic of Hungary*, at 142–143 (emphasis in the original).

[25] *Italian State v X & Court of Appeal of the Canton of the City of Basle*, 82 ILR 24 (English translation), 42 *Annuaire suisse de droit international* 60 (1986) (French translation) (Swiss Federal Tribunal, 6 Feb. 1985).

[26] *Italian State v X*, at 28, para. 5b.

[27] *Italian State v X*, at 26, para. 4a.

the case concerned a claim 'formulated by the Italian State in the exercise of its sovereign powers (*jure imperii*)'.[28] The Tribunal further denied that this implied an impermissible *application* of foreign public law.[29] It finally excluded that Italy was in violation of the ECMACM and that therefore immunity ought to be withdrawn on that account.[30]

The substantive conclusion reached by the Tribunal may be shared, although its reasoning was questionable. Immunity seemed warranted in this case because the latter's immediate subject-matter was the failure to return cultural property by a state which had used that property as evidence in criminal proceedings, and not wrongful acts committed in the context of commercial activities. The disputed Italian governmental determination taken in the context of judicial activities was by definition an expression of sovereign authority. That the property at issue had been previously the subject of contractual arrangements and transfers of ownership[31] may be deemed irrelevant. The same applies to the subsequent Italian conduct evidencing the intention to (re)appropriate the property in accordance with Italian law. But the Swiss Federal Tribunal's position that immunity was the automatic consequence of reliance on national cultural heritage laws went too far. This would imply granting immunity in any case where a foreign sovereign seeks to justify its retention of artworks on the basis of the alleged necessity to comply with those laws, regardless of the circumstances under which the objects were acquired or entered the national territory.[32]

B. The Expropriation Exception in the US FSIA

The most interesting practice in the field of state immunity in art-recovery suits has arisen in the US as a result of the application of a norm that is peculiar to

[28] *Italian State v X*, at 26, para. 4a.

[29] '[T]he distinction between acts *jure imperii* and *jure gestionis* ... cannot be applied without taking account of foreign public law', *Italian State v X*, at 27, para. 4b.

[30] According to the Tribunal, a breach of the ECMACM would only result from Italy's refusal to return the property *upon a specific request* from the Swiss authorities, *Italian State v X*, at 29, para. 5c. Although this part of the decision is rather unclear, it can be read as a further confirmation of the point made in the text accompanying notes 6–9, namely, that (customary) immunity may not be granted when the breach of a treaty, such as the ECMACM, is at issue.

[31] With no participation of Italian authorities and indeed in breach of Italian law.

[32] Although involving a situation which is somewhat the reverse of the cases discussed here, that is, a claim by a foreign state for the recovery of antiquities in the possession of a private art gallery, several observations made by the English Court of Appeal in its *Barakat Galleries* decision are of utmost interest also in our context. The Court excluded that a state's assertions of title to property pursuant to its cultural heritage laws had necessarily to be regarded as a *jure imperii* exercise of sovereign authority, *Government of the Islamic Republic of Iran v The Barakat Galleries*, [2007] EWCA Civ 1374 (per Lord Phillips of Worth Matravers CJ), para. 149 ('[Iran] asserts a claim based upon title to antiquities which form part of Iran's national heritage .... This is a patrimonial claim, not a claim to enforce a public law or to assert sovereign rights.'); *see also Government of the Islamic Republic of Iran v The Barakat Galleries*, paras. 114 and 126. On the facts of the case, this finding paved the way for the acceptance of Iran's right to recovery of the antiquities, but in immunity disputes it may well work out as an argument to defeat an immunity claim generically grounded upon reliance on states' patrimony legislation.

the US legal system, namely, the expropriation or takings exception to sovereign immunity under section 1605(a)(3) FSIA. This reads:

A foreign state shall not be immune from the jurisdiction of courts of the United States or of the States in any case ... in which rights in property taken in violation of international law are in issue and that property or any property exchanged for such property is present in the United States in connection with a commercial activity carried on in the United States by the foreign state; or that property or any property exchanged for such property is owned or operated by an agency or instrumentality of the foreign state and that agency or instrumentality is engaged in a commercial activity in the United States.

We are witnessing an expanding jurisprudence applying this exception to art-restitution claims that seek redress for state misappropriations of cultural property which, more or less patently, are amenable to the notion of a taking in violation of international law. Most importantly, this jurisprudence relates to unsettled cases dating back to infamously known historical instances of systematic, large-scale, and blatantly discriminatory deprivation of artworks, such as the Nazi Germany and Bolshevik Russia eras of plunder and nationalization of property. This is the upshot of the 2004 milestone decision of the US Supreme Court in *Altmann*,[33] which determined that the FSIA applied retroactively so as to cover state conduct pre-dating its enactment in 1976, including conduct carried out before the US adoption of the restrictive doctrine of sovereign immunity with the 1952 Tate Letter.[34]

Altmann, a Nazi-era case, has so far been most significantly followed up by *Chabad*[35] (expropriation and looting of historical and religious books and manuscripts by Russia at different times starting with the October Revolution); *Cassirer*[36] (Nazi confiscation of a Pissarro painting); *de Csepel*[37] (Nazi Hungary's expropriation of a large number of art objects comprising the Herzog Collection); and *Malewicz*[38] (1950s acquisition by the Netherlands of Abstract-art paintings and drawings left behind by their author/owner when fleeing Stalinist- and Nazi-era persecution). This jurisprudence has been widely commented upon especially by American scholars, who have sought to balance its meritorious effect of paving the way for redress for past wrongs with the need to respect the function of, and values inherent in, immunity rules when applied to cultural

[33] *Altmann, see earlier* note 11.

[34] Letter of Jack B. Tate, Acting Legal Advisor, Dep't of State, to Acting Attorney General Philip B. Perlman, 19 May 1952, reprinted in 26 Dep't State Bull. 984 (1952) and in *Alfred Dunhill of London, Inc. v Republic of Cuba*, 425 U.S. 682, at 711–715 app. 2 (S. Ct. 1976).

[35] *Agudas Chasidei Chabad v Russian Fed'n*, 466 F. Supp. 2d 6 (D.D.C. 2006, per Lamberth CJ), 528 F.3d 934 (D.C. Cir. 2008, per Williams SCJ). For detailed information on this complex dispute and its background, *see* Bazyler and Gerber, '*Chabad v Russian Federation*: A Case Study in the Use of American Courts to Recover Looted Cultural Property', 17 *IJCP* (2010) 361.

[36] *Cassirer, see earlier* note 19.

[37] *De Csepel, see earlier* note 21.

[38] *Malewicz, see earlier* notes 17, 20.

heritage issues.[39] It will be sufficient here to recapitulate the salient features of these decisions.

First of all, it should be pointed out that, for US courts, an expropriation contrary to international law is a broad concept, which covers any state deprivation of property rights, either directly or indirectly and carried out either for a non-public purpose or for a public purpose but without payment of prompt, fair, and adequate compensation. An important condition is that the targeted individuals must not be nationals of the expropriating state at the time of the taking. This hurdle has been easily defeated for Jewish-owned cultural objects expropriated under Nazi rule, by emphasizing that Nazi laws and Nazi-occupied countries' laws had stripped Jews of their citizenship rights.[40]

Second, as the presence of the disputed property in the US is only required under the first clause of section 1605(a)(3), the denial of immunity in the cases at hand have most prominently resulted from reliance on the second clause of that provision, which merely presupposes that the property be 'owned or operated by an agency or instrumentality of the foreign state', such as a museum or cultural institution. Thus, the expropriation exception is capable of reaching art located abroad, provided the 'commerciality' condition discussed in the next paragraph is satisfied. However, the *Malewicz* litigation demonstrates that also the first clause may successfully be invoked in our context. This may occur when suit is filed while the contested objects are present in the US in the context of a temporary loan for cultural purposes by a foreign museum *and* even if they are protected from seizure by a US Government decision under the 1965 Immunity from Seizure Act (IFSA).[41] In other words, in such a case, a loan may constitute a valuable occasion to ambush 'tainted' cultural property. Despite all arguments against the propriety of such a procedure,[42] Judge Collyer, in the 2005 decision

[39] *See* Redman, 'The Foreign Sovereign Immunities Act: Using a "Shield" Statute as a "Sword" for Obtaining Federal Jurisdiction in Art and Antiquities Cases', 31 *Fordham Int'l L.J.* (2008) 781 (depicting art and antiquities claims as the 'hottest new investment opportunity' (at 781) and a likely 'tobacco litigation of this decade' (at 781)); Caprio, 'Artwork, Cultural Heritage Property, and the Foreign Sovereign Immunities Act', 13 IJCP (2006) 285 (one of the first pieces seeking to systematically appraise both the US cases now at issue and those concerning immunity of cultural property from execution examined at Part III.B); DeFrancia, 'Sovereign Immunity and Restitution: The American Experience', (Fall/Winter 2010) *Cultural Heritage & Arts Rev.* 32. As for non-American scholars, a comprehensive survey and appraisal of (*inter alia*) the US case law in question is included in the recent monograph by van Woudenberg, *State Immunity and Cultural Objects on Loan* (Leiden/Boston: Martinus Nijhoff, 2012), 107–200.

[40] *Cassirer v Kingdom of Spain*, 461 F. Supp. 2d 1157, at 1165–1166 (C.D. Cal. 2006); *de Csepel*, *see earlier* note 21, at 130. For another example of a decision showing the attitude of US courts of downplaying the nationality requirement at issue, see *Chabad*, *see earlier* note 35, at 943.

[41] 22 U.S.C. § 2459; *see also* Parts III.A and III. B.3.

[42] *See, eg*, Caprio, 'Artwork', at 293–294, 303. Although much discussed, the proposed amendment to the FSIA currently tabled with the US Congress is particularly narrow, as it seems to only foreclose cases similar to the *Malewicz* situation (ie artwork present in the US *in connection with* a commercial activity in the US). The amendment would indeed only prohibit considering as

in *Malewicz*, persuasively took the view that immunity from seizure was not a bar to proceedings seeking restitution of the property; immunity only prohibited the taking of measures of constraint against the disputed art, which should therefore leave US territory unimpeded, but cannot cause dismissal of the restitution suit.[43]

Third, the commercial activity nexus set out by the expropriation exception has also not represented a major obstacle to the expansion of the case law at hand. This is the consequence of the 'nature test' applied to the notion of 'commerciality', which implies that cultural and educational activities are not spared from the scope of the notion. In addition, the second clause of section 1605(a)(3) does not prescribe any particular connection between the disputed property and the commercial activity in the US by the foreign agency or instrumentality. For instance, the following have been considered relevant activities triggering the requirement in question: (i) publication of a museum's guidebook including the contested paintings and advertisement of the museum's initiatives in the US (*Altmann*); (ii) contracts between foreign entities and US companies for joint publications and sales, as well as for duplication and sale of the former's exhibited materials (*Chabad*); (iii) shipping giftshop items to US purchasers, or showing a programme filmed at a museum on Iberia flights between Spain and the US, or the maintenance of a museum's website available to US citizens to buy admission tickets and view the collection (*Cassirer*); (iv) loans of art to museums in the US, promotion of US tourism, sales of books covering the disputed paintings through the Internet, as well as a foreign university's participation in student exchange programmes with the US, including the Fulbright Program (*de Csepel*). By contrast, the 'commerciality' condition under the first clause of section 1605(a)(3) requires a 'substantial contact'[44] with the US, as well as a degree of connection between the contested property and the commercial activity. But in the 2007 *Malewicz* decision even this more demanding test was deemed fulfilled by an art loan agreement that had yielded non-negligible fees to the foreign museum and required the presence of the museum's officials in the US for safety and supervision purposes.[45]

Fourth, prior exhaustion of domestic remedies in the state pleading immunity (or in the state responsible for the taking) has not been regarded as a condition

'commercial activity' under the expropriation exception loans of artworks to the US protected by the IFSA. It would not halt litigation along the lines of the *Altmann* and *Cassirer* decisions, in which a connection between the property at issue and commercial activity in the US is not required (*see later* notes 44–45 and accompanying text) and IFSA protection is irrelevant because the art is located abroad. The bill in question was introduced in the US Congress on 20 March 2012, Bill S. 2212, Foreign Cultural Exchange Jurisdictional Immunity Clarification Act, *available at* <www.govtrack.us/congress/bills/112/s2212/text>; *see* 'Dispute over Bill on Borrowed Art', *NY Times*, 22 May 2012 (New York edn). The heated debates on the bill relate to its savings clause for Nazi-era claims only.

[43] *Malewicz*, *see earlier* note 17, at 309–312.

[44] *See* section 1603(e) FSIA ('A "commercial activity carried on in the United States by a foreign state" means commercial activity carried on by such state and having substantial contact with the United States').

[45] *Malewicz*, *see earlier* note 20, at 332–333.

on the exercise of jurisdiction pursuant to the expropriation exception. While in *Malewicz* and *Chabad* this alleged requirement was rejected on grounds of inadequacy of the foreign remedies,[46] in *Cassirer* the Ninth Circuit Court of Appeals ruled in general terms that exhaustion was *not* mandated by the FSIA, even though it could be considered at the stage of the merits on a prudential or discretionary basis.[47] The defendant state's insistence that exhaustion was dictated by international law as a prerequisite for the state of nationality's espousal of individual claims arising from takings of property was found unpersuasive, insofar as, first, this only concerned interstate dispute settlement processes and not actions before domestic courts by private individuals, and second, the FSIA had not however incorporated that prerequisite.[48]

Despite the ICJ *Jurisdictional Immunities* judgment's flat dismissal of an alternative-remedy argument or a balancing exercise in the area of state immunity,[49] I remain convinced that the availability of alternative forums – including in the state claiming immunity – that might provide access to justice and relief should be seen as a key factor when seeking to reconcile the antagonist values at play in immunity cases involving the violation of individual rights.[50] However, this perspective does not seem viable in the US legal system. Indeed, a crucial feature of US practice in the field of sovereign immunity is that US courts perceive the FSIA as a self-contained piece of legislation, essentially exempt from external dictates and pressures, and are accordingly most faithful to its wording read in

[46] *Malewicz, see earlier* note 17, at 306–308; *Malewicz, see earlier* note 20, at 333–335 (inadequacy due to applicability of statutes of limitations under Dutch law); *Chabad, see earlier* note 35, at 948–950 (inadequacy for the recovery of part of the Chabad Collection of the potential remedy set out in the Russian Law on Cultural Valuables Displaced to the USSR as a Result of the Second World War and Located on the Territory of the Russian Federation, Federal Law No. 64-FZ of 15 April 1998 as subsequently amended, English translation in 17 IJCP 413 (2010), *see* particularly Art. 19(2) which authorizes transfer of cultural property constituting family heirlooms to representatives of the family upon the latter's payment of its value as well as reimbursement of the costs of its identification, expert appraisal, storage, and so on; the latter requirement is in line with the core provision of the Law pursuant to which title to artworks confiscated by the Soviet Red Army at the end of the Second World War is, with a few exceptions, vested in the Russian Federation, Art. 6(1); 'obviously Russia's mere willingness to *sell* the plaintiff's property back to it could not remedy the alleged wrong', *Chabad, see earlier* note 35, at 949–950 (emphasis in the original)).

[47] *Cassirer, see earlier* note 19, at 1499–1501.

[48] *Chabad, see earlier* note 35, at 949; *Cassirer, see earlier* note 19, at 1504 note 26.

[49] *Jurisdictional Immunities of the State, see earlier* note 1, paras. 101–102 (no state practice about, and inappropriateness of, purported limitation of State immunity grounded on the non-availability of effective alternative means of redress), and 106 ('Immunity cannot ... be made dependent upon the outcome of a balancing exercise of the specific circumstances of each case to be conducted by the national court before which immunity is claimed.'). *Contra, Jurisdictional Immunities of the State, see earlier* note 1, dissenting opinion of Judge Yusuf, paras. 4–11, 20, 29, 42, 51–59, and Conforti, 'The Judgment of the International Court of Justice on the Immunity of Foreign States: A Missed Opportunity', 21 *Italian Y.B. Int'l L.* (2011) 135, at 138–141.

[50] Pavoni, 'Human Rights and the Immunities of Foreign States and International Organizations', in E. de Wet and J. Vidmar (eds), *Hierarchy in International Law: The Place of Human Rights* (Oxford: Oxford University Press, 2012) 71, at 74–77, 83–98.

the light of US legal doctrines and materials. This point is clearly discernible also in the following development arising from the case law at stake.

As first declared by the Ninth Circuit Court of Appeals in *Cassirer* with a decision that the US Supreme Court has refused to review,[51] the expropriation exception applies to any defendant state currently possessing the disputed property, irrespective of whether the artworks were originally taken by another state with no complicity whatsoever by the former state.[52] Putting it simply, defendant and taker need not be the same in art-restitution suits under section 1605(a)(3). This is clearly the most far-reaching conclusion arrived at in the art-restitution case law involving foreign states, one greatly expanding the possibilities to recover illegally seized art objects that have traversed various transactions and passages of title before ending up in the hands of a *prima facie* innocent sovereign. In a remarkable dissenting opinion appended to the *Cassirer* appeal decision, Judge Gould forcefully stated the conviction, based inter alia on 'history and reason and comity',[53] that immunity should only be denied to the states actually responsible for expropriatory actions. This was deemed in line with the international law criteria for attributing conduct under the law of state responsibility, namely, that an expropriation of alien property can be considered an act of a state only when the latter has failed to take preventive or punitive measures to avoid or suppress it, which would clearly not be the case with Spain's conduct in the case at hand.[54] By contrast, the Court's majority considered the foregoing argument only pertinent as a defence at the merits stage, where Spain's potential good faith could be thoroughly investigated.[55] The chief elements militating in favour of this conclusion were again the plain language and legislative history of the FSIA. Regardless of international law, the Court found additional support on the common law's rejection of the *a non domino* rule, namely, the 'familiar notion that a purchaser cannot get good title if property has been stolen at any place along the line'.[56]

[51] On 27 June 2011, the Supreme Court denied *certiorari* in the *Cassirer* case, 131 S. Ct. 3057 (2011). For a first follow-up application of the *Cassirer* principle, see *de Csepel, see earlier* note 21, at 130 (alternatively dismissing Hungary's reliance on the Hungarian nationality of the victims of the Herzog Collection's seizure on the grounds that Nazi Germany took part in the latter). By contrast, the *Cassirer* ruling was unhelpful to the plaintiff in *Orkin v Swiss Confederation*, 2011 U.S. app. LEXIS 20639 (2nd Cir. 12 Oct. 2011). This case concerned a claim for the restitution of a van Gogh drawing sold in 1933, allegedly under duress, to a Swiss collector by the plaintiff's great-grandmother, and currently housed by a Swiss museum. The Court of Appeals refused to assert jurisdiction on the basis of the expropriation exception. It distinguished *Cassirer* as a decision still requiring that the original taking be carried out by a foreign state or with its complicity, and not by a private individual in a private capacity as in the case at hand. This should not be taken as a setback for the *Altmann/Cassirer* jurisprudence, but rather as an obvious application of the notion of an expropriation in violation of international law (in principle, states are not internationally responsible for the wrongful acts of private parties).

[52] *Cassirer, see earlier* note 19, at 1497–1498.

[53] *Cassirer, see earlier* note 19, per Gould CJ dissenting joined by Kozinski Chief Judge, at 1507.

[54] *Cassirer, see earlier* note 19, at 1507.

[55] *Cassirer, see earlier* note 19, at 1498.

[56] *Cassirer, see earlier* note 19, at 1502 note 14.

Judge Gould sarcastically asked in his dissenting opinion: 'The question is, in enacting § 1605(a)(3), did Congress mean to so infringe international law in its very provision finding violation of international law a basis for waiver of sovereign immunity?'[57] Quite apart from the consistency of the dissent's observations with international law, the answer to that question must emphatically be 'yes': the US Congress might have well intended to ignore international law *altogether* when introducing the expropriation exception. The dissent fails to mention, not only that sovereign immunity issues are normally examined by US courts through the lens of domestic legislation and as a matter of *grace and comity*,[58] but more particularly that that exception is unique to the US.[59] It instead constitutes a key element for scholars[60] seeking confirmation of the evolution of the law into a system where human rights and the prohibition of international crimes take precedence over *jure imperii* acts, such as a taking of property by state actors.[61] Regrettably, in *Jurisdictional Immunities of the State*,[62] the ICJ entirely failed to consider the US *Altmann* jurisprudence, although (or *because*) it would have significantly supported the Italian theses of the priority of human rights over state immunity and of the loss of immunity when territorial torts committed in armed conflict are at stake.[63]

III. Immunity of Cultural Property from Execution: An Absolute Rule?

There is a growing consensus on the existence of an international customary rule affording immunity from seizure and similar measures of constraint to art objects

[57] *Cassirer*, *see earlier* note 19, per Gould CJ dissenting joined by Kozinski Chief Judge, at 1507.

[58] *Altmann v Republic of Austria* (S. Ct. 2004), *see earlier* note 11, at 1431 ('But the principal purpose of foreign sovereign immunity has never been to permit foreign states ... to shape their conduct in reliance on the promise of future immunity from suit in United States courts. Rather, such immunity reflects current political realities and relationships, and aims to give foreign states ... some present "protection from the inconvenience of suit as a gesture of comity"' (quoting *Dole Food Co. v Patrickson*, 538 U.S. 468, 479 (2003)); *Malewicz*, *see earlier* note 17, at 304 ('Foreign sovereign immunity will be deemed waived (or, more precisely, the comity of recognizing foreign sovereignty will not be extended) ....').

[59] H. Fox, *The Law of State Immunity* 2nd edn, (Oxford: Oxford University Press, 2008), at 372 ('[I]n giving a remedy for State takings of property contrary to international law the US Act goes beyond any recognized position under international law.'); *see also* at 350, 598.

[60] *See*, *eg*, Bianchi, 'L'immunité des États et les violations graves des droits de l'homme: la fonction de l'interprète dans la détermination du droit international', 50 *Revue générale de droit international public* (2004) 63, at 68.

[61] US courts are usually reticent or ambiguous with respect to this crucial aspect of the expropriation exception. *See* however, also for further references, *Garb v Republic of Poland*, 440 F.3d 579, 586–588 (2nd Cir. 2006, per Cabranes CJ) ('Expropriation is a decidedly sovereign—rather than commercial—activity', at 586).

[62] *Jurisdictional Immunities of the State*, *see earlier* note 1.

[63] *See* Pavoni, 'An American Anomaly? On the ICJ's Selective Reading of United States Practice in *Jurisdictional Immunities of the State*', 21 *Italian Y.B. Int'l L.* (2011) 143; DeFrancia, 'Introductory Note to U.S. Ninth Circuit Court of Appeals: *Cassirer v Kingdom of Spain*', 49 ILM (2010) 1487, at 1488. In the Italian case law, see *Federal Republic of Germany v Autonomous Prefecture of Vojotia*, International Law in Domestic Courts (ILDC) 1815 (IT 2011) (Court of Cassation, 20 May 2011 No. 11163), paras. 37–40.

that are part of the cultural heritage of a state, when they are situated on the territory of another state. The following sub-parts will examine the most significant manifestations of practice in this area, both at the normative and judicial levels. In doing so, the underlying assumptions must necessarily be distinguished from those that guide the analysis of the problem of immunity from jurisdiction in art-recovery suits. It is well known that the denial of sovereign-property immunity from execution is considered a greater affront to the dignity and sovereign equality of states as compared to the removal of their immunity from jurisdiction. Diplomatic and political tensions are at their highest when a court allows enforcement measures against foreign sovereign property. Despite the abandonment of a general rule of absolute enforcement immunity, the foregoing conception is still reflected in law and practice, which make clear that the lifting of immunity from jurisdiction by no means implies that the resulting judgment may be unconditionally executed against the property of the defendant state.[64] Likewise, enforcement immunity contemplates a few essential exceptions frequently surrounded by a host of requirements that make successful completion of execution proceedings against foreign states a rare and unlikely outcome. The basic principle is that property in use or intended for use for government/*jure imperii* purposes is exempt from enforcement proceedings.

Accordingly, immunity of cultural heritage property from measures of constraint may be regarded as an obvious and indispensible rule. That property by definition appears inextricably linked to the fulfilment of sovereign purposes. Furthermore, immunity does not only cover artistic objects per se, but more generally any property by which a state pursues cultural and educational activities, such as museums and cultural institutions. The ICJ judgment in *Jurisdictional Immunities of the State* vigorously supported this perspective. The Court unhesitatingly found that Italy breached international law by allowing a measure of constraint (that is, a legal charge, *ipoteca giudiziale*) against Villa Vigoni, a German property located near Lake Como and made available at no cost to a private association which turned it into an Italian-German centre for European excellence in the fields of research, science, culture, and education.[65]

Yet the practice reviewed in the following paragraphs and the necessity to differentiate the circumstances under which cultural property has come under attack from judgments' creditors warrant a closer look at this problem. At the outset, it is again necessary to point out that the rule exempting cultural property from measures of constraint may well be derogated from by way of treaties allowing the taking of such measures. For instance, in the *Odyssey Marine Exploration* case,

[64] For a restatement of the implications of these principles, *Jurisdictional Immunities of the State*, *see earlier* note 1, paras. 113–114.

[65] *Jurisdictional Immunities of the State*, *see earlier* note 1, paras. 118–120. The jurisprudence of the European Court of Human Rights supports this approach: *see* especially *Kalogeropoulou & Others v Greece & Germany*, Appl. No. 59021/00 (Eur. Ct. Human Rts. 12 Dec. 2002), where the Court ruled that the Greek Government's refusal to authorize the enforcement of a judgment awarding damages

before concluding that a Spanish shipwreck fulfilling the notion of underwater cultural heritage was immune from arrest, US courts enquired as to whether certain treaties dictated otherwise.[66] At the international level, this problem concerns the coordination between the rules on state immunity and treaties aimed at the restitution of unlawfully exported or stolen cultural property, such as especially the UNIDROIT Convention. The stakes are higher as compared to immunity from jurisdiction, because they do not simply involve the permissibility of restitution proceedings notwithstanding immunity rules. They have to do with the power of a court to order the seizure or confiscation of art objects located in the forum jurisdiction and their consequent transfer to the rightful owners. It is not a question of title, but of material apprehension of purportedly immune property. Technically, the relationship between the allegedly customary rule on the immunity of artworks from enforcement and cultural property treaties is not amenable to unequivocal solutions according to general principles of international law.[67] I am inclined to think that, in view of the prominent place acquired in the international society by the fight against illicit trafficking of cultural objects and pursuant to a fair balance of the interests in question, a state is entitled, save special countervailing factors, to give precedence to its treaty restitution obligations.[68]

Nevertheless, the shortage of jurisprudence on the interplay between cultural property treaties and immunity rules, as well as certain features of the UNIDROIT Convention (eg, its non-retrospective scope),[69] imply that the law and practice on the problem at issue has emerged from instruments and cases strictly addressing the scope and limits of state immunity from execution.

to the victims of the Distomo massacre against German property located in Greece, including the Goethe Institute in Athens, was compatible with international law and the European Convention on Human Rights.

66 *Odyssey Marine Exploration v The Unidentified Shipwrecked Vessel*, 657 F.3d 1159, at 1176–1178 (11th Cir. 2011, per Black CJ). The claimants invoked Art. 9 of the 1958 Geneva Convention on the High Seas (affording immunity to warships on the high seas only if they are used on government non-commercial service) and the 1926 Brussels Convention for the Unification of Certain Rules Relating to the Immunity of State-Owned Vessels. *See also* Arts. 32 and 95–96 of the UN Convention on the Law of the Sea. The question was one of coordination between the FSIA and international agreements (*cf.* section 1609 FSIA: 'Subject to existing international agreements ....'), and not between international norms *inter se*. Moreover, it involved treaty rules specifically concerned with issues of immunity, and not cultural property treaties without immunity provisions. It would be most interesting to see whether US courts are prepared to apply the savings clause in section 1609 to art-restitution treaties to which the US is a party.

67 *See*, also for further references, Gattini, *see earlier* note 5, at 437–439 (pointing to the possibility to regard the rule against seizure of cultural heritage property as a 'customary *lex specialis*', at 438).

68 This seems the choice retained by the United Kingdom as part of the art-antiseizure rules enacted in the 2007 Tribunals, Courts and Enforcement Act. Section 135(1) thereof reads: 'While an object is protected under this section it may not be seized ..., unless (a) it is seized ... by virtue of an order made by a court in the United Kingdom, and (b) the court is required to make the order under ... any international treaty'. However, for the time being, these treaties do not include the UNIDROIT Convention, which the United Kingdom has not ratified.

69 Art. 10 UNIDROIT Convention; *see also* note 8 above and accompanying text.

A. Antiseizure Legislation and the UNCSI's Cultural Property Carve-Out

The basic rule in the field of state immunity from execution stipulates that the property of a foreign state located in the territory of another state cannot be subjected to attachment, arrest, and comparable measures,[70] unless the property is used or intended for use by the former state for commercial purposes.[71] As cultural objects protected under state patrimony legislation seem by definition extraneous to the commercial property exception, it may be assumed that they should never be targeted with enforcement measures when sent abroad for scientific or educational purposes, either on a long- or short-term basis. However, this assumption must be tested against the modern expansion of state laws establishing procedures for granting immunity from seizure to artworks entering the national territory under loan agreements. These laws testify that states are not persuaded that their cultural property will unconditionally be afforded immunity by the courts of other states on the grounds of its *jure imperii* character. Accordingly, a growing trend consists in the withholding of loans to foreign institutions by art-lending states, unless the cultural objects in question are specifically and officially accorded immunity.

The US, with the 1965 IFSA, has been a forerunner in this area. IFSA provides that, whenever art objects are imported into the US on a non-profit basis for temporary exhibition or display by any US cultural or educational institution, a prior government decision may immunize such objects from 'any judicial process ... having the effect of *depriving such institution ... of* [their] *custody or control*'.[72] The requirements for granting immunity are the cultural significance of the artworks and the national interest in having them exhibited within the US. The US example has increasingly been followed. At least ten more countries have enacted immunity from seizure legislation.[73]

[70] As in the area of immunity from jurisdiction, it is always possible that a foreign state waives its enforcement immunity, for instance by an arbitration agreement or a written declaration before the courts of the forum state. *See, eg*, Arts. 18(a) and 19(a) UNCSI and section 1610(a)(1) FSIA. The earmarking or allocation of property for the satisfaction of particular claims by a foreign state as per Arts. 18(b) and 19(b) UNCSI may also be seen as a form of (implicit) waiver.

[71] *See* Art. 19(c) UNCSI and section 1610(a) FSIA. Importantly, in the UNCSI this general exception to state immunity for 'commercial property' is only provided for *post*-judgment measures of constraint, and not for interim or conservatory measures such as a seizure prior to the entry of judgment (so called pre-judgment measures of constraint). In the latter case, immunity is only lifted upon waiver by the foreign state, *cf.* Art. 18 UNCSI. Arguably, this exclusion of non-consensual pre-judgment measures of constraint does *not* reflect customary international law. For instance, section 1610(d)(2) FSIA allows pre-judgment attachments of state commercial property, provided 'the purpose of the attachment is to secure satisfaction of a judgment that has been or may ultimately be entered against the foreign state, and not to obtain jurisdiction'.

[72] 22 U.S.C. § 2459(a) (emphasis added).

[73] In chronological order by year of enactment of the relevant legislation, these countries are: Canada (with various provincial statutes starting with the Manitoba IFSA 1976), Australia (1986), France (1994), Ireland (1994), Germany (1999), Austria (2003), Belgium (2004), Switzerland

Unsurprisingly, these are developed countries with high stakes in cross-national exchanges of art.[74]

In this context, the UNCSI is a breakthrough. Unlike existing international instruments[75] and national statutes relating to state immunity,[76] the UNCSI singles out artworks as a category of property to be considered in use for non-commercial purposes, thus immune from execution. Pursuant to Article 21(1) UNCSI, this absolute presumption of immunity applies to: '(d) property forming part of the cultural heritage of the State or part of its archives and not placed or intended to be placed on sale', and '(e) property forming part of an exhibition of objects of scientific, cultural or historical interest and not placed or intended to be placed on sale'.

There is a certain degree of overlapping between the two clauses quoted,[77] but the important point is that the inclusion of cultural heritage property in this

(2005), Israel (2007), and the United Kingdom (2007). For an overview, see Gattini, *see earlier* note 5, at 425–430. For a detailed account of Canadian laws, *see* Getz, 'The History of Canadian Immunity from Seizure Legislation', 18 IJCP (2011) 201.

[74] Glaringly absent from the countries listed in the previous note is Italy, which has therefore been exposed to embarrassing incidents in relation to artworks sent on loan by foreign museums. Most prominently, a motion seeking the seizure of Matisse's masterpiece 'La Danse' was filed with the Tribunal of Rome in June 2000 by Marc Delocque-Fourcaud, while the painting was on loan from Russia for an exhibition hosting various Hermitage Museum's artworks. Delocque-Fourcaud is the heir of the famous art patron Sergei Shchukin, whose invaluable art collection was nationalized by the Bolsheviks in the aftermath of the 1918 Russian Revolution. His motion for the seizure of 'La Danse' prompted the latter's immediate 'repatriation' at the insistence of the Hermitage authorities and irrespective of an agreement according to which the masterpiece had to be sent to Milan for another exhibition at the Brera art gallery. Given the departure of the painting from Italian territory, the Tribunal of Rome dismissed the motion on 21 July 2000; *see* 'Matisse, la "Danse" contesa torna all'Ermitage', *Il Corriere della Sera*, 13 June 2000, 35; 'La Danse fugge ed evita il sequestro', *La Repubblica*, 14 June 2000, 52. Since then, it appears that Russia is particularly wary of art loans to Italy; for the telling example of a 2008 Venice exhibition dedicated to Titian which did not include two Hermitage paintings, see Gattini, *see earlier* note 5, at 421. For the hitherto unsuccessful antiseizure legislative initiatives tabled in the Italian Parliament, *see* Frigo, 'Protection of Cultural Property on Loan—Anti-Seizure and State Immunity Laws: An Italian Perspective', 14 *Art Antiquity & L.* 49 (2009/1).

[75] An exception is the 1991 Basel Resolution of the *Institut de droit international* on Contemporary Problems Concerning the Immunity of States in Relation to Questions of Jurisdiction and Enforcement, *available at* <http://www.idi-iil.org/idiE/resolutionsE/1991_bal_03_En.PDF> Article 4(2)(d) of the Resolution specifically considers 'property identified as part of the cultural heritage of the State, or of its archives, and not placed or intended to be placed on sale' as immune from enforcement measures.

[76] The only exceptions are constituted by recent laws which attest to the impact of the UNCSI's provisions. These are Japan's Act on the Civil Jurisdiction with Respect to a Foreign State (Act No. 24 of 24 Apr. 2009), which exempts cultural heritage property and exhibits of a scientific, cultural or historical significance from enforcement proceedings (Art. 18(2)(iii)(a) and (b)) (this Act essentially reproduces the UNCSI, which Japan has ratified on 11 May 2010); and Canada's 'terrorism amendment' to the State Immunity Act enacted by the Justice for Victims of Terrorism Act (Part I of the Safe Streets and Communities Act, Bill C-10, 13 Mar. 2012), which *generally* allows measures of constraint against the property of States supporters of terrorism, 'other than property that has cultural or historical value' (section 12(1)(d)).

[77] On this and other controversial aspects arising from the UNCSI's provision at issue read in the context of its drafting history, *see* Gattini, *see earlier* note 5, at 430–437.

provision aims at foreclosing 'any presumption or implication of consent to measures of constraint'[78] against it, as well as 'any interpretation'[79] to the effect that it is commercial property, with a significant limitation: cultural property must not be (or be intended to be) on sale at the time it is threatened by enforcement measures; for instance, when it is on loan to a foreign country for exhibition purposes *or* when it has been or will be on loan to yet other countries. There is however a substantial difference between this limitation and the approach taken in the *Malewicz* case,[80] according to which art-related activities—such as art loans—are commercial transactions, regardless of their cultural purposes and of the cultural importance of the objects at stake. True, that case was about immunity from jurisdiction, but, as shown in the following section, this US court attitude towards the issue of commerciality and cultural property finds reflection also in the practice regarding immunity from execution.

The UNCSI is thus a chiefly significant piece of practice for the progressive crystallization of a customary rule exempting cultural heritage property from enforcement measures. It may diminish the relevance of existing antiseizure legislation, while at the same time providing similar protection for artworks located in states without such legislation, as well as for artworks which are not—however—covered by such laws. Yet the current prospects for the UNCSI's entry into force are uncertain. Moreover, certain key players in art transactions, like the US and the United Kingdom, are unlikely to ratify the UNCSI, at least in the short term, because this would require a major overhaul of their immunity statutes. These countries may alternatively consider amending such statutes in order to introduce a specific cultural property exemption from enforcement proceedings along the lines of the UNCSI.

For the time being, practice shows that, both in the latter category of countries and elsewhere, art objects are not a priori and under any circumstances excluded from measures of constraint.

B. Cases Involving Attempted Execution against Cultural Property

Although in a few cases measures of constraint have actually been taken against cultural heritage property, such execution proceedings have ultimately failed, and the property in question has thus not been transferred to the applicants. The existing practice can be conveniently distinguished according to the claim underlying the judgment sought to be executed against art objects.

[78] Commentaries of the International Law Commission to the 1991 Draft Articles on Jurisdictional Immunities of States and Their Property, (1991-II/2) *Y.B. Int'l L. Comm'n* 13, at 58.

[79] Commentaries of the International Law Commission to the 1991 Draft Articles on Jurisdictional Immunities of States and Their Property, (1991-II/2) *Y.B. Int'l L. Comm'n* 13, at 58.

[80] *See earlier* text accompanying notes 18, 20, and 45.

1. Breach of Contractual Obligations

A first situation is that of the attempted enforcement against cultural property of damages awarded for breach of contractual or investment obligations. Here, the underlying claim is unrelated to the property targeted with attachment requests. The widely known *NOGA/Pushkin Museum Paintings* case belongs to this category. It involved a motion for the seizure of fifty-four paintings of French Masters, such as Cézanne, Gauguin, and Corot, that were on loan for an exhibition in Switzerland from the Pushkin State Art Museum of Moscow. The paintings were not protected under the Swiss antiseizure rules,[81] which were not effective when the loan agreement was negotiated. The request had been filed by NOGA, a Swiss company to which, in 1997, the Stockholm Court of Arbitration had awarded millions of US dollars as compensation for damage resulting from Russia's repudiation of contracts for the supply of goods.[82] On 11 November 2005, the motion was granted and the paintings seized upon a decision of the competent Swiss authorities, that is, the Martigny Office for Debt Enforcement (*Office des poursuites*). After a series of alternate decisions and venturous circumstances,[83] the *impasse* was overcome and the paintings departed for Russia thanks to the decisive intervention of the Swiss Executive. The Public International Law Directorate of the Swiss Ministry of Foreign Affairs had tried to persuade the competent authorities to unseize the paintings, on the grounds that cultural heritage property fulfilled sovereign functions and was therefore immune from execution *as attested to by the UNCSI*.[84] When this advice proved unable to halt the procedure, the Swiss *Conseil fédéral* stepped in and adopted an unappealable decision imposing the immediate release of the paintings. The decision was based on the Swiss Constitution's provision[85] empowering the Executive to take measures to safeguard the national interest and was succinctly motivated as follows: 'Conformément au

[81] Arts. 10–13 of the *Loi fédérale sur le transfert international des biens culturels*, 20 June 2003, in force 1 June 2005. The delayed entry into force of this law was due to the necessity of implementing regulations, which were adopted with the *Ordonnance sur le transfert international des biens culturels*, 13 Apr. 2005. The exhibition at issue was held from 17 June to 13 November 2005 at the Gianadda Foundation in Martigny.

[82] For further background information, *see* Gattini, *see earlier* note 5, at 422 note 4; Fox, *see earlier* note 59, at 653–655.

[83] Including the Swiss police's diversion of the trucks transporting the paintings and the latter's subsequent storage in the Geneva Airport duty-free area. For a detailed account, see *Office des poursuites et faillites du district de Martigny v Compagnie Noga d'importation et d'exportation SA*, No. 5A.334/2007/frs (Swiss Federal Tribunal, 29 Jan. 2008).

[84] *Cf. Office des poursuites et faillites du district de Martigny v Compagnie Noga d'importation et d'exportation SA*, No 5A.334/2007/frs (Swiss Federal Tribunal, 29 Jan. 2008), para.A.b.

[85] Art. 184(3) of the Swiss Constitution provides: 'When the safeguard of the interests of the country so require, the Federal Government may issue ordinances and orders. Ordinances have to be limited in time'.

droit international public, les biens culturels d'un Etat font partie du patrimoine public, qui est par principe insaisissable'.[86]

Two lessons may be taken from this case. First, it is a major example of the impact of the UNCSI's cultural property carve-out in the immunity from execution, a treaty that at the time[87] had not been ratified by Switzerland (and was however not in force). Second, it testifies that the concern with, and stakes on, the protection of cultural heritage property in the context of art loans are so prominent that states' Executives are prepared to exercise all of their powers so as to thwart even judicial or similar proceedings endangering that protection. It should be recalled that, although Executives' involvement or interference in judicial matters is a frequent occurrence in the area of state immunity at large, this raises acute problems of constitutional legality (at least) in countries such as Switzerland.

The *NOGA* affair has set an influential precedent in international law. Lately, it has been explicitly endorsed in Austria by the courts and authorities dealing with the very similar *Diag Human* case, which involved the attempted execution upon cultural property on loan of damages awarded to an investor against the Czech Republic.[88] Two arbitral rulings had found the latter state responsible for the disruption of a blood plasma joint venture deal with a Czech-Swiss businessman and his company (Diag Human). The company was ultimately awarded near 9 million Czech crowns in damages. When in early 2011 the Czech Republic lent to the Austrian National Gallery Belvedere three artworks (two paintings by Filla and Beneš, and a sculpture by Gutfreund) for the purposes of an exhibition, Diag Human applied to a district court in Vienna for the recognition of the arbitral award and the seizure of the cultural property displayed at Belvedere. The Czech Republic had been imprudent in not conditioning the loan to the release of an immunity guarantee under the Austrian antiseizure legislation. As in the *NOGA* case, the Viennese Court at first ordered the seizure of the artworks, but soon after, it overturned the decision by accepting the submissions of the defendant state *and* the Austrian Ministry of Foreign Affairs.[89] This paved the way for the return of the cultural objects to the Czech Republic, which occurred on 22 November 2011.

The essential position of the Viennese Court (and Austria's Executive) was again that state cultural property on loan was shielded from enforcement proceedings by a customary rule of international law *and* that this rule was codified by the UNCSI.[90] This provides further evidence of the remarkable impact of the UNCSI's cultural property exemption on the attitude of states. Although it is not

[86] Decision of 16 Nov. 2005, *available at* <http://www.admin.ch/cp/f/437b71c6_1@fwsrvg.html>.

[87] Switzerland ratified the UNCSI on 16 Apr. 2010.

[88] For more detail, see van Woudenberg, *see earlier* note 39, at 302–305.

[89] *Diag Human v Czech Republic*, Case No. 72 E 1855/11 z-20 (District Court of Vienna, 21 June 2011). A challenge to this decision before the Court of Appeals in Vienna was entirely unsuccessful, as the Court dismissed the case for lack of jurisdiction (decision of 18 Nov. 2011).

[90] Austria ratified the UNCSI on 14 Sept. 2006.

in force, that UNCSI provision is increasingly applied by states as a matter of customary law. Yet the latter conclusion has been reached in disputes concerning contractual breaches and transactions wholly unconnected to the cultural objects sought to be attached.

One may only speculate as to whether the approach of the Swiss and Austrian authorities would have been any different had these cases involved claims arising from serious violations of human rights or cultural objects expropriations committed by the foreign-state judgment debtor.

2. *Gross Violations of Human Rights and the US Terrorism Exception*

In a second situation, execution against state cultural property may be attempted by creditors of judgments awarding damages for gross violations of human rights that are (again) unconnected to the property. Although unrelated to the property, the underlying claim is here certainly more significant than in the preceding situation, as it calls into question fundamental tenets of modern constitutions and international law. As is well-known, the *Ferrini* jurisprudence[91] of the Italian Supreme Court had posited that sovereign immunity for *jure imperii* acts was lost when the plaintiff's cause of action concerned serious breaches of human rights and humanitarian law, also in view of the *jus cogens* status of the norms under consideration. A setback for the further expansion of this jurisprudence arises from the ICJ judgment in *Jurisdictional Immunities of the State*, which found that under current customary law, state immunity for *jure imperii* conduct remains in place, regardless of the gravity of the violations and/or *jus cogens* nature of the obligations at issue.[92] For present purposes, it should be noted that the vicissitudes surrounding the attempted execution against the Villa Vigoni Italian-German cultural centre of a Greek judgment awarding damages to the victims of a Nazi Second World War massacre make one think that Italian courts were even prepared to extend the jurisprudence to immunity from execution (that is, to allow measures of constraint against sovereign property that serves *jure imperii* functions, such as in principle cultural property).[93]

In this context, significant insights are provided by a much-discussed[94] US case triggered by the terrorism exception to sovereign immunity laid down in section 1605A FSIA.[95] In *Rubin*, the plaintiffs are survivors or relatives of victims of a 1997 suicide bombing in Jerusalem organized by Hamas with the complicity of

[91] *Ferrini v Germany*, 87 *Rivista di diritto internazionale* 539 (2004), English translation in ILDC 19 (IT 2004), 128 ILR 659 (Court of Cassation, 11 Mar. 2004, No. 5044).

[92] *Jurisdictional Immunities of the State*, *see earlier* note 1, paras. 91 and 97.

[93] *See earlier* text accompanying note 65.

[94] *See eg*, Curavic, 'Compensating Victims of Terrorism or Frustrating Cultural Diplomacy? The Unintended Consequences of the Foreign Sovereign Immunities Act's Terrorism Provisions', 43 *Cornell ILJ* (2010) 381; Caprio, *see earlier* note 39, at 294–302.

[95] This section denies immunity 'in any case ... in which money damages are sought against a foreign state for personal injury or death that was caused by an act of torture, extrajudicial killing,

Iran. They obtained a judgment awarding compensatory damages against Iran in the amount of approximately US$71 million.[96] In the face of Iran's refusal to honour this judgment, the plaintiffs relentlessly chased after Iranian attachable assets located in the US. They eventually identified various collections of Persian antiquities held by a number of US museums and cultural institutions and mounted a legal battle to recover their damages against them. In particular, they lodged motions for writs of attachment in Massachusetts and Illinois. In the former case, they are seeking execution against Persian artefacts housed by the Museum of Fine Arts in Boston and several Harvard University museums, while in the latter case they are applying to attach two collections held on long-term academic loan by the University of Chicago's Oriental Institute (that is, the Persepolis Fortification Texts and the Chogha Mish Collection), as well as a third group of antiquities (known as the Herzfeld Collection) in Chicago's Field Museum of Natural History which the Museum purchased in 1945 from the German archaeologist Ernst Herzfeld.[97]

The striking point emerging from the host of decisions already made by the courts in the *Rubin* litigation is the absence of any pronouncement to the effect that the artworks at stake should be exempt from execution proceedings by definition, in view of their inherent quality as heritage property fulfilling sovereign purposes and the common interest of humanity. True, US courts abide by the letter of the FSIA and this does *not* expressly foreclose attachment of cultural property.[98] Nor does it foreclose attachment of non-commercial property in any circumstances.[99] The *Rubin* plaintiffs have so far relied on the commercial property exception set out in section 1610(a)(7) FSIA, according to which:

> The property in the United States of a foreign state, ... used for a commercial activity in the United States, shall not be immune from attachment ..., if the judgment relates to a claim

aircraft sabotage, hostage taking, or the provision of material support or resources for such an act ... '. The defendant state must have been designated as a state sponsor of terrorism by the US Department of State and the claimant must be a US national, a member of its armed forces, or a US employee or contractor (section 1605A(a)(2)(A)(i)(ii)). The State Department currently lists Cuba, Iran, Sudan, and Syria as state sponsors of terrorism.

96 *Campuzano v Iran*, 281 F. Supp. 2d 258 (D.D.C. 2003).

97 For a variety of reasons, the antiquities at stake have not and could not be granted protection from seizure under the IFSA. In the first place, their acquisition predates the enactment of the latter. In the second, Iran's ownership title over most of them is contested by the museums. As for the case of the Oriental Institute, even assuming IFSA's applicability *ratione temporis*, the latter would not in any event cover long-term loans for academic purposes.

98 The categories of property specifically exempted from attachment under section 1611 FSIA are basically the assets of foreign central banks or monetary authorities and property of a military character.

99 Crucially, *any* property of agencies and instrumentalities of foreign states, such as museums and similar cultural institutions, is subject to execution of judgments concerning claims arising from the most important exceptions to immunity from jurisdiction, section 1610(b) FSIA. The same applies to judgments resulting from the terrorism exception recalled in the text, subsequent to amendments to the FSIA passed in 2008 in order to expand the possibilities of recovery of damages for victims of state-sponsored terrorism, *cf.* section 1610(f)(g) and section 1605A(g) FSIA.

for which the foreign state is not immune under [the terrorism exception], regardless of whether the property is or was involved with the act upon which the claim is based.

The plaintiffs argued that the selling of books and academic publications in the US resulting from research on the Persian antiquities by the museums and the Oriental Institute constituted commercial activity. The district courts were only able to defeat this argument by pointing out that only the activities of foreign states themselves were relevant for the purposes of this exception, not those of other entities (that is, the institutions).[100] However, and most importantly, the Massachusetts District Court[101] denied immunity from attachment for the Museum of Fine Arts' and Harvard's Persian antiquities on the grounds that they were Iranian 'blocked assets' according to the 2002 Terrorism Risk Insurance Act (TRIA).[102] TRIA makes such assets subject to execution in satisfaction of judgments against terrorist states. This is a perfect example of a US court engaging in a formalistic interpretation of a terrorism-related piece of legislation setting at naught the sovereign-property immunities provided by the FSIA, all without any effort at sparing cultural heritage property from the reach of such legislation.

Most recently,[103] the same US court managed to dismiss *on the merits* the motion for attachment filed by the *Rubin* plaintiffs, when it ruled that the latter had not demonstrated that the antiquities at issue belonged to Iran. With a telegraphic opinion, Judge O'Toole found that the applicable Iranian laws did not automatically vest ownership on excavated antiquities in the State of Iran. The fact that those excavations took the form of open looting at ancient sites such as Persepolis, with ensuing illicit exportation of the recovered materials, did not alter his conclusion.[104] The Judge relied on the English decisions in *Barakat Galleries* for the proposition that the Iranian laws at stake did not confer title to excavated objects on Iran. This is at best an unfortunate example of transjudicial dialogue. The English Court of Appeal did not take a definite position on the legal effect of the laws relevant to the *Rubin* litigation. It considered them unclear

[100] For the Illinois litigation, *see Rubin v Iran*, 349 F. Supp. 2d 1108 (N.D. Ill. 2004); for the Massachusetts litigation, *see Rubin v Iran*, 456 F. Supp. 2d 228 (D. Mass. 2006). This holding did not persuade the plaintiffs to give up the argument at stake: they are insisting that the institutions possessing the antiquities may be regarded as agents of Iran, by undertaking commercial use of the artefacts (also) on Iran's behalf. This strategy has however been hindered by the rejection of discovery requests addressed to the institutions for the purpose of investigating the profits generated by the sale of publications and any arrangement about the associated royalties, *cf.* Caprio, *see earlier* note 39, at 295.

[101] *Rubin v Iran, see earlier* note 100, *affirmed*, 541 F. Supp. 2d 416 (D. Mass. 2008).

[102] Pub. L. No. 107–297, 116 Stat. 2322, Title II, section 201(a), codified at 28 U.S.C. § 1610 (note). The blocking of Iranian assets in the US goes back to the decisions made in the aftermath of the 1979 Tehran hostage crisis. Despite subsequent developments leading to the unfreezing of most Iranian assets, 'contested assets' remain blocked under US legislation. The Massachusetts District Court found indeed that the Persian antiquities at stake fulfilled that definition because title over them was disputed, *Rubin v Iran, see earlier* note 100, *affirmed*, 541 F. Supp. 2d 416 (D. Mass. 2008).

[103] *Rubin v Iran*, 810 F. Supp. 2d 402 (D. Mass. 2011, per O'Toole, Jr DJ).

[104] *Rubin v Iran*, 810 F. Supp. 2d, at 404–406.

and irrelevant[105] because a subsequent Iranian law[106] had evidently established the principle of state ownership of unrecovered antiquities. More generally, the *Barakat Galleries* appeal judgment is duly noted for its sensitivity toward the international legal framework aimed at countering the illicit trafficking in cultural objects, which was considered a crucial public policy reason for recognizing Iran's right to the restitution of the disputed property.[107] This stands in marked contrast to the US *Rubin* decisions. The 2011 opinion by Judge O'Toole, rather than an accurate statement of the law, is thus best regarded as an exit strategy to avoid the dangers of privatization and commercial dispersion of very significant Persian antiquities.[108]

At any rate, while waiting for the next stages in the *Rubin/Persian Collections* saga,[109] this litigation may also be seen under a different light. Arguably, it suggests that, whenever particularly important societal and legal imperatives are at stake (for example, redress for human rights violations resulting from terrorist activities),[110] certain legislatures and courts may be inclined to accord priority to those imperatives over otherwise sacrosanct immunity principles, such as the one affording enforcement immunity to cultural property.

3. *Expropriation*

This brings us to the third situation where attachment of state cultural property may be attempted, namely, when an individual holds a judgment against a foreign state which has unlawfully expropriated her/his cultural objects. Unlike the previous situations, there exists in this case a close connection between the underlying claim and the property sought to be attached. Therefore, the imposition of measures of constraint may appear more reasonable and supported by the international norms outlawing illicit appropriations of cultural property and mandating its restitution to the rightful owners. Yet this situation is subject to several variations,

[105] *Barakat Galleries, see earlier* note 32, para. 62; *see also* para. 165.

[106] Legal Bill Regarding Prevention of Unauthorised Excavations and Diggings, 17 May 1979. This Bill was probably considered inapplicable on the facts of the *Rubin* case because of its non-retrospective effect. It only deals with antiquities that have not yet been recovered as of the date of its enactment. This was at least the interpretation of the English Court of Appeal, *see Barakat Galleries, see earlier* note 32, para. 111.

[107] *Barakat Galleries, see earlier* note 32, paras. 151–163.

[108] Admittedly, the Judge's opinion was facilitated by the absence of claims of ownership by Iran, which has not yet appeared in the Massachusetts' litigation.

[109] The saga is far from approaching a close. As to the Illinois litigation, see recently *Rubin v Iran*, 637 F.3d 783 (7th Cir. 2011, per Sykes CJ) (striking down decisions of the district court that had declared that Iran alone could plead its immunity and had granted, upon appearance of Iran in the litigation, a plaintiff's request for the discovery of all Iranian-owned assets in the US).

[110] This is intended as a general remark, and not as a broad defence of the FSIA's terrorism exception. The shortcomings of the exception are well-known, both in terms of legal coherence (ie, reliance on targeted State Department determinations, limitation of standing to US nationals or employees) and capability to bring effective relief. On the latter aspect, see most tellingly, *In re: Islamic Republic of Iran Terrorism Litig.*, 659 F. Supp. 2d 31(D.D.C. 2009, per Lamberth CJ).

the unifying element of which is the foreign state's established responsibility for art expropriation suffered by the judgment holder.[111]

The simplest hypothesis is where an individual seeks to attach the very same cultural objects that she/he owned before they were confiscated by state authorities. The *Prince of Liechtenstein* litigation over the painting *Der Grosse Kalkofen* by the 17th-century Flemish artist Pieter van Laer was a case of first impression in that respect. In 1991, the Cologne Regional Court (*Landgericht*) ordered the seizure of the painting when it was on loan for an exhibition at the Wallraf-Richartz Museum from the Brno Historical Monuments Office in the Czech Republic.[112] The order granted a request lodged by Prince Hans-Adam II of Liechtenstein, whose late father had been the owner of the work of art until it was confiscated by the former Czechoslovakia in 1946. However, the proceedings brought by the Prince for the recovery of the painting on the occasion of its loan to the Cologne museum were unsuccessful, as all German courts denied jurisdiction pursuant to a clause in the 1952/1954 Settlement Convention which bars any objections by Germany to confiscations of German external assets carried out by the Second World War Allied countries for war reparation purposes.[113] The painting was thus returned to the Cologne Municipality and eventually to the Czech authorities upon an order of the Cologne Regional Court of 9 June 1998. An application to the European Court of Human Rights by the Prince failed, as the Court unanimously ruled that Germany had not breached the applicant's right of access to justice and right to property.[114]

This is a quite exceptional piece of practice where a *pre-trial* seizure of cultural property has been ordered by a domestic court and maintained for about seven and a half years, before returning the artwork to the institution that had lent it for exhibition purposes. Notably, the lawsuit by the Prince was dismissed for reasons that have nothing to do with the purportedly immune status of the painting. Immunity issues were never considered by the courts, save a rapid reference in Judge Ress's concurring opinion to the European Court's judgment where he highlighted the desirability of reviewing this type of case in the light of the

[111] Additionally, the foreign state's responsibility may be invoked in a claim of expropriation that has yet to be adjudicated on the merits. In this case, the discussion concerns the possibility of obtaining pre-judgment measures of constraint against artworks. This is exactly the situation occurring in the following case considered in the text.

[112] *Prince of Liechtenstein v Municipality of Cologne* (Cologne Regional Ct., 11 Nov. 1991). On 17 December 1991, when the exhibition ended, the painting was handed over to a bailiff. For background information, *see* Gattini, 'A Trojan Horse for Sudeten Claims?', 13 *Eur J. Int'l L.* (2002) 513; *see also* Fassbender, 'Prince of Liechtenstein v Federal Supreme Court', 93 *Am. J. Int'l L.* (1999) 215.

[113] Art. 3 of Chapter 6 of the Convention on the Settlement of Matters Arising out of the War and the Occupation, 26 May 1952, as amended by Schedule IV to the Protocol on the Termination of the Occupation Regime, 23 Oct. 1954.

[114] *Prince Hans-Adam II of Liechtenstein v Germany*, Appl. No. 42527/98 (12 July 2001). The case also prompted proceedings before the ICJ, which however found that it did not have jurisdiction to entertain the application, *Certain Property (Liechtenstein v Germany)*, (2005) ICJ Reports 6 (10 Feb. 2005).

public interest in international art exhibitions.[115] Obviously, the painting at stake was not protected in accordance with antiseizure legislation, which indeed Germany hastened to pass in the aftermath of the *Prince of Liechtenstein* case.[116] Consequently, this litigation arguably shows that a cultural property immunity defence does not per se necessarily bar execution proceedings targeting the expropriated artworks that form the basis of a restitution claim.

What about attempted attachments of cultural property other than that which was illegally expropriated? This question may conveniently be addressed by reference to US practice, in view of ongoing developments within that jurisdiction. At first glance and given the possibilities offered by the FSIA, it may be submitted that any artwork that receives protection under the IFSA is thereby shielded from execution measures, regardless of the claim underlying the suit. This has been affirmed in *Malewicz* with respect to the very paintings which were allegedly misappropriated by the foreign state[117] and would thus *a fortiori* appear to be valid for cultural property that was not the subject of the expropriation at issue. Judge Collyer held in *Malewicz* that, in general, when IFSA protection has been granted, 'a litigant with a claim against a foreign sovereign may *not* seize that sovereign's property that is in this country on a cultural exchange and the litigant may *not* serve the receiving museum with judicial process to interfere in any way with the physical custody or control of the artworks'.[118]

Nevertheless, the *Chabad* case offers a spectacular example of outstanding uncertainties in this field. In July 2010, the Columbia District Court finally established that the applicant's religious books and archival materials had been expropriated by Russia[119] and simultaneously ordered the defendant state

> to surrender to the United States Embassy in Moscow or to the duly appointed representatives of Plaintiff Agudas Chasidei Chabad of United States the complete collection of religious books, manuscripts, documents and things that comprise the 'Library' and the 'Archive' presently being held by the Defendants at the Russian State Library and the Russian State Military Archive or elsewhere ....[120]

Russia has expressed its resolve not to comply with this order. Most importantly, in early 2011 it has declared that it will since refrain from lending artworks to US institutions for fear that they will be subjected to enforcement measures in

[115] *Prince Hans-Adam II of Liechtenstein v Germany, see earlier* note 114, concurring opinion of Judge Ress joined by Judge Zupančič.

[116] By way of a 1999 amendment to the Act on Cultural Property Protection, *see* Art. 20 of the *Gesetz zum Schutz deutschen Kulturgutes gegen Abwanderung.*

[117] *Malewicz, see earlier* note 17, at 311 ('It is undisputed that the Malewicz Heirs could not seek to seize the artwork while it was in this country under a grant of [antiseizure] immunity', at 310).

[118] *Malewicz, see earlier* note 17, at 311 (emphasis in the original).

[119] *Agudas Chasidei Chabad v Russian Fed'n,* 729 F. Supp. 2d 141 (D.D.C. 2010, per Lamberth CJ). This was a default judgment because Russia had previously withdrawn from the litigation.

[120] *Agudas Chasidei Chabad v Russian Fed'n,* Order and Judgment (D.D.C. 30 July 2010, per Lamberth CJ).

satisfaction of the *Chabad* decision.[121] In this context, the plaintiff asked the Columbia District Court to grant a motion seeking a *generic* permission to pursue execution of Russian assets in the US, as well as a motion requesting the imposition of monetary sanctions (so-called civil contempt sanctions) against the defendant for failure to abide by the July 2010 Order. In July 2011,[122] the Court denied the second motion on the grounds that Russia should be afforded a further opportunity to show cause why sanctions should not be imposed and be notified accordingly. Instead, the first motion was granted. The Court determined that plaintiff could apply for attachment of specific Russian property because the procedural requirements in the FSIA had been fulfilled.[123] Faced with the intervention of the US Executive conveying grave concern over the disruption of cultural exchanges with Russia that may ensue from the order sought by the plaintiff, Judge Lamberth replied that these were 'imagined problems'.[124] According to the Judge, Russian artworks covered by a grant of immunity under the IFSA would not absolutely be affected by the order, which only generically paves the way for execution proceedings, without prejudging the legality of any specific attachment eventually pursued.[125] Moreover, upon request from the plaintiff, the Judge agreed to include in his order a stipulation to the effect that 'Plaintiff shall not enforce the default judgment in this action by seeking to attach or execute against any art or object of cultural significance which has been granted protection under [the IFSA]'.[126] But was this stipulation necessary? Probably yes, because the relationship between the FSIA's exceptions to immunity from execution and the IFSA has not yet been conclusively determined by the courts. Judge Lamberth was thus wise to point out that

> the Court is unwilling to conclude that Russia's concerns about the safety of its own cultural objects [are] entirely unfounded, given prior—albeit unsuccessful—attempts to attach [IFSA-protected] objects in at least one other case in satisfaction of a FSIA judgment ... While the Court is eager to provide whatever assurances to Moscow are necessary to encourage full future exchanges of art and artifacts between the United States and Russia, ... the Court is not imbued with the authority to pre-judge any potential attachment that might occur.[127]

The case referred to in the foregoing passage is *Magness v Russia*. This earlier case shows yet another most interesting variation on the theme discussed in the present sub-part. A Texan district court had established that in 1994 the plaintiffs' property in St Petersburg, including a historical piano factory and a host of associated

[121] *See* 'Dispute Derails Art Loans from Russia', *N.Y. Times*, 2 Feb. 2011.
[122] *Agudas Chasidei Chabad v Russian Fed'n*, 798 F. Supp. 2d 260 (D.D.C. 2011, per Lamberth CJ).
[123] *Cf.* section 1610(c) FSIA.
[124] *Chabad*, *see earlier* note 122, at 271.
[125] *Chabad*, *see earlier* note 122, at 270–271.
[126] *Chabad*, *see earlier* note 122, at 266, 272.
[127] *Chabad*, *see earlier* note 122, at 272 note 3.

antiquities, had unlawfully been confiscated by Russian authorities.[128] Instead of restitution, plaintiffs sought pecuniary compensation, which that court awarded in the amount of nearly US$235 million. The judgment holders attempted execution in Alabama, where Russian cultural objects of 'like kind and character'[129] vis-à-vis those expropriated were stationed as part of an itinerant exhibit ('Nicholas and Alexandra: The Last Imperial Family of Tsarist Russia') scheduled to visit various US cities. Such objects comprised the Golden Coronation Carriage (circa 1793), the Grand Piano of Empress Alexandra Feodorova (circa 1898), and the Miniature Copy of Imperial Regalia by Faberge Jewels (circa 1899–1900).[130] Judge Butler denied the writ of execution on the grounds that the exhibit at issue had been granted protection under IFSA pursuant to a 1998 governmental determination to that effect.[131] The Judge seemed to conceive IFSA as a *lex specialis* vis-à-vis the FSIA.[132] The plaintiffs, however, sought to challenge the 1998 governmental decision by pointing out that the exhibit and related antiquities, despite the decision's declarations, were used for commercial purposes. The Judge rejected the argument by relying on the need to pay due deference to the Executive's determinations.[133] This is a very controversial finding when seen in the context of post-FSIA immunity case law. It is well-known that one of the main objectives in enacting the FSIA was to depoliticize immunity disputes by entrusting the courts with the exclusive and independent authority to render decisions in this area.[134]

It is difficult not to consider with the utmost attention the claim advanced by the *Magness* plaintiffs. Not only were they arbitrarily deprived of their cultural property, but they also had to endure the mocking occurrence of antique objects, some of which were *similar in all respects* to those that were confiscated from them, travelling around the US, that is, their country of nationality. The *Magness* decision confirms that the relationship between the unlawful expropriation of artworks and enforcement immunity for cultural property (even if protected from seizure) is an unsettled matter.[135] It will be unsurprising to witness further

[128] *Magness, see earlier* note 15.

[129] *Magness, see earlier* note 15, at 703.

[130] *Magness v Russian Fed'n*, 84 F.Supp. 2d 1357, at 1358 (S.D. Ala. 2000, per Butler CJ).

[131] *Magness v Russian Fed'n, see earlier* note 130, at 1360.

[132] *Magness v Russian Fed'n, see earlier* note 130, at 1359.

[133] *Magness v Russian Fed'n, see earlier* note 130, at 1360 ('In view of the fact that an agency's determination is entitled to deference ... this Court will not attempt to go behind that determination and, thus, put in jeopardy the Exhibition which was originally brought into this country in reliance on such a determination').

[134] *See, eg,* section 1602 FSIA. Admittedly, the debate over the degree of deference due to the US Executive's opinions in matters of state immunity has been revamped by ambiguous statements contained in the Supreme Court decision in *Altmann, see earlier* note 11, at 1433, 1435 note 23 (majority), and 1450–1452 (per Kennedy J, dissenting). For a very important decision (also) in our context, which grants deference to the Executive's submissions on sovereign immunity, see *Whiteman v Dorotheum GMBH & Co. KG*, 431 F.3d 57 (2nd Cir. 2005, per Cabranes CJ).

[135] It is telling that, in the context of an essay mostly criticizing the current US trend towards removing immunity in art-related suits, Caprio proposed a cultural property exemption clause amending

cases where creditors of judgments recognizing their title to cultural property that was illegally expropriated will attempt to attach yet other art object in the possession of foreign states.

IV. Conclusion

The intersection of the law of state immunity and cultural property issues raises profound dilemmas that are well illustrated in the stunning concluding passage of Judge Lamberth's 2011 opinion in *Chabad*:

> The Court hopes that today's opinion will help facilitate a return to business as usual in the sharing of artifacts and history between nations that is crucial to the promotion of cross-cultural understanding in a global world, that the ability to attach and execute property not otherwise subject to immunity under FSIA or any other federal statute may aid plaintiff in its pursuit of the return of the lost Library and Archive containing the cultural heritage and history of the Chasidim movement, and that the show cause order may prompt Russia to rethink its decision to retain items of immense historical and religious significance, seized during times of great crisis and in violation of international law, in warehouses rather than return them to their rightful owners.[136]

The unimpeded cross-national sharing of cultural artefacts for educational and scientific purposes and the respect for property that is part of states' cultural heritage compete with individual claims for redress for spoliations carried out in breach of human rights and international law. A clear-cut, all-encompassing answer to the existing dilemmas is not forthcoming. Equally, a perspective based on cultural human rights is inconclusive. Again, the *Chabad* case exemplifies this point: if, for the sake of a collective right to culture, one was to defend Russia's immunity from jurisdiction and the absolute protection of its cultural objects from the spectre of enforcement measures, this would inevitably run against the Chasidim organization's members' right to enjoy religious heritage property essential for their religious beliefs and practice. It would also condone cultural crimes and blatantly discriminatory acts perpetrated in times of armed conflict.

In the foregoing excerpt, Judge Lamberth pointed to the possibility of the plaintiff attaching Russian property, other than cultural objects, in satisfaction of the underlying judgment. Surely, this may be a non-negligible consideration in cases such as *NOGA* and *Rubin* where the primary claim is unconnected to cultural property deprivation. In the latter situation, a line of equilibrium could arguably be to allow execution against artworks as a last resort, when all other efforts at

the FSIA's enforcement immunity rules that would be without prejudice to attachment against artworks—*including those protected under IFSA*—that are 'found to be the rightful possession of another through a claim of ownership', Caprio, *see earlier* note 39, at 305. See *earlier* note 42 on the ongoing US Congress's discussion of a bill that, unlike Caprio's proposal, aims to amend the expropriation exception to immunity from *jurisdiction*.

[136] *Chabad, see earlier* note 122, at 274.

recovering a judgment debt have proven unsuccessful. But in the *Chabad* case the threat of attaching non-cultural assets (either in the US or elsewhere upon recognition of the judgment) must fundamentally serve the purpose of exerting pressure to achieve the ultimate aim of restitution of the looted art.

In this context, it appears necessary to take issue with the frequent argument that litigation before domestic courts against foreign sovereigns in cases involving egregious breaches of human rights, such as those inherent in most of the disputes reviewed in this chapter, would be a misconceived tool to bring about effective relief for the victims without jeopardizing the pacific relations among states. It would instead upset those relations and corrupt the principles governing the law of state immunity. Regardless of one's views on this question of international law and policy, that argument misses the broader picture. It fails to consider that in these cases the denial of sovereign immunity may fulfil the function of urging states to come back to the negotiating table and accept means to settle past accounts that are alternative to litigation in foreign courts instigated by unredressed victims of wrongful actions. It is also for this reason that I support the thesis that, in such situations, immunity may be lifted when alternative remedies are, or have reasonably been proven, unavailable to wronged individuals.[137]

Significant examples coming from the art-and-immunity practice discussed in this chapter encourage that perspective. As is well-known, *Altmann* was finally resolved through binding arbitration agreed upon by the parties to the dispute.[138] Similarly, an out-of-court settlement was reached in *Malewicz*, and five of the claimed paintings were transferred to Malewicz's heirs.[139] It is crystal clear that, in the absence of the US courts' bold assertions of jurisdiction over these cases, the latter would have remained instances of unredressed wrongs.

[137] Pavoni, *see earlier* note 50.

[138] The arbitration court ruled that the Austrian Gallery had to return five of the six disputed Klimt paintings to Altmann, Arbitration Court, *Altmann & Others v Republic of Austria*, 15 Jan. 2006 and 7 May 2006.

[139] *See* Kaye, 'Art Loans and Immunity from Seizure in the United States and the United Kingdom', 17 *IJCP* (2010) 335, at 343. Similarly, in 2010 the famous *Portrait of Wally* case, which was not reviewed in this chapter because it did not directly involve state immunity issues (the disputed Egon Schiele's painting was allegedly owned by a private museum), ended after ten years of litigation thanks to an out-of-court settlement between the parties, cf. Kaye, 'Art Loans', at 346.

6

The Enforcement of Foreign Law

Reclaiming One Nation's Cultural Heritage in Another Nation's Courts

James Gordley[*]

I. Introduction

Many nations have enacted laws to protect their cultural heritage against export. No-one doubts their right to do so. Yet when objects are exported in violation of those laws, a nation faces two supposedly insurmountable legal obstacles to seeking their return. One is the proposition that the export laws of one nation will not be enforced in the courts of another. The other is that a government cannot repatriate an object without proving that it owns it in the same way as a private owner, having a right to possess and use it as he chooses. Here, it will be argued that both of these propositions are bad law—not only bad policy, but bad law. A court should disregard them.

II. The Enforcement of the Export Laws of One Nation in the Courts of Another

A. The Authorities

As to the first proposition, '[t]he fundamental rule', according to Professor Paul Bator, is that 'illegal export does not itself render the importer (or one who took from him) in any way actionable in a US court; the possession of an art object cannot be lawfully disturbed in the United States solely because it was illegally exported from another country'.[1] In *Jeannerette v Vichy*, Judge Friendly quoted

* W. R. Irby Professor of Law, Tulane University School of Law.

[1] Paul M. Bator, 'An Essay on the International Trade in Art', 34 *Stan. L. Rev.* (1982) 275–384, at 287.

Bator's statement as an accurate expression of the law.[2] In *United States v McClain*, Judge Wisdom stated American law in the same way, again quoting Bator.[3] In *Attorney General of New Zealand v Ortiz*, Lord Denning did not quote Bator but Justice Joseph Story, and said, 'I am of the opinion that if any country should have legislation prohibiting the export of works of art ... that falls into the category of "public laws" which will not be enforced by the courts of the country to which it is exported, or any other country, because it is an act done in the exercise of sovereign authority which will not be enforced outside its own territory.'[4] That rule applied, he said, although, as in the case before him, foreign law provided for the forfeiture of works of art if they were illegally exported.

These are the three cases typically cited for the proposition that a foreign government cannot claim repatriation in the United States or England of illegally exported works of art. None of them is compelling as a precedent, and they rest on slim authority.

None is compelling as a precedent. Judge Friendly would have reached the same result in *Jeannerette* if he had disregarded Bator, and held that a nation cannot obtain repatriation of an object by claiming a 'tremendous loss to its national heritage' absent any proof that such a loss occurred. The plaintiff, an art dealer, bought a painting by Matisse from the defendant, who did not obtain valid export papers. An Italian law prohibited the export of objects of such importance that their export would represent a tremendous loss to the national patrimony. It required would-be exporters to submit a request to the Export Office to determine whether objects could be exported. The defendant failed to do so. When the plaintiff learned that the painting had been exported without proper papers, she sued for breach of warranty of title under the Uniform Commercial Code. After the sale, the Italian Assistant Minister of Culture declared that the painting was of 'particular artistic and historical interest' within the meaning of the Italian law. Judge Friendly did say that because an American court would not enforce foreign export laws, the warranty of title had not been breached. Nevertheless, he also said:

> The somewhat surprising conclusion that exportation of a painting by a prolific French post-impressionist master would represent a 'tremendous loss to the national heritage' of Italy was sought to be justified on the grounds that it had been shown at the Venice Biennale in 1952 'in the large exposition dedicated to art' and 'because it is part of the era of 'a return to normalcy' which pervaded all Europe at the end of the first world war, characterized by a return to classic and Renaissance motifs particularly evident in this balanced, well composed painting by a master of contemporary art and specially rare among Italian collections of significant works of that period.' One is tempted to wonder why, if Italian

[2] 693 F.2d 259, 267 (2d Cir. 1982).

[3] 545F.2d 988, 996 (5th Cir. 1977) citing Paul M. Bator, 'International Trade in National Art Treasures: Regulation and Deregulation', in L. D. DuBoff (ed.), *Art Law Domestic and International* (South Hackensack, NJ: William S. Hein,, 1975) 295, at 300.

[4] [1982] 3 All ER 432, at 459.

collectors do not care enough for Matisse to buy his paintings, one of these, not claimed to be an outstanding masterpiece, should be thought to constitute such an important part of the Italian national heritage.[5]

Friendly's flat statement that United States courts will not enforce foreign export laws thus amounts to an alternate holding. The result of the case would have been the same even if the United States enforced these laws when necessary to prevent 'a tremendous loss to the national heritage', provided such a loss had occurred.

In *McClain*, Mexico claimed title to pre-Columbian artefacts that the defendants had illegally exported. Because Mexico claimed title to them, defendants were prosecuted for violating the National Stolen Property Act. By way of dictum, Judge Wisdom said that an American court would not enforce foreign export laws. But, he noted: 'The question posed … is not whether the federal government will enforce a foreign nation's export law, or whether property brought into this country in violation of another country's exportation law is stolen property'.[6] He held that it did not since the artefacts were not the property of the Mexican government within the meaning of the Act.

In *Ortiz*, New Zealand sought the return of a valuable Maori carving. It had been illegally exported, and, according to New Zealand law, had therefore been forfeited. The House of Lords reversed Judge Staughton's judgment that New Zealand could claim the carving. The reason given by all but three of the Lord Justices was that under the New Zealand law, forfeiture was not automatic but took place only upon actual seizure. Therefore New Zealand has no proprietary claim to the carvings. Lords Ackner and O'Connor said that the law could not be enforced because it was penal. Only Lord Denning said that the reason was that an English court would not enforce foreign export laws. The other justices said that they were expressing no opinion on whether Lords Ackner and O'Connor or Lord Denning were right.[7]

Thus in these cases, we have, in *Jeannerette*, an alternative holding, or close to it; in *McClain*, a dictum; and in *Ortiz*, the opinion of one justice on an issue on which the majority of the court refused to rule.

Nor are the authorities cited in these opinions compelling. The only authority cited by Judge Friendly in *Jeannerette* was Bator, writing in the *Stanford Law Review*.[8] In that article, Bator cited only one authority: a book by Sharon William in 1978, *The International and National Protection of Moveable Cultural Property*.[9] She cited only one authority:[10] a 1918 case, *King of Italy v Marquis Cosimo de*

[5] 693 F.2d at 263 note 6.

[6] 545 F.2d at 996.

[7] [1982] 3 All ER at 467.

[8] 693 F.2d 259, 267 (2d Cir. 1982) (citing Bator, *see earlier* note 1).

[9] Bator, *see earlier* note 1, at 287 note 30. In 'International Trade in National Art Treasures' he cites no authority at all.

[10] Sharon Williams, *The International and National Protection of Moveable Cultural Property: A Comparative Study* (Dobbs Ferry, NY: Oceana Publications, 1978), at 106–108.

Medici Tornaquinci,[11] to which we will return. The only authority cited by Judge Wisdom in *McClain* was another article by Bator in which Bator cited no authority.[12] In *Ortiz*, Lord Denning cited as authority some cases that do not deal with the export of art. He also cited the then-current edition of Dicey and Morrison and a 1918 case just mentioned on which these writers and Sharon William had based their own opinion: *King of Italy v Marquis Cosimo de Medici Tornaquinci*.[13] In that case, the court refused to enjoin the Marquis from selling family papers which he had inherited and which he had taken to England in violation of Italian export laws. The report of the case is sketchy. At any rate, despite that, the majority of justices did not adopt Lord Denning's opinion. Later editions of Dicey and Morrison, edited by Sir Lawrence Collins, revised their earlier view. In *King of Italy*, the treatise now explains, 'the grounds of decision are not clear'.[14] English law, it says, is as yet to be determined. When it is determined, the treatise urges, English courts should be flexible.

> The essential issue is whether the courts will refuse to enforce all public laws, as Lord Denning M.R. thought, or whether there should be a degree of flexibility based on special grounds of public policy which require the law in question not to be enforced, as Staughton, J. thought. The matter has been the subject of attention by the Institut de droit international and the International Law Association each of which recommended a degree of flexibility in dealing with claims to enforce foreign public law. It is suggested that this is an approach which should commend itself to the English court....[15]

Lord Denning's authority, then, and that of Sharon Williams, was a single case dealing with illegally exported papers and the opinion in a treatise based on that case, a treatise which, in later editions, denied the authority of the case and repudiated its earlier opinion.

B. The Principle

If the rule lacks authority, might it not rest on principle? Although Bator did not discuss the question, Lord Denning and Sharon Williams did. The principle, according to Lord Denning, is the 'territorial theory of jurisdiction' of Justice Story:

> It was said long ago by Story J. in the Supreme Court of the United States in *The Apollon* (1824) 9 Wheat. 362, 370: 'The laws of no nation can justly extend beyond its own territories, except so far as regards its own citizens.' And in his book, Story's Conflict of Laws, 2nd ed. (1841), p. 26, he said: 'no state or nation can, by its laws, directly affect or bind property

[11] (1918) 34 T.L.R. 623.

[12] *See earlier* note 3.

[13] (1918) 34 T.L.R. 623.

[14] *Dicey, Morris, and Collins on the Conflict of Laws* 1, 14th edn (London: Stevens, 2006) at 109 note 65.

[15] *Dicey, Morris, and Collins on the Conflict of Laws*, at 112–113.

out of its own territory, or bind persons not resident therein', except that, see p. 28, 'every nation has a right to bind its own subjects by its own laws in every other place.'[16]

Denning concluded:

> [I]f any country should have legislation prohibiting the export of works of art ... then that falls into the category of 'public laws' which will not be enforced by the courts of the country to which it is exported, or any other country, because it is an act done in the exercise of sovereign authority which will not be enforced outside its own territory.[17]

Similarly, Williams agreed that by the principle of 'territorial sovereignty', '[t]he forum will not generally enforce a claim which is the manifestation of a state's sovereignty over its own territorial domain'. Thus it will not enforce foreign 'penal, revenue or public law',[18] including, in her opinion, a law prohibiting the export of art.

Story's principle was that 'it is an essential attribute of every sovereignty that it has no admitted superior, and that it gives the supreme law within its own dominions on all subjects appertaining to its sovereignty'.[19] Therefore, 'the laws of one country can have no intrinsic force, *proprio vigore*, except within the territorial limits and jurisdiction of that country'.[20] One sovereign nation would apply another's laws only because, for reasons of 'comity,' it chose to do so.[21] 'What it yields, it is its own choice to yield.... '.[22]

This principle was a latecomer to the field of conflict of laws, and Story applied it with more subtlety than Williams and Denning. Rules of conflict of laws with which we are still familiar were developed by medieval jurists who did not believe laws which conflicted were made by sovereign states or princes. Jacobus de Arena described some of these rules: that in a conflict of laws that 'arises in procedure', a court follows 'law of the court' in which suit was brought; in cases of contract, 'then the place of the contract is to be consulted'; 'in delict, then the place of the delict is to be regarded'; in disputes of 'powers over things, ... then one must look to ... the place where the thing is'.[23] These rules were repeated almost verbatim by his pupil Cinus of Pistoia,[24] and refined by his pupil Bartolus of Saxoferrato,[25] whose work had enormous influence in the centuries that followed.

Yet these pioneers of the conflict of laws held an opinion about sovereignty that seems strange today: sovereignty, in the sense of the ultimate power to make

[16] [1982] 3 All ER at 455–6.

[17] [1982] 3 All ER at 459.

[18] Williams, *see earlier* note 10, at 106.

[19] Joseph Story, *Commentaries on the Conflict of Laws Foreign and Domestic,* 3rd edn (Boston: Little, Brown & Co., 1846), § 8.

[20] Story, *Commentaries on the Conflict of Laws Foreign and Domestic,* § 7.

[21] Story, *Commentaries on the Conflict of Laws Foreign and Domestic,* § 33.

[22] Story, *Commentaries on the Conflict of Laws Foreign and Domestic,* § 8.

[23] Iacobus de Arena Parmensis, *Super iure civile* (Lyon, 1541) to C. 8.53.1.

[24] Cinus de Pistoia, *Super codice cum additionibus* (Frankfort-am-Main, 1493) to C. 8.53.1.

[25] Bartolus de Saxoferrato, *Commentaria Corpus iuris civilis* (Venice, 1615), to C. 1.1.

law, belonged to the Roman emperor, whom the jurists identified as the Holy Roman Emperor of their own time. The Roman law that they taught was the *ius commune* or common law that was in force, in principle, throughout the world because it had been promulgated by the 6th-century Emperor Justinian in what they called the *Corpus iuris civilis*. They supported their opinion by citing a text of the *Corpus iuris*: 'Only the Emperor is permitted to make laws'.[26] According to Bartolus, a particular city or prince could make laws only by the express or tacit permission of the Emperor.[27] The problem of conflict of laws arose when these laws conflicted.

Story's view of territorial sovereignty certainly seems more plausible to us. But if the principle is taken to mean that the territorial sovereign is the exclusive source of law, it can lead to trouble. To begin with, the territorial sovereign then seems to be the exclusive source of all law; for example, of the entire law of contracts, property, and torts. The medieval jurists recognized a trans-territorial body of law, the *ius commune*, that was everywhere the same. Their problem was what to do when rules that were local and interstitial conflicted with each other. Modern conflicts scholars who work on the assumption that the territorial sovereign is the exclusive source of law have to decide whether an entire national legal system shall apply to a transaction based on where a contract was made, or a tort committed, or property is situated. The problem of conflict of laws is then far less manageable, as I have discussed elsewhere.[28] In any event, Story himself was more subtle. In *Swift v Tyson*,[29] he took the view, later repudiated in *Erie R.R. v Tompkins*,[30] that the common law was a trans-territorial law, not that of a particular state. Absent local and interstitial legislation, a federal court could have its own opinion on what that law was. The *Erie* court rejected that view, quoting Oliver Wendell Holmes' statement:

> 'The common law is not a brooding omnipresence in the sky but the articulate voice of some sovereign or quasi sovereign that can be identified'.[31]

Another problem that arose, and the one of importance here, is that of limiting the situations in which the law of one territorial state will be applied by the courts of another. As we have seen, a limit set by Story was that courts would not enforce penal, revenue, or other public laws of another sovereign. Yet, again, Story was more subtle than some of his successors.

[26] C. 1.17.11.

[27] Bartolus, *Commentaria* to D. 1.1.9 no. 4. I have argued that this was also the view of his student Baldus, despite claims to the contrary. James Gordley, 'The Achievement of Baldus de Ubaldis (132?-1400),' [2000] *Zeitschrift für Europäisches Privatrecht* 820–36.

[28] 'Extraterritorial Legal Problems in a World without Nations: What the Medieval Jurists Could Teach Us' in G. Handl, J. Zekoll, and P. Zumbansen (eds), *"Extraterritoriality Transnational Legal Authority in an Age of Globalization* (Leiden: Martinus Nijhoff, 2012), 325–52.

[29] 41 U.S. 1 (1842).

[30] 304 U.S. 64 (1938).

[31] S. Pac. Co. v Jensen, 244 U.S.205, 222 (1916).

He explained how the principle of territorial sovereignty should apply in 1822, in his decision in *United States v La Jeune Eugenie*.[32] An American naval vessel had seized a schooner engaged in the slave trade off the coast of Africa. The schooner was claimed by its owners, who said that they and the schooner were French, and that, as it had been operating outside American waters, American law did not apply. Story said that engaging in the slave trade was a violation of the law of nature and of nations, and of the law of France. Applying these laws, he ordered that the schooner be turned over to the consular agent of the King of France to be dealt with 'according to his sense of justice and right'.

He argued that slavery violated the principles of the law of nature and of nations, and then raised another possibility:

> But supposing that the opinions already expressed by the court are as erroneous, as the counsel for the claimant contends them to be, and that the law of nations is to be exclusively derived from the practice of nations, and the practice is in favor of the African slave trade; still there remains another obstacle to the recovery of the property by the claimants, which must be displaced before his title is unimpeachable. And that is, that the African slave trade stands prohibited by the positive municipal regulations of France.[33]

He explained:

> In respect to mere municipal regulations, the general rule certainly is, that courts do not take notice of them with a view to their direct enforcement. It is often said, that no country takes notice of the revenue laws of a foreign country, or holds itself bound to repudiate commercial transactions, which violate them. But this is a rule adopted from a motive of policy or comity; and is not an essential ingredient in any system of the law of nations. If any nation were disposed to discountenance any smuggling in violation of the laws of a foreign country, and in cases coming regularly before its own courts were to refuse to recognize any rights of property founded on such violation, I am not able to perceive, what just ground of complaint the offended nation could have against such conduct. It seems to me, that it might with more justice complain of the refusal to enforce such laws, and to discountenance such violations. But where a title to property originates in what a nation deems in its own subjects a public crime, more especially if it be an aggravated crime founded on fraud and rapine; and it finds, that another nation deems it a crime of a like nature, and prohibits it as such, and confiscates the property of its subjects engaged in the commission of it, I do not perceive, why such property, so polluted by crimes, should, if it falls into the custody of a court of the former nation, be so sacred from judicial touch, that it must be restored to the wrongdoer. And I would ask, where is the authority, that requires such a court to act in this manner, when the public policy of its own, as well as of the foreign, government is avowedly engaged in endeavoring to suppress that crime? … [To refuse to do so] enforces the policy, common to both nations, of repressing an odious traffic, which is denounced by

[32] Cir. Ct., D. Mass. Circuit Court, D. Mass., 26 F. Cas. 832 (1822). Story later held, in the famous case of *United States v The Schooner Amistad*, 40 U.S. 518 (1841), that persons who had been kidnapped in Africa by a slave trader and who had taken control of the ship which had been seized in United States territorial waters were not slaves, even under the laws of Spain, and were therefore entitled to release.

[33] *La Jeune Eugenie*, 26 F. Cas. at 849.

both. It makes our own country, not a principal, but an auxiliary, in enforcing the interdict of France, and subserves the great interests of universal justice.[34]

The rule that Story laid down in this case, as Hans Baade phrased it, is that 'where there was an international public policy to "suppress" conduct odious to both the lex fori and the lex causae (such as, in casu, the slave trade) a court would "have extreme difficulty in recognizing" a title acquired through such conduct'.[35] This rule has not disappeared. As Baade noted, it 'is close to being recognized as mandated by public international law, especially where laws that violate fundamental human rights are sought to be given indirect effect'.[36]

The question of whether an American or English court can recognize a title acquired by violation of a foreign export regulation should therefore depend on whether, as in *La Jeune Eugenie*, there is 'an international policy to suppress conduct odious to the lex forae and the lex causae'. In the case of export laws concerning objects of cultural significance, that question turns not simply on whether foreign export laws have been violated, but whether that violation is odious according to the standards of the forum and in contravention of international policy.

The answer must be yes if the object illegally exported constitutes what is called an 'impoverishment of the cultural heritage of the countr[y] of origin' by Article 1 of the UNESCO Convention of 1970 on the Means of Prohibiting the Illicit Import, Export, and Transfer of Ownership of Cultural Property, a convention to which the United States and the United Kingdom are signatories. The reason is not that the Convention itself requires its signatories to return cultural objects illegally exported. It does not. The reason is that, if the rule laid down by Story in *La Jeune Eugenie* is correct, one cannot acquire property through conduct which violates a foreign law when the conduct is also odious to the forum in which suit is brought. Thus an American court should refuse to acknowledge title to property acquired by violation of a foreign export law when it constitutes conduct which the United States condemned when it signed the UNESCO Convention, conduct which impoverishes the cultural heritage of the country of origin.

As mentioned, the Convention itself does not require its signatories to require the return of cultural objects illegally exported. It requires them 'to take all necessary measures, consistent with national legislation, to prevent museums and similar institutions from acquiring cultural property ... which has been illegally exported'.[37] The obstacle in the United States to enacting legislation to give force to the Convention has been the fear of writing what Bator has called a 'blank cheque' to foreign nations to determine what cultural objects must be returned.[38]

[34] *La Jeune Eugenie*, at 850.

[35] Hans W. Baade, 'The Operation of Foreign Public Law', 30 *Tex. Int'l L.J.* (1995), 429–98, at 438 (citing 26 F. Cas. at 850).

[36] Hans W. Baade, 'The Operation of Foreign Public Law', 30 *Tex. Int'l L.J.* (1995), 429–98, at 438.

[37] Art. 7a.

[38] James R. McAlee, 'From the Boston Raphael to Peruvian Pots: Limitations on the Importation of Art into the United States', 85 *Dickenson L. Rev.* (1981), 565–605, at 599–605.

As Bator testified before the Senate Subcommittee on International Trade when it considered one such bill:

Do these provisions [of the bill] paint an adequate picture that import restrictions are to be imposed only in cases of a critical threat to important cultural values? I'm concerned that … there will be a tendency to equate every situation of widespread pot hunting with a situation of jeopardy to some country's artistic patrimony.[39]

Bator favoured legislation governing illegally exported cultural objects that 'critically threat[ened] important cultural values' and 'jeopard[ized] … a country's artistic patrimony'. It did not follow, he recognized, that any violation of a country's export laws impoverished that country's cultural heritage, or that that country should be the final judge of whether it did.

Yet, if the rule laid down by Story in *La Jeune Eugenie* were followed, there is no need for legislation to be enacted or to be afraid of blank cheques. A court would enforce a foreign export law only when its violation is condemned, not only by foreign law, but by the standards of the forum. The forum would have to decide whether the violation was an impoverishment of a foreign country's cultural heritage.

That rule, of course, lacks definitiveness. . Legislation might be desirable, not to enact the rule, but to clarify it, either by making the rule more precise, or by allowing some non-judicial authority, presumably one within the executive branch, to determine whether it has been violated. It is hard to imagine, however, any precise rules that could determine when the exportation of a cultural object impoverishes the cultural heritage of a country. Moreover, assigning government officials the power to make that determination raises problems of its own. When a bill was presented to Congress that would have assigned this power to the executive branch, critics charged that the determination would too strongly reflect the foreign policy concerns of the State Department.[40]

In any event, the rule is not too indefinite for courts to apply absent legislation. Judge Friendly could have done so, if necessary, in *Jeanerette.* Courts apply equally indefinite standards to decide, for example, if a physician correctly performed a medical operation or an engineer defectively designed a jet plane.

Indeed, in the case of illegal exports, the lack of definitiveness is more tolerable than in other areas of law. The physician or engineer must guess whether a court will later hold that his conduct was negligent or his product defective. Fear of liability may inhibit him from acting as he should. In contrast, the illegal exporter of art knows that he is violating the law, and those who buy from him may know as well. They should bear the risk that a court will later hold not only that the law was violated, but in a way that its violation impoverishes the cultural heritage of

39 Paul M. Bator, 'Memorandum,' *Hearings on H.R. 5643 and S. 2261 before the Subcommittee on International Trade on the Senate Committee on Finance*, 95th Cong., 2d Sess. (1978), 191, at 192.

40 McAlee, *see earlier* note 38, at 602.

the country that enacted it. If they are unwilling to take that risk, they should not deal in illegally exported property.

III. The Repatriation of Cultural Heritage

A. Repatriation and Conventional Concepts of Property Rights

A legal alternative for a country that does not wish objects belonging to its cultural heritage to be exported is to expropriate them. The country can then try to claim the return of such an object in a foreign court, not because its export laws have been violated, but because it owns the object. The legal obstacle it will encounter, as mentioned earlier, is that courts have refused to recognize that a country owns an object unless it has the rights of exclusive use and possession that we associate with ownership.

One difficulty that this approach creates is that a government may not want to have the exclusive right to use and possess these objects. It may merely want to prevent them from leaving the country. Consequently, to accomplish the objective that such a government wishes to achieve, it must assert rights that it does not wish to have.

Countries that have tried to escape this difficulty have encountered others. In *McClain*, Mexico had 'expropriated' all pre-Columbian artefacts while allowing private owners to retain them in their own custody and to sell the right to do so to others. The court held that the artefacts were not 'property' of Mexico within the meaning of the National Stolen Property Act. In *Government of Peru v Johnson*,[41] Peruvian law provided that the government 'owned' all pre-Columbian artefacts but could not exercise any of the rights usually connected with ownership. The court held that Peru could not recover illegally exported artefacts because its claim of ownership amounted to a form of export control. The court cited *McClain*, and only *McClain*, for the proposition that an American court would not enforce foreign export controls. It expressed its regret as to the result.

> Irrespective of the decision in this matter, the court has considerable sympathy for Peru with respect to the problems that it confronts as manifested by this litigation. It is evident that many priceless and beautiful Pre-Columbian artifacts excavated from historical monuments in that country have been and are being smuggled abroad and sold to museums and other collectors of art. Such conduct is destructive of a major segment of the cultural heritage of Peru, and the plaintiff is entitled to the support of the courts of the United States in its determination to prevent further looting of its patrimony.[42]

Nevertheless the court did not offer the Government of Peru its support. Only its sympathy.

[41] 720 F. Supp. 810 (D.C. Cal. 1989).
[42] 720 F. Supp. at 811–12.

A state wishing to protect its cultural heritage must therefore go further. In *Ortiz*, the House of Lords considered the effect of a New Zealand law that expropriated any illegally exported cultural artefact. It held that New Zealand could not claim the return of such an artefact because, as the Lords construed the law, the artefact belonged to New Zealand only upon seizure and not merely upon illegal export.

Suppose, then, that the law of a state provided that an artefact was expropriated without seizure at the moment it was illegally exported. The law of Guatemala did so. As a lower federal court explained in *United States v Pre-Columbian Artifacts and the Republic of Guatemala*, 'the moment the artifacts left Guatemala, the artifacts became the property of the Republic'.[43] Citing *McClain* and *Government of Peru*, the court said that although the National Stolen Property Act was not contravened by '[m]ere violation of export restrictions', nevertheless, the illegally exported artefacts were owned by Guatemala, and so could be reclaimed under the Act.

There are problems with that result. One is that the purpose of the law in question was to prevent the export of pre-Columbian artefacts. So far as that law is concerned, it is a matter of indifference who owns the artefacts as long as they stay in the country. It may also be a matter of indifference whether they are privately owned as long as they are brought back. The government was vested with all the incidents of ownership only so that it could ensure their repatriation. It is not consistent for a court to refuse to enforce foreign export laws and then to enforce a property right that exists only in order to make these laws enforceable. Moreover, this approach has all the disadvantages, mentioned by Bator, of writing a blank cheque. There would be no limit to the objects that a country could declare to be expropriated at the moment that they are illegally exported.

Moreover, since the cost to the dealer whose object is expropriated depends on its world market price, not on its value to the national cultural heritage of a country, this approach may often provide the wrong sanctions. The value of the *Matisse* in *McClain*, as Judge Friendly suggested, probably exceeded its value to the Italian cultural heritage. Conversely, the harm done when a figure is chipped off a Mayan temple and sold separately may exceed its market value.

Finally, this approach imposes heavy penalties on those who make mistakes. A drafter must be careful about his language if he wants his statute to be construed as in *Republic of Guatemala* rather than as in *Ortiz*. He must guess how far he must go in giving the government rights it may not want. For example, could he allow an object to be de-expropriated if it were repatriated by sale to a collector or museum within the country, or by an illegal exporter who wished to bring it back without forfeiting it? Could the drafter provide that an object became state property immediately upon its illegal export, but that the state must sell it, or, perhaps, de-expropriate it, after the state had secured its return?

[43] 845 F. Supp. 544, 547 (N.D. Ill. 1993).

Then there are mistakes that dealers in these objects might make. Some exports are flagrantly illegal and others are technical violations of a labyrinthine authorization procedure. The Guatemalan statute applied to any export that was not 'authorized'. Moreover, if a drafter can make mistakes about the legal effect of his statute, so can the dealer. Finally, the dealer can be mistaken about whether other American courts will rule as the Northern District of Illinois in deciding *Republic of Guatemala*.

B. Repatriation and an Alternative Conception of Property Rights

This is a mess. There are two ways to deal with it. One, which I have suggested in this chapter, is to adhere to the law as Justice Story declared it. Foreign laws are enforceable when violation of them is odious not only to the country that made them but to the forum state as well. The 'impoverishment of the cultural heritage' of another nation is wrong according to the treaty commitments of the United States and the opinions of American courts. An American court would have to be convinced by the plaintiff that a given instance of illegal export constituted such an 'impoverishment'. They might be the most suitable forum to do so, but if not, Congress could provide another. Until it does, the courts should enforce the law.

The other alternative, with which I have much sympathy, is to alter our ideas about the sort of property right that will enable a foreign nation to claim repatriation of illegally exported art. We are accustomed to think that, by definition, a property right to an object means that an owner can dispose of it according to its will. This conception of property goes back to the will theorists of the 19th century,[44] the same era in which law was taken to be, by definition, the will of a territorial sovereign.

There is no reason why property must be defined that way. Roman law recognized various kinds of property and different limited interests which one might have in it. Rivers and harbours are 'public things'. They belong to the public, and everyone can fish or boat on them.[45] The banks are owned by those whose lands border on them, yet everyone using the river is free to beach boats, dry nets, and haul fish onto the banks, and to tie up to trees there even though the trees belong to the owner of the land.[46] The sea and seashore are 'common things' that belong

[44] *Eg*, Christopher Columbus Langdell, 'Classification of Rights and Wrongs', pt. 1, 13 *Harv. L. Rev.* (1900) 537–56, at 537–8; Frederick Pollock, *A First Book of Jurisprudence for Students of the Common Law* (London: Macmillan & Co, 1896) at 160; Charles Aubry and Charles Rau, *Cours de droit civil français d'après la méthode de Zacharia* 2, 4th edn (Paris: Marchal & Bilard, 1869), § 190; François Laurent, *Principes de droit civil français* 6, 3rd edn (Paris: A. Durand, 1875), § 101; Charles Demolombe, *Cours de Code Napoléon* 9, 3rd edn, (Paris: A. Durand, 1882), § 543; Bernhard Windscheid, *Lehrbuch des Pandektenrechts* 3, 7th edn, (Frankfort-on-Main: Rütter & Loenig, 1891), § 167.

[45] I. 2.1.2; Dig. 1.8.5.pr.

[46] I. 2.1.4; Dig. 1.8.5.pr.

to everyone, and so everyone can use them.[47] But an individual owns gems or pebbles he takes from the shore.[48] Moreover, an individual can build a hut on the shore.[49] Others must keep clear of the hut.[50] But his ownership lasts only as long as the building remains. If it collapses, someone else can build on the site.[51]

My former colleague Joseph Sax has suggested that, in conceptualizing the law of property as it applies to environmental protection, we could learn a good deal from the Romans.[52] We can conceive of seashores, for example, not as areas subject to unlimited private rights, but as places over which the state exercises a trust for the benefit of the public. That view is now reflected in some American cases.[53] Sax suggested another limit in his book, *Playing Darts with a Rembrandt*.[54] Can it really be that the law of property gives a person the right to acquire an artistic masterpiece for the sole purpose of destroying it for his personal enjoyment? If so, we are construing the law similarly to will theorists who described private rights as unlimited because by definition they must be so, without asking what purpose is served by recognizing such rights in the first place.

Elsewhere, I have argued that, in order to explain the law of landmark preservation in the United States, we must recognize that the owner of property of cultural significance does not have the right to destroy it.[55] The Supreme Court should have said so in the leading case of *Penn Central Transportation Co. v City of New York*,[56] rather than concerning itself with whether the owner of Grand Central Station could sell someone its unused airspace or whether its 'investment-backed expectations' were frustrated—whatever that phrase may mean. The dissent had a clearer perception of what was at stake. Unlike other cases of land use regulation, the City was not 'prohibiting a nuisance' or 'merely prohibit[ing] Penn Central from using its property in a narrow set of noxious ways'. The City was seeking 'to preserve what they believe to be an outstanding example of beaux-arts architecture. Penn Central is prevented from further developing its property basically because *too good* a job was done in designing and building it'.[57] On that point, the dissent was correct. But one should not conclude that an owner can destroy such a building, whatever its cultural significance, whenever he sees a profit in it,

47 I. 2.1.1; I. 2.1.5; Dig. 1.8.2.1.

48 Dig. 1.8.3.

49 I. 2.1.5; Dig. 1.8.3.

50 Dig. 1.8.4.

51 Dig. 1.8.6.pr.

52 Joseph L. Sax, 'The Public Trust Doctrine in Natural Resource Law: Effective Judicial Intervention', 68 *Mich. L. Rev.* (1970), 471–566.

53 *Eg*, Matthews v Bay Head Improvement Ass'n, 471 A.2d 355 (N.J. 1984), *cert. denied*, 469 U.S. 821 (1984).

54 Joseph L. Sax, *Playing Darts with a Rembrandt* (Ann Arbor: University of Michigan Press, 1999).

55 Gordley, 'Takings', 82 *Tul. L. Rev.* (2008) 1505–32, at 1519–21.

56 438 U.S. 104 (1978).

57 438 U.S. 145–6.

unless the state pays him the amount of that profit. One should conclude that his rights of ownership do not extend so far.

Another way of saying that the owner's rights to such property are limited is to say that the state has a paramount authority over its preservation. In a well-written and well-known lower court opinion in which Ecuador recovered illegally exported artefacts,[58] the Tribunale of Torino recognized a doctrine that it called *dominio eminente*. The doctrine has nothing to do with the American concept of eminent domain and could be translated as 'paramount ownership' or 'paramount authority'. Ecuadorian law provided that 'the state will have equal dominion over archaeological treasures without harm to the rights of private parties which, according to statute, belong to them by their discovery or claim'. It provided that the Ecuadorian House of Culture could issue a declaration 'which confers the quality of treasure pertaining to the national artistic patrimony on any object among those described in an earlier article, but does not deprive its owner of the exercise of all relative rights to dominion subject to the limitations established by this law'. According to the court:

> Established is a so-called paramount domain (*dominio eminente*) characterized by the system of subjection of public goods to the 'entitlement' (*titularità*) or protective dominion of the State, a legal institution which is distinct from 'civil property' and from 'common property', for which reason public goods also come to be defined as 'State goods'.
>
> The positive regulation of public goods, in which the 'dominion' of the State is imprescriptible and inalienable, is achieved chief by public administrative law.
>
> Private rights over such goods are acknowledged, but they are unalterably 'limited' by the eminent position of the State, to whose care this class of goods is subjected for the benefit of the social collectivity.
>
> The practical effect of the public system of public goods consists in the prohibition of their free exchange.
>
> Indeed, under article 5 of the law on artistic patrimony (LPA) of 1945, 'one may not transfer the ownership of objects belonging to the national artistic patrimony by gift or by exchange or change the location of such objects without the permission of the Ecuadorian House of Culture,' which has the task of preserving the artistic patrimony and may deny authorization.
>
> Another practical effect consists in the concrete limit of the possibility of obtaining original title to such public goods by private persons. Indeed, under article 13, paragraph one of the law on artistic patrimony (LPA) of 1945 'one may undertake the work of excavation for archaeological or paleological purposes without the authorization of the Ecuadorian House of Culture'.[59]

This system of regulation is not like the jury-rigged laws discussed earlier, in which the state calls itself the owner of objects only to escape the reluctance of foreign courts to enforce its export laws. It is, as the court said, a recognition that

[58] Trib. Torino, 25 Mar.1982, Giur. it. 1982, 625.

[59] Trib. Torino, 25 Mar.1982, Giur. it. 1982, at 629–30.

two rights of ownership or entitlement may exist simultaneously in an object that is part of a country's national heritage: that of a private party to possess the object but to treat it with the respect that it deserves, and that of the state to preserve it. It may be that the Ecuadorian law goes too far in supervising the freedom of exchange or in insisting that an excavator can acquire no title by discovery. But the question is whether a state can legitimately recognize that there are two such rights. If so, a foreign court, without writing it a blank cheque, can enforce them.

IV. Conclusion

This chapter has suggested two grounds on which a country could claim return of objects belonging to its cultural heritage before a foreign court. One is that our courts have too strictly construed the notion of territorial sovereignty, more strictly than Justice Story, so as to refuse to enforce them even when, as Story would have put it, the forum itself deems the violation of the foreign law to be odious. The second is that our courts have too strictly construed the ownership right a foreign nation must have to demand that such an object be returned, applying a modern idea of ownership as something single and entire, not permitting partition between a right of possession and use, on the one hand, and, on the other, a right of guardianship over how an object is used. Actually, they are not two distinct grounds. A country's cultural heritage could be impoverished, either by export, or by harm done within the state. If the state has a right to guard its cultural heritage, then export controls are one aspect, but only one, of that right of guardianship. It does not matter whether a foreign court requires that an object be returned because it recognizes the right of guardianship as a matter of proprietary right or because it regards the subversion of that right by illegal export as odious. If there is such a right of guardianship, it is a proprietary right. If there is none, there is no reason to regard export controls that prevent the impoverishment of cultural heritage as odious.

7

The Enforcement of Underwater Cultural Heritage by Courts

*Patrizia Vigni**

I. Introduction

The protection of underwater cultural heritage affects diverse interests, such as private property rights, state sovereign powers, and the interest of the international community as a whole in the preservation of cultural objects. In fact, these objects cannot only be considered as private property. They also have an intrinsic value as part of the culture and traditions of peoples. For this reason, the legal systems of several states regulate the management and preservation of these objects by means of administrative and criminal norms in order to stress their importance as 'common goods'. Moreover, international provisions, both of a customary and treaty nature, affirm the concept of cultural heritage in order to recognize the intrinsic value of historical objects for humankind as a whole. The very reference to the term 'heritage' with respect to cultural and archaeological objects seems to highlight the non-exclusively commercial character of the interests relating to these objects.

The regulation of the preservation of underwater cultural heritage encounters additional problems due to the fact that historic objects may be located—and thus discovered—in marine areas far from the states and private persons to whom these objects belonged. Thus, other legal persons, such as the finders of historic objects and states enjoying sovereign rights over these marine areas, may claim rights over the objects themselves.

The first aim of the present chapter therefore is to identify who, under international and domestic law, can legitimately claim rights with respect to cultural

* '*Ricercatore*' of International Law and Lecturer of International Dispute Settlement, Law Faculty of the University of Siena.

objects at sea. In particular, special attention will be paid to sovereign and property rights of states and private persons over historic shipwrecks. This issue seems to be particularly intriguing since it may entail the application of international and domestic norms other than the law of cultural property, such as, for example, the provisions of the law of the sea and admiralty law.

Second, this chapter will attempt to ascertain how domestic courts have so far settled disputes affecting cultural objects at sea in order to determine whether and to what extent these courts have enforced international provisions concerning the protection of underwater cultural heritage. Even at first glance, one must admit that domestic courts are the most appropriate organs to enforce the principles of international law that have so far been developed with regard to cultural heritage. In fact, the diverse interests in question can be safeguarded much better by domestic courts which are competent to deal with disputes involving both private and public parties, than ruled by international tribunals the jurisdiction of which is traditionally devoted to inter-state disputes.

II. Claimants to Rights over Cultural Objects at Sea

A. The State of Origin

1. General Remarks

Among the possible claimants to rights over cultural objects at sea, the state of origin of these objects must first be mentioned. For the purposes of the present chapter, the state of origin is the state where a historic object was produced and where it was used before it disappeared into the sea. The claim of this state is justified by the fact that the cultural object is the expression of its historical and cultural traditions. The interest of the state of origin has a public nature and, thus, may in some circumstances prevail over other rights. As an example, the 1970 UNESCO Convention on the Means of Prohibiting and Preventing the Illicit Import, Export and Transfer of Ownership of Cultural Property (hereafter 1970 UNESCO Convention) considers the prevention of 'the impoverishment of the cultural heritage of the countries of origin of such property' as one of its main objectives.[1] Similarly, the 2004 Italian Code on Cultural Properties and Landscape (hereafter the 2004 Italian Code)[2] obliges private owners of cultural properties to endeavor to preserve them with the purpose of maintaining the memory of the traditions of the country.

[1] 1970 UNESCO Convention art. 2.

[2] Decree Establishing the 'Codice dei beni culturali e del paesaggio', 22 Jan. 2004, n. 42. Gazzetta Ufficiale della Repubblica Italiana, 24 Feb. 2004, n. 45.

Although the rights of the state of origin are generally recognized by domestic and international law, some judicial decisions have not paid much attention to this rule. For example, in the *Lisippo bronze* case,[3] the judges of the Tribunal of Pesaro completely set aside the interest of the state of origin of the cultural object at hand—a Greek statue which is currently located at the Getty Museum in Malibu, but which Italy claims to be part of its underwater cultural heritage. The statue was found by Italian fishermen in the Adriatic Sea adjacent to the Italian coast in 1964. In breach of Italian criminal law, the statue was sold to some antiquarians and presumably exported. Finally, it appeared in the Getty Museum in 1977.[4] In 2009, before the Tribunal of Pesaro, the Italian Government claimed the illicit character of the export of the Lisippo bronze. As a consequence, Pesaro's preliminary investigation judge ordered the seizure of the statue assuming that it was a part of the 'Italian unalienable cultural heritage' since it had been found at sea by an Italian ship and brought to Italian territory. In the view of the Pesaro's judge, if the Italian organs had been informed of the finding of the statue at the time of the discovery, as required by Italian law, Italy could have exercised its right of pre-emption over this object.[5] This reasoning was confirmed in 2010 by the decision of another preliminary investigation judge of the Tribunal of Pesaro, who was competent for the enforcement of the seizure's order.[6] Finally, the rights of Greece as the state of origin of the bronze have also been ignored in the most recent decision affecting this case that was yet again delivered by the preliminary investigation judge of Pesaro in May 2012.[7] In this order, the judge reaffirmed that the statue was an 'Italian inalienable cultural property' because its discoverers initially transferred it into the Italian territory.[8] Thus, despite the fact that the

[3] The statue is also known as the 'Victorious Youth'.

[4] Actually, in 1973, Italian police were informed about the presence, in Munich, of a statue that was presumably the Lisippo bronze. As a consequence, Italian judges asked Germany to allow them to examine the possessor of the statue that was charged by Italy for the illicit export of artistic objects. German judges rejected the Italian request on the assumption that German law did not allow extradition for a similar crime. For an overview of the *Lisippo bronze* case, see Lanciotti, 'The Dilemma of the Right to Ownership of Underwater Cultural Heritage: The Case of the "Getty Bronze"', in S. Borelli and F. Lenzerini (eds), *Cultural Heritage, Cultural Rights, Cultural Diversity. New Developments in International Law* (Leiden: Nijhoff Publishers, 2012) 301–26.

[5] Order of 12 June 2009, in Rivista di Diritto Internazionale Privato e Processuale, 2011(1), at 149–52.

[6] Order of 10 February 2010, <http://www.europeanrights.eu/getFile.php?name=public/sentenze/1-LISIPPO_confisca_GIP_trib._pesaro.doc> (last accessed 4 February 2013), *quoted in* Lanciotti, *The Dilemma of the Right to Ownership*, at 302.

[7] This order is the consequence of the claim of the Getty Museum challenging the 2009 seizure's order of the judge of Pesaro before the Italian Supreme Court of Cassazione. The Museum argued that the Greek origin of this object did not allow Italy to claim sovereign rights over it. The Court of Cassazione readdressed the case to the judge of merits asking him for ascertaining the concrete grounds of both the claims of the Getty Museum and Italy in-depth. Decision n. 169/2011 of the Italian Supreme Court of Cassazione, 'Udienza in Camera di Consiglio', 18 Jan. 2011, *quoted in* Lanciotti, *The Dilemma of the Right to Ownership*, at 305.

[8] Order of the Preliminary Investigation Judge, Tribunal of Pesaro, 3 May 2012, at 22, <http://www.scribd.com/doc/92449731/ORDINANZA-LISIPPO-2012–05–03> (last accessed 4 February 2013), hereinafter Order of 3 May 2012.

origin of the statue is indisputably Greek, the Italian judges did not recognize any relevance of the interest of the state of origin as a legal criterion in the determination of the legitimate owner of this cultural object.

By contrast, as to the recognition of the rights of the state of origin of historic shipwrecks, judicial claims are most frequently brought by flag states on the basis of their sovereign rights over sunken vessels. In fact, the nationality link between a ship and its flag state is the primary legal basis for justifying a claim by a state over such a ship both under international and domestic law. Thus, the criterion of the state of origin seems to be entirely respected with regard to historic vessels.

In short, domestic courts seem to provide different meanings of the principle of the 'state of origin' in respect of the diverse objects and interests that are at issue.

2. *The Rights of 'the State of Origin' of Historic Shipwrecks*

a. The 'Origin' of Historic Shipwrecks

In order to allow the concrete exercise of the rights of the state of origin over cultural objects at sea, one must first of all ascertain their geographical origin. Apart from the cases in which the cultural objects are universally known masterpieces, some scientific and historical studies are generally necessary to identify their origin. Moreover, as affirmed previously, it is quite common to discover these objects in waters that are far from the mainland of the states of origin. Thus, the geographic position can sometimes be misleading for the determination of the origin of underwater cultural objects.

As far as shipwrecks are concerned, many vessels have sunk in very restricted marine areas over the centuries. Moreover, except for historical data, not much information is available about these vessels and their demise. Thus, the identity of different ships can often be mistaken. In order to ascertain the identity of a ship and its flag state, specific research activities must be carried out. Recent case law has provided several examples of this uncertainty in identifying shipwrecks: in this regard, the case relating to the excavation of the Nuestra Señora de las Mercedes, a Spanish vessel that sank at the beginning of the 19th century, is worth mentioning. This case concerns the complaint that Spain brought before the Tampa District Court against Odyssey Marine Exploration (hereafter Odyssey), a treasure-hunting venture that had carried out an excavation. While Spain claimed that the vessel had been illicitly excavated, Odyssey denied that this ship was the Nuestra Señora de las Mercedes. Thus, the district court had, first of all, to determine that the vessel was the Nuestra Señora de las Mercedes on the basis of historical information concerning the location, shape, and cargo of the ship itself and, thus, to declare Spain as the legitimate flag state.[9]

[9] *Odyssey Marine Exploration Inc. v The Unidentified Shipwreck Vessel & the Kingdom of Spain, the Republic of Peru*, United States District Court, Middle District of Florida, Tampa Division, 3 June

Similarly, in the abovementioned *Lisippo bronze* case, a few years after the discovery and illicit export of the statue, several Italian courts encountered problems in defining the cultural and historical origin of this object.[10] In particular, in 1970, when the Supreme Court of Cassazione had to examine the charge for illicit trade against the fishermen who had found and sold the statue, it did not reach a guilty verdict against the fishermen because, as the court declared, it was difficult to demonstrate the exact marine area where the object had been found. Surprisingly enough, the Court of Cassazione also showed reservations about the artistic value of this object due to scarce available information relating to it. In fact, no party, including the public attorney, had been able to provide images of the statue. Conversely, in 2010, when the information relating to the origin and value of the Lisippo bronze was sufficiently accurate,[11] the judge of Pesaro was able to ascertain that the statue belonging to the Getty Museum corresponds to the bronze that had been discovered by Italian fishermen in 1964.[12]

Thus, domestic courts must evidently rely upon the thorough and precise information of historical and artistic experts in order to resolve cases concerning the recognition of rights over cultural objects.

b. The Scope of the Right of Flag States over Historic Shipwrecks

Under the norms of the international law of the sea, sunken ships are equated to other vessels. These norms are mainly based on the principle of state sovereignty. Thus, customary international law and the 1982 UN Law of the Sea Convention (UNCLOS) recognize the sovereign rights of flag states over their vessels. Similarly, admiralty law[13] acknowledges the right of flag states to claim sovereignty over their ships except in case of express abandonment. Special attention must be paid to warships. The law of the sea[14] and admiralty law[15] both recognize the sovereign immunity of these types of vessels. The recognition of the immunity of sunken governmental vessels would automatically exclude the jurisdiction of states other than the flag state with respect to these vessels. However, one must admit that the very purpose of the recognition of the immunity of governmental

2009, at 5–12, <http://docs.justia.com/cases/federal/district-courts/florida/flmdce/8:2007cv00614/197978/209/> (last accessed 4 February 2013). Actually, this decision is the opinion of a US magistrate, Judge Pizzo, which was supported by the decision of the Tampa District Court of 22 December 2009, <http://docs.justia.com/cases/federal/district-courts/florida/flmdce/8:2007cv00614/197978/270/> (last accessed 4 February 2013).

[10] The case was examined by the Tribunal of Gubbio, the Court of Appeals of Perugia, and, finally, the Italian Supreme Court of Cassazione.

[11] Some pictures of the Lisippo bronze were discovered and compared with the Getty property in 1977.

[12] Order of 10 Feb. 2010, *see earlier* in this chapter.

[13] Admiralty law is the part of private law that regulates the relations between private maritime operators that voluntarily or accidentally share some interests relating to maritime activities.

[14] *See* UNCLOS arts. 95–96.

[15] *See* International Convention on Salvage, done in London on 28 Apr. 1989, art. 4, <http://www.imo.org/Conventions/mainframe.asp?topic_id=259&doc_id=687> (last accessed 4 February 2013).

ships is to avoid interference with the exercise of states' public functions. Sunken vessels no longer seem to exercise these types of functions. Nevertheless, in some circumstances, the sovereign immunity of sunken governmental ships must be still recognized, in particular, when shipwrecks contain secret information, the dissemination of which might entail some risk for the present security and safety of the flag state. This happens only when the sinking of a state vessel occurred in the recent past. National security does not seem at risk when the dissemination concerns information that was collected in ships that had sunk centuries ago.

Nevertheless, the argument relating to the sovereign immunity of warships has also been raised with regard to historic shipwrecks. In the abovementioned *Nuestra Señora de las Mercedes* case, the Tampa District Court recognized the immunity of the Spanish vessel on the basis of article 8 of the 1958 Geneva Convention on the High Seas,[16] which recognizes the immunity of warships, and the 1902 US–Spanish Friendship Agreement that provides for the mutual recognition of the immunity of sunken warships. Thus, the Nuestra Señora de las Mercedes was considered as a warship that enjoyed sovereign immunity. The same conclusions were also reached by the Eleventh District Court of Appeals before which Odyssey challenged the Tampa Court's ruling of the *Nuestra Señora de las Mercedes* case.[17]

In addition, international provisions other than the law of the sea also recognize the preferential rights of flag states over their vessels, such as, for example, article 2(8) of the 2001 UNESCO Convention on the protection of Underwater Cultural Heritage (hereafter UHC).[18]

Thus, as far as shipwrecks are concerned, the rights of flag states would appear to enjoy priority over other interests.

c. The Origin of the Cargo of Shipwrecks

Even if the flag state of a sunken vessel is certain, the nationality of the cargo can be questioned. Commercial vessels used to, in fact, carry both national and foreign goods. The nationality of the objects of the cargo can most easily be ascertained when sunken vessels moved from one country to another. In this

[16] Done in Geneva on 29 Aprril 1958, 450 U.N.T.S.11.

[17] Odyssey appealed the Tampa court's ruling concerning the *Nuestra Señora de las Mercedes* case on 15 January 2010. Docket n. 10–10269J. The Court of Appeals allowed the request of Odyssey for oral arguments on 2 November 2010. The discussion of oral arguments before the Court of Appeals was scheduled for the week of 28 February 2011, but it was postponed because of the intervention of the US Congress against the view expressed by the Department of State supporting Spain's arguments. The Court of Appeals decided the case on 21 September 2011. US Court of Appeals, Eleventh District, *Odyssey Marine Exploration, Inc. v Kingdom of Spain*, Docket n. 10–10269, 21 September 2011, <http://www.ca11.uscourts.gov/opinions/ops/201010269.pdf> (last accessed 4 February 2013).

[18] Article 2(8) of the 2001 UNESCO Convention states: 'Consistent with State practice and international law, including the United Nations Convention on the Law of the Sea, nothing in this Convention shall be interpreted as modifying the rules of international law and State practice pertaining to sovereign immunities, nor any State's rights with respect to its State vessels and aircraft'.

case the flag state, state of origin, and state of destination of the cargo did not coincide. Conversely, some difficulties may arise when determining the nationality of the cargo of the sunken vessel, moving from the territory of a colony of a state towards its mainland, because, in this case, no proper trans-boundary movement took place and, thus, the flag state, state of origin, and state of destination of the cargo usually coincided at the time of the sinking. However, over the centuries, colonies achieved independence and, thus, problems may arise when determining whether the nationality of the cargo of a shipwreck discovered at the present time is the same as it was at the time of sinking. In fact, one may argue that the cargo now has the nationality of the territory of origin, which in the meantime became an independent state. The solution to this problem reveals its importance particularly in cases in which the cargo of sunken vessels consisted of objects of a cultural and artistic nature. In fact, the interest of the ex-colony in the return of these objects does not only concern their economic value, but also the cultural value that links these goods to the people of the ex-colony. In this case, in order to enhance the legitimacy of its claim, the ex-colony may argue that the objects belonging to the cargo form part of its cultural heritage. Thus, both sovereign and cultural rights are at issue.

As an example, in the *Nuestra Señora de las Mercedes* case, the cargo, which mainly consisted of gold and silver coins, was deemed to be carried by the vessel from the Peru Viceroyalty to the mainland of the Kingdom of Spain. For this reason, Peru joined the claim of Spain against Odyssey before the Tampa District Court and Eleventh Circuit Court of Appeals, asserting its sovereign rights as the state of origin of the cargo of the Nuestra Señora de las Mercedes. Peru raised several arguments in support of its claim. First of all, it affirmed that state practice should be consistent with the general principle of international law that condemns colonialism and, in particular, the pillage of the resources of occupied territories. Moreover, Peru claimed that the cargo of the Nuestra Señora de las Mercedes was part of its cultural and historic heritage and, thus, Peru's right to the return of the objects should prevail over other interests because of the nature of such a right.

Thus, although the state of origin of a sunken vessel may sometimes be easily determined, the same certainty cannot be affirmed with regard to the 'nationality and legal appurtenance' of its cargo.

B. Private Rights over Underwater Historic Objects

The recognition of state sovereign rights over cultural objects does not exclude that private property rights may exist. For this reason, some legal instruments regulate the management of both private and public cultural properties. As an example, the abovementioned 1970 UNESCO Convention and 1995 UNIDROIT Convention on Stolen or Illegally Exported Cultural Objects (hereafter the 1995 UNIDROIT Convention) deal with the illicit trade of both public and private cultural properties.[19] Similarly, the 2004 Italian Code on Cultural Properties includes private properties within its scope in order to provide a thorough protection of the national cultural heritage.

Claims to private rights ought not to be confused with the claims that some private persons may bring with respect to the cultural objects that they deem to belong to the heritage of their cultural or ethnic group. This type of claim is frequently joined to the claim of the state of origin with the purpose of emphasizing the importance of the claimed object for the preservation of the cultural identity of the population of the state concerned. In this case, the interest is aimed at safeguarding a collective right.[20]

As regards cultural objects at sea, private rights can be claimed if they had existed before these cultural objects disappeared into the sea. If the legitimate owners of cultural objects at sea cannot be identified, the law of finds may apply.[21] Thus, in this case, the private rights of the discoverers of cultural objects at sea are also relevant.

Moreover, private rights over cultural objects are recognized under domestic and international law only when these rights arise from the licit acquisition of cultural properties. In this regard, the 1995 UNIDROIT Convention does not recognize any right of the possessor of any cultural property who cannot demonstrate her/his good faith.[22] On the basis of this argument, in thc 2010 *Lisippo bronze* case, the Pesaro's judge stated that the Getty Museum had not legitimately acquired the statue and, thus, its ownership should have been considered void from the onset.[23] Most precisely, in the 2012 order, the preliminary investigation judge specified that the 2004 Italian Code does not recognize the rights of 'good faith owners' in cases affecting the illicit transfer of national 'unalienable cultural properties'. In these cases, the rights of private persons may be exceptionally safeguarded if they can demonstrate to be not related to the illicit transfer. In 2012, the Pesaro's judge affirmed that the Getty Museum could not be considered to be 'not related to the crime of illicit export of the Lisippo bronze', since the Museum's administrators have at all times known that Italian competent organs had never issued valid export documents with respect to the statue.[24]

[19] 1970 UNESCO Convention art. 5(b).

[20] For a thorough analysis on this matter, see Ahrén, 'Protecting Peoples' Cultural Rights: a Question of Properly Understanding the Notion of States and Nations?', in F. Francioni and M. Scheinin (eds), *Cultural Human Rights* (Leiden: Nijhoff, 2008), 91–118.

[21] For an overview, see Vadi, 'Investing in Culture: Underwater Cultural Heritage and International Investment Law', in *Vand. J. Transnat'l L.* (2009) 853–904, at 870.

[22] 1995 UNIDROIT Convention art. 4.

[23] Order of 10 February 2010, *see earlier* in this chapter.

[24] In this regard, the 2004 Italian Code uses the term 'estraneo al reato' in order to identify the private persons that have the right to challenge a state action such as, for example, the seizure of an artistic object. In the view of the Pesaro's judge, the meaning of this wording must be interpreted in a narrow manner since the safeguard of private rights is an exception vis-à-vis the general obligation of preserving national cultural properties. For the same reason, it is up to the private persons claiming property rights over cultural objects to prove the 'absence of a connection between them and the crime affecting these objects'. Order of 3 May 2012, *see earlier*, at 25 and 39.

State sovereignty and private property rights can also coexist with respect to historic shipwrecks. Private owners can claim property rights both over the ship and its cargo.[25] Although some vessels are very ancient, it is still possible to identify the legitimate owners (or, more accurately, the heirs of the legitimate owners) of some objects belonging to the cargo of a ship through historical information. Clearly, the possibility of ascertaining property rights over these objects decreases in cases in which the discovered shipwrecks are very old. Nevertheless, some families of ancient origin can provide historical evidence of the possessions of their ancestors. In these cases, private rights are recognized by international and domestic law. This conclusion has been reached by some national courts. For example, in the case concerning the discovery of the Titanic, the notorious sunken British vessel, the US Fourth Circuit Court of Appeals affirmed that private property, which had been recovered in a shipwreck, could not be considered as abandoned provided that nobody claimed it after its discovery.[26] In these circumstances, private persons may invoke their property rights over some objects before the courts of the state which has been recognized to have jurisdiction over the objects themselves. By contrast, in the *Nuestra Señora de las Mercedes* case, both the Tampa District Court and Eleventh Circuit Court of Appeals rejected the claims of some private persons who argued to be the direct heirs of the legitimate owners of the objects belonging to the cargo of this ship.[27] The entire decisions of US courts were in fact based on the argument that a ship and its cargo are indissolubly linked. So, since the Nuestra Señora de las Mercedes was declared a Spanish public vessel, US courts affirmed that its cargo had to be considered the property of Spain also.

C. Rights and Duties of Coastal States

Cultural objects might be located in diverse areas of the seabed which, as is well known, have different status under the law of the sea and, in particular, UNCLOS. Thus, the interests of coastal states might also be relevant, at least, with regard to the control over the search operations for cultural objects at sea which are carried out in their territorial sea, contiguous zone, continental shelf, or exclusive economic zone (EEZ). Besides, coastal states might also claim the right to supervise these activities for the purpose of preserving the underwater cultural heritage which occurs to be under their jurisdiction or sphere of control.

[25] For this view, see Forrest, 'An International Perspective on Sunken State Vessels as Underwater Cultural Heritage', in *Ocean Dev. & Int'l L.* (2003) 41–57, at 42.

[26] *R.M.S. Titanic, Inc. v RMS Titanic, in rem*, US Court of Appeals, No 04–1933, 31 January 2006, at 16, <http://pacer.ca4.uscourts.gov/opinion.pdf/041933.P.pdf> (last accessed 4 February 2013).

[27] See the claim by Gonzalo de Aliaga and others at <http://docs.justia.com/cases/federal/district-courts/florida/flmdce/8:2007cv00614/197978/136> and <http://docs.justia.com/cases/federal/district-courts/florida/flmdce/8:2007cv00614/197978/169> (last accessed 21 August 2010)

Coastal states enjoy sovereign rights over their territorial sea and the natural resources of their continental shelf. By contrast, these states only have exclusive powers of control of a different nature in their contiguous zone and EEZ. Similarly, salvage law and, in particular, the 1989 International Convention on Salvage (hereafter 1989 Salvage Convention) recognizes the right of coastal states 'to give directions in relation to salvage operations'.[28] Under salvage law, coastal states exercise this right in accordance with generally recognized principles of international law; namely, the norms of the law of the sea that sanction the diverse powers of states in the different maritime areas.

The 2001 UNESCO Convention also provides for the right of coastal states to regulate activities relating to the underwater cultural heritage in their territorial sea,[29] contiguous zone,[30] and EEZ.[31]

In addition, UNCLOS includes a few general obligations relating to the underwater cultural heritage. Article 303 establishes the duty to preserve the 'objects of an archaeological and historical nature found at sea'. For this purpose, coastal states can apply the general rules of state sovereignty in their maritime areas. For example, paragraph 2 of article 303 recognizes the right of coastal states to control and prevent the removal of such objects from their territorial sea. This norm seems to entail a principle of a customary nature since almost all national legislations recognize it. Moreover, paragraph 2 also states that 'in order to control traffic in (archaeological) objects, the coastal State may, in (exercising policy powers in its contiguous zone, as provided for by article 33 of the UNCLOS), presume that their removal from the seabed in (this) zone without its approval would result in an infringement within its territory or territorial sea of (its domestic) laws and regulations'.

In the 2010 and 2012 *Lisippo bronze* rulings, Pesaro's judges went further as to the recognition of the rights of Italy, the coastal state concerned. In fact, these judges acknowledged that Italy enjoyed the right to restitution of the statue because this cultural object was found by Italian citizens in the waters adjacent to the Italian coast.[32] As a consequence, the judges gave approval for the seizure of the statue.[33] However, the Court of Cassazione, before which the Getty Museum challenged the 2010 seizure's order, did not consider the rights of a coastal state to be the exclusive legal basis for the acquisition of a cultural object at sea. Although

[28] Salvage Convention art. 9.

[29] UHC art. 7. For the view that the UHC seems to adopt the same approach as UNCLOS, see N. Ferri, 'The Protection of the Underwater Cultural Heritage According to the United Nations General Assembly', in *Int'l J. Marine & Coastal L.* (2008) 137–49, at 142.

[30] Article 8 of the UHC expressly mentions article 303(2) of UNCLOS, which provides for a particular regime for the preservation of archaeological objects that are removed from the contiguous zone.

[31] UHC art. 10.

[32] Italian judges did not make any reference to the specific marine area where the statue was found since it has always been unclear whether or not this area was part of the Italian territorial sea.

[33] Order of 12 June 2009, *see* p. 127.

the Court did not annul the seizure's order, it affirmed that the arguments of the parties (in particular, of the Getty Museum) relating to the acquisition of the Lisippo bronze had not been examined by the Tribunal of Pesaro in a sufficient manner so as to recognize Italy's exclusive rights over this cultural object. For this reason, the Court of Cassazione sent the case back to the judge of merits for further examination.[34] However, the preliminary investigation judge confirmed the seizure's order in May 2012.

In sum, under international law, the jurisdiction of coastal states may vary with respect to cultural objects at sea on account of the diverse marine areas in which these objects have been found.

D. The Interest of Humankind

Among the interests relating to cultural objects, the universal interest in protecting the cultural heritage is worth mentioning. In particular, the 2001 UNESCO Convention has contributed to the recognition of the special status of cultural objects at sea as part of the heritage of humankind. UHC provisions are mainly aimed at protecting the cultural heritage for the benefit of humanity and its exceptional intrinsic value. Thus, under this convention, the underwater cultural heritage should not be considered as a commodity, but rather as a common good that must be managed by means of an international regime. The UHC is not the only instrument dealing with the protection of cultural properties which sets aside the traditional approach based on state sovereignty and private property rights. As an example, the 1972 UNESCO Convention Concerning the Protection of the World Cultural and Natural Heritage (hereafter 1972 UNESCO Convention) provides for an international system of protection of the world heritage, and recognizes the duty of the international community as a whole to cooperate and assist states in complying with the obligations of the Convention.[35]

Similarly, article 149 of UNCLOS, which deals with the preservation of archaeological and historic objects found in the 'Area', namely the international deep seabed, which is considered part of the common heritage of humankind under the Convention, states that the protection of these objects must be ensured for the benefit of humankind.

In addition, admiralty or, more precisely, salvage law also seems to recognize the special status of cultural objects at sea, although in a marginal manner.

[34] *See* p. 129.

[35] The seventh paragraph of the Preamble of the 1972 Convention states: 'Considering that parts of the cultural or natural heritage are of outstanding interest and therefore need to be preserved as part of the world heritage of mankind as a whole ...'. For the view that the duty to protect the world heritage, which is established by the 1972 UNESCO Convention, is an *erga omnes* obligation of both customary and treaty nature, see F. Francioni and F. Lenzerini, 'The Obligation to Prevent and Avoid Destruction of Cultural Heritage: From Bamiyan to Iraq', in B. T. Hoffman (ed,), *Art & Cultural Heritage* (Cambridge: Cambridge University Press, 2006) 28–40, at 34–5.

Salvage law is mainly aimed at dealing with the bilateral relationship between the flag state of a ship in peril (or a sunken ship) and the salvor, who is the person that actually carries out salvage operations.[36] The salvor enjoys the right to the reward of the flag state for his/her intervention. This general principle is applicable to all ships except warships. However, the 1989 Salvage Convention allows states parties to make reservations to limit its scope especially with the purpose of providing specific regulation for the preservation of underwater cultural objects. In particular, article 30(1)(d) of the Convention affirms, '[A]ny State may ... reserve the right not to apply the provisions of this Convention ... when the property involved is maritime cultural property of prehistoric, archaeological or historic interest and is situated on the sea-bed'.

Thus, international norms both concerning the cultural heritage and the law of the sea at the very least seem to recognize that cultural objects at sea deserve special forms of regulation due to their particular value.

III. Domestic Courts' Arguments: A Critical Analysis

Although international and domestic law provide for several legal grounds on the basis of which the claims of public and private persons may be recognized with respect to cultural objects at sea, one must observe that domestic courts have so far only made reference to some of these legal criteria.

As affirmed previously, the most frequently acknowledged ground that legitimizes claims relating to cultural objects at sea is the status of 'state of origin'.

As far as historic shipwrecks are concerned, domestic courts have so far recognized that this status may only be accorded to flag states. In fact, in the *Juno* and *La Galga* cases,[37] US courts did not acknowledge any relevance to the fact that some parts of the cargo of these vessels could originally belong to states other than flag states. These cases concerned the discovery of two Spanish sunken vessels, Juno and La Galga, in US territorial waters. In the *Juno* decision, the United States attempted to claim sovereign rights over these vessels since they were found in its 'territory'. However, the Virginia District Court affirmed that the flag state maintains sovereignty over sunken vessels, as long as it has expressed its intention to retain them. In the dispute relating to La Galga, the Fourth Circuit Court clarified that both the ship and its cargo belonged to the flag state unless it expressly

[36] Although salvage law was initially aimed at dealing with activities of assistance to vessels in peril, at the present, it also governs all the activities that somehow affect shipwrecks, including excavation. For the view that a ship is also in peril after its sinking due to the negative action of marine elements, see the decision of the US Fifth Circuit Court of Appeals, in the case involving the Atocha vessel. 569 F 2d. 330, 337(1978), *quoted in* O'Keefe, 'International Waters', in S. Dromgoole (ed.), *Legal Protection of the Underwater Cultural Heritage* (The Hague: Kluwer Law International, 1999) 223–35, at 227.

[37] Case *Virginia v Spain* 00–629 and Case *Sea Hunt Inc. v Spain* 00–652, respectively.

renounced its sovereign rights. Moreover, in the *Nuestra Señora de las Mercedes* case, the language of the Tampa District Court was even more precise on this matter. The court said that the separation of the ship and its cargo was not admissible since ships and their cargos were 'inextricably intertwined'.

Similarly, in the 2010 and 2012 *Lisippo bronze* rulings, Italian judges completely disregarded the fact that the cultural object in question was a product of Greek culture and that, thus, Greece may claim rights over it as the state of origin. By contrast, Italian judges accorded the status of 'state of origin' to Italy by reason of the nationality of the persons who had found this object.

According to this domestic case law, state sovereign rights seem to prevail over other interests. This conclusion has also been strengthened by the argument of US courts, which have recognized the immunity of foreign governmental vessels even when these vessels are historic shipwrecks, such as the Nuestra Señora de las Mercedes. As affirmed previously, the decision of the Tampa District Court relating to this case does not seem to be consistent with either international or domestic law, which both recognize the nature of a vessel as a warship on the basis of its current functions. The Nuestra Señora de las Mercedes, as any ancient sunken ship, no longer exercises any public functions on behalf of the current Kingdom of Spain. Moreover, although states can invoke the immunity of their sunken warships in some circumstances, such as, for example, when these ships contain information that is important for national security, the *Nuestra Señora de las Mercedes* case does not appear to envisage these special circumstances. In fact, any information that may be found in this vessel, which is more than 200 years old, will never endanger the security of the current Government of Spain.

Due to these unconvincing conclusions, the Tampa Court's ruling of the *Nuestra Señora de las Mercedes* case was appealed by Odyssey and other claimants before the Eleventh District Court of Appeals.[38] This case also attracted the attention of the main US political organs. While the US Department of Justice supported the Spanish argument relating to flag state immunity before the Court of Appeals,[39] some Members of the US Congress submitted an *amicus curiae* brief challenging the construction of the concept of immunity as provided by the Tampa District Court.[40] According to Congress's brief, the absolute immunity of state vessels does not correspond to the concept of immunity that is recognized

[38] *See* p. 138.

[39] The *Amicus Curiae* brief of the US Department of Justice was submitted to the Eleventh Circuit Court of Appeals in August 2010. Some Members of the Congress asked the Secretary of State to withdraw the Government's brief with a letter of 20 January 2011. The request was based on the fact that WikiLeaks had revealed some documents from which the US Government appeared to have supported Spain's claim in exchange for Spanish assistance in retrieving a painting belonging to some US citizens and housed in a Spanish museum. The answer of the Department of State of 16 March 2011 excluded any link between the two disputes and *quid pro quo* commitment between the United States and Spain.

[40] Brief *Amicus Curiae* of Members of Congress on the proper construction of the Sunken Military Craft Act in support of neither party. Submitted on 14 May 2010.

both under domestic and international law. Immunity should be only guaranteed with regard to governmental activities that are carried out by foreign state vessels. By contrast, when foreign governmental ships perform commercial activities in US territorial waters, these ships should be subject to US jurisdiction. In the view of the Members of Congress, the definition of immunity provided by the Tampa District Court resulted both in the disproportionate limitation of US sovereignty and the denial of the right of US citizens to defend their rights before domestic courts.

The Court of Appeals confirmed the conclusions of the Tampa court providing more specific reasoning. First, the Court of Appeals recognized that jurisdiction can only be excluded when no legal issue relating to a vessel falls into territorial jurisdiction.[41] As to the *Nuestra Señora de las Mercedes* case, no link seemed to exist between US territory and this vessel, since it was excavated in international waters. Second, the Court supported the view of the district judges according to which a vessel and its cargo cannot be considered separately when immunity is at issue. The ruling of the Eleventh Circuit Court was based both on US legislation that traditionally recognizes the same status of ships and their cargo and the principle of comity. With regard to this principle, the Court of Appeals affirmed that, although the exercise of US jurisdiction over some objects belonging to the cargo of the Nuestra Señora de las Mercedes might be admissible, the exercise of jurisdiction may cause injury to Spain.[42] Thus, the need to cooperate with a foreign country with which the US has friendly relationships compelled the Court of Appeals to recognize the immunity of any claim relating to the Nuestra Señora de las Mercedes.

Thus far, few domestic courts have adopted a different approach towards the recognition of state immunity of sunken historic objects. For example, immunity was denied very clearly by the Eleventh Circuit Court of Appeals in the *Aqua Log* case. This case concerned the excavation by a private company (Aqua Log) of submerged ancient logs that were located in the rivers of the State of Georgia. Georgia denied the jurisdiction of any courts on the basis of the recognition of the immunity of submerged cultural goods as state property. However, the Court of Appeals ruled that the sovereign state can only claim immunity from the courts in an admiralty case when the state is in the actual possession of the salvaged items.[43] If this reasoning relating to the possession requirement was generally applied to historic shipwrecks, immunity would be denied in all the cases where shipwrecks are found and possessed by persons other than the flag state. This

[41] US Court of Appeals, Eleventh District, *Odyssey Marine Exploration, Inc. v Kingdom of Spain*, Docket n. 10–10269, 21 September 2011, at 32, <http://www.ca11.uscourts.gov/opinions/ops/201010269.pdf> (last accessed 4 February 2013).

[42] *Odyssey Marine Exploration, Inc. v Kingdom of Spain*, Docket n. 10–10269, 21 September 2011, at 43–4.

[43] *Aqua Log, Inc. v State of Georgia*, 594 F.3d 1330 (11th Cir. 2010), <http://www.ca11.uscourts.gov/opinions/ops/200816225.pdf> (last accessed 4 February 2013).

argument was also embraced by the Historic Shipwreck Salvors Policy Council in the *amicus curiae* brief that was submitted to the Eleventh Circuit Court of Appeals in the *Nuestra Señora de las Mercedes* case.[44] The Court, rejecting this argument, affirmed that the immunity of Spain, as any foreign state, had only to be ascertained in accordance with the US Foreign State Immunity Act (US FSIA), which does not demand any possession requirement to invoke immunity.[45]

However, the most surprising aspect of the *Nuestra Señora de las Mercedes* case is the fact that no party associated state sovereignty with the concept of cultural origin of shipwrecks. By contrast, this particular concept could have constituted a valid argument for those who supported the priority of the rights of Spain. In fact, these parties could have asserted the exclusive right of the state of origin of the cultural object without mentioning the thorny concept of state immunity. On the other hand, the 'cultural' argument might have helped the applicant and other intervening parties to deny the immunity of sunken state vessels which, as any historic objects, do not perform governmental functions. Similarly, both the Tampa District Court and Eleventh Circuit Court of Appeals did not make any reference to the historic and cultural value of the Nuestra Señora de las Mercedes to resolve this case. In particular, the Court of Appeals patently disregarded the 'cultural' argument when it dealt with the issue of the interaction of the US FSIA and international law. In fact, although § 1609 of the FSIA states that the immunity from arrest of sovereign property is 'subject to existing international agreements with which the United States is a party at the time of enactment', the only international norm that the Court of Appeals mentioned in its ruling was article 9 of the 1958 Geneva Convention on the High Seas concerning the immunity of governmental vessels. Actually, this proviso was originally invoked by Odyssey to demonstrate that the Nuestra Señora de las Mercedes was a state vessel performing commercial activities and which, thus, did not enjoy sovereign immunity. Moreover, Odyssey stressed the point that, even if the Nuestra Señora de las Mercedes was considered as a state ship, it no longer carried out activities in the name of Spain since it had sunk some centuries ago. In this regard, the Court of Appeals might have supported the view that this vessel should not be treated as an ordinary ship due to its historic nature and value. By contrast, the Court affirmed that the governmental nature of the Nuestra Señora de las Mercedes was demonstrated both by the character of the activities that this vessel used to perform and, more importantly, by the fact that it was a warship which, as such, always enjoys immunity under domestic and international law.[46] One must

[44] Brief *Amicus Curiae* of the Historic Shipwreck Salvors Policy Council, the Institute of Marine Archaeological Conservation and Fathom Exploration LLC. Submitted in May 2010.

[45] US Court of Appeals, Eleventh District, *Odyssey Marine Exploration, Inc. v Kingdom of Spain*, Docket n. 10–10269, 21 September 2011, at 40–42, <http://www.ca11.uscourts.gov/opinions/ops/201010269.pdf> (last accessed 4 February 2013).

[46] *Odyssey Marine Exploration, Inc. v Kingdom of Spain*, Docket n. 10–10269, 21 September 2011, at 33–8.

admit that the use that the Court of Appeals made of international law in this case was limited, to say the least. In fact, although the USA is not a party to the 2001 UNESCO Convention on Underwater Cultural Heritage and, thus, US courts are not obliged to take into account this convention to interpret § 1609 of the FSIA as one of the 'existing international agreements with which the United States is a party at the time of enactment', the Court of Appeals' absolute lack of concern for the cultural value of historic shipwrecks does not appear to reflect the spirit of the FSIA itself. In particular, § 1609 seems to exhort domestic judges to take into account the interests that international law intends to safeguard other than sovereign rights. In the light of this interpretation of the FSIA, one may argue that, if the Court of Appeals had recognized the cultural value of the Nuestra Señora de las Mercedes as a historic object, it might also have identified a possible legal ground to assert its jurisdiction. In fact, under general international law, any state has the interest and duty of safeguarding cultural objects that have been found in the deep seabed.

Conversely, in the view of the Tampa District Court and Court of Appeals, when historic shipwrecks are at issue, the law of the sea is the only relevant international legal framework to ascertain state jurisdiction. Actually, the Eleventh Circuit Court of Appeals already showed this approach in its ruling of an ancillary dispute to the *Nuestra Señora de las Mercedes* case.[47] This dispute concerned the claim of Mr Bray, a British researcher of sunken vessels, who had provided professional aid to Odyssey in the search of the shipwreck of the Merchant Royal, an ancient Spanish vessel, in exchange for certain proceeds deriving from the discovery of this shipwreck. A few years later, Odyssey declared its intention to stop its search and Mr Bray received a cash sum as payment for his research file. However, in Mr Bray's view, Odyssey had continued the search of the Merchant Royal and discovered Nuestra Señora de las Mercedes thanks to his research file. Thus, he intervened in the dispute between Odyssey and Spain to obtain part of the earnings of the discovery. While the Tampa District Court dismissed Bray's intervening complaint for lack of subject-matter jurisdiction, the Eleventh District Court of Appeals, reversing this decision, recognized the federal admiralty jurisdiction with regard to this specific claim. In fact, the Court considered that the general matter of this dispute mainly related to admiralty law.

This approach was also adopted by the US Supreme Court. Odyssey requested an en banc hearing against the decision of the Eleventh Circuit Court of Appeals in the *Nuestra Señora de las Mercedes* case. The Supreme Court rejecting the

[47] US Court of Appeals, Eleventh District, *Odyssey Marine Exploration, Inc. (Keith Bray, Intervenor Plaintiff) v Spain*, Docket n. 10–14396, 31 March 2011. For a first comment to this decision, see Pacenti, 'Federal Appeals Court Ruling Allows English Researcher Claim to Sunken Treasure', 27 April 2011, <http://www.law.com/jsp/law/article.jsp?id=1202491736730&Federal_Appeals_Court_Ruling_Allows_English_Researcher_Claim_to_Sunken_Treasure> (last accessed 4 February 2013).

request denied any right of Odyssey and recognized the exclusive jurisdiction of Spain over this shipwreck.[48]

In sum, domestic courts have frequently considered the status of 'state of origin' as the preferential ground to determine the legitimate owners of historic shipwrecks, because this legal criterion is based on the traditional principle of state sovereignty. However, these courts did not pay attention to the fact that other sovereign states, such as the states of cultural origin of historic shipwrecks, also have rights over these cultural objects which are the expression of their traditions. In the view of domestic courts, state 'cultural rights' apparently deserve to be sacrificed in order to safeguard those sovereign rights that are based on the principles of nationality and territoriality.

As affirmed previously, private persons may also legitimately claim rights over cultural objects at sea. However, the domestic case law analysed in this chapter has shown scant concern for private rights. With the exception of the abovementioned *Titanic* case, where the Fourth Circuit Court of Appeals recognized the rights of the heirs of the original owners of the objects pertaining to the cargo of this shipwreck, no private claim has thus far been successful. This approach of domestic courts might discourage private persons from investing their money in the acquisition and preservation of cultural objects originating from other countries.

In short, when states show their interest in the objects belonging to the underwater cultural heritage, private claims are apparently destined to be set aside unless they have been recognized before states present their claims.

In addition, coastal states may claim some rights over cultural objects at sea. However, US courts have always supported the view that the interest of the state of origin of an object (in particular, when the object is a shipwreck) indisputably prevails over the coastal state's rights. The only exception to this view is provided by the unsuccessful attempt by the US to claim sovereign rights over historic objects that were found in its territorial sea in the *Juno* case.

As to the recognition of the right of coastal states, Italian judges appeared to be more audacious than their US colleagues. In particular, in the 2009 ruling relating to the *Lisippo bronze* case, Pesaro's preliminary investigation judge recognized that Italy, as the relevant coastal state, enjoyed exclusive rights over the statue, although it was controversial as to whether or not the statue had been found in Italian territorial waters. As affirmed earlier, this judge acknowledged Italy's sovereign rights on the basis of the nationality of the persons who discovered the statue and of the fact that the statue was transferred by the discoverers from the sea to Italian territory. It is not surprising that the Court of Cassazione did not consider this

[48] Supreme Court of the United States, *Odyssey Marine Exploration, Inc., Applicant v Kingdom of Spain, et al.*, Decision No. 11A745, 9 February 2012, <http://www.supremecourt.gov/Search.aspx?FileName=/docketfiles/11a745.htm> (last accessed 4 February 2013). For a comment relating to this decision, see Pancracio, 'Cas de la Nuestra Senora de las Mercedes-épisode 3', in *Droit de la mer et des littoraux* (26 février 2012), <http://blogs.univ-poitiers.fr/jp-pancracio/2012/02/26/cas-de-la-nuestra-senora-de-las-mercedes-episode-3/> (last accessed 4 February 2013).

argument sufficiently convincing and asked the judge of merits to examine whether other persons have more concrete rights over the statue.[49] However, in his 2012 order, the preliminary investigation judge reaffirmed the exclusive jurisdiction of Italy over the statue and related judicial proceedings.[50]

Unless the coastal state and the state of origin of the cultural object at sea coincide, the role of coastal states is quite limited under international law. Both UNCLOS[51] and the 2001 UNESCO Convention[52] recognize the power of coastal states to control the preservation of the underwater cultural heritage that happens to be located in the maritime areas where these states enjoy sovereign or exclusive rights. Sometimes, coastal states have been entitled to retain cultural objects found in their maritime areas only when no further claimants exist, such as in the case of the voluntary abandonment of these objects, as US courts declared in the *Juno* and *La Galga* cases.

Finally, one must sadly observe that domestic case law has never made reference to the interest of humankind as a whole in the preservation of underwater cultural heritage. This fact is not surprising if one considers that the 2001 UNESCO Convention, the international instrument that most firmly establishes this interest, only entered into force in January 2009 and has thus far been ratified by a small number of states.[53] However, one must recall that the interest of humankind *vis-à-vis* underwater cultural heritage is also recognized by article 149 of UNCLOS. This norm was invoked by Peru in its claim relating to the *Nuestra Señora de las Mercedes* case. Actually, Peru referred to article 149 because it is one of the few international norms that expressly mentions the rights of the 'country of origin, or the State of cultural origin, or the State of historic and archaeological origin' besides the interest of humankind. However, dismissing Peru's claim due to the lack of jurisdiction, the Tampa District Court affirmed that it did not have any obligation to apply article 149 of UNCLOS since this norm did not establish a principle of customary international law and the US was not yet party to the Convention.[54] Peru renewed its claim before the Court of Appeals without success.[55]

[49] *See* p. 134.

[50] Order of 3 May 2012, *see earlier* in this chapter.

[51] Article 303(2) of UNCLOS affirms, 'In order to control traffic in ... objects (of an archaeological and historical nature found at sea), the coastal State may ... presume that their removal from the seabed ... without its approval would result in an infringement within its territory or territorial sea of (its laws and regulations)'.

[52] Article 7(1) of the 2001 UNESCO Convention states, 'States Parties, in the exercise of their sovereignty, have the exclusive right to regulate and authorize activities directed at underwater cultural heritage in their internal waters, archipelagic waters and territorial sea'.

[53] For the current status of ratifications and acceptations of the UHC, see <http://portal.unesco.org/en/ev.php-URL_ID=13520&URL_DO=DO_TOPIC&URL_SECTION=201.html#ENTRY> (last accessed 22 August 2012).

[54] For the view that Peru's argument deserves to be further discussed before either a national or international court, see Alderman, 'High Seas Shipwreck Pits Treasure Hunters Against a Sovereign Nation: The *Black Swan* Case', in *Am. Society Int'l L. & Cultural Heritage & Arts Rev.* (Legal Studies Research Paper Series, Paper No. 1135, Spring 2010) 1–5, at 5.

[55] The Court of Appeals affirmed that the recognition of the immunity of the Nuestra Señora de las Mercedes, as a Spanish warship, prevented the Court from deciding substantive issues, such as

Actually, the obligation to manage historic objects found in the deep seabed for the benefit of humankind is a specific provision of the UNCLOS regime for the 'Area'. Although the rules and obligations of this regime are too detailed to be considered as reflecting customary international law, nevertheless, at the present time, one can at least assume that there exists general acceptance of the fact that the 'Area' cannot be freely available for appropriation by states, but rather it must be managed consistently with the principle of 'common heritage of mankind' as proclaimed by article 136 of UNCLOS. In short, even though article 149 of the Convention cannot be deemed as a norm of customary international law and, thus, generally applicable, this article has the merit of pointing out the diverse rights and interests of all public and private persons who are involved in the preservation of archaeological objects at sea.

While state organs, including courts, have so far been reluctant to recognize the interest of humankind in the preservation of underwater cultural heritage, private citizens seem to be eager in affirming such an interest. In fact, the acknowledgment of this general interest may ensure that the protection of underwater cultural heritage is carried out with the aim of safeguarding common needs, such as, for example, public access to this heritage, rather than the selfish interest of either private or public persons in the acquisition of cultural objects. As an example, one can mention the case concerning the 2002 agreement between the United Kingdom and Odyssey, the exploration company, relating to the search and excavation of the Sussex, a historic shipwreck.[56] The UK was severely criticized by scientific and non-governmental associations who believed that the agreement did not take into account existing domestic and international provisions relating to the preservation of the cultural heritage, but rather, it was mainly aimed at the exploitation of excavated objects for commercial purposes. Although the British government replied that the agreement intended to rescue historic objects and make them available for educational exhibitions, it was clear that the UK had not taken any inspiration from the 2001 UNESCO Convention to draft this agreement, as the scientific associations wished.[57] In particular, the agreement did not express any concern for the benefit of humanity, which, conversely, is the main

the effective appurtenance of the cargo of this ship. US Court of Appeals, Eleventh District, *Odyssey Marine Exploration, Inc. v Kingdom of Spain*, Docket n. 10–10269, 21 September 2011, at 42–3, <http://www.ca11.uscourts.gov/opinions/ops/201010269.pdf> (last accessed 4 February 2013).

[56] The UK was particularly interested in the Sussex's cargo which mainly consisted of gold and silver coins. For an overview of this case, see Dromgoole, 'Murky Waters for Governmental Policy: The Case of a 17th Century British Warship and 10 Tonnes of Gold Coins', in *Marine Policy* (2004) 189–98.

[57] First of all, no attention was paid to the preference of the UHC for *in situ* protection. Secondly, while commercial exploitation is totally banned by Rule 2 of the Annex to the UHC, the UK-Odyssey partnership agreement expressly established that the British government should have given part of the excavated objects to Odyssey as compensation. Last but not least, the agreement disregarded the fact that the interests of private or public persons other than the UK should have been respected.

objective of the UHC. This is even more important due to the fact that the Sussex was found in the seabed outside the external limit of Gibraltar's territorial sea, an area where UNCLOS itself stresses the importance of protecting the interest of humankind in addition to state sovereign rights.

International legal instruments, such as the UHC, the 1972 UNESCO Convention and, to a certain extent, the part of UNCLOS relating to the management of the 'Area', provide domestic courts with several provisions which highlight the existence of an obligation of safeguarding the interest of humankind in the preservation of cultural heritage. This interest appears to be one of the most important principles to have been recently recognized by international law and, thus, cannot be sacrificed to the safeguarding of the selfish needs of private or public persons.

Domestic courts have so far demonstrated that they may sometimes set aside the sovereign rights of their national state to protect the legitimate interests of other persons, such as foreign states or private persons, in the acquisition of objects pertaining to the underwater cultural heritage. At present, the rights of the state of origin, in particular, the flag state of historic shipwrecks, seem to be indisputably recognized. Similarly, the property rights of legitimate private claimants have been acknowledged even if the cultural objects at issue were not actually possessed by these private persons. The only lacuna arising from this (although superficial) examination of domestic case law seems to be the absolute silence relating to the cultural value of historic objects and, even more disappointing, to the interest of humankind in the preservation of these objects as the expression of the history and traditions of peoples.

IV. Some Unanswered Questions

The complexity of the protection of underwater cultural heritage and the recent adoption of specific international instruments dealing with this issue still leave some important questions unsettled. In addition, this uncertainty within the international legal system prevents domestic courts from enforcing international provisions in a more effective manner.

One of these unresolved questions concerns the fact that international law does not provide a uniform definition of underwater cultural heritage which easily permits the identification of the objects of cultural and historic value found at sea. As observed previously, while historic shipwrecks are considered to be cultural objects by the UHC, they are treated as ordinary vessels under the international law of the sea and, in particular, salvage law, as has been demonstrated by the *Nuestra Señora de las Mercedes*, *LaGalga*, and *Juno* cases. Similarly, domestic courts may reject the cultural value of objects found at sea unless they are well-known masterpieces, as occurred in 1970 in one of the earliest decisions concerning the *Lisippo bronze* case. In fact, the Italian Court of Cassazione argued that the cultural value of this statue was uncertain since its characteristics and, thus, its origin, could not be identified. Although this case is quite exceptional, since no image of the bronze was available at the time of the 1970 judgment, one must admit that a proper definition of cultural objects would be extremely useful. In particular, the concept of underwater cultural heritage is only defined by article 1(1) of the 2001 UNESCO Convention. Under this article, underwater cultural heritage includes 'all traces of human existence having a cultural, historical or archaeological character which have been partially or totally under water, periodically or continuously, for at least 100 years'. Although few states are at present bound by the UHC, the definition provided by the 2001 UNESCO Convention could be generally adopted by both international and domestic organs to deal with disputes relating to historic objects found at sea. In fact, the terms of this definition are quite general and thus acceptable, even for states that are not parties to the UHC. Moreover, this definition seems to be particularly effective since it takes into account cultural objects affecting the interest of both public and private persons and, most importantly, of humankind as a whole. Therefore, if the definition of underwater cultural heritage sanctioned by the UHC were generally recognized, domestic courts would be obliged to resolve the disputes affecting these diverse interests paying attention to all of them and not only to some, as has occurred in some recent state judicial decisions.

Secondly, domestic case law has so far shown some uncertainty concerning the recognition of private claims of cultural objects at sea, in particular when the private persons involved are not the original owners of these objects. This problem mainly affects the rights of the heirs of the original owners. This is especially true in cases relating to objects belonging to historic shipwrecks. In fact, domestic courts have so far recognized the preferential right of the flag state of the sunken vessel with respect to the interests of other public or private claimants. This approach seems to be unfair because it does not pay due regard to the desire of the heirs of the original owners to have some tangible memories of their ancestors. Thus, in order to avoid injuries to the interests of private persons, domestic courts should take into account the real significance of objects found at sea for the state of origin. For example, when the objects belonging to the cargo of sunken vessels did not have any artistic value at the time of sinking, but were just personal belongings of the passengers of these vessels, national courts should recognize the priority of the private rights of the heirs of the legitimate owners of these objects over the sovereign rights of the state of origin. However, when the objects found at sea are unique masterpieces or old, common items that at present consist only in the memories of the cultural traditions of a state, the supremacy of the public interest of the state of origin should be acknowledged over other claims relating to the same objects. Certainly, the priority of public interests should not completely set aside private rights. For example, although private persons may be considered as the legitimate owners of cultural objects, they might be obliged to make these objects accessible to the public by means of permanent or cyclical exhibitions.

This difficulty of distinguishing between private and public interests demonstrates that, when cultural objects are at issue, the traditional approach of international law, which is mainly based on the principle of state sovereignty, is not effective. By contrast, international instruments, such as the 1995 UNIDROIT Convention, which expressly deals with cases involving private property rights, appear to be most suitable to resolve disputes where private and public interests may collide. Unluckily, the convention may not be applied to resolve several cases that are currently at issue, such as, for example, the *Lisippo bronze* case, because the provisions of this convention are not retroactive.[58] When international norms and standards are not applicable, national courts may encounter problems affecting the conflict of the laws of different countries. National judges patently prefer to apply domestic norms rather than foreign law in particular when public interests are at issue.[59] Nevertheless, this may provoke the lack of uniformity of the decisions of diverse national courts concerning similar matters and, thus, encourage some practice of forum-shopping of private claimants in order to find the most favorable judge. Therefore, existing general principles of international law relating to the safeguard of cultural heritage should at least function as interpretative instruments in order to harmonize the decisions of different state courts concerning these peculiar types of properties.

Thirdly, a further unsettled question affecting cultural objects at sea and, in particular, historic shipwrecks, concerns whether or not the discoverers of cultural objects at sea have any rights under international and domestic law. Under admiralty law, which is traditionally applied by domestic courts in these cases, the rights of discoverers over these objects only arise when the intention of the state of nationality (or flag state) of abandoning the objects themselves has been expressly declared. This argument is certainly aimed at safeguarding state sovereign rights. However, in most cases, state courts have also denied the right to reward of the discoverers, which is by contrast recognized by salvage law as a form of compensation for the rescue expenses that salvors incurred. It is clear that domestic courts have adopted this approach because discoverers are usually treasure-hunting speculators that carry out the excavation of shipwrecks and cultural objects at sea for commercial purposes.[60] The lucrative interest of treasure-hunting companies is certainly not consistent with either state sovereign rights or the purpose of

[58] For the view that both the 1970 UNESCO and 1995 UNIDROIT Conventions are not applicable to the *Lisippo bronze* case, see Lanciotti, *The Dilemma of the Right to Ownership*, at 318.

[59] As an example, one can mention the case in which German judges rejected the request of Italian police of examining the German citizen that was charged for the illicit export of the Lisippo bronze due to the discrepancy between German and Italian criminal law. *See* p. 127.

[60] The concern for the approach that domestic courts adopted in these cases has been shown by some marine associations in the *amicus curiae* brief that they submitted before the Court of Appeals in the *Nuestra Señora de las Mercedes* case, Brief *Amicus Curiae* of the Historic Shipwreck Salvors Policy Council, the Institute of Marine Archaeological Conservation and Fathom Exploration LLC, *see* p. 137.

preserving underwater cultural heritage as the expression of human traditions. For this reason, following the recent decision of the US Supreme Court in the *Nuestra Señora de las Mercedes* case, Odyssey was immediately compelled to hand over the shipwreck and its cargo to Spain.[61] However, one cannot ignore the fact that, although many states are aware of the presence of their sunken vessels or cultural objects on the seabed, they intentionally avoid rescuing them because of the high costs of excavation activities. So far, the states of origin of cultural objects have claimed sovereign rights over them only when excavation activities had already been completed. This belated interest of the states of origin in the restitution of their cultural objects found at sea hardly seems to be inspired by good faith; rather, it appears as an attempt on the part of states to obtain these objects without paying the very high costs of rescue. Thus, in order to provide a satisfactory solution for all public and private persons involved in the excavation of cultural objects at sea, domestic courts should firstly ask treasure-hunting speculators to be more transparent in the planning and performance of excavation activities. On the other hand, states of origin could both demonstrate their good faith and strengthen their legal position by means of a prior public statement of their intention of claiming any object belonging to their cultural heritage that is found at sea in the past, present, and future. However, when the activities of treasure-hunting speculators have been undoubtedly carried out in good faith, national courts should recognize some form of compensation for the expenses relating to such activities. Even if these proposed solutions are not sanctioned by any norm of customary international law, they can be inferred from the provisions and general principles of the 1995 UNIDROIT Convention which attempts to safeguard the interests both of the legitimate owners and persons who act lawfully with the purpose of rescuing and conserving cultural objects.[62]

Finally, the distinctiveness of underwater cultural heritage and the regime established by the UHC clearly make the task of domestic courts to safeguard the interest of humankind in the preservation of cultural objects at sea difficult. So far, state courts have attempted to reach this objective by enforcing the norms of the law of the sea and admiralty law. Notwithstanding this, these norms appear to be inappropriate to deal with this matter because of their overly general content and simplistic approach.[63] The greatest difficulty affecting the application of these

[61] For the follow-up of the *Nuestra Señora de las Mercedes* case, see Pancracio, 'Cas de la Nuestra Senora de las Mercedes-épisode 4', in *Droit de la mer et des littoraux* (28 février 2012), <http://blogs.univ-poitiers.fr/jp-pancracio/2012/02/28/cas-de-la-nuestra-senora-de-las-mercedes-episode-4/> (last accessed 4 February 2013).

[62] *See* 1995 UNIDROIT Convention arts. 4, 6. For the view that the provisions of the 1995 UNIDROIT Convention may be enforced to balance private and public interests, see Francioni, 'The Role of International Law in the Protection of Cultural Heritage', in G. Camarda-T. Scovazzi (eds), *The Protection of the Underwater Cultural Heritage* (2002) 6, and UNIDROIT Secretariat, 'UNIDROIT Convention on Stolen or Illegally Exported Cultural Objects: Explanatory Report', in *Uniform L. Rev.* (2001) 476–564, at 504.

[63] For the view that salvage law is not appropriate to deal with issues concerning the underwater cultural heritage, see Scovazzi, 'The Application of Salvage Law and Other Rules of Admiralty

provisions to the protection of the interest of humankind in underwater cultural heritage consists in the fact that they are mainly based on the principle of state sovereignty and bilateral relationships, such as the recognition of the economic private rights of the operators who contributed to safeguarding cultural objects belonging to states. Conversely, the UHC provides for a global regime which, in order to prevent any form of appropriation of the underwater cultural heritage, gives preference to *in situ* protection in the interest of humankind as a whole.[64] This type of protection requires states and private persons to undertake very complex and costly activities, such as research, management plans, and monitoring of historic objects at sea, in order to avoid the negative impact of natural agents[65] and, more perilously, the pillage by treasure-hunters of these objects.

Notwithstanding the holistic purpose of the UHC, penniless governments cannot easily ensure this type of protection. Thus, the choice of *in situ* protection might result in the underwater cultural heritage, in particular shipwrecks, not only remaining undisturbed at sea, but also remaining defenseless. To a certain extent, the excavation of shipwrecks might guarantee the preservation of cultural objects at sea in a more direct manner than *in situ* protection. In fact, excavated objects may be treated by professional hands and preserved forever. However, as already affirmed, excavation activities are most frequently carried out by private investors and operators for lucrative purposes which relegate rescued objects to private collections and, thus, make them inaccessible to the public. In order to safeguard both the interest of humankind in gaining access to underwater cultural heritage, and the rights of private persons who invested their money and work for the salvage of cultural objects at sea, domestic courts should stress the cooperation between states and private operators. For example, while public access to underwater cultural heritage should be acknowledged in absolute terms, some reward might be granted for private investors and operators who supported states in the rescue of their cultural objects at sea. Cooperation is provided for in the UHC between all persons involved in the management of underwater cultural heritage.[66] Although this convention has so far achieved limited participation of states and, thus, cannot be considered to be universally applicable, domestic courts

to the Underwater Cultural Heritage: Some Relevant Cases', in R. Garabello-T. Scovazzi (eds), *The Protection of the Underwater Cultural Heritage—Before and After the 2001 UNESCO Convention* (Leiden: Nijhoff, 2003), 19–78, at 30–2.

64 *See* Rule 25 of the Annex to the UHC.

65 This issue has been highlighted by Dromgoole, 'Murky Waters for Governmental Policy…', at 193. The concern for the deterioration of cultural heritage due to natural agents is also expressed in the Preamble of the European Convention on the Protection of the Archaeological Heritage (Revised). Done at La Valetta, 16 Jan. 1992, <http://conventions.coe.int/Treaty/en/Treaties/Html/143.htm>, (last accessed 4 February 2013), which revised the European Convention on the Protection of the Archaeological Heritage, done in London on 6 May 1969, <http://conventions.coe.int/Treaty/en/Treaties/Html/066.htm> (last accessed 4 February 2013).

66 Rule 8 of the UHC states: 'International cooperation in the conduct of activities directed at underwater cultural heritage shall be encouraged in order to further the effective exchange or use of archaeologists and other relevant professionals'.

may nevertheless use the norms and general principles of the 2001 UNESCO Convention as interpretative criteria for the enforcement of national legislation and international provisions, such as the law of the sea and admiralty law, in order to safeguard the interest of humankind in the preservation of underwater cultural heritage. In fact, no one can deny the legitimacy and importance of this interest at the global level.

In short, although international law has increasingly provided new instruments for the protection and conservation of underwater cultural heritage, such as the 2001 UNESCO Convention, the role of domestic courts is still essential for coordinating the various norms, whether domestic or international, that are applicable in the disputes affecting these particular goods.[67] The recognition of general interests could become meaningless if states do not provide effective means to safeguard these interests both within domestic and international legal regimes.

[67] For the view that cooperation between the political, administrative, and judicial organs of different states is necessary to resolve the problems affecting the transfer of cultural objects, see Lanciotti, *The Dilemma of the Right to Ownership*, at 325. A cooperative resolution of the *Lisippo bronze* case has been attempted through the 2006 Italy–US Treaty on Mutual Assistance in Criminal Matters. The treaty also establishes the duty of either party to enforce the seizure's orders relating to imported cultural objects provided that seizure is consistent with its domestic law.

8

Enforcement by Domestic Courts

Criminal Law and Forfeiture in the Recovery of Cultural Objects

Patty Gerstenblith *

I. Introduction

Illegal conduct involving cultural objects encompasses traditional theft of objects from public and private collections, the looting of archaeological and ethnographic objects from sites and cultural communities, and smuggling across borders (illegal export and import). It is widely recognized that much of this illegal conduct is carried out for the purpose of supplying the international art market with objects for sale. The art market itself has been booming in recent years, and so, even while methods of detecting stolen artworks and law enforcement efforts have grown in number and sophistication, the financial incentive to supply the market has also increased. While any of these types of illegal conduct are to be deplored, the activity that imposes the greatest cost on society is the looting of archaeological sites. When a site is looted, not only is the object itself lost, but the context of that object is forever lost as well. This means that our ability to reconstruct and understand the past is irreparably harmed and our knowledge about ourselves is diminished.[1]

Simon Mackenzie summarized the relationship between looting of archaeological sites, the losses to the historical and cultural record, and the need for the

* Distinguished Research Professor, DePaul University College of Law, and Chair, US Cultural Property Advisory Committee. The views expressed in this chapter are those of the author and not necessarily the views of the Department of State or the United States government.

[1] For more detailed discussion of the value of controlled exploration of archaeological sites and of the preservation of original contexts, see Gerstenblith, 'The Public Interest in the Restitution of Cultural Objects', 16 *Conn. J. Int'l L.* (2001) 197–246, at 198–201, and Gerstenblith, 'Controlling the International Market in Antiquities: Reducing the Harm, Preserving the Past', 8 *Chi. J. Int'l L.* (2007) 169–95, at 170–74 (hereinafter Gerstenblith, 'Controlling the International Market in Antiquities').

law to impose detrimental consequences on those who directly or indirectly provide incentives for the looting of sites:

> [W]e can define looted antiquities as those taken illicitly from the ground, or from their place as an integral part of, or attachment to, a temple or other ancient structure. This looting happens routinely throughout the world. Looters, while digging, often destroy objects that they perceive to be of lesser value than the gold, silver and jewels that they prize. More serious, perhaps, is their destruction of stratified context. This refers to the placement of artifacts in a tomb, or the particular layer of the earth in which they are found: information valuable to a trained excavator that can add greatly to our knowledge about the human past. Archaeology is dedicated to the collection of such knowledge and its publication.
>
> A further detrimental effect of looting is in the loss to a country of its cultural assets as they travel to overseas markets. However, this loss is theoretically remediable if looted and smuggled objects are traced and returned to their country of origin.... The market structure of the global movement of antiquities leads us to see the reduction of demand for the purchase of looted antiquities as a productive avenue to the reduction of looting itself.
>
> ... [T]he United Kingdom is home to one of the world's largest market centres, in terms of volume of trade, for the sale of antiquities. Antiquities looted from source countries routinely travel here to be sold by international dealers and auction houses to other dealers, private collectors and museums. The other main international centre for the purchase of high-end antiquities is New York.[2]

As the purpose of the law is to deter conduct that harms society, it is necessary for the law to impose negative consequences on traders and purchasers of looted antiquities in the market nations in order to decrease demand for antiquities. As demand decreases, the incentive to supply the market will diminish, thereby reducing the economic motivation for looting and helping to preserve archaeological sites. While those who loot sites are the primary actors and their conduct is generally criminalized in the nations where the sites are located, it is incumbent on market nations—the destinations for the looted objects—to deter the end-market in such objects. As Mackenzie points out, London and New York are the two largest destination markets for antiquities in the world; this chapter will therefore focus on the legal structure that has developed in the United States and, to a lesser extent, in the United Kingdom, to deter the market in archaeological objects that have been illegally obtained in the attempt to evaluate which elements in this structure are the most efficacious in diminishing these incentives.

[2] Mackenzie, 'Dig a Bit Deeper: Law, Regulation and the Illicit Antiquities Market', 45 *Brit. J. Criminol.* (2005) 249–68, at 251–2.

II. Types of Illegal Conduct in the Movement of Antiquities

It is necessary to consider first the types of illegal and other undesirable conduct in which archaeological artefacts may be involved. Three terms are often used interchangeably in reference to antiquities: looted, undocumented, and illegal. These terms are not synonymous, although the categories may overlap. Before examining the different legal actions that may be involved in the recovery of an object, it is necessary first to clarify what these terms mean and how they should be used.

A looted antiquity is one recovered from the ground in an unscientific manner. The antiquity is decontextualized and what it can tell us about the past is limited to the information intrinsic within the object itself, rather than what might have been learned from the object's full associated context. Looting also jeopardizes the object's physical integrity because the process of looting often destroys or damages fragile objects and those not desired by the market.

An illegal antiquity is one whose history or handling involves some violation of law. The antiquity may be characterized as stolen property if it is removed from its country of modern discovery in violation of a national law vesting title to antiquities in the nation.[3] An illegal antiquity may also be contraband if it has been imported in violation of an import restriction or was not properly declared upon entry.

An undocumented antiquity is one that has poor or only recent evidence of its ownership history (provenance) and how it was obtained. The term is also often used more specifically in voluntary codes of museums and professional associations to indicate an antiquity whose existence out of the country of discovery is not documented before 1970 (the date of adoption of the 1970 UNESCO Convention on the Means of Prohibiting and Preventing the Illicit Import, Export and Transfer of Ownership of Cultural Property) or which was not legally obtained and exported from its country of discovery after 1970.[4]

[3] *See, eg, United States v Schultz*, 333 F.3d 393 (2d Cir. 2003); *Gov't of the Islamic Republic of Iran v The Barakat Galleries Ltd.*, [2007] E.W.C.A. Civ. 1374; [2007] 1 All E.R. 1177. The 1995 Unidroit Convention on Stolen or Illegally Exported Cultural Objects equates illegal excavation or illegal retention of an archaeological object with theft in Article 3(2), *see* later note 27 and accompanying text.

[4] *See, eg*, Archaeological Institute of America Code of Ethics (adopted 29 December 1990, amended December 1997), *available at* <http://archaeological.org/news/advocacy/130> (last accessed 4 February 2013); American Alliance of Museums' Standards Regarding Archaeological Material and Ancient Art, approved July 2008, *available at* <http://aam-us.org/museumresources/ethics/upload/Standards%20Regarding%20Archaeological%20Material%20and%20Ancient%20Art.pdf> (last accessed 4 February 2013); Association of Art Museum Directors' Report of the AAMD Task Force on the Acquisition of Archaeological Materials and Ancient Art (revised 2008), *available at* <http://aamd.org/newsroom/documents/2008ReportAndRelease.pdf> (last accessed 4 February 2013).

Objects often fit into all three of these categories, but an object can also, for example, be looted but documented (if the object was recovered unscientifically, but its ownership history is known for a sufficiently long period of time) or legal (depending on the laws of the country of discovery and those of the country where the antiquity is currently located).[5] A documented history back to 1970 is often used as a proxy to indicate legality, although it does not guarantee legality, or to indicate that any initial looting happened long enough ago that its acquisition will not provide further financial incentive to the contemporary looting of sites.

There are two basic types of illegal conduct that will render an antiquity 'illegal'; theft and smuggling. While other types of cultural objects may be subject to these same broad categories of illegal conduct, particular legal doctrines have been crafted, both statutorily and judicially, that apply to antiquities because the looting of antiquities raises particular societal concerns.

A. Theft

Theft occurs when a rightful owner is deprived of possession of property[6] without permission. Theft, in the traditional sense, occurs when an object is located in either a private collection or a public one (such as a museum, library, archive, or religious institution) and is stolen. Such theft does not, however, form the primary subject of this chapter because relevant law already exists that applies to all types of personal movable property, including cultural objects, and there is no particular reason to distinguish such thefts based on the type of property at issue.[7]

The law, however, has developed particular doctrines to deal with the theft of archaeological objects that have been looted directly from a site and had not been reduced to actual possession in modern times. Beginning in the mid-19th century, many nations that are rich in archaeological resources and ancient monuments enacted national ownership laws that vest ownership of such objects

[5] For example, an object that was stolen in one country may be transferred to a good faith purchaser in a country that recognizes the 'good faith purchaser' doctrine by which such a purchaser may acquire valid title, even though there is a theft in the chain of title. *See, eg, Autocephalous Greek-Orthodox Church of Cyprus & the Republic of Cyprus v Goldberg & Feldman Fine Arts, Inc.*, 927 F.2d 278 (7th Cir. 1990) (discussing but rejecting applicability of the Swiss good faith purchaser doctrine); *Bakalar v Vavra*, 619 F.3d 136 (2d Cir. 2010) (same); *Greek Orthodox Patriarchate v Christies, Inc.*, 1999 U.S. Dist. LEXIS 13257 (S.D.N.Y. 1999) (barring claim of original owner of Archimedes palimpsest); *Winkworth v Christie, Manson & Woods Ltd.*, [1980] 1 Ch. 496, [1980] 1 All E.R. 1121 (applying Italian law of good faith purchase to bar the claim of the original owner to recover artworks stolen in England but sold in Italy).

[6] For purposes of this chapter, 'property' here refers to movable personal property or chattels.

[7] Much of the litigation concerning recovery of artworks stolen from an identifiable collection concerns the question of whether the statute of limitations or the equitable defense of laches bars the original owner's claim. Recent cases focus on the alleged theft and attempted recovery of artworks looted during the Holocaust. *See, eg, Vineberg v Bissonnette*, 548 F.3d 50 (1st Cir. 2008); *Bakalar v Vavra*, 819 F. Supp. 2d 298 (S.D.N.Y. 2011), *aff'd*, 2012 U.S. App. LEXIS 21042 (2d Cir. 2012); *In re Peters*, 821 N.Y.S.2d 61 (App. Div. 2006).

in the nation. Reducing the economic value of looted antiquities by making them unsaleable, these laws have the purpose of deterring the initial theft. These laws serve the dual purposes of preventing unfettered export of antiquities[8] and of protecting archaeological sites in which antiquities are buried. As the knowledge that could be recovered through controlled, scientific excavation of sites increased throughout the 19th and 20th centuries, the role of national ownership laws in protecting the contextual integrity of archaeological sites eclipsed their role in preventing removal of ancient artefacts from a particular country.

When ownership of an antiquity is vested in a nation, one who removes the antiquity without permission is a thief and the antiquities are stolen property. This enables both punishment of the looter and recovery of possession of the antiquity from either the looter or a subsequent purchaser. Vesting laws thus create ownership rights that are recognized even when such antiquities are removed from their country of discovery and are traded in foreign nations. National ownership laws[9] were typically enacted as part of a larger legal regime that aimed to protect sites, limit permitted excavation to those with certain qualifications, and provide for the disposition of artefacts recovered through excavation. Some of the earliest such laws were passed in Greece,[10] Egypt,[11] and Turkey.[12]

Laws protecting the archaeological heritage are not limited to the nations typically viewed as rich in archaeological resources, such as those around the Mediterranean rim or in the Middle East. In nations that follow the common law

[8] Earlier laws prevented the removal and export of antiquities, but these did not take the form of a national ownership law. Perhaps the earliest of these attempts to protect the integrity of ancient monuments was a statute issued by Pope Pius II in 1462. *See* Alain Schnapp, *The Discovery of the Past* (Harry N. Abrams, Inc.: New York, 1996) at 339–40.

[9] For more extensive discussion of national ownership laws applied to archaeological objects, see Gerstenblith, '*Schultz* and *Barakat*: Universal Recognition of National Ownership of Antiquities', 14:1 *Art Antiquity & L.* (2009) 29–57.

[10] Greece enacted its first laws protecting its archaeological heritage in 1834, but national ownership was embodied in its Law 5351/32 'On Antiquities' of 1932. Brodie, 'Historical and Social Perspectives on the Regulation of the International Trade in Archaeological Objects: The Examples of Greece and India', 38 *Vand. J. Transnat'l L.* (2005) 1051–66, at 1057.

[11] Egypt has enacted a series of laws protecting its cultural heritage, beginning with an ordinance of 1835, Ordonnance du 15 août 1835 portant mesures de protection des antiquités. Siehr, 'The Beautiful One Has Come—to Return: The Return of the Bust of Nefertiti from Berlin to Cairo', in John Henry Merryman (ed.), *Imperialism, Art and Restitution* (Cambridge: Cambridge University Press, 2006) 114–34, at 117 n.14. Its earliest vesting law seems to date to 1883. *See* Urice, 'The Beautiful One Has Come—to Stay', in Merryman (ed.), *Imperialism, Art and Restitution* (2006) 135–92, at 141–2.

[12] The Ottoman Empire passed a type of national ownership law in 1874, which vested title to newly discovered antiquities in the nation but also recognized that rights were to be divided among the government, the finder and the landowner. *See* Osman, 'Occupiers' Title to Cultural Property: Nineteenth-Century Removal of Egyptian Artifacts', 37 *Colum. J. Transnat'l L.* (1999) 969–1002, at 990. The 1884 Ottoman law established national ownership of all artefacts excavated in the Ottoman Empire and protected archaeological sites by requiring excavation permits. Kersel, 'The Trade in Palestinian Antiquities', 33 *Jerusalem Q.* (2008) 21–38, at 24. Turkey has vested ownership of antiquities in the nation at least from the time of a 1906 decree. *Republic of Turkey v OKS Partners*, 1994 U.S. Dist. LEXIS 17032, at *3 (D. Mass. 1994).

of property, including Britain and the United States, the law of finds governs the disposition of embedded or lost articles.[13] However, the United States enacted a limited national ownership law, the Antiquities Act, in 1906.[14] The Archaeological Resources Protection Act (ARPA), enacted in 1979, vests ownership of archaeological resources found on federal and tribal lands,[15] with exceptions now provided in the Native American Graves Protection and Repatriation Act,[16] in the national government and requires that anyone who wishes to excavate or remove archaeological resources first obtain a permit. ARPA also prohibits the trafficking in interstate and foreign commerce of any archaeological resource taken or held

[13] Izuel, 'Property Owners' Constructive Possession of Treasure Trove: Rethinking the Finders Keepers Rule', 38 *UCLA L. Rev.* (1991) 1659–702, at 1670–73; Gerstenblith, 'Identity and Cultural Property: The Status of Cultural Property in the United States', 75 *Boston U. L. Rev.* (1995) 559–688. Archaeological objects are typically characterized as embedded property and therefore belong to the landowner. *See, eg, Allred v Biegel*, 240 Mo. App. 818 (Ct. App. 1949) (holding that a Native American canoe embedded in the soil belonged to the landowner, rather than to the finder). However, England, Wales, and Northern Ireland recognize that treasure trove belongs to the Crown and, in the interest of maintaining national ownership of historic and archaeological artefacts, have gradually expanded its definition. The Treasure Act of 1996 changed the common law definition of 'treasure trove' to include any object which is at least 300 years old with a precious metal content of at least 10 per cent; coins at least 300 years old with a gold or silver content of at least 10 per cent by weight (if there are ten or more coins, then the metallic content is ignored), and any object found in geographic and temporal proximity to an object in the first two categories. Carleton, 'Protecting the National Heritage: Implications of the British Treasure Act 1996', 6 *Int'l J. Cultural Prop.* (1997) 343–52. Prehistoric base-metal assemblages found after January 2003 also qualify as treasure. *See* 'Summary of the Treasure Act', *available at* <http://finds.org.uk/treasure/advice/summary> (last accessed 4 February 2013). Gaps in the use of treasure trove to protect cultural heritage were again revealed with the discovery of the Crosby Garrett helmet, a Roman cavalry helmet in remarkably good condition, found by a metal detectorist in 2010. Because it was composed primarily of copper, the helmet did not qualify as treasure, and the landowner and finder were deemed the owner. The helmet was auctioned at Christie's for US$3.6 million. 'Crosby Garrett Helmet Found in Britain Sells for £2.3m', *The Telegraph*, 7 Oct. 2010, *available at* <http://www.telegraph.co.uk/news/8048670/Crosby-Garrett-Helmet-found-in-Britain-sells-for-2.3m.html> (last accessed 4 February 2013).

[14] 16 U.S.C. §§ 431–433. The Antiquities Act authorizes the President to set aside as national monuments 'historic landmarks, historic and prehistoric structures, and other objects of historic or scientific interest' located on lands owned or controlled by the federal government, including Indian tribal lands, forest reserves, and military reservations. The Act also penalizes the destruction, damage, excavation, appropriation, or injury of any historic or prehistoric ruin, monument, or object of antiquity. This latter part of the Act was declared unconstitutional in *United States v Diaz*, 499 F.2d 113 (9th Cir. 1974), because the term 'object of antiquity' was considered to be unconstitutionally vague, and has been largely superseded by the Archaeological Resources Protection Act.

[15] Because of the federal system in the United States, which limits the authority of the federal government, the Antiquities Act and the Archaeological Resources Protection Act generally apply only to federal and tribal lands. 16 U.S.C. §§ 470aa-hh. Each state has enacted an ARPA-equivalent statute pertaining to state-owned land and approximately half of the states now regulate Native American burials found on private land as well. *See* Gerstenblith, 'Protection of Cultural Heritage Found on Private Lands: The Paradigm of the Miami Circle and Regulatory Takings Doctrine after *Lucas*', 13 *St. Thomas L. Rev.* (2000) 65–111, at 101–103. Archaeological sites and historic structures are also protected through the National Historic Preservation Act, 16 U.S.C. §§ 470–470w.

[16] 25 U.S.C. § 3002 (vesting ownership of human remains and cultural items found on federal or tribal lands after 1990 in the lineal descendant or, when there is no identified lineal descendant, in an Indian tribe or Native Hawaiian organization).

in violation of federal, state, or local law, regardless of whether it was found on federal lands.[17]

A series of judicial decisions in the United States, beginning with the federal criminal prosecutions in *United States v McClain*,[18] established that archaeological objects removed in violation of a nation's vesting statute retain their characterization as stolen property, even after they are brought to the United States. This triggers the availability of various legal actions, including civil replevin, forfeiture, and criminal prosecution, depending on the relevant factual circumstances. The most recently litigated case is the prosecution and conviction of the New York dealer, Frederick Schultz, who conspired, in violation of the National Stolen Property Act,[19] to deal in antiquities looted in Egypt.[20] This doctrine is now accepted in the circuits that most often confront market issues related to antiquities, including the Second, Ninth, Fifth, and Eleventh Circuits.[21]

The principle of national ownership of antiquities was adopted more recently in British courts with the decision in *Islamic Republic of Iran v Barakat Galleries Ltd.*, decided in 2007.[22] This case involved a civil replevin action undertaken by Iran to recover antiquities allegedly looted from the Jiroft region of south-western Iran. The decision recognized Iran's law as vesting ownership of undiscovered antiquities in the nation and as a basis for suit. This decision could also be used in the future as the basis for possible criminal prosecution.

In late 2003, the United Kingdom enacted new criminal legislation, the Dealing in Cultural Objects (Offences) Act 2003, which created a new offense for dealing in 'tainted cultural objects'.[23] One commits this offense if he or she 'dishonestly deals in a cultural object that is tainted, knowing or believing that the object is tainted'.[24] The statute defines a 'tainted object' under the following circumstances: '(2) A cultural object is tainted if, after the commencement of this

[17] 16 U.S.C. § 470ee(c); *see United States v Gerber*, 999 F.2d 1112 (7th Cir. 1993) (holding that ARPA applies to archaeological resources removed from private land without the owner's permission and taken across state lines).

[18] 545 F.2d 988 (5th Cir. 1977); 593 F.2d 658 (5th Cir. 1979).

[19] 18 U.S.C. § 2315 ('Whoever receives, possesses, conceals, stores, barters, sells, or disposes of any goods ... of the value of $5,000 or more ... which have crossed a State or United States boundary after being stolen, unlawfully converted, or taken, knowing the same to have been stolen, unlawfully converted, or taken ... shall be fined under this title or imprisoned not more than ten years, or both').

[20] 333 F.3d 393 (2d Cir. 2003).

[21] Gerstenblith, *see earlier* note 9, at 34–6. Several district courts have also recognized the efficacy of foreign national ownership laws and these laws have served as the basis for settlement of foreign national claims.

[22] *Gov't of the Islamic Republic of Iran v The Barakat Galleries Ltd.*, [2007] E.W.C.A. Civ. 1374; [2007] 1 All E.R. 1177.

[23] Dealing in Cultural Objects (Offences) Act 2003, ch. 27. This statute was enacted following the United Kingdom's ratification of the 1970 UNESCO Convention on the Means of Prohibiting and Preventing the Illicit Import, Export and Transfer of Ownership of Cultural Property. The new criminal offence was not viewed as a direct means of implementing the 1970 UNESCO Convention.

[24] Dealing in Cultural Objects (Offences) Act 2003, ch. 27, § 1(1).

Act—(a) a person removes the object in a case falling within subsection (4) or he excavates the object, and (b) the removal or excavation constitutes an offence'.[25] Subsection 4 refers to objects removed from 'a building or structure of historical, architectural or archaeological interest', or from an excavation. For purposes of the statute, it does not matter whether the excavation or removal takes place in the United Kingdom or in another country or whether the law violated is a domestic or foreign law.[26]

The 1995 Unidroit Convention on Stolen or Illegally Exported Cultural Objects effectively adopts a similar approach. Article 3(2) states: '… a cultural object which has been unlawfully excavated or lawfully excavated but unlawfully retained shall be considered stolen, when consistent with the law of the State where the excavation took place'.[27] However, the Unidroit Convention is a part of private (rather than public) international law and thus seems primarily concerned with creating a mechanism for restitution of such objects, rather than the basis for a criminal prosecution.

B. Smuggling

Customs laws of most nations require the declaration of country of origin and value of objects to be imported. While in the more typical case of importation of commercial goods, the primary purpose of these declaration requirements is to determine customs duties,[28] these requirements also assist in the regulation of importation of goods when these may be subject to some other form of import restriction or simply to maintain the integrity of the import process.[29] More specifically, the Customs statute of the United States prohibits the importation of goods that have been 'stolen, smuggled, or clandestinely imported' if they have been 'imported into the United States contrary to law'.[30] More general import

[25] Dealing in Cultural Objects (Offences) Act 2003, ch. 27, § 2(2).

[26] Dealing in Cultural Objects (Offences) Act 2003, ch. 27, § 2(3). These provisions seem based on Article 3(2) of the 1995 UNIDROIT Convention on Stolen or Illegally Exported Cultural Objects, which states that a cultural object which has been unlawfully excavated or lawfully excavated but unlawfully retained shall be considered stolen.

[27] The text of the convention is available at: <http://www.unidroit.org/english/conventions/1995culturalproperty/main.htm> (last accessed 4 February 2013). For analysis of the convention's provisions, *see* Lyndel V Prott, *Commentary On The Unidroit Convention* (Institute of Art and Law: Leicester, 1997).

[28] But see the Payne-Aldrich Tariff Act of 1909, ch. 6, 36 Stat. 11, 81–2, which exempts from the payment of customs duty all works of art imported into the United States that are more than one hundred years old. Therefore, antiquities are generally exempted.

[29] *See, eg, United States v An Antique Platter of Gold, known as a Gold Phiale Mesomphalos c. 400 B.C.*, 184 F.3d 131 (2d Cir. 1999) (affirming forfeiture of an ancient *phiale,* whose value and country of origin were misdeclared, in order to preserve the integrity of the importation process).

[30] 19 U.S.C. § 1595a(c)(1)(A). In the case of stolen objects, the National Stolen Property Act can be the underlying law in the 'contrary to law' provision. Since enactment of the Civil Asset Forfeiture Reform Act in 2000, stolen property can also be forfeited directly under the NSPA, 18 U.S.C. § 981(a)(1)(C). Export of goods contrary to law is now prohibited under both 18 U.S.C. § 554 and 19 U.S.C. § 1595a(d).

bans may be imposed under the International Emergency Economic Powers Act.[31] The general Customs provisions provide for either criminal prosecution[32] or civil forfeiture,[33] depending upon the circumstances.

Importation of certain categories of cultural objects into the United States is restricted under the Convention on Cultural Property Implementation Act (CPIA),[34] the United States legislation that implements the 1970 UNESCO Convention on the Means of Prohibiting and Preventing the Illicit Import, Export and Transfer of Ownership of Cultural Property.[35] The United States implemented only two sections of the 1970 UNESCO Convention. One prohibits the import into the United States of any cultural object that was inventoried in the collection of a public religious or secular institution, and that was stolen after the later of the dates on which the country of origin and the United States ratified the Convention.[36] The second provision, implementing Article 9 of the Convention, allows the President of the United States to impose import restrictions, following a request by another state party, upon designated categories of archaeological and ethnological materials[37] pursuant to either an emergency action[38] or a bilateral agreement (or memorandum of understanding (MOU)) between the United States and the requesting nation.[39] Import restrictions imposed in emergency situations

[31] 50 U.S.C. §§ 1701–1707. For example, the original trade sanctions imposed against Iraq in August 1990 were enacted under Executive Orders promulgated under this statute.

[32] 18 U.S.C. §§ 542, 545.

[33] 19 U.S.C. § 1595a(c)(1)(A).

[34] 19 U.S.C. §§ 2601–2613.

[35] 823 U.N.T.S. 231 (14 Nov. 1970).

[36] 19 U.S.C. § 2607 (implementing Article 7(b) of the Convention). The date of ratification for the United States is 1983, although the Senate had given its unanimous consent to ratification in 1972. The CPIA also adopts the definition of 'cultural property' from Article 1 of the Convention, 19 U.S.C. § 2601(6).

[37] The term 'archaeological or ethnological material of the State Party' means:

- (A) any object of archaeological interest;
- (B) any object of ethnological interest; or
- (C) any fragment or part of any object referred to in subparagraph (A) or (B); which was first discovered within, and is subject to export control by, the State Party. For purposes of this paragraph—
  - (i) no object may be considered to be an object of archaeological interest unless such object—
    - (I) is of cultural significance;
    - (II) is at least two hundred and fifty years old; and
    - (III) was normally discovered as a result of scientific excavation, clandestine or accidental digging, or exploration on land or under water; and
  - (ii) no object may be considered to be an object of ethnological interest unless such object is—
    - (I) the product of a tribal or nonindustrial society, and
    - (II) important to the cultural heritage of a people because of its distinctive characteristics, comparative rarity, or its contribution to the knowledge of the origins, development, or history of that people.

19 U.S.C.§ 2601(2).

[38] 19 U.S.C. § 2603.

[39] 19 U.S.C. § 2602.

can last a maximum of eight years (an initial period of five years with one renewal period for three years);[40] import restrictions imposed under an MOU can last a maximum of five years but may be renewed an unlimited number of times.[41] The only remedy available under the CPIA is civil forfeiture.[42]

Although it was not enacted as a means of restricting the importation of cultural objects into the United Kingdom, the Dealing in Cultural Objects (Offences) Act 2003[43] has now been used as a means of seizing 'tainted objects' upon entry. The offense of dealing in tainted cultural objects includes the import or export of such objects, in which case Her Majesty's Customs and Excise (HMCE) is empowered to investigate the potential offense and to seize such objects as part of the investigation.[44] Section 49(1)(b) of the Customs and Excise Management Act 1979 allows for the forfeiture of goods that are imported contrary to a statute, in this case the Dealing in Cultural Objects (Offences) Act. If forfeited, the goods would be returned to their country of origin. Since 2005, archaeological objects from Afghanistan, Iran, Greece, India, and possibly other countries have been seized.[45]

The primary mechanism for regulating the movement of cultural objects within Europe is provided by the Council Directive on the return of cultural objects unlawfully removed from a the territory of a member state[46] and the Regulation on the export of cultural goods.[47] While free movement of goods

40 19 U.S.C. § 2603(c)(3).

41 19 U.S.C. § 2602(e).

42 19 U.S.C. § 2609. An archaeological or ethnological object, which is subject to import restriction, may be imported into the United States if it is accompanied by an export license, at § 2606(a), or if satisfactory evidence can be presented that the object left the country of origin more than ten years before the date of entry or on or before the date the import restriction went into effect, at § 2606(b).

43 *See earlier* notes 23–26 and accompanying text.

44 The explanatory notes and guidance issued in conjunction with the Act state that section 4 of the Act gives HM Customs and Excise the 'necessary powers of enforcement where an offence involves the importation or exportation of a tainted cultural object. These include search and seizure powers under the Police and Criminal Evidence Act 1984'. Department of Culture, Media and Sport Cultural Property Unit, Dealing in Tainted Cultural Objects—Guidance on the Dealing in Cultural Objects (Offences) Act 2003, at 9, *available at* <http://www.culture.gov.uk/images/publications/Dealincultural.pdf> (last accessed 4 February 2013). A Government report issued in February 2004 in response to queries from the Select Committee stated:

> The new Dealing in Cultural Objects (Offences) Act 2003 has given HM Customs and Excise new powers of seizure under the Police and Criminal Evidence Act (PACE) for cultural objects they suspect to be tainted at the time of import. HM Customs and Excise can also rely on their seizure powers under the Customs and Excise Management Act 1979 where the import of any cultural objects also involves the commission of a Customs offence.

45 Sophie Vigneron, 'Trafic illicite et restitution des biens culturels, Royaume Uni', in M. Cornu and J. Fromageau (eds), *Protection de la propriété culturelle et circulation des biens culturels. Étude de droit comparé Europe/Asie* (2008) 259–322, at 292–3, 295, *available at* <http://www.gip-recherche-justice.fr/IMG/pdf/173-RF-Cornu_Protection_propriete_culturelle.pdf> (last accessed 4 February 2013).

46 Council Directive No. 93/7 of March 15, 1993, OJ L 74 of 27 March 1993.

47 Council Regulation (EEC) No. 3911/92 of December 9, 1992. The Regulation with several amendments was codified in Council Regulation (EC) 116/2009 of 18 December 2008 (OJ L 39 of 10 February 2009) on the export of cultural goods.

within the European Union is one of the goals of the European Community Treaty, Article 36 of the Treaty on the Functioning of the European Union allows 'prohibitions or restrictions on imports, exports or goods in transit justified on grounds of ... the protection of national treasures possessing artistic, historic, or archaeological value...'.[48] The Regulation created uniform export controls at the European Union's external borders to prevent the export out of the European Union of cultural goods, via a different member state, that had been illegally exported from the member state that is the country of origin.[49] The Directive provides a means by which one member state can recover from another member state cultural goods that have been illegally removed from the former's territory.[50] The Directive and Regulation make use of an Annex, which lists those cultural objects that are subject to the Directive and Regulation; archaeological objects, dismembered monuments, incunabula, manuscripts, and archives are included regardless of their monetary value. Neither the Directive nor the Regulation provides a basis for criminal prosecution but, rather, focus only on preventing export and restitution of cultural objects.[51]

III. Legal Actions

A. Civil Replevin

When a cultural object is stolen from its true owner, the owner may seek to recover the object from the current possessor in an action for replevin, detinue, or conversion. This principle applies regardless of whether the object is stolen in the traditional sense or it is an archaeological object whose ownership is vested in the nation.[52] Unlike the European civil law good faith purchaser doctrine, under

[48] Centre d'Etudes sur la Coopération Juridique Internationale-Centre National de Recherches Scientifiques (CECOJI-CNRA), Report, Study on preventing and fighting illicit trafficking in cultural goods in the European Union 40–3 (2011).

[49] Centre d'Etudes sur la Coopération Juridique Internationale-Centre National de Recherches Scientifiques (CECOJI-CNRA), Report, Study on preventing and fighting illicit trafficking in cultural goods in the European Union at 43–4.

[50] Centre d'Etudes sur la Coopération Juridique Internationale-Centre National de Recherches Scientifiques (CECOJI-CNRA), Report, Study on preventing and fighting illicit trafficking in cultural goods in the European Union 44.

[51] General domestic law providing criminal sanctions for theft, dealing in stolen property, and violation of Customs provisions would apply within European Union member states to cultural objects, 130–8. There are, in addition, European Union legal instruments that provide for assistance and cooperation among member states in criminal matters, Centre d'Etudes sur la Coopération Juridique Internationale-Centre National de Recherches Scientifiques (CECOJI-CNRA), Report, Study on preventing and fighting illicit trafficking in cultural goods in the European Union 48–55.

[52] For examples of such private actions brought by a nation pursuant to a national vesting ownership law, see *Republic of Turkey v OKS Partners*, 1994 U.S. Dist. LEXIS 17032 (D. Mass. 1994) (suit to recover hoard of 1750 rare ancient coins); *Republic of Turkey v Metro. Museum*, 762 F. Supp. 44 (S.D.N.Y. 1990) (suit to recover group of 360 antiquities, known as the 'Lydian hoard'). Both cases settled with virtually all objects returned to Turkey after preliminary litigation. For restitution of

general common law property principles, a thief cannot transfer title to stolen property, and even a subsequent good faith purchaser does not acquire title to stolen property.[53] The original owner's suit to recover stolen property may only be barred by the jurisdiction's statute of limitations for the recovery of personal property or by an equitable defense, such as that of laches.[54]

Many of what may be called the 'first generation' cases involving restitution of archaeological objects were private replevin actions undertaken by the foreign country as owner.[55] Such suits involve difficult questions of fact and law, with the claimant-nation bearing the burden of proving by the preponderance of the evidence that the artefacts at issue were found within the modern boundaries of the nation; the artefacts were located within the country at the time the vesting law was enacted; the vesting law is sufficiently clear in declaring national ownership, and the vesting law is internally enforced within the country of origin.[56]

the Lydian hoard, see Kaye and Main, 'The Saga of the Lydian Hoard: from Uşak to New York and Back Again', in K.W. Tubb (ed.), *Antiquities: Trade or Betrayed—Legal, Ethical and Conservation Issues* (Archetype Publisher: London, 1995) 150–61.

[53] *See, eg,* Uniform Commercial Code § 2–403 (stating that a thief cannot transfer title to stolen property).

[54] Most states have adopted a due diligence/discovery rule to define accrual of the cause of action for recovery of stolen artworks and other cultural objects. *O'Keeffe v Snyder*, 416 A.2d 862 (N.J. 1980); *see also Autocephalous Greek-Orthodox Church of Cyprus & the Republic of Cyprus v Goldberg & Feldman Fine Arts, Inc.*, 717 F. Supp. 1374 (S.D. Ind. 1989), *aff'd*, 917 F.2d 278 (7th Cir. 1990) (affirming use of due diligence/discovery rule). This rule states that the cause of action accrues when the owner discovers or, with the use of due diligence, should have discovered the current location of the stolen artwork. New York defines accrual as the time when the claimant demands return of the stolen property and the current possessor refuses. However, New York courts also permit a defendant to use the equitable defense of laches, which examines any unreasonable delay on the part of the claimant balanced against any legal prejudice caused to the possessor by the delay. *Solomon R. Guggenheim Found. v Lubell*, 569 N.E.2d 426 (N.Y. 1991); *Bakalar v Vavra*, 819 F. Supp. 2d 298 (S.D.N.Y. 2011), *aff'd*, 2012 U.S. App. LEXIS 21042 (2d Cir. 2012). California takes a unique approach, most recently in extending the statutory time period for recovery of works of fine art stolen during the past one hundred years. Cal. Code Civ. Proc. § 338(c)(3). As for other objects of 'historical, interpretive, scientific, or artistic significance', the pre-existing California statute specifically provides that the cause of action accrues from the time of discovery, and this was further clarified in the recently adopted legislation. Cal. Code Civ. Proc. § 338(c)(2).

[55] *See earlier* note 52; *see also Autocephalous Greek-Orthodox Church of Cyprus & the Republic of Cyprus v Goldberg & Feldman Fine Arts, Inc.*, 717 F. Supp. 1374 (S.D. Ind. 1989), *aff'd*, 917 F.2d 278 (7th Cir. 1990); *Peru v Johnson*, 720 F. Supp. 810 (C.D. Calif. 1989), *aff'd*, 933 F.2d 1013 (9th Cir. 1991) (rejecting Peru's claim to recover antiquities because the national ownership law was not sufficiently clear and Peru failed to meet its burden to establish that the Pre-Columbian antiquities at issue had been found within Peru's modern boundaries); *Republic of Croatia v Tr. of the Marquess of Northampton 1987 Settlement*, 610 N.Y.S.2d 263 (1st Dep't 1994), *appeal denied*, 642 N.E.2d 325 (N.Y. 1994) (rejecting Hungary's attempt to recover the 'Sevso treasure' because it failed to meet its burden to show that the treasure was discovered in Hungary).

[56] It is clear that the first two factors must be established in a civil replevin action as such vesting laws do not have either retroactive or extraterritorial effect. These factors were at issue in the *Peru v Johnson* and *Republic of Croatia* cases, and the failure of the plaintiff-nations to satisfy their burden was the reason for their inability to recover the artefacts. The third and fourth factors did not feature as legal issues in these cases. The third and fourth factors derive from the criminal prosecution in the *Schultz* case. It is not clear the extent to which these factors would play a role in a civil, as opposed to criminal, case, especially the requirement of giving notice of what conduct may constitute a crime to

For reasons that will be discussed in Section IV these types of actions have rarely, if ever, been undertaken in the United States during the past ten years or more, although the *Barakat* case in Britain was a private recovery action.

B. Criminal Prosecution

Probably the best-known (and most controversial) legal actions undertaken in US courts involving archaeological artefacts are the two criminal prosecutions, *United States v McClain*[57] and *United States v Schultz.*[58] These were preceded by a less well-known case, *United States v Hollinshead*, involving the taking of part of a Maya stele from Guatemala.[59] All three of these prosecutions were brought under the National Stolen Property Act (NSPA),[60] for trafficking or conspiring to traffic in stolen property worth more than US$5000.

In addition to use of the NSPA in trafficking cases, US courts have interpreted one of the trafficking provisions of ARPA as applying to archaeological resources from foreign countries.[61] The first and perhaps most interesting case to apply ARPA in the international context was the prosecution of a professor who had stolen illuminated manuscripts from various European collections, including the Vatican.[62] This same provision of ARPA was used to prosecute a Virginia collector who tried to sell his collection of antiquities from Peru. The defendant pled guilty and so the case did not come to trial.[63]

a possible defendant. The fourth factor is used to distinguish a national ownership law from an export control. While the question of whether one country's export controls are enforceable by another country is open to debate, this issue falls outside the scope of this chapter.

57 In *McClain*, the Fifth Circuit reversed the defendants' convictions on substantive counts twice, finally allowing only their conviction for conspiracy to violate the National Stolen Property Act to stand because the court held that only Mexico's latest vesting statute, enacted in 1972, was clearly an ownership law. 593 F.2d 658, 670–2 (5th Cir. 1979).

58 333 F.3d 393 (2d Cir. 2003).

59 495 F.2d 1154 (9th Cir. 1974).

60 18 U.S.C. §§ 2314–2315.

61 16 U.S.C. § 470EE(c) ('[N]o person may sell, purchase, exchange, transport, receive, or offer to sell purchase, or exchange, in interstate or foreign commerce, any archaeological resource excavated, removed, sold, purchased, exchanged, transported, or received in violation of any provision, rule, regulation, ordinance, or permit in effect under State or local law'). The first case to apply this provision to artefacts that did not originate on federal lands was *United States v Gerber*, 999 F.2d 1112 (7th Cir. 1993). Unlike the NSPA, ARPA does not require the artefacts to have any particular monetary value.

62 *United States v Melnikas*, 929 F. Supp. 276 (S.D. Ohio 1996). Manuscripts fit the definition of 'archaeological resource' under ARPA as items of historical and scientific interest that are more than one-hundred-years old. 16 U.S.C. § 470BB(1). The prosecution initially was based on handling of stolen property under the NSPA, but the ARPA count was added later. *See* Marous and Marous, 'ARPA in the International Context: Protecting the Articles of Faith', in S. Hutt et al. (eds), *Presenting Archaeology in Court: Legal Strategies for Protecting Cultural Resources* (AltaMira Press: Lanham, MD, 2006) at 39–45.

63 Eck and Gerstenblith, 'International Legal Developments in Review: 2003: Cultural Property', 38 *Int'l Law.* (2004), 469–76; Vardi, 'The Return of the Mummy', *Forbes*, 22 Dec. 2003, at 156; Glod, 'Arlington Man Pleads Guilty To Selling Protected Artifacts', *Wash. Post*, 25 Sept. 2003, at B3.

An undercover investigation carried out over several years by US federal agencies culminated in a series of raids to execute search warrants on four southern California museums (the Los Angeles County Museum of Art, the Pacific Asia Museum in Pasadena, the Bowers Museum in Santa Ana, and the Mingei International Museum in San Diego), the Malter Gallery in Encino, the Silk Road Gallery owned by Jonathan and Cari Markell in Los Angeles, and the home of Barry MacLean, a private collector in Chicago.[64] The affidavits submitted to obtain the warrants alleged an elaborate scheme in which an undercover agent, posing as a collector, was taken to the storerooms of an alleged smuggler who sold artefacts stolen and smuggled out of several Asian and South-East Asian countries, including China, Thailand, Cambodia, and Myanmar. Given the valuation of the artefacts at just below US$5000, if a criminal prosecution were to go forward, then the indictments would be likely to fall, at least in part, under the trafficking provision of ARPA.[65]

Criminal prosecution is also possible for intentional violation of the Customs statute requiring truthful declaration of merchandise upon import or prohibiting importation 'contrary to law'.[66] These criminal provisions, however, have not been used frequently with respect to importation of antiquities (or other cultural objects), although an intentional misdeclaration of country of origin seems to be a likely ploy to avoid import restrictions or other legal impediments that pertain if the true country of origin were declared. It is often difficult to determine the country of origin of a particular archaeological artefact. Therefore, criminal prosecutions may be rare because it is difficult to prove that an importer intentionally falsified the country of origin on import documents. An exception to this occurred when Hicham Aboutaam was charged in 2004 with falsifying Customs import documents when he imported an ancient silver rhyton, which originated in Iran but he declared as coming from Syria. Aboutaam admitted to falsifying the documents and pled guilty to a misdemeanor.[67] In a more recent case, the

[64] Zagaris, 'U.S. Tax Investigation Turns Up Apparently Stolen Cultural Artifacts', 24 *Int'l L. Enforcement Rep.*, Apr. 2008, 149–51; Wyatt, 'Four Museums Are Raided in Looted Antiquities Case', *N.Y. Times*, 25 Jan. 2008, at A14; Wyatt, 'Papers Show Wider Focus in Inquiry of Artifacts', *N.Y. Times*, 30 Jan. 2008, at A11.

[65] Now more than five years after the execution of these search warrants, it is not clear whether the government will proceed to indictment.

[66] The customs statute provides, inter alia, that '[w]hoever enters or introduces ... into the commerce of the United States any imported merchandise by means of any fraudulent or false invoice, declaration ... or by means of any false statement, written or verbal, ... or makes any false statement in any declaration without reasonable cause to believe the truth of such statement [shall be guilty of a crime]', 18 U.S.C. § 542, and '[w]hoever fraudulently or knowingly imports or brings into the United States, any merchandise contrary to law ..., knowing the same to be have been imported or brought into the United States contrary to law [shall be subject to criminal penalties]', 18 U.S.C. § 545.

[67] Meier, 'Art Dealer Pleads Guilty in Import Case', *N.Y. Times*, 24 June 2004, at E1. For the suggestion that the rhyton was not an authentic antiquity, see Muscarella, 'Archaeologists and Acquisitionists', 18 *Int'l J. Classical Tradition* 449–63, 454–5 (2011).

United States prosecuted two dealers and a collector for making false statements as to value and country of origin of antiquities from Iraq and Egypt. One of the defendants pled guilty to a misdemeanor, one was sentenced to house arrest, and prosecution of the third was deferred.[68]

The greatest challenge in bringing a criminal prosecution is meeting the government's burden to establish that the defendant knew that his or her conduct was illegal under the prevailing criminal standard of 'beyond a reasonable doubt'. In cases involving undocumented antiquities, it is often very difficult to satisfy this burden. While a considerable majority of the antiquities on the market at any given time are likely to carry insufficient provenance information to affirmatively establish their legitimate legal status, the lack of such information concerning a particular artefact does not prove that it is illegal under this criminal standard or that someone trafficking in the artefact knew that some illegal conduct attached to the object. On the other hand, when a criminal prosecution succeeds, it will have the greatest deterrent effect. Those involved in illegal aspects of the antiquities trade are white-collar criminals. As Simon Mackenzie has pointed out, white-collar criminals are most susceptible to the deterrent effect caused by the possibility of criminal conviction and incarceration.[69] The adverse consequences imposed on a defendant convicted of a crime involving cultural heritage resources were increased under the Cultural Heritage Resource Crimes Sentencing Guideline,[70] which came into effect in late 2002, thus presumably providing a greater deterrent effect.

[68] In July 2011, the government indicted four individuals, Mousa Khouli, Joseph A. Lewis II, Salem Alshdaifat, and Ayman Ramadan, who were allegedly involved in an antiquities smuggling ring. Many of the antiquities involved in the case seem to have originated in Egypt, Iraq and other Middle Eastern countries. St. Hilaire, 'A Closer Look at the Case against Moussa "Morris" Khouli and the Greco-Roman Coffin' (18 July 2011), *available at* <http://culturalheritagelawyer.blogspot.com/2011/07/closer-look-at-case-against-moussa.html> (last accessed 4 February 2013). One of the defendants, Mousa Khouli, subsequently pled guilty to smuggling antiquities through the making of false declarations. United States Attorney Eastern District of New York Press Release, Antiquities Dealer Pleads Guilty to Smuggling Egyptian Cultural Property (April 18, 2012), *available at* <https://docs.google.com/file/d/0B6ciLv_9mHWJY0RTb1d5U0FVOHc/edit?pli=1>. Early in 2013, the government entered into an agreement to defer prosecution of the remaining defendant, collector Joseph Lewis. This makes a prosecution unlikely. St. Hilaire, 'U.S. v. Khouli et al. Update: Motion to Defer Prosecution Ushers Rapid End to Antiquities Case' (8 January 2013), *available at*: <http://culturalheritagelawyer.blogspot.com/> (last accessed 4 February 2013). Another example of criminal prosecution for misdeclaration of value involved a dealer who imported Pre-Columbian artefacts from Honduras, declaring them to be ceramic ornaments worth US$37. In fact, the dealer had paid US$11,000 for the artefacts and the government presented evidence at trial that he intended to sell them for US$100,000–US$120,000. Mayhood, 'Man Guilty of Smuggling Ancient Artifacts', *Columbus Dispatch*, 23 Oct. 2002, at 4E; *United States v Hall*, 104 F. Appx 475 (6th Cir. 2004).

[69] Simon R. M. Mackenzie, *Going, Going, Gone: Regulating the Market in Illicit Antiquities* (Institute of Art and Law: Leicester UK, 2005), at 149–56.

[70] 18 U.S.C. App.§ 2B1.5.

C. Forfeiture

Forfeiture actions are *in rem* legal proceedings brought by the government against a particular item of property (either real or personal). The result of a forfeiture action is to transfer title to the United States government, after which the government decides the disposition of the property. When the forfeited property is cultural property, the government typically returns the object to its rightful owner.[71] Forfeiture actions may be brought as part of a criminal proceeding; once the defendant is convicted, whatever property was involved in the crime may be forfeited as part of the defendant's sentence.[72] The more typical use of forfeiture in the context of cultural objects is civil; in a civil forfeiture, depending on the statute under which the forfeiture proceeds,[73] the government may not have to establish that the owner, possessor, or importer knew that the property was stolen or was illegal in some other way.

Civil forfeiture of cultural property most frequently occurs when an object has been imported illegally into the United States.[74] There are typically three circumstances in which a cultural object may be imported illegally: in violation of the Convention on Cultural Property Implementation Act (CPIA);[75] by means of a false statement concerning the object as to country of origin or value, leading to a violation of the Customs Act,[76] and importation 'contrary

[71] Articles of cultural property and archaeological and ethnological materials forfeited under the CPIA must first be offered for return to the relevant State Party. 19 U.S.C. § 2609(b)(1), (c)(2)(A).

[72] 18 U.S.C. § 982.

[73] There is no general statute providing for forfeiture; rather, forfeiture authority is found in individual statutes. Civil forfeiture is used when the government is unable to prosecute the wrongdoer or in cases that are serious 'but not serious enough to justify a criminal conviction and a prison term'. Cassella, 'Using the Forfeiture Laws to Protect Archaeological Resources', 41 *Idaho L. Rev.* (2004) 129–45, at 132.

[74] Forfeiture may also be used in ARPA violations for artefacts removed illegally from federal and tribal lands. 16 U.S.C. § 470GG(b); *see* Cassella, 'Using the Forfeiture Laws to Protect Archaeological Resources', in S. Hutt et al. (eds), *Presenting Archaeology in Court* (AltaMira Press: Lanham MD, 2006) 169–89, at 174–84. Forfeiture under ARPA can also be used for illegally imported archaeological resources. In the first forfeiture of archaeological resources from a foreign country under ARPA, in 1996, the United States government seized and forfeited a set of Etruscan pottery, alleged by the Italian government to have come from an archaeological site, the Etruscan necropolis of Crustumerium, near Rome, and dated approximately to the 7th century BC. The US Government's forfeiture complaint was filed under § 470ee(c) of ARPA, which bars interstate and international trafficking in archaeological resources held in violation of state and local law. The local law on which the government relied was New York Penal Law § 165.45, which prohibits knowingly handling stolen property. The gallery that had possession of the artefacts waived any claim to them and the pottery was ultimately returned to Italy. The government's legal theory was thus never tested. *United States v An Archaic Etruscan Pottery Ceremonial Vase c. Late 7th Century, B.C. and a Set of Rare Villanovan and Archaic Etruscan Blackware with Bucchero and Impasto Ware, c. 8th–7th Century, B.C., Located at Antiquarium, Ltd., 948 Madison Avenue, New York, New York 10021*, 96 Civ. 9437, verified complaint dated 12 Dec. 1996.

[75] *See earlier* notes 34–42 and accompanying text.

[76] *See, eg, United States v An Antique Platter of Gold, Known as a Gold Phiale Mesomphalos c. 400 B.C.*, 184 F.3d 131 (2d Cir. 1999) (involving violation of 18 U.S.C. § 542, prohibiting import into the United States of 'any imported merchandise by means of any fraudulent or false invoice [or] declaration').

to law'.[77] When imported goods are imported in violation of a Customs statute, the government's burden of proof is one of probable cause, a relatively low standard.[78]

A complex question has arisen in recent cases as to whether the government must establish a knowledge or scienter requirement for forfeiture of objects imported 'contrary to law' when the underlying law involved is the National Stolen Property Act, which, as a criminal statute, contains a knowledge requirement. In several cases, particularly those originating in the Southern District of New York, the government alleged, and thereby acknowledged that it needed to establish, that someone involved in the importation knew that the objects were stolen.[79] In other forfeiture actions filed elsewhere, however, the United States government did not seem to feel the necessity to establish scienter.[80] In contrast, it is clear that forfeitures under the CPIA do not require proof of any knowledge. The question of whether the government needs to establish knowledge for a civil forfeiture can have a significant impact on the number of forfeitures that can proceed, but it is unlikely that the courts would accept an approach that eliminates the scienter requirement.

[77] Merchandise that has been introduced into the United States contrary to law if it is 'stolen, smuggled, or clandestinely imported or introduced' may be forfeited under 19 U.S.C. § 1595a(c) or 18 U.S.C. § 545.

[78] The Civil Asset Forfeiture Reform Act, 18 U.S.C. §§ 981 *et seq*., raised this burden of proof for most forfeiture actions and added an innocent owner defense but exempted forfeitures under the Customs statute, Title 19, from all of CAFRA's provisions, 18 U.S.C. § 983(i)(2)(A).

[79] *See, eg, United States v Portrait of Wally, A Painting by Egon Schiele*, 2009 U.S. Dist. LEXIS 91464 (S.D.N.Y. 2009) (setting for trial the question of whether the Leopold Museum could rebut the government's showing that Rudolf Leopold knew the painting had been stolen); *United States v Davis*, 648 F.2d 84 (2d Cir. 2011), *aff'g*, *United States v Painting Known as 'Le Marché'*, 2010 U.S. Dist. LEXIS 53420 (S.D.N.Y. 2010). The government does not seem to have specifically alleged that the Pissarro monotype was imported into the United States by someone with knowledge of its theft from a museum in France. However, the government's allegations included that it was the thief who brought the painting to the United States and sold it to a dealer in Texas, thus implicitly satisfying a knowledge requirement. The question of knowledge is one of the central issues in a forfeiture action filed in New York against a Cambodian sculpture that Sotheby's was intending to sell. *United States v A 10th Century Cambodian Sandstone Sculpture, Currently Located at Sotheby's in New York*, New York, 12 Civ. 2600, at paras. 48–9 (S.D.N.Y. April 4, 2012) (alleging that Sotheby's knew the Cambodian sculpture was stolen at the time it was imported into the United States).

[80] *See, eg, United States v Mask of Ka-Nefer-Nefer*, Complaint filed 16 Mar. 2011, Case 4:11-cv-00504-HEA, at 4 (hereinafter U.S. Complaint) (alleging that the mask was stolen but not alleging that anyone involved in importation of the mask knew it was stolen); *United States v One Ancient Egyptian, Yellow Background, Wooden Sarcophagus, Dating to the Third Intermediate Period*, Complaint filed 8 Oct. 2009, Case 09–23020, at 6 (S.D. Fla. 2009) (alleging that the sarcophagus 'was introduced or was attempted to be introduced into the United States contrary to law' but without stating what law pertained to the 'contrary to law' provision or alleging that someone involved with the importation knew the sarcophagus was stolen). The importer did not contest the forfeiture. Default Judgment of Forfeiture, Case No. 09–23030-CIV-Huck, entered 31 Dec. 2009. In *Mask of Ka-Nefer-Nefer*, 2012 U.S. Dist. LEXIS 47012 (E.D. Mo. 2012), after its complaint was dismissed, the United States attempted to amend its complaint, in part, so as to include an allegation that the St Louis Art Museum had consciously avoided learning the mask's legal status, thus satisfying a knowledge

IV. Shifts in Recovery Methods and Deterrent Effect: Unintended Consequences

As previously mentioned, the 'first generation' of cultural property restitution cases seemed to involve primarily civil replevin actions brought by the foreign country or the institution from which the property was stolen as the original owner of stolen property,[81] in addition to a relatively small number of criminal prosecutions. Such private replevin actions place the burden of proof on the claimant under the civil standard to establish that the property was stolen, although there is no need to establish that the current possessor knew the property was stolen. In addition, the claimant must often contend with the statute of limitations and, in some jurisdictions, the equitable defense of laches,[82] and these cases were often decided on these procedural issues. Overcoming defenses based on statutory limitations and laches may pose a considerable burden on the claimant, especially as such thefts and the current location of the property are often difficult to establish, taking many years and raising a convenient procedural defense. This means that considerable burdens, including the expenses of litigation, hiring of attorneys, investigation of the theft circumstances, procuring of evidence and witnesses, and

requirement. The court has not, however, permitted the amended complaint to be filed. Ricardo St. Hilaire, 'Judge Once Again Dismisses Ka Nefer Nefer Forfeiture Case,' June 29, 2012, available at: <http://culturalheritagelawyer.blogspot.com/> (last accessed 4 February 2013).While in the forfeiture of the monotype 'Le Marché', the government alleged sufficient facts to establish knowledge, the Second Circuit, in discussing CAFRA's exemption of forfeitures under the Customs statute from the innocent owner defense, stated:

> [C]ivil forfeiture claimants are rarely afforded the same procedural and substantive protections applicable in criminal forfeiture proceedings. For example, in many cases the burden rests on the claimant to demonstrate that her property is not subject to forfeiture. Similarly, the claimant's culpability is often irrelevant: 'a long and unbroken line of cases holds that an owner's interest in property may be forfeited by reason of the use to which the property is put even though the owner did not know that it was put to such use.' *Bennis v Michigan*, 516 U.S. 442, 446, 116 S. Ct. 994, 134 L. Ed. 2d 68 (1996).

648 F.3d 84, 92 (citations omitted). Thus, Congress's exemption of forfeitures under the Customs statute from the innocent owner defense under CAFRA indicates a strong policy interest in regulating the importation of goods into the United States. Nonetheless, forfeiture under 19 U.S.C. § 1595a(c), when the NSPA is the underlying law in the 'contrary to law' provision, still requires the government to establish knowledge on the part of someone involved in the importation process, even if only to the probable cause standard.

[81] *See, eg, Republic of Turkey v OKS Partners*, 1994 U.S. Dist. LEXIS 17032 (D. Mass. 1994) (analysing Turkey's national ownership law); *Republic of Turkey v Metro. Museum*, 762 F. Supp. 44 (S.D.N.Y. 1990) (holding that Turkey's claim to recover the Lydian hoard was not barred by the statute of limitations); *Autocephalous Greek-Orthodox Church of Cyprus v Goldberg & Feldman Fine Arts, Inc.*, 917 F.2d 278 (7th Cir. 1990) (analysing Indiana statute of limitations to hold that claim of Church to recover stolen Byzantine mosaics is not barred); *Greek Orthodox Patriarchate v Christies, Inc.*, 1999 U.S. Dist. LEXIS 13257 (S.D.N.Y. 1999) (in alternative holding, barring claim for recovery of stolen Archimedes palimpsest under the defense of laches).

[82] *See earlier* notes 54, 81.

learning the legal system of a foreign nation, were imposed on a nation seeking to recover its stolen cultural property.

In the past decade, this picture has changed substantially. Research reveals fewer private replevin actions instituted by a nation or a foreign institution to recover stolen antiquities.[83] Instead, the considerable majority of actions for recovery of such cultural objects have been civil forfeiture actions instituted by the United States government.[84] One significant advantage is that when the US government brings a civil forfeiture action, the statute of limitations is five years from the time the US government *learns* of the illegal importation or the transfer of stolen property across international or state lines.[85] In addition, the statutory time period runs from the time of illegal import or transfer across state lines, not from the time of the original theft. This substantially reduces the likelihood that a claim will be barred by the statute of limitations. In turn, this effectively means that the US government now bears much of the cost of litigation involving

[83] The one significant exception is the action instituted by Peru to recover cultural artefacts taken by Hiram Bingham from Machu Picchu close to a century ago. *Republic of Peru v Yale Univ.*, Compl. filed 5 Dec. 2008, Case 1:08-cv-02109-HHK (D.D.C. 2008). Nonetheless, the theory of the case did not depend on national ownership laws or import violation, because the artefacts were removed with permission from Peru. This dispute settled with the return of some artefacts and the promise to return the remainder. Roman, 'Peru-Yale Center for the Study of Machu Picchu and Inca Culture Opens', *Yale NEWS*, 6 Oct. 2011, *available at* <http://news.yale.edu/2011/10/06/peru-yale-center-study-machu-picchu-and-inca-culture-opens> (last accessed 4 February 2013). The most recent cultural property dispute that may be resolved based on the statute of limitations concerns several pages taken from the Zeyt'un Gospels, claimed by the Armenian Orthodox Church and currently housed at the J. Paul Getty Museum, which purchased the pages for US$950,000 in 1994. Boehm, 'The Getty Museum Is in a Legal Fight over Armenian Bible Pages', *L.A. Times*, 4 Nov. 2011, *available at* <http://www.latimes.com/entertainment/news/la-et-armenian-bible-20111104,0,4956662.story> (last accessed 4 February 2013). The statement that private replevin actions have decreased does not include the numerous examples of private replevin actions instituted by the heirs and descendants of Holocaust victims instituted to recover artworks looted during the Holocaust. The ongoing case of *In re Flamenbaum*, 945 N.Y.S.2d 183 (App. Div. 2012), while involving an ancient artefact, is more easily classified as a case involving an artefact looted during the Holocaust. On the other hand, it is likely that the potential of a foreign nation to institute civil replevin actions alleging theft of antiquities in violation of a national ownership law resulted in the considerable number of voluntary restitutions of antiquities in recent years to Italy and to Greece from US museums.

[84] The number of antiquities recovered through civil forfeiture actions has increased significantly in recent years as the number of bilateral agreements under the CPIA has increased. One may note, as examples, the forfeitures and repatriation of fourteen artefacts to China and other artefacts to Peru. Dep't of Homeland Sec., ICE-HSI, 'Priceless Chinese Antiquities Unlawfully Imported to U.S. Returned to Chinese Government', 13 Mar. 2011, *available at* <http://newsroom-magazine.com/2011/executive-branch/homeland-security-department/ice-hsi/priceless-chinese-antiquities-unlawfully-imported-to-u-s-returned-to-chinese-government/> (last accessed 4 February 2013); 'ICE and CBP Officials Return Cultural Artifacts to Peru', 12 May 2011, *available at* <http://www.ice.gov/news/releases/1105/110512washingtondc.htm> (last accessed 4 February 2013).

[85] *See, eg*, 19 U.S.C. § 1621 (stating that no action for forfeiture of property can be commenced more than 'five years after the time when the alleged offense was discovered, or in the case of forfeiture, within two years after the time when the involvement of the property in the alleged offense was discovered, whichever was later').

archaeological artefacts, and the foreign nation is spared these costs and other difficulties incurred in such litigation.[86]

The action filed by the United States government to forfeit the Ka-Nefer-Nefer Mask located in the St. Louis Art Museum is a good example of this. In this case, there seems to be general agreement that the mask was excavated in Egypt in 1952, placed in a storage facility at Saqqara and later sent (or the mask was intended to be sent) to Cairo for display.[87] At some point, it was stolen, although it is not certain when. The St. Louis Art Museum purchased the mask from the Aboutaam Brothers in 1998.[88] In late 2005 or early 2006, information began to circulate on Internet list-serves concerning the background of the mask and alleging that it had been stolen. In the past, this would have been the type of case in which Egypt would have filed a replevin action against the Museum to recover the mask; it is likely that Egypt would have had to litigate the questions of whether it used due diligence in searching for the mask or whether the defense of laches was available to the Museum. However, the question of the Museum's knowledge or intent would not have been relevant.

As the case developed, the US government filed a forfeiture action, while Egypt took no legal steps to recover the mask. The case might have posed an interesting question of the running of the statute of limitations because the Museum claimed that the US government received notice of the mask in late 2005/early 2006, and thus more than five years had elapsed between the time the US government allegedly learned of the illegal importation and the filing of the forfeiture complaint.[89] On the other hand, the question of the lapse of time from the original theft is not relevant. However, the government's forfeiture complaint was dismissed for failure to allege the necessary facts with sufficient specificity, including the circumstances of the alleged theft and the exact law on which the government was relying for forfeiture.[90]

A more significant effect and unintended consequence that results from the extensive use of civil forfeiture actions by the US government (in what has been characterized as a 'catch and release' approach) is that the relative ease of civil

[86] In addition, if the action is brought under the Customs statute, the government must only meet the probable cause standard in establishing its case, whereas a private claimant must meet the civil standard of the preponderance of the evidence. *See earlier* note 78.

[87] U.S. Complaint, *see earlier* note 80, paras. 8–17; *The Art Museum Subdistrict of the Metro. Zoological Park and Museum Dist. of the City of Saint Louis & the County of Saint Louis v United States of Am.*, Case 4:11-cv-00291, filed 15 Feb. 2011, paras. 10–11 (E.D. Mo. 2011) (hereinafter Art Museum Complaint) (stating that the mask was excavated in 1952 in the Saqqara necropolis by Mohammed Zakaria Goneim without explaining how the mask was subsequently transferred to a collection in Europe); *see also* Gay, 'Out of Egypt: From a Long-Buried Pyramid to the Saint Louis Art Museum: The Mysterious Voyage of the Ka-Nefer-Nefer Mask', *Riverfront Times*, 15 Feb. 2006.

[88] Art Museum Complaint, *see earlier* note 87, para. 11.

[89] Art Museum Complaint, *see earlier* note 87, paras. 15–16.

[90] *United States v Mask of Ka-Nefer-Nefer*, 2012 U.S. Dist. LEXIS 47012, at *8–10 (E.D. Mo. 2012).

forfeiture may serve as a disincentive to the prosecution of criminal cases. Another potential disincentive is the relatively light sentences such defendants receive.[91] Criminal cases are difficult to win because of the need for the government to establish criminal intent or knowledge beyond a reasonable doubt.[92] In cases involving undocumented antiquities, the essence is that, as undocumented antiquities, it is difficult to establish beyond a reasonable doubt that someone *knew* that the particular artefact was stolen.

This impediment can be overcome, to some extent, through use of a jury instruction based on the doctrine of conscious avoidance. Also dubbed the 'ostrich' instruction, its purpose is 'to expand the traditional understanding of "knowledge" for purposes of determining whether a defendant "knowingly" committed a certain act'.[93] In the *Schultz* prosecution, the jury was instructed as follows:

> [A] defendant may not purposefully remain ignorant of either the facts or the law in order to escape the consequences of the law. Therefore, if you [the jury] find that the defendant, not by mere negligence or imprudence but as a matter of choice, consciously avoided learning what Egyptian law provided as to the ownership of Egyptian antiquities, you may [infer], if you wish, that he did so because he implicitly knew that there was a high probability that the law of Egypt invested ownership of these antiquities in the Egyptian government. You may treat such deliberate avoidance of positive knowledge as the equivalent of such knowledge, unless you find that the defendant actually believed that the antiquities were not the property of the Egyptian government.[94]

A jury instruction based on 'conscious avoidance' requires that the jury find that the defendant was aware of the high probability of the existence of a particular fact, unless the defendant actually believed that the fact does not exist. In discussing Schultz's defense based on a mistake of US law, the court examined Schultz's position as former president of the National Association of Dealers in Ancient, Oriental and Primitive Art and evidence that Schultz was aware of the *McClain* decision and application of the NSPA to antiquities taken in violation of national

[91] *See earlier* note 68.

[92] The United Kingdom Statutory Instrument 2003 No. 1519, adopted to implement UNSCR 1483, reversed the burden of proof in the case of cultural materials illegally removed from Iraq, stating, 'Any person who deals in any item of illegally removed cultural property [from Iraq] shall be guilty of an offence under this Order, *unless he proves that he did not know and had no reason to suppose* that the item in question was illegally removed Iraqi cultural property.' Iraq (United Nations Sanctions) Order 2003, § 8(3) (emphasis added). The question of whether this provision complies with the European Convention on Human Rights was analysed by Kevin Chamberlain, 'The Iraq (United Nations Sanctions) Order 2003—Is It Human Rights Compatible?', 8 *Art Antiquity & L.* (2003) 357–368, at 361–8 (concluding that the unusual circumstances of the looting in Iraq justified this reversal of the burden of proof).

[93] *United States v Caliendo*, 910 F.2d 429, 433 (7th Cir. 1990); *see also United States v Hooshmand*, 931 F.2d 725, 734 (11th Cir. 1991) ('To justify a conscious avoidance instruction, the facts must "point in the direction of deliberate ignorance"' (citing *United States v Aleman*, 728 F.2d 492, 494 (11th Cir. 1984))).

[94] *Schultz*, 333 F.3d at 413.

ownership laws.[95] The result in the *Schultz* case and, in particular, the court's discussion of how to establish knowledge to satisfy the *mens rea* requirement in criminal proceedings demonstrate that the more knowledgeable the dealer, the more difficult it is for the dealer to demonstrate that he or she was ignorant of the law, and therefore the easier that it should be for the government to bring a criminal prosecution.

Nonetheless, the relative ease with which a looted cultural object can be civilly forfeited seems to indicate that the government will routinely choose this avenue to achieve restitution but that it will not go to the extra trouble that it takes to conduct a criminal prosecution. One also needs to factor into this equation the difficulty of a prosecutor learning a fairly obscure area of the law—one that the prosecutor is unlikely to encounter again, unless the prosecutor is located in a jurisdiction such as that of New York, the heart of the US art market. The paucity of criminal prosecutions seems to indicate this is correct.[96]

When the government files a civil forfeiture action, in most situations, the current possessor or the importer seems to 'walk away' from the property without contest. This may sometimes be in exchange for a promise from the government that it will not pursue criminal charges or it may not be financially worthwhile for the possessor or importer to fight the forfeiture. A third possibility is that the possessor does not want to risk receiving a subpoena of all business records if the forfeiture is contested. Whatever the reason, it may be that civil forfeiture has become a 'replacement' for criminal prosecution.

If that is correct, it is also unfortunate. As has previously been demonstrated, to the extent that such information is available, the cost of acquiring an antiquity in a foreign country is relatively small compared to the amount for which the antiquity can be sold on the international market.[97] Absorbing the loss of some antiquities through an uncontested forfeiture may be viewed as simply the cost of doing business. Thus forfeiture does not provide a significant disincentive to engaging in the trade in looted antiquities.

Simon Mackenzie's study of participants in the art market based on extensive interviews reveals that there are three factors a would-be white-collar criminal considers in deciding whether to engage in criminal conduct. The first and threshold factor is what Mackenzie labels the practical balance sheet; that is, a determination as to the likelihood that a perpetrator will be caught and punished. As Mackenzie described:

> The market interview sample displayed a high level of desire to buy unprovenanced antiquities, a perception of adverse consequences (penal and other) at or approaching

[95] *Schultz*, 333 F.3d at 412 and n.12.

[96] The fact that a criminal prosecution seemed likely in the Southern California museum raids, *see earlier* notes 64–65 and accompanying text, and that an undercover investigation was conducted for several years, indicating a significant investment of resources, but that no indictments have yet been issued may support this conclusion.

[97] Gerstenblith, 'Controlling the International Market in Antiquities', *see earlier* note 1, at 180–1.

nil, and a routine approach to the purchase of unprovenanced antiquities which suggested that the act had an established place in their 'comfort zone' of action.

If a positive balance is obtained on the subject's Practical Balance Sheet, he has the capacity to make the offending purchase. He has decided that he is unlikely to suffer any evil practical consequences from the performance of the act, or that his desire to perform the act outweighs any considered adverse consequences.[98]

The practical balance sheet constitutes the threshold to entry into criminal conduct. Only if a potential perpetrator 'passes' that threshold will he or she consider the other two factors—the moral balance sheet and the social balance sheet.[99] The potential for punishment through prosecution is the primary determinant that enters into the calculation of the practical balance sheet.

Mackenzie has demonstrated that crimes involving looted or stolen antiquities are carried out by white-collar criminals and that white-collar criminals are much more susceptible to the deterrent effect of possible criminal prosecution because they have more to lose in terms of prestige and their place in society.[100] Mackenzie concludes:

While the continuing dearth of provenance information passed in the course of transactions allows [potential purchasers] to alter their personal balance sheets in various ways so as always to arrive at an asset result in relation to the question of whether or not to buy any given object, then so long as their desire to trade persists, they will continue to do so, unless either: (i) legislation is put in place which so affects their Practical Balance Sheet calculations that they can no longer arrive at an asset result when considering the purchase of an antiquity. For this to work, the risk associated with purchase must become so great as to outweigh the possible gain, both emotional and financial, from the purchase (which is currently not the case with existing legislation) ....[101]

The best way to influence the potential wrongdoer's decision as to whether to engage in criminal conduct is to alter the practical balance sheet calculation. Only when the likelihood of criminal prosecution and punishment is relatively high will the law serve as an effective deterrent. The question is thus how can the 'risk' of criminal prosecution be increased?

Mackenzie focuses on the need for new legislation as the solution to insufficient criminal prosecution.[102] He suggests that because of the difficulty of establishing the requisite intent or knowledge, criminal punishment is rarely used. Mackenzie is correct to the extent that the lack of provenance information will routinely insulate the end-buyers and often the middlemen from criminal liability. However, the likelihood of enacting new legislation and practical difficulties in adopting

[98] Mackenzie, *see earlier* note 69, at 213.

[99] Mackenzie, *see earlier* note 69, at 213–26.

[100] Mackenzie, *see earlier* note 69, at 149–56.

[101] Mackenzie, *see earlier* note 69, at 227.

[102] Mackenzie, *see earlier* note 69, at 243–6 (proposing legislation to create a registry of antiquities and criminalize the possession of unregistered antiquities).

the specific scheme that Mackenzie proposes render his proposal an unsuitable solution.[103] Rather than being concerned with whether sufficient laws are in place to combat trade in looted antiquities, one needs to focus instead on shifting the practical balance sheet calculation through greater and more certain enforcement of the laws that already exist.

There are several reasons that might be suggested for insufficient law enforcement efforts. One is the lack of resources for law enforcement personnel and, in particular, the relatively low place in the government's priorities for prosecuting cultural heritage resource crimes. This ordering of priorities should shift in alignment with the recognition that international cultural heritage preservation is an increasingly key component in US foreign relations, in particular within the sphere of public and cultural diplomacy. However, if a foreign nation is more concerned with return of its cultural objects than with punishment of the wrongdoers, then foreign relations and diplomacy concerns will not play a significant role in encouraging more prosecutions.

Second, there seems to be insufficient knowledge, training, and awareness concerning existing laws among law enforcement personnel, including Assistant United States Attorneys, concerning how to prosecute such crimes. For example, one can posit the benefits of establishing national jurisdiction for a group of prosecutors who would be empowered to prosecute cultural heritage resource crimes anywhere in the nation. The FBI created the Art Crime Team in 2004[104] and has several agents located throughout the country who are specifically trained in cultural heritage resource crimes. However, at this time only one Assistant United States Attorney is assigned to this team,[105] and there is now no equivalent team within the Customs and Border Protection Agency or Immigration and Customs Enforcement/Homeland Security Investigations within the Department of Homeland Security. As most cases of international trafficking of illegal antiquities will involve an illegal importation offense, this failure within the Customs-related agencies is a major lacuna. Prosecutions could also be undertaken at the state and local levels, at least where stolen cultural objects are involved.[106] It is likely that

[103] One may also criticize Mackenzie's proposal because it leads to 'whitewashing' many of the antiquities that were stolen in the past. In addition, the granting of 'amnesty' to these antiquities may encourage continued illegal conduct because of the possibility that 'amnesties' will be granted to newly surfaced antiquities at some future date.

[104] *See* <http://www.fbi.gov/about-us/investigate/vc_majorthefts/arttheft/art-crime-team> (last accessed 4 February 2013).

[105] Consistent with its jurisdiction, the FBI Art Crime Team focuses more on thefts of fine art and other types of cultural objects such as historical documents and cases of fraud, rather than on cases involving international smuggling. Despite these limitations, the FBI has been involved in recoveries of Iraqi antiquities and in the civil forfeiture under the CPIA of two Spanish Colonial period paintings from Peru. Flegel, 'Iraqi Artifacts Going Home', *CNN*, 7 July 2011, *available at* <http://articles.cnn.com/2011–07–07/us/iraqi.artifacts_1_iraqi-artifacts-iraqi-museum-iran-iraq-war?_s=PM:US> (last accessed 4 February 2013); *United States v Eighteenth Century Peruvian Oil on Canvas Painting*, 597 F. Supp. 2d 618 (E.D. Va. 2009).

[106] Two recent prosecutions that involved international transport of allegedly stolen cultural objects have been undertaken by New York County prosecutors, rather than federal prosecutors. One

additional methods could be formulated for encouraging more prosecutions of these crimes.

This brief study is an attempt to demonstrate that the US government has stepped up its interest in pursuing illegal cultural objects, replacing, to a considerable extent, the civil replevin actions that were much more common a decade and more ago. While this is, in part, a welcome development, it seems that US law enforcement agencies have also opted for the relatively easy route of achieving restitution through civil forfeiture of cultural objects. This brings attention to the US government's efforts and wins favour with foreign nations, to whom the cultural objects are returned, but fails in the more important underlying purpose of law enforcement of providing a sufficient deterrent effect so that potential perpetrators make the calculation not to engage in the prohibited activity. Without this deterrent effect, the goal of reducing the looting of archaeological sites and the accompanying negative effects imposed on all society will not be achieved to the fullest extent possible.

involved coins allegedly stolen from Italy in violation of its national ownership law and ended with a plea agreement. *See* Wartenberg Kagan, 'An Editorial Comment on Caveat Emptor', *ANS Mag.* (2012) 32–3. In the second case, the Manhattan District Attorney issued an arrest warrant charging Subhash Kapoor with receiving cultural objects stolen from religious sites in India and elsewhere in Asia. Pogrebin and Flynn, 'Museums Studying Dealer's Artifacts,' *N.Y. Times*, July 28, 2012, at C1.

PART III

ALTERNATIVE METHODS OF ENFORCEMENT

9

Plurality and Coordination of Dispute Settlement Methods in the Field of Cultural Heritage

Alessandro Chechi *

I. Introduction

The international practice of the past forty years shows the proliferation of a great variety of disputes concerning the restitution[1] of cultural assets. A large number of these controversies originated from the pillage of cultural relics during war times. The illicit trafficking of works of art in peacetime is another cause of disputes. The worldwide interest in culture has not only fuelled a wealthy art trade, but also a profitable black market where materials illicitly removed from collections and archaeological sites are regularly traded.

This chapter discusses the problem of the resolution of disputes arising from restitution claims concerning cultural assets by examining the role of non-adversarial dispute settlement procedures alternative to domestic court proceedings. However, this chapter does not advocate that disputes should be dealt with by non-confrontational processes in preference to litigation. As it will be demonstrated, both avenues are characterized by important shortcomings. Moreover, because cultural heritage disputes come in many varieties, it would be irrational to advocate one method of dispute resolution.[2] Rather, the aim of this chapter is to demonstrate that domestic courts increasingly endorse the culture-sensitive solutions that can be attained by litigants through extra-judicial means. Crucially, these solutions have often been grounded on models produced outside classical intergovernmental law-making processes. Indeed, available practice evidences that domestic courts appear increasingly eager to adopt culture-sensitive decisions by

* Post-doctoral researcher, Art-Law Centre, University of Geneva; PhD, European University Institute.

[1] The terms 'restitution', 'return', and 'repatriation' will be used interchangeably.

[2] Byrne-Sutton, 'Introduction: Alternative Paths to Explore', in Q. Byrne-Sutton and F. Geisinger-Mariéthoz (eds), *Resolution Methods for Art-Related Disputes* (1999) 3, at 12.

deviating from the mechanical application of the letter of the law through the resort to various tools, such as the argument of public policy. In sum, this chapter intends to demonstrate a convergence of views of non-judicial and judicial adjudicators[3] toward the enhancement of the enforcement of cultural heritage law.

For these purposes, the first part of the *exposé* describes the main features of the existing legal framework. This permits us to illustrate the complexity of the existing regime and to assess its virtues and failings (Parts II–III). The chapter then provides an overview and a critical appraisal of the available means of dispute settlement and confirms that alternative dispute resolution (ADR) methods to litigation are, in general, better suited to adjudicate restitution cases (Parts IV–V). However, this chapter also points out that domestic courts contribute decisively to the enforcement of cultural heritage law. In this respect, Part VI examines the available judicial practice and investigates the rationale and the aims behind the work of domestic courts. Finally, Part VII concludes by arguing that a culture-sensitive jurisprudential trend is developing as a result of the consolidation of an international public policy based on the needs to protect cultural heritage from the risk of dispersion and to warrant restitution of wrongfully removed art objects.

II. The Legal Framework for Cultural Heritage Protection

Since the end of the 19th century, several national and international legal tools have been adopted in order to safeguard cultural heritage. Notably, the international community acted toward the adoption of international norms because of the perception that domestic laws did not suffice to cope with the different challenges characterizing this specific field. This part describes the state of the law and identifies its virtues and failings. However, it is not possible, within the limited space of this chapter, to examine in detail the existing legal framework. Thus, it analyses some relevant types of domestic legislation and the most pertinent treaties in order to provide the obligatory background of a study concerning the interrelated issues of the implementation of cultural heritage law and the settlement of disputes concerning the restitution of cultural assets.

A. Domestic Laws

1. Almost all states have adopted legislation that recognizes the uniqueness of cultural objects, and they decide if and to what extent such materials should be subject to specific legal regimes. These vary in their content but share some

[3] The term 'adjudicator' will be used to indicate any person or body that is entrusted by one or more litigants to render a decision on a dispute and will encompass both judicial and non- (or quasi-) judicial means.

common features. For instance, they aim to protect cultural heritage from illicit trafficking and provide more protective and less trade-oriented rules.[4] More specifically, source nations[5] have attempted to curb illicit trafficking in movable cultural materials through the enforcement of two types of legislation. First, there are patrimony laws. These provide that ownership of certain categories of cultural objects is vested *ipso iure* in the state. The role of the state is that of exclusive owner. This entails that the person removing such objects without permission is a thief and that such objects are stolen property. Second, there are export regulations. These prohibit or restrict the export of cultural materials, either belonging to state patrimony or to private ownership.

The formal distinction between patrimony laws and export regulations is critical because only the former category enjoys extra-territorial effect. This is due to the fact that theft is universally recognized as a crime to be subject to criminal sanction. On the contrary, a state is not obliged to recognize and enforce the export regulations of another state absent a treaty or a statute. In other words, although source nations can legitimately enact export control laws, they cannot create an international obligation to recognize and enforce those measures.

Nevertheless, a number of importing countries have passed legislation in order to assist source countries in the enforcement of their domestic laws. For instance, in 2003, the United Kingdom passed the Dealing in Cultural Objects (Offences) Act. This Act creates a new offence. It outlaws the handling of items knowing that they were illegally removed or excavated either within or outside the United Kingdom, while it does not matter whether the law infringed is domestic or foreign.[6] In the United States, the National Stolen Property Act (NSPA)[7] has been used several times by the government to seize stolen objects—even if it was not adopted to counter the trade in stolen art—thereby leading to the extra-territorial implementation of foreign patrimony laws.

2. The statutory norms barring the exercise of legal actions are also relevant for the present study. These norms include the procedural rules that subject the starting of judicial proceedings to certain time limits,[8] or that regulate prescription[9]

[4] Carducci, 'The Growing Complexity of International Art Law: Conflict of Laws, Uniform Law, Mandatory Rules, UNSC Resolutions and EU Regulations', in B. Hoffman (ed.), *Art and Cultural Heritage* (2006) 68, at 69–70.

[5] For the distinction between 'source' (or 'exporting') and 'market' (or 'importing') nations, see Merryman, 'Two Ways of Thinking About Cultural Property', *AJIL* (1986) 831, at 832.

[6] Department of Culture, Media and Sport, *Dealing in Cultural Objects (Offences) Act 2003—Explanatory Notes, available at* <http://www.culture.gov.uk/what_we_do/cultural_property/3295.aspx> (last accessed 4 February 2013).

[7] 18 U.S.C. §§ 2314–2315 (1934).

[8] Statutes of limitations subject the starting of proceedings to certain time limits, eg, from the time of the theft or from the discovery of the location of the object. Redmond-Cooper, 'Limitation of Actions in Art and Antiquity Claims', *Art Antiquity & L.* (2000), at 185 ff.

[9] The rules of prescription (or adverse possession) serve the state to make legal the possession of abandoned property or property the possession of which has been lost against the true owner's will. These rules allow a possessor who has held an object openly for a considerable length of time to acquire title.

or standing,[10] as well as the statutes that grant immunity from seizure to items temporarily on loan from abroad. The principal function of anti-seizure legislation is to protect the international exchange of works of art. As international exhibitions expose art to the public and, inevitably, to the scrutiny of potential claimants, these statutes aim to remove any doubt regarding the categories of acts and objects that may attract immunity.[11] Accordingly, anti-seizure statutes produce at least two legal effects: (i) no judicial proceeding can be brought in the borrowing state with regard to objects on loan[12]—in this manner the security of cultural exchanges prevails at the expense of the (alleged) ownership title of claimants and of their right of access to court; and (ii) the efficacy of the international legal instruments deployed to curb the illicit trade in cultural objects is jeopardized.

Given the cross-border nature of cultural heritage disputes, another category of norms that has to be considered is that of private international law.[13] This consists of the domestic rules that delimit the scope of national jurisdiction and help judges to choose the applicable law when a dispute involves a foreign element. This element may relate to the parties, to the facts, or to the object of the litigation. The *lex rei sitae* is one of the most problematic rules. Under this rule, the validity of a transfer of movable property is regulated by the law of the country where the property is located at the time of the last transaction. This rule entails unpredictable outcomes given the differences between civil law and common law countries. In civil law jurisdictions, which favour the security of commercial transaction, the domestic rules on the protection of *bona fide* purchasers establish that once the possessor has satisfied the good faith requirement (which is presumed—it is for the claimant to prove the bad faith of the possessor) and the statutory time period has expired, he acquires good title (even from a thief), while the original owner loses the right to recover. Conversely, common law jurisdictions follow the *nemo dat quod non habet* principle (no-one can transfer title on stolen property), according to which the mere fact that a person acquires a stolen object in good faith does not extinguish the title of the true owner.

B. International Conventions

1. The large-scale destruction of cities and monuments and the magnitude of the systematic Nazi plundering during the Second World War led to the adoption of the Convention for the Protection of Cultural Property in the Event of Armed

[10] According to these rules, claimants may be admitted as a proper plaintiff only if it is recognized by the judge of the forum as a legal person capable of suing under the law of the forum.

[11] Siehr, 'Commercial Transactions and the Forfeiture of State Immunity Under Private International Law', *Art Antiquity & L.* (2008) No. 4, 339, at 349.

[12] Weller, 'Immunity for Artworks on Loan? A Review of International Customary Law and Municipal Anti-Seizure Statutes in Light of the *Liechtenstein* Litigation', *Vand. J. Transnat'l L.* (2005) 997, at 1013 ff.

[13] In common-law countries, the terms 'choice-of-law' and 'conflict of laws' are preferred.

Conflict (1954 Hague Convention)[14] by the United Nations Educational, Scientific, and Cultural Organization (UNESCO). This treaty obliges the states parties to take special care to avoid damage to 'movable or immovable property of great importance to the cultural heritage of every people' (Article 1(a)). Cultural property is thus placed under special legal protection. The Convention prohibits the destruction of cultural property during armed conflict and during periods of belligerent occupation (Articles 4 and 5). Other provisions are set out in relation to the removal of cultural assets from occupied territories. Article 4(3) declares that states parties must prohibit, prevent and, if necessary, put a stop to any form of theft, pillage, or misappropriation of cultural property. However, the Convention does not cover the issue of restitution. This matter is regulated by the First Protocol of 1954.[15] The Protocol contemplates the obligations for occupying powers to prevent and avoid any exportation of cultural objects from occupied territories, and, in the event that such exportation would occur, to provide restitution (Article I(3)). Moreover, the Protocol codifies the principle according to which cultural property 'shall never be retained as war reparations' (Article I(3)). In 1999, the system of the 1954 Hague Convention was completed by the adoption of the Second Protocol.[16] This Protocol: (i) extended the scope of the regime to non-international armed conflicts (Article 22); (ii) introduced the new system of 'enhanced protection' (Article 10 ff.); (iii) established individual criminal responsibility for serious violations (Article 15 ff.); and (iv) set up the Committee for the Protection of Cultural Property in the Event of Armed Conflict to supervise the operation of the Protocol (Article 24).

2. The decades following the end of the Second World War saw two important developments that determined a further reform of the international legal regime for movable cultural objects: first, the booming demand for artefacts, which caused the worsening of illicit trafficking, and, second, the independence of many colonies, which led to the multiplication of repatriation claims concerning the materials removed during colonial times. To respond to these challenges, UNESCO adopted the Convention on the Means of Prohibiting and Preventing the Illicit Import, Export and Transfer of Cultural Property (1970 UNESCO Convention).[17]

The 1970 UNESCO Convention aims to prevent the peacetime impoverishment of the cultural heritage of the countries of origin and operates mainly by imposing obligations on States Parties. As far as restitution is concerned, the 1970 UNESCO Convention imposes no general duty to procure the return of illegally removed antiquities. This results from the wording of Articles 7 and 13. The latter norm imposes on states parties a few general obligations: 'to prevent transfers of ownership of cultural property likely to promote the illicit import or

[14] 14 May 1954, 249 U.N.T.S. 215.
[15] 14 May 1954, 249 U.N.T.S. 358.
[16] 26 Mar. 1999, (1999) 38 I.L.M. 769.
[17] 17 Nov. 1970, 823 U.N.T.S. 231.

export of such property', 'to ensure [...] restitution of illicitly exported cultural property', 'to admit actions for recovery of lost or stolen items', 'to recognize the indefeasible right of each State Party to this Convention to classify and declare certain cultural property as inalienable [...], and to facilitate recovery of such property [...]'. However, these obligations are limited in that states parties should act consistent with their respective municipal laws. Under Article 7(a), states parties undertake to adopt measures to discourage domestic museums from acquiring cultural property illegally exported from another state party. Article 7(b)(i) circumscribes the duty of return to cultural objects stolen 'from a museum or a religious or secular public monument or similar institution', 'provided that such property is documented as appertaining to the inventory of that institution'. Moreover, the obligation to return is conditional on the payment by the requesting state of 'just compensation' to the innocent buyer or to any person who has valid title to the object (Article 7(b)(ii)). Last, the restitution procedure is based on intergovernmental action, as only states parties can trigger the procedure. It is in light of these deficiencies that Article 7 is routinely criticized for being at variance with the general interest in the protection of cultural heritage from the risk of dispersion.

3. Upon request of UNESCO, in 1995 the International Institute for the Unification of Private Law (UNIDROIT) adopted the Convention on Stolen or Illegally Exported Cultural Objects (1995 UNIDROIT Convention).[18] As a specialized organization for the harmonization of national laws, the UNIDROIT was requested to produce a self-executing treaty aiming to improve the international protection of cultural objects through the resolution of the problems resulting from the differences among national rules and from the weaknesses of the 1970 UNESCO Convention.

Specifically, the UNIDROIT Convention applies to claims of international character and deals with both theft and illicit exportation. As far as theft is concerned, the UNIDROIT Convention sets forth an outright obligation of restitution of stolen objects, even if they are recovered in those systems of law that protect the good faith possessor (Article 3(1)). Any claim for restitution must be made within specific time limits (Article 3(3) and (4)). Upon recovery of the claimed artefact, the Convention entitles the *bona fide* purchaser to a 'fair and reasonable compensation' if it is proved that he 'exercised due diligence when acquiring the object' (Articles 4). As for illegal exportation, the 1995 UNIDROIT Convention provides that a 'State may request the court or other competent authority of another Contracting State to order the return of a cultural object illegally exported from the territory of the requesting State' (Article 5(1)). Therefore, the UNIDROIT Convention is based on the premise that the law of the country of origin is the controlling law. Hence, the Convention does not formulate an independent supranational policy of international art trade, but dictates the enforcement of

[18] 24 June 1995, (1995) 34 I.L.M.1322.

the export prohibitions of the country of origin regardless of what the law of the state of location provides.

4. In 2001, the General Conference of UNESCO adopted the Convention on the Protection of the Underwater Cultural Heritage (2001 UNESCO Convention).[19] There are three main reasons why UNESCO elaborated this new treaty. First, there was a growing awareness that the pillaging and dispersion of archaeological heritage was no longer restricted to land-based sites. The looting and destruction of underwater sites by treasure hunters are increasing rapidly due to the technical progress that, at present, leads to an unprecedented accessibility of the seabed.[20] Second, owing to the specific nature and location of underwater cultural heritage, it was clear that existing national laws did not suffice to safeguard it. Domestic legislation can offer legal protection only to sites located within the territorial sea, that is, the part of the sea adjacent to the territory that falls within the exclusive jurisdiction of the coastal state. Instead, on the High Sea there is no state jurisdiction. Third, the 2001 UNESCO Convention was adopted because the United Nations Convention on the Law of the Sea (UNCLOS)[21] does not articulate an adequate level of protection.

The 2001 UNESCO Convention is inspired by the objectives and general principles listed in Article 2: (i) 'States Parties shall preserve underwater cultural heritage for the benefit of humanity' (Article 2(3)); (ii) 'preservation *in situ* […] shall be considered the first option' (Article 2(5)); and (iii) '[u]nderwater cultural heritage shall not be commercially exploited' (Article 2(7)). The 2001 UNESCO Convention also sets up a specific international cooperation regime encompassing reporting, consultations and coordination in the implementation of protective measures (Articles 9 to 11). Obligations extend to control and prevention of the illicit trafficking in cultural heritage (Article 14), seizure and disposition (Article 18), cooperation and information-sharing (Article 19), public awareness (Article 20), training (Article 21), and the establishment of competent domestic authorities (Article 22).

III. A Critical Appraisal of the Legal Parameters

The foregoing parts demonstrate that during the last hundred years, the law of cultural heritage evolved at both the domestic and international levels. UNESCO's action permitted the transformation of the protection of cultural heritage into an essential element of contemporary international law. One of the notable corollaries of this evolution is that some general principles have formed as part of general

[19] 2 November 2001, (2002) 41 I.L.M. 37.

[20] *See* UNESCO, *Information Kit for the 2001 UNESCO Convention on the Protection of the Underwater Cultural Heritage* 4–5, *available at* <www.unesco.org/en/under water-cultural-heritage/>.

[21] 10 December 1982, (1982) 21 I.L.M. 1261.

international law and, which are binding upon all states independently of their consent to be bound by UNESCO treaties. These principles are: the prohibition of acts of violence against cultural heritage and the corresponding obligation to protect cultural heritage from the vicissitudes of armed conflict, the prohibition of plundering artworks and the ensuing obligation of restitution, and the prohibition on retaining cultural objects as war reparations.[22]

By way of contrast, the customary nature of the obligation to return artworks wrongfully removed in peacetime is doubtful. For the limited purposes of this chapter, it is not necessary to embark on an in-depth examination of the arguments against the affirmation of such an obligation. Nevertheless, it is possible to pinpoint the most troublesome obstacles.

The first problem is that domestic patrimony laws and export regulations have proved difficult to enforce. As a matter of fact, these rules have neither deterred nor stopped the illicit trafficking principally because: (i) they are excessively broad and strict—no government can police every archaeological site in its country, nor can it monitor every border crossing to enforce export controls; and (ii) they are not systematically recognized and enforced in market countries. The same problem concerns international instruments: all too often national governments and domestic courts exclude the direct applicability of treaty norms because their character is supposedly indeterminate and their nature non-self-executing. The problem of enforcement particularly affects the international treaties that accord rights to individuals. If these treaties are not implemented nationally, individuals are not able to invoke such rights and, consequently, judges are obliged to dismiss the legal actions grounded on their provisions.[23] Second, domestic laws and international treaties do not apply backwards. Hence, neither domestic nor international law applies to claims regarding artefacts removed, for instance, in remote colonial times. Third, UNESCO treaties neither regulate the issue of the applicable law nor the reach of domestic laws. This means that thieves and traffickers can profit from their wrongdoing by transferring and selling stolen items in countries where the tainted title is laundered through the domestic norms that protect *bona fide* purchasers or where legal action is barred as a result of the expiry of statutory limitation periods.[24] In turn, this means that the non-coordinated

[22] In this sense, the 1954 Hague Convention can be seen as a codification of the customary norms that have developed since the adoption of the Hague Convention (II) with Respect to the Laws and Customs of War on Land (29 July 1899, *AJIL* (1907) 66) and the Hague Convention (IV) Respecting the Laws and Customs of War on Land (18 Oct. 1907, *AJIL* (1908) 165). *See* Francioni, 'Au-delà des traités: l'émergence d'un nouveau droit coutumier pour la protection du patrimoine culturel', *RGDIP* (2007) 19, at 29; W. Sandholtz, *Prohibiting Plunder. How Norms Change* (Oxford 2007) 9, at 223, 256–7; M. Frigo, *La circolazione internazionale dei beni culturali* (2001), at 84; Siehr, 'International Art Trade and the Law', *RCADI* (1993-VI), at 120.

[23] *See, eg, Autocephalous Greek Orthodox Church in Cyprus v Willem O.A. Lans* (District Court, Rb Rotterdam, 4 Feb. 1999; confirmed in Appeal, Hof Den Haag, 7 March 2002, 99/693); *République fédérale du Nigeria c. Montbrison* (Court of Cassation, 2006, JCP 2006, IV, 3005, 1917).

[24] Siehr, 'The Protection of Cultural Heritage and International Commerce', *IJCP* (1997), at 304 ff.

components of the existing legal framework fuel the illicit activities that they are supposed to prevent and hence contribute to the proliferation of disputes.

The fourth shortcoming necessary to mention is that cultural heritage law lacks specific and effective procedures for the resolution of disputes. None of the existing treaties sets up a special tribunal or adequate system of control to ensure the consistent application of their norms. The 1954 Hague Convention merely states that the 'Protecting Powers shall lend their good offices in all cases where they may deem it useful in the interest of cultural property' (Article 22), whereas the Regulations provide for arbitration in relation to objections to the registration of cultural heritage for Special Protection.[25] The Second Protocol to the Hague Convention has introduced some possibilities for resolution of disputes. Articles 35 and 36 detail the conciliation and mediation powers of the Protecting Powers and of the Director-General. The 1970 UNESCO Convention specifically addresses the problem of dispute settlement at only one point: Article 17(5) provides that when two states parties to the Convention are engaged in a dispute over its implementation, UNESCO can offer its 'good offices to reach a settlement between them'. The only relevant provision of the 1995 UNIDROIT Convention is Article 8. This states that claims concerning its application may be brought before 'the courts or other competent authorities of the Contracting State where the cultural object is located, in addition to the courts or other competent authorities otherwise having jurisdiction under the rules in force in Contracting States'. In addition, pursuant to Article 8(2), the parties are permitted to submit their dispute to arbitration. Unfortunately, this provision does not give guidance on how to design arbitration procedures. Article 25(1)(2) of the 2001 UNESCO Convention requires the states parties involved in a dispute concerning the interpretation and application of the Convention to resort to peaceful means of settlement of their own choice. If a settlement is not reached, Article 25(3)(4) authorizes the states parties ('whether or not they are also Parties to the United Nations Convention on the Law of the Sea') to choose between the four dispute settlement procedures listed in Article 287(1) UNCLOS.[26] However, this dispute settlement system only encompasses inter-state claims, whereas disputes between states and non-state entities, such as commercial salvage companies, lie beyond the treaty's competence.[27]

The only exception to this discouraging situation is represented by the domestic laws concerning the restitution of indigenous peoples' cultural heritage

[25] Article 14 of the Regulations for the Execution of the Convention for the Protection of Cultural Property in the Event of Armed Conflict.

[26] These options are: (i) the International Tribunal for the Law of the Sea established in accordance with Annex VI UNCLOS; (ii) the International Court of Justice; (iii) an arbitral tribunal constituted in accordance with Annex VII UNCLOS; or (iv) a special arbitral tribunal constituted in accordance with Annex VIII UNCLOS for one or more of the categories of disputes specified therein.

[27] E. Boesten, *Archaeological and/or Historic Valuable Shipwrecks in International Waters* (2002) 188–90.

and of Holocaust-related art. In the former case, most of the states with significant indigenous peoples have passed legislation providing for non-forensic procedures designed to facilitate restitution and indigenous peoples' participation in all curatorial decisions that relate to their heritage.[28] As regards Nazi-looted art, special non-forensic commissions have been created in various states with the task of evaluating both the legal and moral aspects of disputes and suggesting restitution or other forms of relief.[29]

The obvious consequence of this state of affairs is that controversies are to be settled through political or diplomatic negotiation or, if these fail or are not available, through traditional dispute settlement mechanisms, which include mediation, arbitration, and litigation before domestic courts or international tribunals. This ad hoc fashion of dealing with cultural heritage disputes entails that the final settlement mostly depends on the choice of the forum and of the applicable law (outcome-determinative nature of forum selection), which often depends on the arbitrary circumstance of where an object is discovered. This further entails the risk of the adoption of inconsistent decisions, the establishment of harmful precedents and the fragmentary development of the law.

IV. The Enforcement of Cultural Heritage Law through Dispute Settlement Means

In general, the methods of dispute resolution can be divided into two categories: (i) legal means (arbitration and judicial settlement), which result in binding decisions; and (ii) diplomatic means (negotiation, good offices, conciliation, and mediation), according to which the parties retain control over the procedure insofar as they may accept or reject a proposed settlement.[30]

The survey that follows aims to describe the main features of these procedures and to explore the available practice in order to appraise the efficacy of both legal and diplomatic methods with respect to the settlement of restitution claims and, thus, the implementation of cultural heritage law. Indeed, as pointed out by Nafziger, the enforcement of international cultural heritage law relies mostly on—non-criminal—'sanctions' such as the restitution of wrongfully removed assets.[31]

[28] *See, eg*, Canadian First Nations Sacred Ceremonial Objects Repatriation Act (RSA, Ch. F-14, 2000); United States Native American Graves Protection and Repatriation Act (25 U.S.C. § 3001 et seq. (1990)), *commented in* Nafziger, 'Cultural Heritage Law: The International Regime', in J. A. R. Nafziger and T. Scovazzi (eds), *The Cultural Heritage of Mankind* (2008) 145, at 213–4.

[29] *See* Part IV.B.2 Mediation.

[30] Von Schorlemer, 'UNESCO Dispute Settlement', in A. A. Yusuf (ed.), *Standard-Setting in UNESCO, Normative Action in Education, Science and Culture* (Vol. I) (2007) 73, at 74 ff.

[31] Nafziger, 'International Penal Aspects of Protecting Cultural Property', *Int'l Law.* (1985) 835 ff.

Litigation and arbitration will not be dealt with under the same heading. Even if these share some features (both are decisional, as they do not seek to compromise disputes, and their decisions are final and binding), arbitration is treated as one of the alternative dispute resolution (ADR) methods to litigation. In addition, this examination will only consider litigation before domestic courts, thereby excluding a discussion over the role of international tribunals. This is not motivated only by the paucity of international decisions.[32] The most decisive reason is that existing international fora are structurally unable either to grant standing to non-state entities such as individuals, museums, and communities or to accommodate their interests in transnational cases of restitution.

A. Legal Means—Litigation before Domestic Courts

The initiation of legal proceedings before domestic courts is the main avenue for the settlement of the majority of transnational art cases. The most obvious reason is that litigation ends with a definitive ruling that can be enforced through state machinery.

States normally sue before foreign domestic courts by relying either on patrimony laws or export statutes. On the other hand, non-state entities like collectors and museums resort to domestic courts mostly seeking restitution as a remedy for the violation of the right to property. Criminal cases are not uncommon. However, the judicial practice demonstrates that it is not easy to prove that the defendant was involved in a theft or illicit trafficking or that he acquired a stolen object knowingly because of the murky practices of the art market.

Having said that, it must be underlined that domestic courts have been able to warrant restitution of contested items of cultural heritage (even) through the application of existing rules.[33] The *Goldberg* case is just one prominent example.[34] In this case, the Court of Appeals of Indiana ruled that the possession of four Byzantine mosaics had to be awarded to the plaintiffs, the Autocephalous Greek-Orthodox Church of Cyprus and the Republic of Cyprus, as against the defendant, the art dealer Peg Goldberg. The four mosaics had been stolen from the Cypriot Church of the Panagia Kanakaria in Lythrankomi following the Turkish invasion of 1974. The *Elicofon* case[35] was concerned with two portraits by Albrecht Dürer stolen

[32] For instance, the International Court of Justice has dealt with restitution claims only twice since its inception, in the cases *Temple of Preah Vihear (Cambodia v Thailand)*, Judgment of 15 June 1962, ICJ Reports, 1962, at 6, where the issue of restitution of cultural assets was incidental to that of the delimitation of national boundaries, and *Certain Property (Liechtenstein v Germany)* (Preliminary Objections, Judgment of 10 February 2005, ICJ Reports, 2005, at 6), which was not discussed on the merits because the applicant's claim was rejected on the grounds of lack of jurisdiction *ratione temporis*.

[33] Other examples are described Parts VI–VII.

[34] *Autocephalous Greek Orthodox Church of Cyprus v Goldberg*, 717 F. Supp. 1374 (S.D. Ind. 1989), *aff'd*, 917 F.2d 278 (7th Cir. 1990).

[35] *Kunstsammlungenzu Weimar v Elicofon*, 478 F.2d 231 (1973), 536 F. Supp. 829 (E.D.N.Y. 1981), *aff'd*, 678 F.2d 1150 (2d Cir.1982).

in 1945 from the Schwarzburg Castle in Germany. While American troops occupied the castle, the paintings disappeared. In 1966, they were discovered in the possession of a New York collector, Edward Elicofon, who had bought them in 1946 from an American serviceman. In 1966, upon learning of the Dürer paintings' location, the Federal Republic of Germany and the Kunstsammlungenzu Weimar (Weimar Art Collection) filed suit seeking restitution. In 1981, the US District Court for the Eastern District of New York ruled that the Dürers had been stolen, that the Kunstsammlungenzu Weimar was the rightful owner and that Elicofon had to deliver the paintings to the Weimar Art Collection.

B. Diplomatic Means

1. Negotiation

Negotiation is the means more frequently used for the settlement of disputes over the restitution of cultural assets. This is a voluntary, non-binding mechanism that allows the parties to retain control over the process without the intermediation of any neutral third party. As such, it allows like-minded disputants to create win-win solutions, where creative and mutually satisfactory outcomes are envisaged[36] and existing legal obstacles are set aside.[37]

Various instances demonstrate that negotiation has been extensively used with regard to restitution requests. However, given that today, hardly a week goes by without a new case being reported in the press, only the most representative examples will be discussed.[38] With respect to Holocaust-related art, it is worth considering the case involving the painting *Madonna and Child in a Landscape* by Lucas Cranach the Elder. In 2000, the North Carolina Museum of Art surprised the art world by returning the painting immediately after having been presented with evidence that it had been confiscated by the Nazis from the Viennese collector Philipp von Gomperz. Hence, the museum did not force the heirs to prove their claim in court. Gomperz's heirs did not even have to hire a lawyer. They were so contented with the museum's response that they agreed to sell the painting back to the museum at a substantially below-market price.[39] By way of contrast, the dispute over Egon Schiele's *Portrait of Wally* was settled through negotiation

[36] I. Fellrath Gazzini, *Cultural Property Disputes: The Role of Arbitration in Resolving Non-Contractual Disputes* (2004), at 62.

[37] Cornu and Renold, 'Le renouveau des restitutions de biens culturels: les modes alternatifs de règlement des litiges', *JDI* (2009) 493, at 517.

[38] *See* the examples listed in the database *ArThemis*, *available at* <http://unige.ch/art-adr> (last accessed 4 February 2013). *ArThemis* was set up in 2011 by the Art-Law Centre of the University of Geneva.

[39] Yellin, 'North Carolina Art Museum Says It Will Return Painting Tied to Nazi Theft', *N.Y. Times*, 6 February 2000.

only after twelve years of litigation.[40] On July 2010, the parties (the Estate of Lea Bondi, the US Government, and the Leopold Museum of Vienna) announced the out-of-court settlement of the case. The major terms of the agreement are as follows: (i) the Leopold Museum pays the Estate US$19 million; (ii) the Estate releases its claim to the painting; (iii) the US government dismisses the civil forfeiture action; and (iv) the Leopold Museum permanently displays signage next to the painting that sets forth its true provenance.[41]

Negotiation has proved useful also to prevent (or end) costly and lengthy legal battles over stolen or illicitly exported cultural objects. This is proved by the numerous bilateral agreements concluded by source and market nations, and between source nations and foreign museums. Among the various examples available, it is worth considering the agreement between Italy and the United States.[42] This agreement was concluded under the Convention on Cultural Property Implementation Act (CCPIA), which was adopted by the United States in 1983 to implement the 1970 UNESCO Convention. The CCPIA provides a mechanism by which the United States and other states parties to the 1970 UNESCO Convention may enter into bilateral agreements to impose import restrictions on archaeological or ethnological materials that are subject to pillage. On the one hand, the Italy-United States agreement helps protect Italian cultural heritage because the designated materials could enter the United States only if accompanied by an export permit issued by the Italian Government or by verifiable documentation demonstrating that the exportation occurred prior to 19 January 2001. On the other hand, the agreement helps enrich American cultural life through research, educational programs and loans. Significantly, the Agreement established that 'Italy permits the interchange of archaeological materials for cultural, exhibition, educational and scientific purposes' through 'agreements for long-term loans […], agreed upon, on a case by case basis, by American and Italian museums […]' (Article II(E)).

The principles underpinning the Italy-United States agreement have been transposed into the accords concluded between 2006 and 2008 by the Italian

[40] *United States v Portrait of Wally*, 105 F.Supp. 2d 288 (S.D.N.Y. 2000), 2000 U.S. Dist. LEXIS 18713 (S.D.N.Y. 28 Dec. 2000), 2002 U.S. Dist. LEXIS 6445 (S.D.N.Y. 2002), 663 F. Supp. 2d 232 (S.D.N.Y. 2009), No. 99-CV-09940 (S.D.N.Y. filed 29 July 2010). For the details of the case, see Spiegler, 'What the Lady Has Wrought: The Ramifications of the Portrait of Wally Case', *Art & Advocacy, The Art Law Newsletter of Herrick, Feinstein LLP*. (2010), vol. 7, at 1–5; and Dobrzynski, 'The Zealous Collector: A Singular Passion for Amassing Art, One Way or Another', *N.Y. Times*, 24 December 1997.

[41] Press Release, The Art Law Group of Herrick, Feinstein LLP, 'The United States of America, the Estate of Lea Bondi Jaray and the Leopold Museum Settle the Long-Standing Case Involving "Portrait of Wally" by Egon Schiele', 20 July 2010, *available at* <http://info.herrick.com/rs/vm.ashx?ct=24F76A15D4AE4EE0CDD881AFD42F921E91907ABFDA9818CF5AE175767CEAC80BDF416> (last accessed 4 February 2013).

[42] 'Agreement Concerning the Imposition of Import Restrictions on Categories of Archaeological Material Representing the Pre-Classical, Classical, and Imperial Roman Periods of Italy', 19 January 2001, (2001) I.L.M. 1031 ff. In 2011, the agreement was extended for five years, until January 2016.

Government with China, Switzerland,[43] and with a number of foreign museums, including the Boston Museum of Fine Arts, the New York Metropolitan Museum of Art, and the J. Paul Getty Museum of Los Angeles. In addition, similar accords have been signed by various source countries.[44] All in all, these agreements constitute efficient out-of-court settlements that have permitted: (i) the return of several precious antiquities despite the fact that the Italian Government had little legal means to compel museums to return claimed objects[45] and (ii) the development of a continuing program of cultural cooperation involving reciprocal loans and collaboration in the areas of scholarship, conservation, and archaeological investigation. Indeed, such accords aim to foster cooperation and not simply restitution.

2. *Mediation*

Mediation is the intervention of a neutral third party in a dispute with the purpose of assisting the litigants to reach a mutually satisfactory agreement, in a flexible, expeditious, confidential, and less costly manner, also by taking into consideration extra-legal factors. It is when the antagonism between the parties impedes direct negotiations that a mediator is essential to assist them in de-escalating contentiousness, promoting bargains and reciprocal concessions, and maintaining business relationships. As rightly suggested by Palmer, 'Mediation seeks to resolve disputes, not according to the legal analysis and redress of past conduct, but according to the identification of common ground, the development of future relationships and the attainment of future goals',[46]

It is not easy to discover the existence of a mediated claim. This is due to the confidentiality that mediation guarantees the parties. Nevertheless, the following examples demonstrate that mediation represents a useful model to settle restitution claims. The first example relates to the controversy between the Swiss cantons of Zurich and St. Gallen over around one hundred manuscripts, books, and other artefacts stolen during the War of Villmergen of 1712. Given the failure of all attempts to bring about an amicable solution, in 2002 the canton of St. Gallen invoked the mediation of the Confederation relying on Article 44(3) of the Constitution, which states, '[*L*]*es différends entre les cantons ou entre les cantons et la Confédération sont, autant que possible, réglés par la négociation ou la*

[43] The agreement with China is available at <www.rio.beniculturali.it/index.php?it/129/furti-scavi-illeciti-importazione-ed-esportazione-illegale>. The agreement with Switzerland can be found in GU Suppl. to No.171 of 23 July 2008.

[44] *See*, *eg*, the agreement between the Government of Peru and Yale University concluded in November 2010. *See* <http://opac.yale.edu/peru/english/mou.html> (last accessed 4 February 2013); *see also* Taylor, 'Yale and Peru Sign Accord on Machu Picchu Artifacts', *N.Y. Times*, 11 February 2011.

[45] Scovazzi, '*Diviser c'est détruire*: Ethical Principles and Legal Rules in the Field of Return of Cultural Properties', *Rivista di diritto internazionale* (2010) 341, at 380.

[46] N. Palmer, *Museums and the Holocaust: Laws, Principles, and Practice* (2007), at 107.

mediation', An agreement was reached in April 2006. It establishes, *inter alia*, that: (i) the canton of Zurich is the legitimate owner of the items, (ii) the canton of St. Gallen recognizes Zurich's title, (iii) thirty-five valuable manuscripts are loaned to St. Gallen for a renewable thirty-eight-year period, and (iv) St. Gallen will receive a replica of a globe of heaven and earth at the expense of the canton of Zurich. Although it concerned an intra-national dispute, this mediated settlement is noteworthy because it took into consideration the relevance of the disputed objects for the historical and cultural heritage of both cantons.[47]

Although not concerning cultural objects, the settlement of the dispute over the return of a number of human remains from the Natural History Museum of London shows that mediation can find a solution relatively quickly and without high costs. These remains were removed from Tasmanian burial sites around 1850 and subsequently transported to the United Kingdom. The Tasmanian Aboriginal Centre submitted various restitution requests beginning in the 1980s, but the museum always refused these claims. Consequently, the Tasmanian Centre initiated a lawsuit in London against the museum. The centre sought to prevent invasive scientific examinations on the remains, including extractions of DNA, chemical analyses of slivers of bone, as these would have violated Aboriginal customary rights. In view of the lengthy trial and the mounting legal costs, the museum's board of trustees agreed to proceed by means of mediation. The dispute was settled in May 2007 after a three-day-mediation session during which the centre and the museum's representatives jointly determined the extent of permissible scientific investigations on the human remains before their return to Tasmania.[48]

With respect to Holocaust claims, it is necessary to consider that, since the eruption of the restitution movement at the end of the 1990s, various non-forensic institutions have been set up to resolve disputes through mediation. These include the French Restitution Committee and the UK Spoliation Advisory Panel (SAP). Importantly, the municipal laws establishing such commissions were prompted by the principles adopted on the occasion of the Washington Conference on Holocaust-Era Assets.[49] Although non-binding, these principles call for a just solution and impose upon states a moral commitment to assist the return of stolen artworks to their original owners. For instance, Principle 11 establishes: 'Nations are encouraged to develop [...] alternative dispute resolution mechanisms for resolving ownership issues'.

All the non-forensic domestic bodies created in the past two decades have achieved major practical importance, even though their decisions are mere non-binding recommendations. For instance, the SAP provides a form of institutionalized mediation to resolve claims from people or their descendants who

[47] B. Schönenberger, *The Restitution of Cultural Assets* (2009), at 10–11.

[48] L. V. Prott (ed.), *Witnesses to History. A Compendium of Documents and Writings on the Return of Cultural Objects* (2009), at 401 ff.

[49] *Available at* <http://www.lootedart.com/MG7QA043892> (last accessed 4 February 2013).

lost possession of cultural objects during the period 1933–1945 and which are now held in national collections.[50] Although its powers are merely advisory, the panel has been entrusted with the duty of evaluating the legal, factual, and moral aspects of disputes, such as the conduct, the circumstances of the acquisition, the degree of scrupulousness shown in the acquisition and the level of effort in claiming the looted materials.[51] Moreover, as the SAP is not bound by the legal rules of evidence, it can consider facts that a court of law might not be able to access.

Art Resolve is another institution offering mediation for the resolution of disputes about authenticity and attribution, title, and provenance or any other question concerning cultural objects.[52] This non-profit company, which was established in 2000, offers other confidential and effective out-of-court options for the resolution of disputes besides mediation, including early neutral evaluation, expert determination, and arbitration.

It may be argued that mediation will be increasingly used as a result of the amendment of the Statutes of the UNESCO Intergovernmental Committee for Promoting the Return of Cultural Property to its Countries of Origin or its Restitution in Case of Illicit Appropriation (ICPRCP). Created in 1978, the ICPRCP was entrusted with the mandate to assist UNESCO member states in dealing with cases falling outside the scope *ratione temporis* of the 1970 UNESCO Convention. However, this permanent body was not entrusted with jurisdictional powers to rule in inter-state disputes. Rather, it can simply act in an advisory capacity offering a framework for discussion and bilateral negotiation. Therefore, states are neither compelled to bring a case before it, nor to abide by its recommendations. As hinted previously, the UNESCO General Conference amended the ICPRCP Statutes in 2005. Now the ICPRCP is responsible for 'seeking ways and means of facilitating bilateral negotiations for the restitution or return of cultural property to its countries of origin' also through the exercise of—non-binding—mediation (and conciliation) functions. Admittedly, the goal is to enhance the role of the ICPRCP as a specialized interlocutor for the resolution of restitution claims. In effect, over the years it has been called on to solve eight cases only.[53]

3. *Arbitration*

Arbitration is one of the principal non-forensic methods of settling international disputes. The parties to a dispute can settle their controversy by arbitration if they

[50] Spoliation Advisory Panel, 'Constitution and Terms of Reference', *available at* <http://www.culture.gov.uk/what_we_do/cultural_property/3296.aspx> (last accessed 4 February 2013).

[51] As of July 2012, the SAP has made recommendations in twelve cases. *See* Spoliation Advisory Panel, 'Constitution and Terms of Reference', note 50.

[52] *See* <http://www.artresolve.org/index.htm> (last accessed 4 February 2013).

[53] *See* Prott, 'The History and Development of Processes for the Recovery of Cultural Heritage', in Prott (ed.), *see earlier* note 48, at 16. But the most debated case is still pending: the request of Greece for the repatriation of the Parthenon Marbles from the British Museum. Instead, the examination by the ICPRCP of the *Khorvin* case was suspended when the case was brought before Belgian courts,

rely on an arbitration clause contained in a general undertaking (such as a treaty or a contract) or by stipulating a submission agreement (*compromis*).

Notwithstanding the form that it can take, the primary benefit of arbitration resides in the parties' power to shape the process to fit their needs. Disputants can agree, *inter alia*, on the selection of one or more arbitrators, the applicable law and the rules of evidence to be applied.[54] If the parties have failed to subject the agreement to a law of their choice, the *lex fori*, the law of the place of arbitration, applies on a subsidiary basis.[55] Litigants are permitted to include clauses which allow arbitrators to decide according to 'equity', 'good conscience' as well as principles others than those embodied in the rules of the selected system of law. This is not only the case when no national system of law seems appropriate, but also when it is necessary to refer to supra-national rules.[56]

In light of these considerations, arbitration can be considered as a suitable technique to facilitate the settlement of a variety of cultural heritage disputes. First, it seems appropriate to solve cases concerning contractual claims over authenticity. This is due to the confidentiality that arbitration grants, which is important for the professionals involved. Second, arbitration may provide significant advantages in disputes concerning objects requested by the state of origin because arbitrators are in the neutral position to decide questions of sovereignty, national, and international law as well as moral and ethical arguments. This is confirmed by Article 9(2) of the abovementioned agreement entered into by the Italian Ministry of Cultural Heritage and the Metropolitan Museum of Art, according to which 'disputed issues shall be settled in private by arbitration'. Third, arbitration may help to solve the problems arising in the context of international loans, where problems come up not only because of the differences in national laws, but also because borrowers and lenders normally omit to spell out in their loan agreements matters of foremost importance, such as those pertaining to the lender's title, duty to exhibit, and authenticity.[57] Finally, arbitration provides an efficient way to settle Holocaust-related art disputes. This is testified by the case *Maria Altmann v Republic of Austria*.[58] This controversy involved six paintings by Gustav Klimt, which were confiscated by the Nazis in 1938 from Ferdinand Bloch-Bauer, the Jewish uncle of the claimant. Maria Altmann brought suit in the United States

until such time as all internal means of redress have been exhausted. This case was submitted to the ICPRCP in 1985 by Iran and concerns a collection of archaeological objects in the possession of a private collector. *See* ICPRCP, Final Report of the Seventeenth Session, UNESCO Doc. CLT-2011/CONF.208/COM.17/6, May 2011, at 6.

[54] N. Palmer, *Art Loans* (1997), at 373 ff.

[55] Shengchang and Lijun, 'The Role of National Courts and *Lex Fori* in International Commercial Arbitration', in L. Mistelis and J. D. M. Lew (eds), *Pervasive Problems in International Arbitration* (2006) 155–83.

[56] Palmer, *see earlier* note 54, at 380 ff.

[57] Palmer, *see earlier* note 54, at 11, 405–06.

[58] *Maria Altmann v Republic of Austria*, 142 F.Supp.2d 1187 (C.D.Cal. 1999), *aff'd*, 317 F.3d 954 (9th Cir. 2002), *as amended*, 327 F.3d 1246 (9th Cir. 2003), 541 U.S. 677 (2004).

against the holders; that is the Republic of Austria and the Austrian National Gallery. However, the case was not resolved with a judicial decision. The disputants reached an agreement to end the litigation and submit the dispute to arbitration in Austria. Pursuant to the agreement, the panel of three Austrian arbitrators applied Austrian substantive and procedural law. With an award in January 2006, the arbitral panel ruled that Austria was obliged to return the Klimt's masterpieces to Maria Altmann, as the sole descendent of Ferdinand Bloch-Bauer.

V. Critical Appraisal of the Dispute Resolution Methods

Admittedly, the analysis set out in this chapter may convey the impression that both legal and diplomatic avenues could be used to adjudicate restitution cases. However, it should be made clear that, just as for many disputes there is no possible substitute for ordinary court proceedings—especially taking into consideration the enforcement and sanctioning powers of domestic courts—it is rather unlikely that all controversies can be effectively resolved through ADR methods. Moreover, both legal and diplomatic means present deficiencies that frustrate the resolution of claims. This part of the chapter aims to pinpoint such weaknesses.

Starting with litigation, access to municipal courts is the first problem. Although the decision to go to court is for the litigants, lawsuits may be barred by the expiry of limitation periods or the application of anti-seizure legislation or the rules on state immunity.[59] Second, litigation, as an adversarial system, entails zero-sum solutions that often cause antagonism between winners and losers, particularly in cases involving a theft victim and an innocent purchaser. In these cases, judges are forced by the applicable law to assign a financial loss either to the dispossessed owner or the current good faith possessor.[60] Third, resort to litigation entails considerable economic and human expenses. Litigants may not only suffer the loss of time, but also the burden of paying the legal costs for expensive and lengthy proceedings as a consequence of the intricate issues of fact and law involved. Last, judges lack experience in art and cultural matters. Not only do judges err by equating artefacts to chattel, but they also have an insufficient understanding of the dynamics of the illicit trade in antiquities. In effect, there are many decisions where the domestic rules developed for ordinary goods have been applied to disputes involving outstanding cultural treasures and singular problems of evidence, ethics, and morality.[61]

[59] *See earlier* Part II.A.2.

[60] Minyard, 'Adding Tools to the Arsenal: Options for Restitution from the Intermediary Seller and Recovery for Good-Faith Possessors of Nazi-Looted Art', *Tex. Int'l L.J.* (2007–2008) 115, at 116.

[61] Paterson, 'Resolving Material Culture Disputes: Human Rights, Property Rights, and Crimes against Humanity', in J. A. R. Nafziger and A. M. Nicgorski (eds), *Cultural Heritage Issues: The Legacy of Conquest, Colonization, and Commerce* (2009) 371, at 379.

These shortcomings show that litigation before domestic courts cannot be entirely effective. This is why lawyers counsel their clients to settle out of court.[62] In this regard, it is interesting to recall the statement made by Lord Denning in the *Ortiz* case that the retrieval of works of art situated outside the national territory 'must be achieved by diplomatic means'.[63] Moreover, it is worth emphasizing that cultural heritage disputes do not lend themselves to classical adversarial dispute settlement. The safeguarding of the—non-economic—values enfolded in cultural assets requires more than definite and enforceable rulings. The fact that litigation permits the achievement of a settlement imposed *ab extra* by a neutral judge according to strict law is not necessarily an advantage. As a matter of fact, the culture-insensitiveness of ordinary laws and procedures, even if impartially applied, may bring about negative results.

Yet resort to ADR means is not widespread. On the one hand, the rarity of contractual clauses providing in advance for the resolution of disputes through ADR methods is due to the choice to avoid the legal costs of drafting comprehensive contracts. For instance, museum officials prefer to avoid dealing with purely legal matters. This is particularly striking in case of art loans. There is the conviction that museums can resolve controversies among themselves by appealing to professional loyalty and common interest.[64] On the other hand, as said previously, ADR means are not commonly used because they are characterized by some shortcomings.

The voluntary essence of ADR methods constitutes the most significant handicap. Outside the realm of contractual disputes, litigants may be reluctant to resort to negotiation, mediation or arbitration in the absence of significant incentives. This is illustrated by the *Altmann* case, where the Republic of Austria rejected the initial proposal of Maria Altmann to submit the dispute to arbitration. The same holds true as regards negotiation and mediation.

A related problem is that of enforcement. Negotiation cannot guarantee that a dispute will eventually be settled and cannot secure a definitive and immediately enforceable solution. Likewise, there is not a mechanism by which parties can be compelled to honour a mediated settlement. Instead, arbitration awards are generally binding on the parties. This is because the 1958 New York Convention[65] has been signed by over 150 States. This Convention provides for virtually automatic enforcement of arbitration awards by the courts of signatory states. However, the losing party may still fail to honour the award. In this case, the prevailing party

[62] Lowenthal, 'Recovering Looted Jewish Cultural Property', in International Bureau of the Permanent Court of Arbitration (ed.), *Resolution of Cultural Property Disputes* (2004) 139, at 156.

[63] *Attorney General of New Zealand v Ortiz* [1982] 3 QB 432, *rev'd*, [1984] A.C. 1, *add'd*, [1983] 2 All E.R. 93.

[64] Palmer, 'Extra-Curial Resolution of Contract Issues Involving Art and Antiquities: The English Experience', in Byrne-Sutton and Geisinger-Mariéthoz (eds), *see earlier* note 2, at 55, 56–7.

[65] Convention on the Recognition and Enforcement of Foreign Arbitral Awards, 10 June 1958, 330 U.N.T.S. 38.

will have to move for the recognition and enforcement of the award through the court system of the losing party. In the same manner, the losing party may oppose this motion or, alternatively, may attempt to set aside or annul the award through the domestic judiciary.[66]

Furthermore, it is routinely assumed that ADR methods are less costly and time-consuming than litigation. This is certainly true as far as negotiation and mediation are concerned. Instead, this benefit is not always attainable by resorting to arbitration. The whole arbitration process, including the recognition and enforcement of the award, is not always expeditious. In part, these explain the marked contrast between the rarity of arbitrated settlements and the abundance of negotiated and mediated agreements. Last, arbitration entails the risk of partiality. This claim does not derive from the fact that each party is entitled to select his arbitrator (or arbitrators) and that this would be inclined to support the interests of the party by which they have been appointed. More specifically, this problem relates to the fact that arbitrators may tend to favour whatever party is most likely to need their services in the future, irrespective of the other interests involved.[67] In this respect, Lalive went as far as to say that ADR methods could be exploited by unethical art professionals or reckless collectors to avoid judicial proceedings and the ensuing sanctions.[68]

VI. Disclosing the Judicial's Ongoing Penchant for Culture-Sensitive Rulings

The inherent limitations of existing dispute settlement mechanisms, coupled with the deficiencies of the existing legal regime, call for the identification of methods for resolving the recurrent disputes over art objects that can take into account the specificity of art and culture, and the unique features of the art market, and that can reconcile the historical, moral, cultural, financial, and legal issues involved.

In this respect, some scholars contend that the establishment of a unified dispute resolution body with an exclusive, compulsory jurisdiction over cultural heritage disputes would be the ideal mechanism to prioritize cultural heritage concerns.[69] The harmonization of troublesome domestic rules—such as those

[66] The grounds for refusing recognition or enforcement of an award are enumerated in Article V of the 1958 New York Convention. Shengchang and Lijun, *see earlier* note 55.

[67] Shapiro, 'Litigation and Art-Related Disputes', in Byrne-Sutton and Geisinger-Mariéthoz (eds), *see earlier* note 2, at 17, 32–3; G. van Harten, *Investment Treaty Arbitration and Public Law* (2007), at 152–3.

[68] Lalive, 'Themes and Perspectives: Litigation—A Declining Solution to Holocaust-Related Claims?', Paper Presented at the Conference *Dispute Resolution and Holocaust-Related Art Claims: New Principles and Techniques* (London, 18 Oct. 2006).

[69] *See, eg,* Parkhomenko, 'Taking Transnational Cultural Heritage Seriously: Towards a Global System for Resolving Disputes over Stolen and Illegally-Exported Art', *Art Antiquity & L.* (2011) 145 ff.; Anglim Kreder, 'A Nazi-Looted Art Tribunal', *World Arb. & Mediation Rev.* (2007) 693 ff.; Pell,

regarding *bona fide* purchases, formalities for valid transfer of title, statutes of limitations, export restrictions, choice-of-law, and so forth—constitutes another option to bring to the fore the unique nature of cultural heritage and exclude the application of the rules conceived for ordinary goods.

However, neither of these options seems attainable for the time being. The lack of will and the differences between exporting and importing countries make these developments more of a vision for the future than realistic options at present.

Nevertheless, the recent practice demonstrates that an important development is underway, one that, to a degree, could surrogate impracticable structural and legal reforms. The realistic observation of contemporary practice evidences that domestic courts do adopt culture-sensitive decisions in the face of existing structural and legal constraints. As a result, the final outcome of many judicial proceedings is not dissimilar from the settlements that disputants may obtain by resorting to ADR methods. Accordingly, one can see a convergence of the views of judicial and non-judicial adjudicators.

The following pages offer an overview of the most significant culture-sensitive decisions offered by the judicial practice. This jurisprudence allows the reflection that the most effective method of enforcing international law—including international cultural heritage law—is at the domestic level. Furthermore, this case law evidences that the protagonists of the jurisprudential development analysed here are mainly the courts of importing countries, that is, the courts of the countries where stolen or illicitly exported objects are found and where lawsuits are brought. The case law has been divided into four major groups.

1. The first group encompasses the judicial decisions ordering the restitution of cultural objects looted in times of war. Importantly, this case law should be considered as one of the proofs confirming the customary nature of the obligation of restitution enshrined in the treaties adopted since the end of the nineteenth century.[70] The first decision to mention relates to the renowned *Menzel v List* case, where the Belgian owners of a Chagal painting that had been seized by the Nazis in 1941 sued the possessors in the United States.[71] The Supreme Court of New York ordered the restitution of the painting by relying on the Regulations annexed to the 1907 Hague Convention[72] and on foreign case law, such as the Nuremberg Tribunal judgments and the decision *Mazzoni c. Finanze dello Stato*.[73]

The *Altmann* decision is highly relevant to the present analysis.[74] As said, Maria Altmann sued the Republic of Austria and the Austrian National Gallery in the

'Using Arbitral Tribunals to Resolve Disputes Relating to Holocaust-Looted Art', in International Bureau of the Permanent Court of Arbitration (ed), *see earlier* note 62, at 307 ff.; Prunty, 'Toward Establishing an International Tribunal for the Settlement of Cultural Property Disputes: How to Keep Greece from Losing Its Marbles', *Georgetown L.J.* (1983–1984) 1155 ff.

[70] *See earlier* note 22.

[71] 267 N.Y.S.2d 804, 809 (Sup.Ct. N.Y. 1966), *rev'd*, 246 N.E.2d 742 (N.Y. 1969).

[72] *See earlier* note 22.

[73] *Tribunale di Venezia*, 8 Jan. 1927, Foro It., 1927, I, 961 ff.

[74] *See earlier* note 58.

Central District of California seeking the Klimt paintings return, alleging expropriation of property in violation of international law. To establish subject matter jurisdiction, Altmann relied upon the expropriation exception of the Foreign Sovereign Immunities Act (FSIA).[75] This expressly exempts from immunity all cases involving 'rights in property taken in violation of international law', provided the property has a commercial connection to the United States or the agency or instrumentality that owns the property is engaged in 'commercial activity carried out in the United States'.[76] The Republic of Austria and the Gallery moved for dismissal, alleging, *inter alia*, lack of subject matter jurisdiction under the doctrine of sovereign immunity. The District Court denied the defendants' motion for dismissal. Defendants appealed the ruling. The matter arrived before the United States Supreme Court. This determined conclusively that the FSIA applied retroactively to events that occurred before the Act's enactment (1976), thereby overruling foreign sovereign immunity. The *Altmann* decision is significant because it reflects the US judiciary's sentiment to stretch the limits of legal interpretation in order to create an environment that provides greater opportunities to recover looted artwork, even if owned by foreign sovereigns and their agents.[77] By doing so, US judges confirmed the unique nature of Holocaust-related art claims and showed support for the opinion that the objects taken by the Nazis must be returned regardless of the defences that may be raised by current possessors.[78] As the Nazi's plunder of artworks constituted one aspect of the systematic stripping of lives aimed to eradicate the Jewish race, the Nazi looting cannot be considered 'traditional' spoils of war and hence Holocaust-related claims cannot be seen as mere title claims.[79]

Interestingly, this argument was endorsed by the District Court of Rhode Island in the *Vineberg* case,[80] which concerned the painting *Girl from the Sabiner Mountain* by Winterhalter, that the original owner was forced to liquidate in 1935. The Court ordered the restitution of the painting and established the principle that all sales made by Jewish owners between 1933 and 1945 are not only presumed to have been done under threats, hence invalid, but are to be considered as theft. The Court acknowledged that the defendant acquired the artwork through no wrongdoing on her part, but because the defendant's predecessor-in-interest did not have title to the painting, the defendant could not assert a valid ownership claim to it.

[75] 28 U.S.C. §§1602–1607 (1976). The FSIA provides the exclusive basis for jurisdiction in US courts over civil actions against foreign governments.

[76] 28 U.S.C. § 1605(a)(3).

[77] The *Altmann* precedent resonated in later cases, including *Malewicz et al. v City of Amsterdam* (U.S. Dist. LEXIS 46312, D.D.C., 27 June 2007) and *Claude Cassirer v The Kingdom of Spain and the Thyssen-Bornemisza Collection Foundation* (461 F.Supp.2d 1157 (C.D. Cal. 2006)).

[78] Paterson, *see earlier* note 61, at 373.

[79] M. J. Kurtz, *America and the Return of Nazi Contraband* (2006), at 26 ff.

[80] *Vineberg et al. v Maria-Louise Bissonnette* et al., 529 F.Supp.2d 300, 301 (27 December 2007).

In 2011, two New York courts settled the case over a van Gogh drawing by narrowing the scope of application of the FSIA.[81] The case concerned the drawing 'View of Les Saintes-Maries-de-la-Mer' that Margare the Mauthner, a German of Jewish descent, allegedly sold under duress during the Nazi era. The District Court and the Court of Appeals rejected the claim and affirmed that the aforementioned FSIA's exception to state immunity did not apply to the case because the drawing was not 'taken' by a sovereign entity, but by a private individual, who subsequently bequeathed the drawing to the Swiss Confederation. In other words, the Courts dismissed the action for lack of subject matter jurisdiction by establishing that the FSIA's exception could only be triggered by the acts of a sovereign state, not of a private individual.[82]

2. The second group includes the jurisprudence with which courts have recognized and implemented the laws of source countries despite the default rule against the extraterritoriality of export laws.[83] In the *Schultz* case,[84] a New York court convicted an art dealer under the NSPA for conspiring to receive stolen Egyptian antiquities. As US courts traditionally do not enforce the export controls of other countries, the defence argued that the pertinent Egyptian law did not vest ownership in the state, so that there was no theft, only a violation of Egypt's export control. However, after listening to testimony from Egyptian officials, the *Schultz* Court established that the Egyptian law was a true patrimony law. Accordingly, the Court confirmed that the NSPA applied to objects stolen in violation of foreign patrimony laws. The *Schultz* decision[85] also demonstrated that US courts allow a sort of 'hidden' implementation of foreign export regulations. In effect, the courts of the United States tend to enforce foreign laws regardless of the state's prior possession. This does not mean that US courts do not differentiate between 'theft' and 'illegal exportation'. Rather, it means that they recognize and deem as worthy of protection situations with a connection to a status similar to ownership.

In the United States, another piece of legislation has been used to implement foreign laws protecting archaeological sites: the Archaeological Resources Protection Act (ARPA).[86] Although the proclaimed purpose of this act is the protection of archaeological resources originating within the United States, since

[81] *Andrew Orkin v The Swiss Confederation, et al.*, 2011 U.S. Dist. Lexis 4357 (13 January 2011); *Andrew Orkin v The Swiss Confederation, et al.*, 770 F. Supp. 2d 612, 2011 U.S. Lexis 24507 (S.D.N.Y. 11 March 2011), *aff'd*, *Andrew Orkin v The Swiss Confederation, et al.*, 2011 U.S. App. (12 October 2011).

[82] *Orkin v The Swiss Confederation* (S.D.N.Y. 11 March 2011), at 7.

[83] *See earlier* Part II.A.1.

[84] *United States v Schultz*, 178 F. Supp. 2d 445 (S.D.N.Y. 2002), *aff'd*, 333 F.3d 393 (2d Cir. 2003).

[85] Among the cases leading up to it there are: *United States v McClain*, 545 F.2d 988, 991–992 (5th Cir. 1977); *United States v Hollinshead*, 495 F.2d 1154 (9th Cir. 1974); *United States v Pre-Columbian Artefacts*, 845 F.Supp.544 (N.D. III. 1993).

[86] 16 U.S.C. §§470aa-470mm (1979).

1996 federal prosecutors have applied ARPA to antiquities stolen from foreign states on at least three occasions: the first involved an ancient vase,[87] the second Peruvian artefacts,[88] the third Asian antiquities.[89]

The appeal decision of the case *Iran v Barakat* brought the law of the United Kingdom into line with the law and jurisprudence of the United States.[90] In this case, Iran sued the London-based Barakat gallery to recover a collection of antiquities affirming that they were taken in violation of its national ownership laws. The Court of Appeals ruled that British courts should recognize Iran's national ownership law in order to allow Iran to recover its antiquities.[91] Notably, the Appellate Court reached this conclusion by relying on the case *United States v Schultz* and on a public policy argument:

> [T]here are positive reasons of policy why a claim by a State to recover antiquities which form part of its national heritage [...] should not be shut out [...]. There is international recognition that States should assist one another to prevent the unlawful removal of cultural objects including antiquities.[92]

According to the Court, states were required to engage in mutual assistance by virtue of the instruments having the purpose of preventing unlawful dealing in property[93]—despite the fact that these were not directly applicable to this case—as these

> illustrate the international acceptance of the desirability of protection of the national heritage. A refusal to recognise the title of a foreign State, conferred by its law, to antiquities unless they had come into the possession of such State, would in most cases render it impossible for this country to recognise any claim by such a State to recover antiquities unlawfully exported to this country.[94]

Finally, the case concerning the *Nuestra Señora de las Mercedes* is relevant to the present analysis to the extent that it involved the questions whether a state can assert ownership over property discovered in international waters and whether a state can impede a salvage company exploiting that property. This dispute began in 2007 when Odyssey Marine Exploration discovered the remains of a 19th-century shipwreck, code-named *Black Swan*, and transferred to Florida a

[87] *United States v An Archaic Etruscan Pottery Ceremonial Vase C. Late 7th Century, B.C.*, No.1:96-cv-09437 (S.D.N.Y. 24 March 1997).

[88] *See* Glod, 'Arlington Man Pleads Guilty to Selling Protected Artifacts', *Wash. Post*, 25 September 2003.

[89] *See* Wyatt, 'Four California Museums Are Raided', *N.Y. Times*, 25 January 2008.

[90] *Government of the Islamic Republic of Iran v The Barakat Galleries Ltd* [2007] EWHC 705 QB, *rev'd*, [2007] EWCA Civ.1374.

[91] Para. 163.

[92] Paras. 154–5.

[93] The Court referred to the 1970 UNESCO Convention, the 1995 UNIDROIT Convention, Directive 93/7 on the Return of Cultural Objects Illegally Exported from the Territory of a Member State (OJ L74/74, 27 March 1993), and the Commonwealth Scheme for the Protection of the Material Cultural Heritage of 1993.

[94] Paras. 155–63.

collection of silver and gold coins and a number of other artefacts. Odyssey did not disclose the exact location of the wreck; it only admitted to have discovered it in international waters in conformity with the law of salvage and UNCLOS. The Spanish Government suspected the find came from the *Nuestra Señora de las Mercedes*, a frigate carrying treasure back from Peru which was sunk by British gunboats in 1804. In the court cases that followed, Odyssey claimed the trove under the law of finds, while Spain asserted its sovereign immunity rights over the treasure. With the decision of 21 September 2011,[95] a Court of Appeals ruled that the objects brought up from the *Black Swan* should be released immediately to Spain, thereby setting a precedent limiting the activities of treasure hunters and excluding a first-come-first-served approach for the heritage found beyond territorial waters. The decision was applauded by archaeologists and the heritage community who contend that treasure hunting contradicts the aims of the 2001 UNESCO Convention,[96] according to which '[u]nderwater cultural heritage shall not be traded, sold, bought or bartered as commercial goods'.[97]

3. The third group reveals a tendency towards the tightening of the obligation to investigate the provenance of art on the part of purchasers. Failure to enquire and research on the part of purchasers entails that the standard of care regarding due diligence has not been met. This jurisprudence demonstrates that the increase in the level of diligence affects the distribution of the burden of proof: whereas a claimant has to prove the existence of suspicious circumstances, the defendant has to present proof that she complied with all obligations of diligence.[98] Article 4(4) of the 1995 UNIDROIT Convention constitutes a useful codification of an international standard of diligence for a flexible assessment of the circumstances of the acquisition:

> In determining whether the possessor exercised due diligence, regard shall be had to all the circumstances of the acquisition, including the character of the parties, the price paid, whether the possessor consulted any reasonably accessible register of stolen cultural objects, and any other relevant information and documentation which it could reasonably have obtained, and whether the possessor consulted accessible agencies or took any other step that a reasonable person would have taken in the circumstances.

Among the cases illustrating that judges demand increased levels of diligence are *Goldberg* and *Schultz*.[99] Yet there are other cases to consider.[100] In 1996, the Swiss Federal Tribunal decided a case concerning a stolen arms collection. It ruled

[95] *Odyssey Marine Exploration, Inc. v The Unidentified Shipwrecked Vessel*, No. 8:07-cv00614-SDM-MAP, 21 September 2011.

[96] Sharpe, 'Cache of Sunken Coins Returned to Spain', *Art Newspaper*, 14 March 2012.

[97] Rule 2 of the Rules Concerning Activities Directed at Underwater Cultural Heritage, annexed to the 2001 UNESCO Convention.

[98] Schönenberger, *see earlier* note 47, at 192–3.

[99] *See earlier* notes 34 and 84, respectively.

[100] Apart from the cases that follow, see also *Demartini c Williams*, Tribunal Correctionnel, 18th Chamber, 6 July 2001, and *Porter v Wertz*, 416 N.Y.S.2d 254, 259 (App. Div. 1979).

that a purchaser of antiquities must show he made all reasonable efforts to determine whether the seller had good title. The Tribunal held that a general obligation for the purchaser to make enquiries not only exists in the case of a specific suspicion but also if there are circumstances that give cause for reasonable doubt.[101] In *De Prevail v Adrian Alan Ltd*, an English court ordered the restitution of two stolen candelabra that were found in the possession of an antique dealer. The court held that the defendant did not act in good faith as he should have put on notice the doubtful provenance of these objects because of their unique character and peculiar features, and should not have bought them without further verifying the vendor's title.[102]

4. The last group of case law shows that domestic courts have found ways to allow claimants to sue even many years after the wrongdoing. As hinted earlier, because art objects are portable and easy to conceal, thieves hide them until limitation periods have elapsed. Most limitations statutes dictate that courts calculate the period within which a plaintiff may bring an action from the time the cause of action accrues. Such statutes are very specific about the length of limitation periods, but often leave the question of the triggering event for the accrual up to the courts. In the United States, courts have taken advantage of this 'gap' to develop two rules: the 'demand and refusal' rule and the 'discovery' rule. According to the former, the cause of action does not accrue until the true owner has made a demand for the return of stolen property and the good faith possessor has refused the demand.[103] This means that an innocent purchaser's possession cannot be deemed right or wrong until the original owner demands a return. The discovery rule provides that actions to recover stolen objects do not accrue until the actual discovery of the whereabouts of the object or the identity of the possessor.[104] In *Goldberg*, the Court held that the claim of Cyprus was timely because the 'discovery rule' and the doctrine of 'fraudulent concealment' prevented the statute of limitations from running. The doctrine of fraudulent concealment has its origins in equity: it stops a defendant from asserting a statute of limitations defence if he has concealed material facts, either by deceit or by a violation of duty, thus preventing the plaintiff from discovering a possible cause of action.[105]

Clearly, these rules favour the protection of dispossessed owners at the expense of the interests of good-faith purchasers in line with common law jurisdictions' predilection for the *nemo dat quod non habet* principle. Moreover, the same

[101] *Insurance X v A.M.*, ATF 122 III 1, 5 March 1996, JdT, 1997, I, 157.

[102] *De Préval v Adrian Alan Ltd* (1997), unreported, commented by Redmond-Cooper, 'Good Faith Acquisition of Stolen Art', *Art Antiquity & L.* (1997), No.1, at 55 ff.

[103] *See, eg, Solomon R. Guggenheim Found. v Lubell*, 567 N.Y.S.2d 623 (Ct. App.1991).

[104] *See, eg, Naftzger v American Numismatic Society*, 42 Cal. App. 4th 421 (1996).

[105] *Autocephalous Greek Orthodox Church of Cyprus v Goldberg*, 717 F. Supp. 1374 (S.D. Ind. 1989), *aff'd*, 917 F.2d 278 (7th Cir. 1990), at 1387–88.

jurisprudential solutions should be seen as important means to limit the harsh results that the application of statutes of limitation generates, thereby clearing the way to the enforcement of cultural heritage law.

VII. International Public Policy and Coordination in Dispute Settlement for the Enforcement of Cultural Heritage Law

Taken as a whole, the culture-sensitive jurisprudence analysed earlier could be seen as one of the materialization of a developing international public policy based on the needs to warrant the restitution of wrongfully removed art objects and in turn to protect cultural heritage from the risk of dispersion. Sometimes referred to as 'transnational public policy', such international public policy can be described as a set of principles that can be employed to nullify or flout the agreements and rules that contravene certain fundamental values or interests as to which a broad consensus has emerged in the international community.[106]

In the cultural heritage realm, the existence of this international public policy argument has been highlighted in numerous cases. Apart from *Barakat*,[107] in the *Nigerian mask* case the *Bundesgerichtshof* (the German Federal Court of Justice) declared that a shipping insurance contract was void because contrary to German 'good morals' in light of the 1970 UNESCO Convention, as an instrument representing the emerging international public policy on the issue of restitution:

> In the interest of the safeguarding of the morality of the international trade in cultural goods, the export of cultural objects in violation of an export prohibition of the State of origin does not deserve the protection by private law including the protection by the insurance of the transportation of cultural goods from the territory of a foreign State in violation of that State's export control laws.[108]

Similarly, in 1997, a Swiss court ordered the return of a stolen painting to France and emphasised that the 1970 UNESCO Convention and the 1995 UNIDROIT Convention contain principles expressing an '*ordre public internationale*' either in force or in formation, and which '*concrétisent l'impératif d'une lutte internationale efficace contre le trafic de biens culturels*'.[109]

Quite clearly, this transnational public policy originates primarily from the treaties promulgated under the aegis of UNESCO. Accordingly, the fact that in the past few years many states with vigorous art markets have ratified the

[106] Mayer, 'Effect of International Public Policy in International Arbitration', in Mistelis and Lew (eds), *see earlier* note 55, at 61–9.

[107] *See earlier* note 90.

[108] *Entscheidungen des Bundeserichtshofs in Zivilsachen*, BGH, 22 June 1972, BGHZ 59 No.14, 82.

[109] *L. v Chambre d'accusation du Canton de Genève*, ATF 123 II 134, 1 April 1997, SJ 1997, 529.

1954 Hague Convention and the 1970 UNESCO Convention signifies that this protective policy is heading toward universal participation.[110]

However, given the shortcomings pinpointed, and that only a few of the obligations contained in cultural heritage treaties are capable of international enforcement,[111] it seems fair to say that the international public policy and the culture-sensitive jurisprudential trend under consideration have not been inspired only by the standard-setting activity of UNESCO. Indeed, the case law evidences that domestic courts have espoused solutions that seem responsive to private regulations and to the non-confrontational models crafted by other stakeholders, including (other) intergovernmental organizations, States, non-governmental organizations and museums. These include: (i) the documents adopted to guide the resolution of claims over cultural objects misappropriated during the Second World War[112] or transferred in violation of the legislation of the country of origin;[113] (ii) the ethical codes adopted by museums, museum associations[114] and associations of art trade professionals;[115](iii) the tailored rules and non-adversarial procedures developed by international and non-governmental organizations aimed at the resolution of cultural heritage-related disputes;[116] and, finally, (iv) the numerous negotiated and mediated agreements entered into by states and museums.

[110] To date, 123 States are parties to the 1970 UNESCO Convention and 126 States are parties to the 1954 Hague Convention. Updated list is available at <http://portal.unesco.org/en/ev.php-URL_ID=12025&URL_DO=DO_TOPIC&URL_SECTION=-471.html> (last accessed 4 February 2013). Instead, thirty-three states have ratified the UNIDROIT Convention thus far. Updated list is available at <www.unidroit.org/english/implement/i-95.pdf> (last accessed 4 February 2013).

[111] C. Forrest, *International Law and the Protection of Cultural Heritage* (2011), at 400.

[112] *See, eg,* the Washington Principles (*see earlier* note 49); the 1999 Council of Europe Parliamentary Assembly Resolution 1205 on Looted Jewish Cultural Property; the 2000 Vilnius Declaration issued as a result of the International Forum on Holocaust Era Looted Cultural Assets; Resolution A5–0408/2003 of 17 December 2003 of the European Parliament; and the 2009 Terezin Declaration issued as a result of the Holocaust Era Assets Conference convened under the auspices of the European Union and of the Czech Presidency.

[113] *See, eg,* ICOM's General Assembly, Resolution No. 4, Preventing Illicit Traffic and Promoting the Physical Return, Repatriation, and Restitution of Cultural Property (2007); ICOM Legal Affairs & Properties Standing Committee, Report on the International Process for the Resolution of Disputes over the Ownership of Objects in Museum Collections (2005).

[114] *See, eg,* Code of the Association of Art Museum Directors; Codes and Guidelines of the American Association of Museums; Acquisition Policy of the J. Paul Getty Museum; Guidelines of the British Department for Culture, Media, and Sport; Code of Ethics of the UK Museums Association; *see also* ICOM Code of Ethics for Museums.

[115] *See, eg,* Code of Practice for the Control of Trading in Works of Art (British Code); Code of Ethics of the International Association of Dealers in Ancient Art (IADAA); Codes of Due Diligence for Auctioneers and Dealers of the Council for the Prevention of Art Theft (CoPAT); *Usages de l'Association des Commerçant d'Art de Suisse*; *see also* International Code of Ethics for Dealers in Cultural Property adopted in 1999 by UNESCO.

[116] See the ICPRCP mediation or conciliation functions (*see earlier* Part IV.B.2 Mediation); the Arbitration and Mediation Center and the ADR Service for Art and Cultural Heritage of the World Intellectual Property Organization (WIPO); the Art and Cultural Heritage Mediation Program

Generally speaking, these solutions necessitate the compliance with the international and national legal standards in force and either call for abandoning overly legalistic approaches in favour of an ethical one or for legislative change.[117]

In addition, the gradual convergence between the approaches of non-judicial adjudicators and domestic courts can be ascribed to the intensifying rate with which the latter engage in cross-fertilization, that is, the practice through which judges—whether or not belonging to the same legal system—refer to and borrow decisions from each other in order to better cope with the disputes pending before them. The result of this judicial interaction is a sort of global jurisprudential networking that enables decision makers to forge a dynamic jurisprudential process of law interpretation and law enforcement for the proper settlement of restitution cases.[118]

In conclusion, this chapter has examined the problem of the enforcement of cultural heritage law from an alternative approach, one that emphasizes the role played by the stakeholders of the cultural heritage milieu and adjudicators in bringing about a virtuous circle: the increasing adoption of non-confrontational solutions to restitution claims by international organizations, states, and non-state entities nourishes the international public policy described in this chapter; in turn, the progressive consolidation of this transnational public policy influences the work of extra-judicial as well as judicial adjudicators, with the latter often seeking guidance from foreign authorities; finally, the ensuing case law reinforces the determination of all stakeholders to resort to non-adversarial solutions as the best method to enhance the enforcement of cultural heritage law.

launched in 2011 by the International Council of Museums (ICOM), together with the WIPO ADR Service for Art and Cultural Heritage.

117 For instance, Article 13 of Resolution 1205 (*see earlier* note 113) calls for 'legislative change with particular regard being paid to: a) extending or removing statutory limitation periods [...]'.

118 For an overview of the practice of cross-fertilization in the field of cultural heritage *see* Chechi, 'The Role of Domestic Courts in Resolving Restitution Cases: Unveiling Judicial Strategies for Culture-Sensitive Settlements', in M.-A. Renold, A. Chechi, and A. L. Bandle (eds), *Resolving Disputes in Cultural Property* (2012) 147.

10

Social Norms and Illicit Cultural Heritage

*Derek Fincham**

I. Introduction

Real change has emerged in the struggle to prevent the theft of art and heritage. In the late 1960s, awareness was raised over the problems posed by looting and the trade,[1] and international and domestic laws were strengthened to respond to these threats.[2] Reform in the law can certainly enact powerful change. However, before we propose even more legal solutions, we should consider the efficacy of reforms that previous transformations in the law have made. Many cultural heritage advocates argue for more laws, often overestimating the ability of law to eliminate looting and theft.[3] Consider criminal prosecutions, which in isolation will have difficulty in stemming the illicit trade in cultural objects.[4] As the criminologist Simon Mackenzie argues, there exist a varied collection of individuals who deal in and are responsible for illicit activity, and a wide range of regulation would be ideal, including not just the regulation of individuals at the high level of activity, such as antiquities dealers, but self-regulation, sanctions, and incentives at mid-level

* Derek Fincham is an Assistant Professor at South Texas College of Law. Since 2008 he has served as a trustee of the Association for Research into Crimes Against Art (ARCA). He earned his PhD in law from the University of Aberdeen, Scotland examining the response of the United States and the United Kingdom to the illicit trade in cultural heritage. He also holds a JD from Wake Forest University and a BA from the University of Kansas.

[1] *See* Coggins, 'Illicit Traffic of Pre-Columbian Antiquities', 29 *Art J.* (1969), at 94–114.

[2] This has taken place in a number of countries. In the United States these laws include the National Historic Preservation Act of 1966, 16 U.S.C. § 470 (2006); the Archaeological Resources Protection Act of 1979, 16 U.S.C. §§ 470aa-470mm (2006); and the Cultural Property Implementation Act, 19 U.S.C. § 2601 et seq. (2006).

[3] As Professor Macey argues in a more general context: 'Over a very wide range of human interaction, the content of the relevant legal rules simply does not matter very much. People do not bother to learn the underlying legal rules that affect their actions and rely instead on norms and customs to govern their behavior'. Macey, 'Public and Private Ordering and the Production of Legitimate Legal Rules', 82 *Cornell L. Rev.* (1997) 1123, at 1126.

[4] The author has made a similar argument with respect to criminal regulation of the illicit trade in antiquities. Fincham, 'Why U.S. Federal Criminal Penalties for Dealing in Illicit Cultural Property Are Ineffective, and a Pragmatic Alternative', 25 *Cordozo Arts & Ent. L.J.* (2007) 597, at 601.

activity such as administrative sanctions.[5] When prosecutions do take place, they have the potential to affect the everyday operation of the antiquities trade and museum practices, yet too often a prosecution or return of a long-ago looted object ends the conversation with calls for further investigation and action. But more laws are not the solution. Rather, we need better regulation, and to achieve this, more attention needs to be paid to how targeted groups have altered their behaviour and why. As Mackenzie argues, better models of understanding the trade will ideally create 'a discussion about effective regulation which can draw on current thinking that is more sophisticated than calls for "more law"'.[6] To move beyond the calls for more laws, let us examine the recent exercise of cultural heritage law and what effects can be observed.

There are of course two competing ideas about how works of art should be controlled, and both have been exhaustively debated.[7] One set adopted by some museums and art dealers conceives of a system in which works of art should be moved internationally, and these objects are best preserved by residing in museums or in the art market.[8] This view often ignores or minimizes the destruction of information and the removal of objects from important heritage sites. In contrast, another set of norms suggests that the demand for antiquities and works of art encourages the looting of sites. The sharp conflict between these different views of heritage has produced an entrenched and often unhelpful debate. By examining how behaviours have changed, we can begin to construct a foundation for arriving at common-sense approaches which reduce the looting of sites and the destruction of history.[9] When it comes to illicit cultural heritage, archaeologists and the collector community do actually agree on a few core ideas: they lament the theft of art, the destruction of archaeological context, and the looting of archaeology. Even the hardened buyers and sellers of material cultural heritage have been forced into a grudging appreciation of the laws which apply to cultural objects.[10] The disagreement emerges when it comes time to propose solutions and consider the causes of the illicit activity. Nevertheless these solutions are

[5] Mackenzie, 'Illicit Deals in Cultural Objects as Crimes of the Powerful', 56 *J. Crime, L. & Social Change* (2011) 133, at 145–6.

[6] Mackenzie, 'Illicit Deals in Cultural Objects as Crimes of the Powerful', at 149.

[7] *See* Merryman, 'Two Ways of Thinking about Cultural Property', 80 *Am. J. Int'l L.* (1986) 831.

[8] *See, eg*, James B. Cuno, *Who Owns Antiquity?: Museums and the Battle over Our Ancient Heritage* (2008); Rothstein, 'Antiquities, the World Is Your Homeland', *N.Y. Times*, 27 May 2008, <http://www.nytimes.com/2008/05/27/arts/design/27conn.html?_r=1&pagewanted=all> (last accessed 4 February 2013).

[9] Fincham, 'A Coordinated Legal and Policy Approach to Undiscovered Antiquities: Adapting the Cultural Heritage Policy of England and Wales to Other Nations of Origin', 15 *Int'l J. Cultural Prop.* (2008) 347, at 366.

[10] Philippe de Montebello, the long-serving former director of New York's Metropolitan Museum of Art, has acknowledged that museums should abide by the law, yet is 'puzzled, by the zeal with which the United States rushes to embrace foreign laws that can ultimately deprive its own citizens of important objects useful to the education and delectation of its own citizens'. Kennedy and Eakin, 'Met Chief, Unbowed, Defends Museum's Role', *N.Y. Times*, 28 February 2006, <http://www.nytimes.com/2006/02/28/artws/28mont.html> (last accessed 4 February 2013).

elusive. National borders are no barrier to works of art, and limited law enforcement resources have been directed at small pockets of the collector and dealer community. We should be paying more attention to the important figures in the cultural heritage community and how their behaviour may be changing.

Two recent events involving prominent members of the dealer and collector community signal the emergence of fundamental changes. The first involved the prosecution of prominent antiquities dealer Frederick Schultz. He was convicted of conspiring to receive stolen Egyptian antiquities, but before his conviction he was a prominent Manhattan art dealer who was publicly critical of the regulation of the antiquities trade.[11] When the law seems unfair or overly restrictive to an antiquities dealer, he or she may decide to violate and evade it. Schultz served as the president of the National Association of Dealers in Antique, Oriental and Primitive Art and was very critical of a 2001 bilateral agreement imposing import restrictions on certain antiquities originating from Italy, arguing, 'It is a very bad precedent in many regards .... These kind of broadly defined restrictions would be impossible to comply with and impossible to enforce'.[12] So he was publicly critical of the use of import restrictions to regulate antiquities, and also violated these laws. He refused to abide by and accept the legal restrictions, erecting his own code, perhaps because the present body of cultural heritage law was in his view too broad to allow him to make a living as an antiquities dealer, or he did not sufficiently value archaeological context or respect the sovereign rights of Egypt to care for its own heritage.

The second involved former Getty Curator Marion True, who was tried in Italy for conspiring to acquire stolen antiquities.[13] True was a complicated figure. On the one hand, she was an advocate for positive change. In a speech made at the annual AAMD gathering in 2000, she criticized antiquities dealers, argued for more accountability on the part of museum staff and their boards, and most notably she argued that 'if serious efforts to establish a clear pedigree for the object's recent past prove futile, it is most likely—if not certain—that it is the produce of the illicit trade and we must accept responsibility for that fact'.[14] And she backed up these calls for reform with real action in one notable case involving looted mosaics from Cyprus. When they were offered to the Getty she refused them as the Seventh Circuit Court of Appeals noted:

> [T]he aptly-named Dr. True explained to the dealers that she had a working relationship with the Republic of Cyprus and that she was duty-bound to contact Cypriot officials about them. Dr. True called Dr. Vassos Karageorghis, the Director of the Republic's Department

[11] *United States v Schultz*, 333 F.3d 393, 395 (2d Cir. 2003).

[12] Bohlen, 'Old Rarities, New Respect: U.S. Works with Italy', *N.Y. Times*, 28 February 2001.

[13] Povoledo, 'Italy and U.S. Sign Antiquities Accord', *N.Y. Times*, 22 February 2006, <http://query.nytimes.com/gst/fullpage.html?res=9904EED7113EF931A15751C0A9609C8B63&pagewanted=all> (last accessed 4 February 2013).

[14] Marion True, Speech Before the AAMD, presented in Denver, Colorado (1 June 2000), *available at* <https://www.documentcloud.org/documents/254275-marion-trues-2000-denver-presentation.html> (last accessed 4 February 2013).

of Antiquities and one of the primary Cypriot officials involved in the worldwide search for the mosaics. Dr. Karageorghis verified that the Republic was in fact hunting for the mosaics that had been described to Dr. True, and he set in motion the investigative and legal machinery that ultimately resulted in the Republic learning that they were in Goldberg's possession in Indianapolis.[15]

But on the other hand, she was using many of the same hidden policies she was criticizing to violate domestic and international law. This ultimately resulted in a public and lengthy trial in Italy and the return of a number of objects from the Getty to Italy. Although her prosecution was dismissed when the statute of limitations expired on her indictment,[16] she has been the subject of a great deal of criticism, and it seems unlikely that she will return to the heritage field.[17]

Both of these prominent prosecutions were warnings that investigations may become more widespread, and when they occur, the consequences are severe. Change has emerged in the wake of these two public prosecutions in the form of informal rules and social norms. Rather than simply encourage more prosecutions and a rigid law-and-order approach, perhaps a more productive short-term strategy would work in tandem with the law to encourage a collective shift in behaviour of the dealer and collector community.

These social norms regulate the actions of individuals, and can also shape the operation of the law.[18] By examining what individuals are actually doing, we can see what areas might need legal reform and how enforcement resources should be allocated. Laws are in place now. All nations forbid theft, and the wholesale destruction of archaeological sites is a major violation of both domestic and international law. The centres of the art trade are increasingly recognizing foreign ownership of cultural heritage.[19] Yet bringing behaviour in line with these laws has proved difficult. Not only are works of art valuable and portable,[20] but the sale of works of art too often involves restricting information.[21] When the law regulating art and heritage fails to change behaviour in the collector community—these norms fill the void.

[15] *Autocephalous Church v Goldberg*, 917 F.2d 278, 283 (7th Cir. 1990).

[16] Felch, 'Charges Dismissed against Ex-Getty Curator Marian True by Italian Judge' (updated), *L.A. Time Culture Monster*, <http://latimesblogs.latimes.com/culturemonster/2010/10/charges-dismissed-against-getty-curator-marion-true-by-italian-judge.html> (last accessed 13 October 2010).

[17] Bell, 'The Beautiful and the True', WSJ.com (2 July 2011), <http://online.wsj.com/article/SB10001424052702303339904576405983959162302.html?mod=googlenews_wsj> (last accessed 4 February 2013).

[18] Robert C. Ellickson, *Order without Law: How Neighbors Settle Disputes* (1991), at 4–6.

[19] *Republic of Iran v Barakat Galleries* [2007] EWCA Civ 1374.

[20] *Schultz v United States*, 333 F.3d 393 (2d Cir. 2003).

[21] Fincham, *see* note 4, at 612. Courts have also criticized the lack of information given by the art trade, particularly with respect to Nazi-era claims. *See, eg, Menzel v List*, 24 N.Y.2d 91, 96–8 (1969) ('Had the Perls taken the trouble to inquire as to title, they could have sold to List subject to any existing lawful claims unknown to them at the time of the sale'.).

This is not to say domestic and international laws have not been instrumental in producing reform. They have. But the next logical step should consider how the law impacts the behaviour of individuals. Social norms are an uneasy yet inevitable partner with the law in impacting behaviour. In some cases, norms conflict with the legal regime; in other cases these norms change the law itself. The laws of nations and international conventions attempt to prevent theft and destruction from the top down. By examining some of the recent shifts in behaviour and attitudes in the heritage community we can see how much change legal instruments have produced. The domestic and international law which affects cultural heritage can change the behaviour of important actors: museum officials, dealers in art, buyers of art, and the individuals who transport antiquities across national borders. There are areas where the law has shifted the culture. By looking at the important role social norms play we can arrive at some observations on how norms are created, how they affect behaviour, and cultivate strategies for future beneficial changes in the actions of dealers, collectors, local populations, and museums.

Many have advocated solutions for preventing cultural heritage crimes. Some advocate continued legal restrictions;[22] others propose that the only solution is an outright end to the trade;[23] while at the other extreme some have proposed a licit market in cultural objects.[24] A varied group of individuals end up producing the norms which govern cultural objects. States have built the legal framework which governs cultural objects.[25] But cultural heritage advocates would be well-served by broadening their approach.[26] In the forty years which have elapsed since the 1970 UNESCO Convention, it remains an open question whether increased repatriation and prosecutions are in fact stopping the looting of archaeological sites and impacting the right individuals. As Colin Renfrew has observed, the world has begun to pay closer attention to the looting of sites, even though calls for repatriation and export controls of objects has not stemmed the destruction.[27]

[22] *See* Gerstenblith, 'Controlling the International Market in Antiquities: Reducing the Harm, Preserving the Past', 8 *Chi. J. Int'l L.* (2007) 169.

[23] *See* Stanish, 'Forging Ahead—How I Learned to Stop Worrying and Love eBay', *Archeology* (2009), <http://www.archaeology.org/0905/etc/insider.html> (last accessed 4 February 2013).

[24] *See* Merryman, 'A Licit International Trade in Cultural Objects', 4 *Int'l J. Cultural Prop.* (1995) 13.

[25] Both the leading multilateral treaties are directly linked to states, including both the Convention on the Means of Prohibiting and Preventing the Illicit Import, Export and Transfer of Ownership of Cultural Property, 14 November 1970,823 U.N.T.S. 231 (hereinafter 1970 UNESCO Convention), as well as the UNIDROIT Convention on Stolen or Illegally Exported Cultural Objects, 24 June 1995, 34 I.L.M. 1330 (hereinafter UNIDROIT Convention).

[26] Repatriation has even been defined as 'a return to patria, which means fatherland understood as a State'. Kowalski, 'Repatriation of Cultural Property Following a Cession of Territory or Dissolution of Multinational States', 6 *Art, Antiquity, & L.* (2001) 139, at 163.

[27] Renfrew, 'Foreword', in Neil Brodie and J. Doole (eds) *Trade in Illicit Antiquities: The Destruction of the World's Archaeological Heritage* (2001).

Social norms regulate behaviour when the law is ineffective—and because the antiquities trade works hard at every turn to evade scrutiny, these norms serve as de facto regulation of the sale of antiquities in many cases. As an example, we need only consider the practices which took root at the Getty in the late 1970s and early 1980s.[28] The extent to which the Getty intentionally chose not to fully examine the histories of objects, and the routine practice of committing tax fraud for many of those illicit objects was pervasive.[29] These practices emerged because these actors felt that the risk of sanction was far less than the benefits that would accrue to them personally and towards the Getty generally. Real change has emerged with the actions of individuals and institutions such as museums, universities, and groups like the AAM and AAMD. When the law is not nimble enough to react to looting of archaeological sites, the trafficking of cultural heritage, or to stolen art, norms increasingly impact the actions of individuals. These guiding principles govern the resolution of cultural heritage disputes in the absence of law, when there are gaps in the law, when a court does not secure jurisdiction, or when a relevant time period has elapsed.

In examining the relationship between cultural heritage norms and the law, the difference between ownership and possession must be considered, because mere possession of an object does not necessarily connote ownership. The law confers ownership, while social norms confer the possession and disposition of objects in many cases. For example, the Sevso Treasure, a hoard of fourteen silver objects which is currently held in trust by the Marquess of Northampton, has not been auctioned because the hoard was most likely looted from either Croatia or Hungary.[30] The objects have only rarely been displayed. Their location, find spot, and provenance are unknown. The Marquess of Northampton acquired them in the early 1980s and put them on display at Bonham's Auction House in London in 2006.[31] After a seven-week trial in 1993 in the New York Supreme Court, a jury found that neither Croatia nor Hungary had established a valid claim over the objects, and the Marquess of Northampton trust retained possession.[32] As a result, these objects have not been auctioned, nor does it appear they will go under the hammer in the near future. Rather, they remain locked away, and their modern discovery remains a mystery.

Norms regulate possession outside courts of law. When an object is returned absent legal process this return is often described as voluntary, when in fact there is nothing voluntary about the return—'[t]he idea that there is a moral duty

[28] Jason Felch and Ralph Frammolino, *Chasing Aphrodite: The Hunt for Looted Antiquities at the World's Richest Museum* 31–56 (2011).

[29] Felch and Frammolino, *Chasing Aphrodite,* 31–56 .

[30] *Republic of Lebanon v Sotheby's*, 167 A.D.2d 142, 143–4 (N.Y. App. Div. 1990).

[31] Riding, '14 Roman Treasures, On View and Debated', *N.Y. Times*, <http://query.nytimes.com/gst/fullpage.html?res-9C00E0D8173FF936A15753C1A9609C8B63> (last accessed 5 May 2011).

[32] *Republic of Croatia et al. v Tr. of the Marquess of Northampton 1987 Settlement*, 203 A.D.2d 167, 167–8 (N.Y. App. Div. 1994).

to make restitution of, or pay compensation for, highly valuable or significant cultural heritage items is strongly gaining ground, especially when the dispossession dates back to a period of colonial domination'.[33] In the case of the long civil forfeiture proceeding over *Portrait of Wally* by Egon Schiele, a settlement was eventually reached.[34] The painting had been purchased by Rudolf Leopold in 1954 and had been locked away for more than ten years while the discovery process stretched on. It was returned to the heirs of Lea Bondi Jaray, who lost the work to the Nazis in 1938. In the settlement the Leopold Museum in Austria maintained possession of the painting, but paid the heirs US$19 million and agreed to display a plaque near the work relating the history of the painting. For many this result was unsatisfying. These broad themes can be seen in the emerging social norms which govern cultural heritage at both the state level via customary international law, and at the individual level via social norms.

International law does not typically apply directly to individuals. And perhaps we should remind ourselves that individuals loot, traffic, and purchase illicit cultural heritage. International law impacts states, and states in turn impact individuals. This disconnect may explain how the current international framework has had difficulty preventing theft and looting. The separation between international law and individuals requires individual states to act and implement international law like the 1970 UNESCO Convention. When states are either unable or unwilling to vigorously implement this international law, norms flow into this gap.[35]

In addition, efforts to broker agreements at the state level have had difficulty impacting sites and the trade itself. The Intergovernmental Committee for Promoting the Return of Cultural Property to Its Countries of Origin or Its Restitution in Case of Unlawful Appropriation in Case of Unlawful Appropriation was established by UNESCO in 1978 and was charged with the responsibility of the facilitation negotiations for the return of objects to their nation of origin.[36] Since 2005, the committee has been charged with helping to

[33] Cornu and Renold, 'New Developments in the Restitution of Cultural Property: Alternative Means of Dispute Resolution', 17 *Int'l J. Cultural Prop.* (2010) 1, at 3.

[34] Kennedy, 'Leopold Museum to Pay $19 Million for Painting Seized by Nazis', *N.Y. Times*, 20 July 2011, <http://artsbeat.blogs.nytimes.com/2010/07/20/leopold-museum-to-pay-19-million-for-painting-seized-by-nazis/?scp-2&sq=portrait%20of%20wally&st=cse> (last accessed 4 February 2013).

[35] Wallach, 'The Alien Tort Statute and the Limits of Individual Accountability in International Law', 46 *Stan. J. Int'l L.* (2009) 121, at 137. Individuals acting in a state capacity, and who violate international obligations, carry their state into a violation of an international obligation. The main exceptions to this rule involve admiralty law, or where all nations have an interest such as the high seas. The Supreme Court has held that US jurisdiction 'must ... be restrained to places where our jurisdiction is complete, to our own waters, or to the ocean, the common highway of all nations'. *See, eg, The Apollon*, 22 U.S. 362, 371 (1824). A useful analogue may be drawn between the oceans, which are the common highway of all nations, and art and antiquities—which are the common heritage of mankind.

[36] Cornu and Renold, *see earlier* note 33, at 2.

facilitate cross-border disputes over cultural objects, but does not appear to have taken an active role in resolving any existing disputes.

Consider the role of international law with respect to the intentional destruction of heritage. Attacks on cultural sites in the former Yugoslavia prompted the UN Security Council to protect against the destruction of cultural property.[37] However, the world was powerless to stop the destruction of the Bamiyan Buddhas in 2001. The Buddhas represent one of the few examples of monumental Buddhist sculpture.[38] They were cut directly from the rock 1,500 years ago on a busy trade route between China and India.[39] On 26 February 2001, Mullah Mohammad Omar ordered all statues in Afghanistan should be demolished.[40] A number of states protested the threats to the statutes. The UN General Assembly quickly adopted a resolution calling for the Taliban 'to prevent the further destruction of the irreplaceable relics, monuments or artefacts of the cultural heritage of Afghanistan'.[41] The Taliban had committed no violation of existing international law. Under established principles, the Taliban was perfectly within its rights as a sovereign state. Joseph Fishman argues that '[i]n positing a norm that circumscribed the territorial state's discretion, the General Assembly claimed an interest that overrode the state's traditionally exclusive authority over its own cultural property'.[42] The Declaration does not create any legal obligation and creates no new positive rights or responsibilities; it merely compels that the full extent of international law should be brought to bear when objects are intentionally destroyed.[43]

Law has a part to play, perhaps even the most important part. But when it reaches its limitations we can observe a number of norms which are impacting the disposition of cultural heritage. These norms can be seen in action, and although they are informed by the law, they are not necessarily wholly driven by it. The practical impact of these norms can be seen in three cases: (1) the increasing view that cultural objects which first appear on the market after 1970 are presumed illicit, (2) objects which are illicitly excavated should be returned to their point of

[37] *See* Abtahi, 'The Protection of Cultural Property in Times of Armed Conflict: The Practice of the International Criminal Tribunal for the Former Yugoslavia', 14 *Harv. Hum. Rts. J.* (2001) 1, at 1–2 (discussing that the destruction of Dubrovnik, the Neretva Bridge in Mostar, the Jasenovac memorial complex in Croatia, and the library of Sarajevo all motivated the international community to act).

[38] Cotter, 'Buddhas of Bamiyan: Keys to Asian History', *N.Y. Times*, 3 March 2001, <http://www.nytimes.com/2001/03/03/world/buddhas-of-bamiyan-keys-to-asian-history.html> (last accessed 4 February 2013).

[39] Cotter, 'Buddhas of Bamiyan', see note 38.

[40] 'Pre-Islan Idols Being Broken under Decree by Afghans', *N.Y. Times*, 2 March 2001, <http://www.nytimes.com/2001/03/02/world/pre-islam-idols-being-broken-under-degree-by-afghans.html> (last accessed 4 February 2013).

[41] The Destruction of Relics and Monuments in Afghanistan, G.A. Res. 55/243, P 3, U.N. GAOR, 55th Sess., U.N. Doc. A/RES/55/243 (9 March 2001).

[42] Fishman, 'Locating the International Interest in Intranational Cultural Property Disputes', 35 *Yale J. Int'l L.* (2010) 347, at 363.

[43] O'Keefe, 'World Cultural Heritage: Obligations to the International Community as a Whole?', 53 *Int'l & Comp. L.Q.* (2004) 189, at 204 note 105.

origin, and (3) the use of aggressive police power on antiquities dealers in isolation will not produce compliance with heritage laws.

II. Antiquities Appearing on the Market Since 1970 are Presumed Illicit

Antiquities which do not have histories pre-dating 1970 are now widely presumed to be illicit, and yet the 1970 threshold has no direct textual grounding in any nation's law. The date, of course, hearkens back to the 1970 UNESCO Convention, but nothing in the Convention explicitly states that museums should use 1970 as a cut-off date. The date has been an unexpected shift in behaviour which has been one of the strongest lasting legacies of the Convention itself. Not only has the accession of new objects decreased substantially, but now objects which have been illicitly removed from their context are also increasingly being returned to their probable nation of origin.

This represents a fundamental change. Museums are now rightfully hesitant to acquire objects without a documented pre-1970 provenance. Antiquities which do have documented histories pre-dating 1970 set auction house records. For example, both the *Bronze Figure of Artemis and the Stag* which sold for US$28.6 million in 2007,[44] or the Guennol lioness which sold for US$57.1 million in December of that year had clean histories dating long before 1970.[45] Many museums have publicly amended their acquisition policies to refrain from acquiring objects which have surfaced after 1970 without sufficient documentation establishing a licit history. When considering the acquisition of an object many museums will not accession objects which do not have clean history dating to the enactment of the 1970 UNESCO Convention. 1970 is used first because it is a watershed date at which museums were put on notice that contemporary buying and selling of antiquities contributes to the looting of archaeological sites. But perhaps more importantly, picking a date that is now quite distant allows museums to ensure their current practices are not leading to the ongoing looting of archaeological sites. Matthew Bogdanos argues the 1970 date is 'crucial' to limiting the illicit trade in antiquities because '[a]s each year passes, it becomes less and less likely that a previously unpublished (and hence unknown) antiquity can appear on the market and be legal… '.[46]

[44] Pollock, 'Bronze Artemis Sells for $28.6 Million, Sets Records (Update 2)', *Bloomberg*, 7 June 2007, <http://www.bloomberg.com/apps/news?pid=newsarchive&sid=agaewu8u95EE> (last accessed 4 February 2013).

[45] Harmansah and Witmore, 'The Endangered Future of the Past: Looting of Antiquities', *Int'l Herald Trib.*, 22 December 2007.

[46] Bogdanos, 'Thieves of Baghdad: Combating Global Traffic in Stolen Iraqi Antiquities', 31 *Fordham Int'l L.J.* (2008) 725, at 729.

Both of the major museum industry groups have amended their own guidelines to signal this shift. In 2008 the AAMD announced a new Report on the Acquisition of Archaeological Materials and Ancient Art.[47] One of the guidelines provides that museums 'should not acquire a work unless its provenance research substantiates that the work was outside its country of probable modern discovery before 1970 or was legally exported from its probable country of modern discovery after 1970'.[48] Guideline F states that when an object has surfaced after 1970, 'the museum must carefully balance the possible financial and reputational harm of taking such a step against the benefit of collecting, presenting, and preserving the work in trust for the educational benefit of present and future generations'.[49] As the then-president of the AAMD noted when the new rules were adopted, the 1970 cut-off date is the date adopted by much of the rest of the world and brought American museum standards into closer harmony with other practices.[50] And to be clear, the AAMD rules are not legally binding.[51] The AAMD might decide to sanction or call out a member institution from violating the rule.[52]

The AAM has a stricter standard. In its 2008 Standards, museums 'should not acquire any object that, to the knowledge of the museum, has been illegally exported from its country of modern discovery or the country where it was last legally owned'.[53] In addition, in respect to existing collections:

> In order to advance further research, public trust, and accountability museums should make available the known ownership history of archaeological material and ancient art in their collections, and make serious efforts to allocate time and funding to conduct research on objects where provenance is incomplete or uncertain. Museums may continue to respect requests for anonymity by donors.[54]

Even the major antiquities-acquiring museum throughout much of the 1980s and 1990s—the Getty—has amended its policies to align itself with the shift to 1970. In 2006 the Getty announced a stringent acquisition policy which adopts

[47] Ass'n of Art Museum Dirs., *New Report on Acquisition of Archaeological Materials and Ancient Art* (4 June 2008), <http://www.aamd.org/newsroom/documents/2008ReportAndRelease.pdf> (last accessed 4 February 2013).

[48] Ass'n of Art Museum Dirs., *New Report on Acquisition of Archaeological Materials and Ancient Art*, pt. II(E).

[49] Ass'n of Art Museum Dirs., *New Report on Acquisition of Archaeological Materials and Ancient Art*, pt. II(F).

[50] Stoilas, 'New Guidelines for US Museums Acquiring Antiquities', *Art Newspaper*, 24 July 2008, <http://www.theartnewspaper.com/articles/New-guidelines-for-US-museums-acquirin g-antiquities%20/8635> (last accessed 4 February 2013).

[51] Stoilas, 'New Guidelines for US Museums Acquiring Antiquities', see note 50.

[52] The National Academy was sanctioned by the AAMD when it considered deaccessioning some of its works in 2008. *See* Pogrebin, 'Bill to Stop Museums from Certain Art Sales May Die', *N.Y. Times*, 10 August 2010, <http://www.nytimes.com/2010/08/11/arts/design/11selloff.html?_ r=1&partner=rss&emc=rss> (last accessed 4 February 2013).

[53] Am. Ass'n of Museums, *Standards Regarding Archaeological Material and Ancient Art* § 2, para. 3 (July 2008), <http://www.aam-us.org/museumresources/ethics/upload/Standards%20Regarding%C2 0Archaeological%C20Material%C20and%C20Ancient%Ärt.pdf> (last accessed 4 February 2013).

[54] Am. Ass'n of Museums, *Standards Regarding Archaeological Material and Ancient Art* § 3.

1970 as the date for determining whether an object should be considered licit.[55] The British Museum has also adopted the 1970 date. The British Museum's acquisitions policy provides that it 'will normally only acquire those archaeological and heritage objects that have documentation to show a legal history back to November 14th 1970', although the policy also provides that the museum's curators can 'use their best [judgment]' for those objects without a documentary history.[56] New York's Metropolitan Museum of Art has also used 1970 as a guideline. It provides that it 'shall not acquire a work unless provenance research substantiates that the work was outside its country of probably modern discovery before 1970 or was legally exported from its probably country of modern discovery after 1970'.[57]

The impetus for this collective shift has been a gradual shaming of many museums. Shame will affect behaviour when moral disapproval of the community at large impacts the collective actions of individuals.[58] Museums claimed boldly that the objects they were proudly displaying were part of an international movement of art which promoted learning and cultural exchange. However, many of those arguments were badly undermined when the looting, deceit, and misinformation were fully revealed.[59] As a result, not only have objects appearing after 1970 been deemed illicit, but objects which have been illicitly excavated have also been increasingly returned to their nation of origin.

III. The Return of Illicitly Excavated Objects

When objects are shown to have been illicitly excavated, nations are asking for the return of these objects. Although the return does punish the end of the illicit supply chain, it does not really serve to undo the damage and destruction which has already been done to archaeological context. David Gill, an archaeologist who has examined the antiquities trade has argued, 'There is sadly little to celebrate over the return of [looted] antiquities. [They] represent destroyed archaeological contexts, scientific knowledge lost forever; and even the best scholarship cannot retrieve this information ... energetic calls for the repatriation of antiquities,

[55] 'Getty Revises Acquisitions Policy' (Getty Press Release), <http://www.getty.edu/news/press/center/revised_acquisition_policy_release_103606.html> (last accessed 4 May 2011).

[56] 'British Museum Policy on Acquisitions' (2007), <http://bit.ly/r51DWg> (last accessed 4 February 2013).

[57] 'Metropolitan Museum of Art Collections Management Policy' (2008), <http://www.metmuseum.org/works_of_art/collection_database/collection_management_policy.aspx#acquisitions> (last accessed 4 February 2013).

[58] Skeel, 'Shaming in Corporate Law', 149 *U. Pa. L. Rev.* (2001) 1811–68, at 1816 ('Because shaming sanctions undermine the offender's reputation, they often serve the traditional functions of criminal law'.).

[59] *See* Felch and Frammolino, *see earlier* note 28.

however justified, would be better spent in calling for the protection of archaeological sites'.[60]

Italy has achieved a number of high-profile returns of objects in recent years, primarily from American museums. Italy boasts an array of heritage sites, including half of the United Nations-designated world heritage sites and important remains of the Roman and Etruscan civilizations as well as the Renaissance.[61] Italy has perhaps the world's finest dedicated art crime unit in the world in the Armadei Carabinieri, established in 1968 to prevent the theft of its tremendous artistic heritage.[62] Despite these efforts, policing and protecting these sites remains an expensive and difficult undertaking. In attempting to protect its heritage and in seeking the return of objects, Italian officials have justifiably voiced concerns when objects are smuggled out of the country.

Italy was able to successfully repatriate a number of illegally excavated objects. The most prominent return was the Euphronioskrater, a large painted object, likely to have been created in ancient Greece, looted from an Etruscan tomb near Ceveteri in Italy, and purchased for a then-record US$1 million in 1972.[63] Italy criticized the acquisition soon after its purchase was announced, although initial investigations into the object were initially unsuccessful.[64] That changed in 1995 with the Italian and Swiss investigation of the warehouse in Geneva, which belonged to Giacomo Medici.[65] In 2004 Medici was convicted of trafficking in looted antiquities, but the real import of the investigation was the thousands of polaroid photographs of the krater and other objects which were on display at the Museum of Fine Arts in Boston, the Getty in California, Princeton, and elsewhere. This massive trove of photographs established concretely that these objects had passed through the hands of a convicted antiquities dealer who had dealt in looted objects in the past.[66] As a result of that very successful investigation, Italy was able to negotiate the return of a great number of objects which were illegally excavated and removed from the country. Italy's then-Culture Minister, Francesco Rutelli, did a terrific job of using press releases, op-eds, and public persuasion to shift the public's perception about the rightful place for these objects.[67]

[60] Bonn-Muller and Powell, 'A Tangled Journey Home', *Archaeology Mag.*, Oct. 2007, <http://www.archaeology.org/0709/etc/returns.html> (last accessed 4 February 2013).

[61] *See* U.S.Dep't of State, *Italy: U.S. Protection of Archaeological Material Representing the Pre-Classical, Classical, and Imperial Roman Periods, Background, available at* <http://exchanges.state.gov/culprop/itfact.html> (last accessed 1 May 2011).

[62] Suro, 'Going Undercover for Art's Sake', *N.Y. Times Mag.* (1987), <http://www.nytimes.com/1987/12/13/magazine/going-undercover-for-art-s-sake.html> (last accessed 4 February 2013).

[63] Povoledo, *see earlier* note 13.

[64] Kennedy and Eakin, 'The Met, Ending 30-Year Stance, Is Set to Yield Prized Vase to Italy', *N.Y. Times*, 3 February 2006, <http://www.nytimes.com/2006/02/03/arts/03muse.html&ref=euphronioskrater> (last accessed 4 February 2013).

[65] Kennedy and Eakin, 'The Met', *see* note 64.

[66] *See* Gill and Chippindale, 'From Boston to Rome: Reflections on Returning Antiquities', 13 *Int'l J. Cultural Prop.* (2006) 311.

[67] *See, eg,* Rutelli, Op-Ed., 'Rogue Gallery', *Wall St. J.*, 17 January 2007.

The returns have set an important precedent which establishes a norm that when objects are shown to have been illicitly excavated, they should be returned.

An agreement between Italy and the Met has set the tone for a number of other agreements between Italy and returning institutions.[68] First, Italy and the Met called for cooperation by agreeing to conduct joint excavations in Italy. Second, the agreement allowed for a transfer in title for all the disputed objects, even though some of the objects would remain on display in New York, including the Euphronioskrater which was not returned until 2008. Third, Italy, in exchange for the Euphronioskrater, would make loans of other objects to the museum of 'equivalent beauty and artistic/historical significance, mutually agreed upon' for four years.[69] And finally, Italy agreed not to bring any civil or legal suits for any of the objects which were slated for return to Italy.

The agreement avoids any direct reliance on criminal law, replevin, or any legal tools. Instead both sides entered into negotiations and reached an agreement which has been replicated with other institutions, most notably the Getty.[70] This and the many other returns from prominent American museums has ushered in a new norm—that objects without sufficient histories, that appear suddenly on the art market, are most likely to have been looted, and will be returned. And the longer an unbending museum refuses to return illicit objects, the greater and louder the potential criticism will be levelled at them from members of the heritage community and nations of origin. Italy, in securing, these returns, has outlined a precedent for a powerful repatriation norm that many other nations have already attempted to emulate.

Yet there still exists real resistance to this kind of return in some corners of the museum community, even given the overwhelming shift in practice in recent years. The St. Louis Art Museum (SLAM) has sued the federal government to preclude it from initiating a forfeiture claim against the Ka-Nefer-Nefer mask.[71] The museum has told the public and Egypt that they would return the mask to Egypt if they were presented evidence that the mask was looted or stolen, and according to them Egypt has not presented this evidence. The mask was acquired by the museum in 1998 and was excavated in 1952. Both Egypt and the museum have very different versions of the subsequent history of the mask. We are not certain what happened in the intervening years. But given what we know about the antiquities trade, we should have strong suspicions that some illicit activity brought the mask to market and display in St Louis.

[68] Agreement Between the Ministry for Cultural Assets and Activities of the Italian Republic and the Metropolitan Museum of Art ('Accord') (21 February 2006) (on file with author).

[69] Agreement Between the Ministry for Cultural Assets and Activities of the Italian Republic and the Metropolitan Museum of Art, art. 4.1(b). See note 68.

[70] Felch, 'Getty's Aphrodite Is Returned to Sicily', *L.A. Times*, 23 March 2011, <http://www.latimes.com/entertainment/news/la-et-return-of-aphrodite-20110323,0,6998689.story> (last accessed 4 February 2013).

[71] Harris, 'Museum Sues USA over Mummy Mask', *Courthouse News Serv.*, 16 February 2011, <http://www.courthousenews.com/2011/02/16/34223.htm> (last accessed 4 February 2013).

The museum was approached in January 2011 by several Assistant US attorneys, who indicated an intention to bring a forfeiture action against the mask. But in this case, rather than waiting for the forfeiture action, the museum has decided to try to preclude a suit by the US attorneys, arguing that from December 2005 to January 2006, the US was a party to several communications regarding questions with respect to the history of the mask.[72] They use as examples, posts and emails sent by Ton Cremers, of the Museum Security Network. He sent at least two emails to Bonnie Magness-Gardiner of the FBI, INTERPOL, as well as James McAndrew at Immigrations and Customs Enforcement (ICE). The museum's complaint quotes emails from Cremers, which were published on the Museum Security Network.[73]

The museum argued in the complaint that the relevant US government officials had knowledge of the potential claim over five years prior, and the five-year statute of limitations period has expired under 19 U.S.C. § 1621.[74] A court will decide whether these emails and queries the museum sent to INTERPOL in the 1990s about the mask are sufficient to have given the US government actual or constructive knowledge of the potential claim. The museum seeks a declaratory judgment under the Tariff Act that the action is barred by the statute of limitations. Even if successful, this suit would only preclude a suit by the US government. This marks an effort by the museum to remove the dispute from the legal arena and requires—according to SLAM—some concerted documentation on the part of the Egyptian museum that the mask was in fact stolen from an Egyptian storehouse.

It would not vindicate the acquisition of the mask. The mask was acquired in 1998 by SLAM from Phoenix Ancient Art for a reported US$500,000. The museum has attempted to demonstrate its diligence in a number of ways when it acquired the mask. It sent a letter to Mohammed Saleh, the retired director of the Cairo Museum, asking about the mask or the existence of similar objects. The museum contacted the Art Loss Register, INTERPOL, and the International Federation of Art Research. In 1998 the SLAM requested a Swiss attorney to conduct a background investigation of Phoenix and the purported previous owner of the mask, which confirmed the address of the alleged previous owner and confirmed there were no liens or encumbrances on business property belonging to Phoenix. The museum also sent a letter to the Missouri Highway Patrol requesting a search of the Interpol database which did not flag the mask as looted or stolen. These efforts to look at the history of the object did take place, but certainly are not the best efforts. The museum did not contact the Supreme Council of Antiquities or the Culture Ministry. The museum argues the government has waited too long to pursue its claims that the object was stolen.

[72] Complaint, *Museum Dist. of the City of St. Louis v United States*, No. 4:11-cv-00291, 2011 WL 903377 (E.D. Mo. 2011).

[73] Complaint, *Museum Dist. of the City of St. Louis v United States*, at 7–8. See note 72.

[74] Complaint, *Museum Dist. of the City of St. Louis v United States*, at 7. See note 72.

At the time of writing, the United States has initiated a civil forfeiture action over the Ka-Nefer-Nefer mask.[75] One may argue that the acquisition procedures of museums are generally lacking, and we can certainly criticize the imperfect procedures implemented by the museum to ask questions of the mask in this case. Although there was no export permit for the mask, the museum is only asserting that the Federal government waited too long to bring a forfeiture claim.

It is likely that perhaps the museum was not terribly eager to look deeply into the history of this object, for fear they would be unable to acquire it, displaying optical due diligence—if there are not direct indications that an object is illicit, the beauty of an object and the importance of its exhibition in a universal museum justify its acquisition. The museum was told by the seller that the mask was seen at an antiquities dealer in 1952, and it remained in the ubiquitous 'Swiss Collection' for the next forty years. An expert hired by the museum, Peter Lacovara, reasoned that the mask was probably awarded to the excavator after the 1952 excavation.[76] This would account for its appearance at a market in Brussels soon after. Nonetheless the mask would have still been removed from Egypt in violation of Egyptian law and should be returned. A legal victory for the government in this case will cause museums confronted with repatriation calls like this in the future to consider avoiding litigation seriously. Perhaps this is why the St. Louis Art Museum has defended the suit so vigorously, but ultimately the result in the case will have an important impact on the actions of museum officials in the near term. If the museum is able to avoid a repatriation like this in the future, it may prompt others to employ similar versions of optical due diligence.

At the other end of the spectrum, a much different repatriation norm may be emerging, one which seeks to remedy other past injustices with repatriation, even though there is no connection to theft or archaeological looting. This repatriation differs substantially from the returns to Italy of recent years, even though it uses these returns as a precedent and potential justification. This kind of repatriation can be tied to what Elezar Barkan describes: 'Control of one's patrimony is seen as a mark of equality and has become a privileged right in today's world. Restitution of cultural property, therefore, occupies a middle ground that can provide the necessary space in which to negotiate identities and a mechanism to mediate between the histories of perpetrators and victims'.[77] Yet the support for repatriation raises 'epistemological contradictions' which are often ignored.[78]

[75] Mann, 'Government Sues to Seize St. Louis Museum's Mummy Mask', *St. Louis Post-Dispatch*, 17 March 2011, <http://www.stltoday.com/news/local/metro/article_98d72244-9976-5b8a-a73d-5c211c6a771b.html> (last accessed 4 February 2013).

[76] Gay, 'Out of Egypt', *Riverfront Times* (2006), <http://www.riverfronttimes.com/2006-02-15/news/out-of-egypt/1/> (last accessed 4 February 2013).

[77] Barkan, 'Amending Historical Injustices: The Restitution of Cultural Property—An Overview', in E. Barkanand R. Bush (eds), *Claiming the Stones, Naming the Bones: Cultural Property and the Negotiation of National and Ethnic Identity* (2002) 16–50, at 16–7.

[78] Eg, it is often unclear which *patria*, or homeland, an object should return to. Consider the Euphronioskrater, or the Horses of St Mark—important works of antiquity which have travelled and

A repatriation agreement which bore similarities to the Italy accords was a response to a very different kind of cultural removal involving not looting, but rather academic study which did not sufficiently respect indigeneity. Yale University has signed an agreement with Peru over the disposition of objects removed from Machu Picchu nearly a century ago.[79] Over the course of three different expeditions in the early part of the 20th century, Hiram Bingham brought back 5,000 objects from Peru to Yale University. Peru has asked them to be returned and has reached a mutually beneficial agreement with Yale to have the objects returned. Early attempts at resolving the dispute and reaching an amicable compromise were unsuccessful. The former First Lady of Peru, Eliane Karp-Toledo, argued in a 2008 op-ed, Peru rightfully owns the objects, and asked:

> Why is it so hard for Yale to let go of these collections after almost a century of loan default? It is time for Peruvian scholars and citizens—especially the indigenous descendants of those who led Bingham to the ancient complex—to have access to the collection. The present agreement should be discarded and new talks should begin, based on the recognition of Peru's sovereign right to all that was taken from Machu Picchu.[80]

The eventual agreement—which averted continued litigation between the two parties—will create a joint Center for the Study of Inca Culture in Cusco, Peru.[81] The Center will preserve the artefacts, make the objects available for study and display, and promote research. There will be a new joint research centre in Cusco, pairing Yale University with the University of San Antonio Abad del Cusco. And although the objects will no longer be in Connecticut, the objects will be available for future study and will still be cared for. A number of prominent US and Peruvian officials offered their support for return. Senator Chris Dodd offered to intervene and said, 'The Machu Picchu artifacts do not belong to any government, to any institution, or to any university', '[t]hey belong to the people of Peru'.[82] There are contradictions in Peru's request for these objects. Some have argued Peru's national vesting law which establishes ownership of these objects 'enables the government to use [cultural objects] to develop a sense of national

been transferred around the Mediterranean for centuries, long before they were looted. A better dialogue, such as exists in the US with NAGPRA, may be a better solution as it emphasized 'affiliation' over location. Bauer et al., 'When Theory, Practice and Policy Collide, or Why Do Archaeologists Support Cultural Property Claims?', in Y. Hamilakis and P. Duke (eds), *Archaeology and Capitalism: From Ethics to Politics* (2009) 45, at 50.

[79] Nutman, 'Yale and University of Cusco Sign Collaboration Agreement', *Yale Daily News*, 11 February 2011, <http://www.yaledailynews.com/news/2011/feb/11/yale-and-university-cusco-sign-collaboration-agree/> (last accessed 4 February 2013).

[80] Karp-Toledo, 'The Lost Treasure of Machu Picchu', *N.Y. Times*, 23 February 2008, <http://www.nytimes.com/2008/02/23/opinion/23karp-toledo.html?_r=1&ref=todayspaper&oref=slogin> (last accessed 4 February 2013).

[81] Nutman, *see earlier* note 79.

[82] Press Release from US Senator Christopher J. Dodd, 'In Peru, Dodd Works to Mediate Dispute over Machu Picchu Artifacts' (2010), <http://dodd.senate.gov/?q=node/5658> (last accessed 4 February 2013).

identity as well as benefit from them monetarily, without either financial or cultural regard for its indigenous communities'.[83] So Peru may undervalue indigenous peoples in its own domestic policies, while earning credibility domestically for seeking the return of objects from a prominent American university.

Similar difficulty plagues the requests made by Egypt for the return of objects from the United States and Germany. Little distinguishes the rhetoric used with respect to an object rightfully removed—the Bust of Nefertiti, with an object that almost certainly was stolen or looted—the Ka-Nefer-Nefer mask. The return of the bust of Nefertiti has been requested, despite its lawful removal. Zahi Hawass when he was still in a prominent position in the Egyptian Antiquities Ministry told German media outlets that '[i]f she left Egypt illegally, which I am convinced she did, then I will officially demand it back from Germany'.[84] Nevertheless the bust has been in Germany since 1913; a German archaeological expedition digging near Amarna found what may have been the house and studio complex of the sculptor Thutmose in 1912; and the bust of Nefertiti was found on the floor of a storeroom along with other plaster casts. Monika Grütters, an art history professor, legislator and a leading cultural expert in Germany has argued Hawass and the Egyptians have an uneven case for return:

> The documentation exists. The arrangements were agreed. The process was legal … There was a complete understanding about what would remain in Egypt and what would be taken to Germany … Maybe there is a bit of jealousy on the part of Egypt over Nefertiti. In any event, I am not so sure Egypt has the best conditions for this statue … And because it is so fragile, I am not sure the statue can even be flown. We have excellent conditions here in Germany.[85]

This stands as a very different case than the St. Louis dispute, which relied on theft or looting. These rules can also be seen in operation domestically in the United States as well, particularly in the wake of a high-profile recent investigation.

IV. The Culture of Antiquities Looting in the American Four Corners Region

Despite firm criminal penalties and a high-profile raid in 1986,[86] looting in the Four Corners Region[87] has continued. This region has seen a shift away from

[83] Bauer et al., *see earlier* note 78, at 52.

[84] Dempsey, 'Egypt Demands Return of Nefertiti Statue', *N.Y. Times*, 19 October 2009, <http://www.nytimes.com/2009/10/19/world/Europe/19iht-germany.html?_r=2&ref=global-home> (last accessed 4 February 2013).

[85] Dempsey, 'Egypt Demands Return of Nefertiti Statue'.

[86] Jones, 'Utah Town Torn Between Law and Tradition', *AP Online*, 14 December 1986.

[87] Parts of this discussion of the Four Corners investigation appear in Fincham, 'Justice and the Cultural Heritage Movement: Using Environmental Justice to Appraise Art and Antiquities Disputes', *Va. J. Social Pol'y& L.* (forthcoming 2013).The Four Corners region is an area of the American south-west known for its remains of indigenous civilizations and an arid climate which preserves the objects absent human destruction.

widespread taking of Native American objects from archaeological sites. In recent years a massive federal investigation has attempted to use police power to crack down on one large antiquities dealing network. The reasons for this crackdown are apparently based on the formidable task confronting those who have responsibility for preventing and punishing the taking of heritage. The National Park Service, US Forest Service, and the Bureau of Land Management collectively estimate that of the 2 million archaeological sites on federal land, one-third has been looted or vandalized.[88] Moreover, half of the 6,000 most important sites on National Forest land in Arizona have been destroyed.[89] There has also been an increase in the reports of connections between antiquities looters and meth dealers.[90] There are massive areas to police, officers are few in number, and the rewards to be made from plundering and looting will often outweigh the chances that looters will be caught.[91] Craig Childs, a naturalist and ecologist who has visited a number of remote sites argues the 'lower right-hand corner of Utah is ... one of the richest zones of North America', and that as many as 'half a million graves lie within 25,000 square miles and more than 100,000 abandoned, dust-buried settlements'.[92]

Looting of these sites has been illegal since the passing of the Antiquities of Act of 1906, but the looting in this area continues, even amongst respected members of the community. Some in San Juan County in Utah would take shovels and buckets to search for artefacts on Sunday picnics.[93] Devar Shumway, the uncle of the notorious looter Earl Shumway, told a reporter in 1986 that '[f]or three summers during the Depression, pot-hunting was my father's only job'.[94] Earl Shumway was charged under ARPA for damaging United States property in both 1994 and in 1995.[95] Shumway was finally convicted of unauthorized

[88] 'Precious Artifacts Stolen, Ancient Culture Shattered: Looters Ravage Indian Ruins to Sell Pottery, Heirlooms on Black Market', *Arizona Republic*, 12 November 2006.

[89] R. D. Hicks, *Time Crime: Protecting the Past for Future Generations* (1997), <http://www2.fbi.gov/publications/leb/1997/july971.htm> (last accessed 4 February 2013).

[90] Patel, 'Drugs, Guns and Dirt', 62 *Archaeology* (2009), <http://www.archaeology.org/0903/etc/drugs.html> (last accessed 4 February 2013).

[91] In the south-west alone, there may be as many as five million archaeological sites. Egan, 'In the Indian Southwest, Heritage Takes a Hit', *N.Y. Times*, 2 November 1995, <http://www.nytimes.com/1995/11/02/us/in-the-indian-southwest-heritage-takes-a-hit.html> (last accessed 4 February 2013).

[92] C. Childs, *Finders Keepers: A Tale of Archaeological Plunder and Obsession* (2010) 79. Childs describes the destruction in detail in an earlier article:

> The caves of Arizona have been emptied down to bedrock. Parts of New Mexico look carpet-bombed. In Utah, I frequently find graves freshly looted, the soft packing if juniper bark ripped out like gift wrapping. Southwest Colorado feels ravaged and beaten .... It is hard not to be angry, witnessing this wholesale removal of human antiquity from the land.

Childs, 'Pillaging the Past', 40 *High Country News* (2008) 10.

[93] Childs, *Finders Keepers: A Tale of Archaeological Plunder and Obsession*, *see earlier* note 92, at 80.

[94] Jones, *see earlier* note 86.

[95] *United States v Shumway*, 112 F.3d 1413, 1417 (9th Cir. 1997).

excavations at two Anasazi archaeological sites located on federal land near the Manti-LaSal National Forest and also pleaded guilty to violating ARPA and to damaging United States property in connection with other wrongdoing. He was given the maximum sentence, six-and-a-half years in prison.[96]

Yet such stiff custodial sentences are very rare. For instance in *United States v Austin*, prosecutors charged Bradley Owen Austin under both ARPA and under another theft of federal property statute.[97] After a two-year investigation in 1986 and 1987 government agents seized 2,800 artefacts, digging tools, and photographs. On appeal, Austin argued that the prosecution was vindictive and that ARPA was overbroad and unconstitutionally vague. The Ninth Circuit affirmed the conviction, yet Austin served only four months in a federal prison.[98]

In another recent case, John Ligon and Carroll Mizell were charged in 2003 with theft of government property and violating ARPA.[99] The Ninth Circuit Court of Appeals reversed the convictions, holding the prosecution had not demonstrated the commercial value of the stolen rock art exceeded US$1,000. The men were acquitted of their crimes, yet after the criminal case was closed the United States Forest Service pursued a penalty action against the two men, who were ordered to pay US$21,523 as the full damage done to the archaeology and to restore and repair the damaged petroglyphs.[100]

The culture in the region maintains the looting of sites and the trafficking in antiquities. To police and change these behaviours, prosecutors have increasingly used undercover agents or informants to police looting. Rodney Tidwell was indicted and charged under NAGPRA, ARPA, and the NSPA for selling Hopi masks and robes from the Acoma Pueblo to an undercover federal agent.[101] The man who provided the masks to Tidwell, Ernest Chapella, was initially charged in the case but committed suicide.[102] So we now have a set of cases and investigations since roughly the mid-1980s which have used ARPA and these other federal criminal statutes to police ancient sites. Yet, the justification for the administration of these penalties rests on an uneasy foundation because with these increased penalties, looting has continued. Looters of sites and dealers of illegally acquired objects should be punished first and foremost to preserve the information which is so often destroyed when looters disturb ancient sites.

In 2006, agents from the FBI and the Bureau of Land management identified Ted Gardiner as a confidential source. Gardiner had been a dealer in archaeological

[96] 'Pothunter Gets 6 1/2-Year Sentence for Desecration', *Denver Rocky Mountain News*, 16 December 1995.

[97] *United States v Austin*, 902 F.2d 743, 743 (9th Cir. 1990); 18 U.S.C. § 641 (2006).

[98] 'Artifact Excavation Law Survives Its First Test', *Seattle Times*, 8 May 1990.

[99] *United States v Ligon*, 440 F.3d 1182, 1183–84 (9th Cir. 2006).

[100] Press Release, 'Peavine Mountain Rock Art Update', 2007 WLNR 15243152 (2007).

[101] *United States v Tidwell*, 191 F.3d 976 (Ariz. Ct. App. 1999).

[102] *United States v Tidwell*, at 979.

objects and had a number of contacts in the trade of these objects.[103] In March 2007 Gardiner began working with the FBI and BLM, and purchased—under surveillance in most cases—approximately 256 archaeological artefacts for over US$335,000. As a result of this investigation, the federal agents discovered a network of individuals who loot archaeological sites in the Four Corners region of the United States and sell these objects to other dealers and collectors. When individuals sell these objects, they often claim falsely that the site where these objects originated was on private or leased property. The objects also usually contain a letter of provenance; however, this provenance information was falsified for many of the transactions Gardiner recorded.

In what has become known as the Four Corners Raids, a massive federal investigation has emerged which uncovered a network of antiquities looting and dealing, yet any enthusiasm over the successful investigation has dampened quickly. Ted Gardiner later committed suicide, as did two others connected with the case.[104] Steven Shrader was a salesman and 'amateur' collector who committed suicide shortly after his arrest. So did physician James Redd. Redd's wife and daughter were sentenced to probation. So in total, there have been at least twenty-six indictments; all are expected to plead guilty and will be sentenced to probation. Naturalist Craig Childs sums up the attitudes in the wake of the two-and-a-half-year investigation by rightly pointing out that in examining antiquities dealers and archaeologists, neither group particularly likes the other: 'In no other field of research have I encountered so many people who have wanted the other party dead'.[105] Senator Orrin Hatch argued the raids and searches were 'unnecessary and brutal' and 'destroyed good feelings towards the government' in San Juan County, Utah,[106] all while archaeologists and heritage advocates championed the raids as a sign of renewed emphasis on the trade. Utah's state archaeologist Kevin Jones said, 'I'm happy to see the federal government paying attention to these sorts of crimes'.[107] Archaeologists view the objects as pieces of heritage, which have multi-generational value that should be researched, preserved, and respected in a very specific way. Dealers and collectors also value these objects, but in a way which hinges upon property rights and personal interests in these objects.

Sentencing of the defendants has been affected by the historical relationship with heritage in the region. Since June 2009, there have been more than two dozen arrests for charges of unearthing and dealing in stolen or looted objects, yet no prison sentences. Taking pottery shards or arrowheads and other artefacts

[103] Foy, 'More Are Sentenced in Four Corners Artifacts Case', AP, 12 July 2010, <http://www.nativetimes.com/index.php?option=com_content&view=article&id=3903:more-are-sentenced-in-four-corners-artifacts-case&catid=55&Itemid=31> (last accessed 4 February 2013).

[104] 'Utah: Third Apparent Suicide in Indian Looting Investigation', *N.Y. Times*, 3 March 2010.

[105] Childs, *see earlier* note 92.

[106] Senate Committee on the Judiciary Hearing on Oversight of the Justice Department, 6/17/09 eMediaMillWorks Pol. Transcripts 19:10:00 (17 June 2009).

[107] Draper, '24 Indicted in Artifact Thefts Officials Say a Network, Including Three Coloradans, Illegally Dug at Sites and Sold What They Found', *Denver Post*, 11 June 2009.

from public lands is seen by a large segment of the public as a harmless hobby, or even an unjustified exercise of federal power. Part of this reaction stems from a traditional practice. Andrew Kerr, who earned a PhD at Harvard, was appointed to the University of Utah in 1915 and he began paying US$2 per pot which was brought to him to grow the University's collection.[108] Yet today these practices are justifiably frowned upon because this activity destroys archaeological context, robbing us of information about these objects and the cultures which produced them.

The criminal penalties in place do not have a general deterrent effect. Their use in this case has promoted specific deterrence perhaps, because it seems unlikely that these individuals will be inclined to deal in these objects in the future, yet how will other dealers and individuals alter their behaviour? The perception of the raids has been tainted by the show of force from federal agents, the three tragic suicides, and the light resulting sentences to those who have plead guilty. The Four Corners arrests will most likely not result in better-preserved sites. In the short term many will alter their behaviour or work harder to evade law enforcement, but the underlying reality of the market remains. As the search warrants and actions of dealers selling to Gardiner while he was an informant show, buyers and sellers of these objects are not required to divulge histories for these objects. Even when they do they are easily fabricated. Until the baseline behaviour of antiquities dealers changes to provide accurate information to help buyers determine if they are selling looted objects, there will likely be more large investigations. The better approach to regulation of the antiquities trade is by punishing the lawbreakers, but in a consistent, evenhanded way, which informs the public about why antiquities should be viewed as heritage, what can be learned from the careful study of these objects, and engages the local community in the practices which best preserve these objects and their associated context. In essence, the underlying attitudes and behaviours must change.

V. Conclusions

The disposition of pieces of cultural heritage has been the subject of much discussion. Perhaps too much of that discussion has centred narrowly on what role the law can play. Collective behaviour informs and is shaped by the law. We have seen these shifts in the ways in which acquisitions policies have changed, how and when objects are returned, and in the shifting culture of native and dealer communities in the American south-west. When we see thefts, looted sites, and

108 Goddard, 'Anticipated Impact of the 2009 Four Corners Raid and Arrests', 56 *Crime, L. Social Change* (2011) 175, at 177–8.

the sale of illicit objects, a reasonable observer would be forgiven for feeling pessimistic about the role law has played in preserving cultural heritage. Yet a careful observer can also see where behaviours have changed and attitudes are shifting. The foundations for better future practices are being formed now, and heritage advocates must maintain their diligence in nudging, prodding, and forcing behaviours to change in positive ways. The law sets standards, and individuals respond to these standards. By observing the collective response policy makers can mitigate the behaviour that maintains looting and theft.

11

The Quest for the Masterpiece

Traditional Practices of Collecting in American Museums

Holly Flora[*]

I. Introduction

When it comes to collecting, American museums are in a state of crisis. Over the past decade, museums have been repeatedly accused of knowingly acquiring looted antiquities and even conspiring to do so with shady dealers and their networks of tomb-robbers. Under pressure from the Italian government and exposed to much negative press, the Getty, Metropolitan Museum of Art, the Museum of Fine Arts in Boston, the Princeton University Art Museum, and others recently returned treasures such as the Euphronios krater and the so-called Morgantina Aphrodite to Italy. Curators Marion True, formerly of the Getty, and Michael Padgett, at the Princeton Art Museum, have been put on trial by the Italian government, blamed for their respective museums' acquisition of supposedly illegally exported archaeological material. In response to these events, leading professional organizations of museums such as the International Council on Museums, the American Association of Museum Directors, and the American Association of Museums issued new codes of ethics denouncing the collecting of antiquities with questionable provenance. Museums, too, have revised their acquisitions policies to reflect the new ethical standards, in an effort to reach beyond legal norms and practice collecting with 'clean hands'. The questions I want to consider in this chapter are, how effective are these new codes of ethics in defending cultural heritage, and, can museums find better ways of reconciling their missions and traditions of acquisition with contemporary ethical standards? First, I want to present a brief history of the ethics of acquisition in American museums, foregrounding the current debate about and rationale behind these recently revised ethical codes. Then I will look at those codes in greater detail in

* Associate Professor, Tulane University. B.A., William Jewell College; M.A., Institute of Fine Arts, New York University; Ph.D., Institute of Fine Arts, New York University.

an effort to assess their effectiveness thus far. Finally, I would like to propose new strategies museums might employ in their efforts to collect ethically.

Many of the world's great museums, especially those regarded as 'encyclopedic', that is, with collections spanning a broad range of times, places, and cultures, were founded under ethical norms far removed from today's standards. Indeed, one could argue that the collections of the Louvre and British Museums, for example, were built in part from the booty looted by imperialist nations.[1] When collections were not the result of war, they nonetheless became the prerogative of wealthy countries that could afford to sponsor archeological digs, as was the case behind a number of German and American museums. Or, wealthy collectors built private collections that later became part of the foundation collections of museums, as was the case for example with the collection of J. P. Morgan at the Metropolitan Museum of Art.[2] Many American museums were effectively built on the industrial wealth of figures like Morgan and the availability of treasures in Europe for their purchase and, at the time, legal export.

Around the turn of the 20th century, European nations began passing laws to prevent works of art declared to be part of their cultural heritage from leaving their respective countries. George Grey Barnard, an American sculptor, collector, and dealer who built the collection now at the core of the Cloisters Museum in New York, famously inspired the French Government to enact such laws when he removed the entire cloister from the monastery of San Michel de Cuxa and exported it to the United States. Barnard exported the pink marble columns and capitals just days before the laws passed that would have prevented him from doing so.[3] From the Museum's point of view, the question of nationalism and ethics of collecting had yet to come up. As long as it was legal to acquire it, and in the early 20th-century, legal norms were just beginning to be established, museums had no problem doing so.

By the middle of the 20th century, the notion of legitimate ownership and protection of cultural heritage was emerging, resulting from a greater sense of national identity by European nations, as well as the establishment of international legal agreements, so much so that the allied forces during the Second World War created the Monuments Men, a corps of art-world professionals including James Rorimer, who was later director of the Metropolitan, who sought not only to protect important buildings and works of art from the ravages of war but also sought the restitution of the multitudes of artworks looted by the Nazis.[4] Thus the notion of a nationalistic right to cultural patrimony was part and parcel of the

[1] *See, eg,* Sharon Waxman, *Loot: The Battle over the Stolen Treasures of the Ancient World* (New York: Times Books, 2008).

[2] Louis Auchincloss, *J.P. Morgan: The Financier as Collector* (New York: Abrams, 1990).

[3] James J. Rorimer, *Medieval Monuments at the Cloisters: As They Were and As They Are* (New York: The Plantin Press, 1941).

[4] Lynn H. Nicholas, *The Rape of Europa: The Fate of Europe's Treasures in the Third Reich and the Second World War* (New York: Vintage, 1995); Robert Edsel, *The Monuments Men: Allied Heroes, Nazi Thieves, and the Greatest Treasure Hunt in History* (New York: Center Street, 2009).

post-war recovery efforts of European nations to reclaim their national identity. I mention this here only as a means of foregrounding the climate in which we find ourselves still living, where European nations claim certain works of art as icons of their cultural distinctiveness. One only has to think of the ongoing efforts by Greece to recover the Parthenon sculptures, also called the Elgin Marbles, to see how firmly tied works of the distant past are tied to current ideas about who we are. We shall return to this issue of nationalism later.

All of this brings us back to the question of museums and their traditional practices of collecting. For American museums at least, the post-war period did not seem to inspire the kind of careful collecting practices one would imagine it would. For example, in the early 1960s the Cloisters Museum famously acquired what is now known as the Cloisters Cross, a 12th-century ivory altar cross intricately carved with over one hundred figures. The dealer who sold the cross to the museum refused to disclose where he had purchased it; he reportedly didn't even confide that information to his wife and later died without revealing the secret to anyone.[5] It has since been speculated that this extremely rare object may have been smuggled out of Eastern Europe after the Second World War, but of course that cannot be proven. And yet, the famously maverick and outspoken then-director of the museum, Thomas Hoving, had no hesitation in acquiring it because of its extraordinary rarity and beauty.

To a large degree, then, the priority of traditional acquisitions policies in museums like the Met could be summed up in two words: acquire masterpieces. Period. Ethical and legal considerations were to some degree secondary, or perhaps it can be more accurately said that the norms were different at the time. Hoving himself even chronicled such practices proudly, and with some degree of embellishment and bravado, in his books *King of the Confessors* and *Making the Mummies Dance*.[6] Collecting for the museum was a grand gentleman-connoisseurs' game, with the winner finding the world's greatest hidden treasures and scoring them for the museum, whatever the cost. Museums were supposed to ensure that objects proposed for acquisition were not stolen and had legitimate provenance, but in many instances, far more importance was placed on the 'quality' of the object itself.

II. Recently Revised Ethical Standards and Acquisition Policies

It is this somewhat unchecked curatorial quest for masterpieces, I believe, that has led to the current climate of reform. In the later part of the 20th century, American museums began feeling pressure from foreign governments, Italy in particular, to ensure that their acquisitions were not recently looted. I should note

[5] Thomas Hoving, *King of the Confessors* (New York: Simon & Schuster, 1981).

[6] Thomas Hoving, *Making the Mummies Dance: Inside the Metropolitan Museum of Art* (New York: Simon & Schuster, 1993).

here that the recent response of museums to such pressure, really only seen in the last decade, has come relatively late, considering that the benchmark UNESCO agreement dates to 1970. Museums such as the Getty and Met have been accused of flagrantly and/or clandestinely disregarding the 1970 agreement.[7]

But the demands by Italy for the return of objects and the litigation brought against Marion True reveal a changed cultural attitude. In turn, the most recent allegations sparked a tug-of-war of blame. No-one denies that the looting of archeological sites is a long-standing problem, and in a place like Italy with so many unexcavated sites, it is impossible for all of them to be properly protected.[8] Italy (as well as other countries) blames museums and wealthy collectors for creating and sustaining a market for such material and thus encouraging looting. Some museum officials, conversely, have argued that the black market in antiquities is the fault of 'retentionist' cultural property laws marking all excavated material as national government property.[9] In defence of museums, Marion True and others have accused the Italians of enacting a very politically charged campaign of intimidation, forcing American museums into returning cultural treasures without requiring sufficient proof of their dubious acquisition.[10] Following the end of her trial, which ended with the expiration of the statute of limitations, True further denounced the Italian government for wasting time and money on 'endless litigation' when they do not have the resources to address collapsing vaults in major ancient structures such as the Colosseum, or to excavate and police their own archeological heritage.[11] Whatever side of the argument you are on, without question, something needs to be done to address the current situation.

In an effort to prevent their potential participation in the black market, and to protect the museum community from bad publicity, leading museums and professional museum organizations have revised their ethical codes in recent years. The aim of such measures is also to go beyond legal norms to enact higher ethical standards. As the American Association of Museums recently stated: '[L]egal standards are a minimum. Museums and those responsible for them must do more than avoid legal liability, they must take affirmative steps to maintain their integrity so as to warrant public confidence. They must act not only legally but also ethically'.[12] Let us take a look at some of the new ethical codes now.

[7] *See, eg*, Peter Watson and Cecilia Todeschini, *The Medici Conspiracy: The Illicit Journey of Looted Antiquities* (New York: Public Affairs/Perseus, 2006).

[8] Jonathan Tokeley, *Rescuing the Past: The Cultural Heritage Crusade* (London: Imprint Academic, 2006).

[9] James Cuno, *Who Owns Antiquity? Museums and the Battle over Our Ancient Heritage* (Princeton: Princeton Univ. Press, 2008), at xxxii.

[10] Eakin, 'Treasure Hunt', *New Yorker*, 17 December 2007; *see also* Eaken, 'Marion True on Her Trial and Ordeal', *New Yorker* online blog post, 14 October 2010, <http://www.newyorker.com/online/blogs/newsdesk/tny41> (last accessed 4 February 2013).

[11] Marion True, '"Neither Condemned Nor Vindicated," Marion True on Why It Is Hard to Accept the Lack of Verdict After Her Five Year Trial', *Art Newspaper*, Issue 220 (5 January 2011).

[12] American Association of Museums Code of Ethics (2000), <http://www.aam-us.org/museum-resources/ethics/coe.cfm> (last accessed 4 February 2013).

Professional organizations of museums led the movement to bring museum collecting standards in line with the 1970 agreement. The International Council on Museums, or ICOM, the largest such organization, paved the way for this early on in a 1970 report on the 'Ethics of Acquisition' in which it declared 'there must be full, clear, and satisfactory documentation in relation to the origin of any object to be acquired'.[13] One can see immediately how this could be very broadly interpreted. In ICOM's revised ethical code published in 2004, the statement is much more specific:

> Every effort must be made before acquisition to ensure that any object or specimen offered for purchase, gift, loan, bequest, or exchange has not been illegally obtained in or exported from, its country of origin or any intermediate country in which it might have been owned legally (including the museum's own country). Due diligence in this regard should establish the full history of the item from discovery or production.[14]

This is perhaps the most rigorous of the professional organizational codes in that it demands that 'due diligence ... should establish the full history of the item'.

American museum associations began drafting similar and yet slightly less stringent, codes. The Association of Art Museum Directors or AAMD, in 2004, recommended that museums thoroughly research the provenance of possible acquisitions, publish a photo and provenance history immediately upon its acquisition, and that all acquisitions should follow the guidelines of the UNESCO agreement.[15] When provenance cannot be clearly established, museums were told to use their 'professional judgment' in deciding whether or not to acquire a work. Although certain acceptable standards are recommended here, much latitude is ultimately given to museums to acquire objects lacking full provenance documentation. This policy was criticized by archeologists who claimed it was not stringent enough.[16]

Several years later, in 2008, the AAMD, following new guidelines proposed by the American Association of Museums, or AAM, the largest American professional organization of museums, issued specific standards for the acquisition of archeological material. The AAMD and AAM codes here reflect the stricter ethical norms prompted by recent events. The AAM Standards require that museums should:

1) rigorously research the provenance of an object prior to acquisition;

[13] International Council on Museums Report on the Ethics of Acquisitions (1970), <http://icom.museum/acquisition.html> (last accessed 4 February 2013).

[14] International Council on Museums Code of Ethics (2004), § 2.3, <http://icom.museum/ethics.html> (last accessed 4 February 2013).

[15] Am. Ass'n of Museum Dirs., 'Report on Acquisition of Archaeological Materials and Ancient Art' (2004), <http://www.aamd.org/papershttp://www.aamd.org/papers/> (last accessed 4 February 2013).

[16] Robert Bagley and Patty Gerstenblith, 'Museums Taxed by New Allegations'(2008), <http://www.archaeology.org/online/features/camuseums> (last accessed 4 February 2013).

2) make a concerted effort to obtain accurate written documentation with respect to the history of the object, including export and import documents; and
3) require sellers, donors, and their representatives to provide all available information and documentation.

However, the AAM guidelines still include this caveat:

AAM recognizes that there are cases in which it may be in the public's interest for a museum to acquire an object, thus bringing it into the public domain, when there is substantial but not full documentation that the provenance meets the conditions outlined above. If a museum accepts material in such cases, it should be transparent about why this is an appropriate decision in alignment with the institution's collections policy and applicable ethical codes.[17]

We can see a very interesting difference, then, in the way American codes of ethics, even in revised form and in regards to the acquisition of antiquities, allow for the discretionary acquisition of objects without full provenance. In contrast, the ICOM code can be interpreted more strictly in this regard. Thus, it seems that American museums recognize that ethical consideration must also include the idea of bringing an object into the public domain, and that is the trump card that can overrule questions of provenance.

In accordance with these new guidelines, American museums have now revised their acquisitions policies. As a case study here, I want to look at two of these, the Met and Getty, because these institutions are the ones that have most famously come into conflict with Italy over issues of acquisition and repatriation in recent years. These new acquisitions policies, as well as the formal agreement the Met made with Italy in 2006, reveal these two institutions' different responses to the current climate.

The Getty actually revised its acquisitions policy to reflect concern about looting long before the Met did. Marion True, in defending herself against accusations that she knowingly acquired looted objects for the Museum, declares that she has long attempted to cooperate with Italian authorities on this matter. It was not until the mid-1990s, however, that the Getty revised its acquisitions policy to state that the museum would not accept objects with unknown records of ownership. Their policy stated that objects imported before November 1995 without proof of prior ownership could be acquired by the museum. The date may seem arbitrary, given the 1970 agreement now accepted as standard, but it was convenient for the Getty, since in 1994 they had published a catalogue of the antiquities collection of Barbara and Lawrence Fleischman, wealthy collectors who became

[17] Am. Ass'n of Museums, 'Standards Regarding Archaeological Material and Ancient Art'(2008), <http://www.aam-us.org>; Am. Ass'n of Museum Dirs., 'Report on Acquisition of Archaeological Materials and Ancient Art'(revised 2008), <http://www.aamd.org/newsroom/documents/ 2008 ReportAndRelease.pdf>.

friends of True's and even later lent her the money to buy a house in Greece, an act later decried as an obvious conflict of interest. Because the objects, most of which had no known provenance before entering the Fleischman collection, were published by 1994, that established a record of ownership that was acceptable under the Getty's 1995 policy. The Getty was therefore able to accept the acquisition of a large portion of the Fleischman collection thereafter, just in time for the opening of the Getty's spectacular new Villa in Malibu, dedicated to its collection of antiquities. The rather self-interested effort toward an ethical acquisitions policy obviously did not work, because the Getty, more than any other museum, has come under fire for its acquisition practices, and True herself was at the centre of the controversies.

After the Italian cultural ministry threatened effectively to excommunicate the Getty, barring all loans and cultural cooperation with the museum, the Getty adopted a new policy in 2006 finally bringing acquisitions standards in line with 1970 UNESCO agreement. Here the requirements for proof of provenance and legal title are clearly articulated. The policy states:

1. No object will be acquired without assurance that valid and legal title can be transferred.
2. The Museum will undertake due diligence to establish the legal status of an object under consideration for acquisition, making every reasonable effort to investigate, substantiate, or clarify the provenance of the object.
3. No object will be acquired that, to the knowledge of the Museum, has been stolen, removed in contravention of treaties and international conventions of which the United States is a signatory, illegally exported from its country of origin or the country where it was last legally owned, or illegally imported into the United States.
4. In addition, for the acquisition of any ancient work of art or archaeological material, the Museum will require:
   a.) Documentation or substantial evidence that the item was in the United States by 17 November 1970 (the date of the UNESCO Convention on the Means of Prohibiting and Preventing the Illicit Import, Export and Transfer of Ownership of Cultural Property) and that there is no reason to suspect it was illegally exported from its country of origin, OR
   b.) Documentation or substantial evidence that the item was out of its country of origin before 17 November 1970 and that it has been or will be legally imported into the United States, OR
   c.) Documentation or substantial evidence that the item was legally exported from its country of origin after 17 November 1970 and that it has been or will be legally imported into the United States.

There are no caveats made in this policy allowing for the acquisition of works for which no provenance can be established. In requiring documentation, the Getty policy is much stricter than the standards adopted by the AAMD and the AAM and is more in line with those stated by ICOM.

The Met offers a case study that reveals significant differences to the responses made by the Getty. Before officially changing their acquisitions policy to reflect the 1970 agreement, which the Met did not do until 2008 (following, as the policy states, the AAMD and AAM's recommendations made also only in that year), the Met made a benchmark agreement directly with the Italian government in 2006. In this accord, the Met agreed to return the Euphronioskrater and several other important antiquities to Italy in exchange for long-term loans from Italy of 'equal beauty and importance'.[18] The Museum released this statement from Philippe de Montebello regarding the agreement:

> This is the appropriate solution to a complex problem, which redresses past improprieties in the acquisitions process through a highly equitable arrangement. The Met is particularly gratified that, through this agreement, its millions of annual visitors will continue to see comparably great works of ancient art on long-term loan from Italy to this institution.[19]

The Met thus found a means of cooperating with Italy while continuing its tradition of presenting 'masterpieces' to the public.

Having made this bargain and thereby placating the Italians, the Met effectively freed itself, in a sense, to adopt a new acquisitions policy in 2008 that reflects the current climate but is also subject to broader interpretation than the stance taken by the Getty in 2006. In their policy the Met states:

a. The Museum normally shall not acquire a work unless provenance research substantiates that the work was outside its country of probable modern discovery before 1970 or was legally exported from its probable country of modern discovery after 1970.
b. The Museum recognizes that even after the most extensive research, some works will lack a complete documented ownership history. In some instances, the Museum may make an informed judgment that the work was outside its probable country of modern discovery before 1970 or legally exported from its probable country of modern discovery after 1970, and therefore may acquire the work. In other instances, given the cumulative facts and circumstances resulting from provenance research, including, but not limited to, the independent exhibition and publication of the work, the length of time it has been on public display, and its recent ownership history, the Museum may make an informed judgment to acquire the work. In both instances, the Museum shall carefully balance the possible financial and reputational harm and the potential for legal liability against the benefit of

[18] 'The Metropolitan Museum of Art—Republic of Italy Agreement of February 21, 2006', 13 *Int'l J. Cultural Prop.* (2006), at 427–34.

[19] Press Release, Metropolitan Museum of Art (21 February 2006), <http://www.metmuseum.org/press_room/full_release.asp?prid=%7BF9704AC3-297B-4704-999B-111ACC8E6804%7D> (last accessed 4 February 2013).

> collecting, presenting, and preserving the work in trust for the educational benefit of present and future generations.[20]

The broad language used here, for example the statement that the museum will not 'normally' acquire works that are not in accordance with UNESCO 1970, as well as the concessions to 'the benefit of present and future generations', allow for the Met to acquire works for which provenance cannot be proven.

Leaving in this concession makes sense in some regard, for, however one might criticize the collecting practices of the Met, Getty, and others, there is no doubt that it has had the beneficial effect of bringing great works of art into the public trust where they are accessible to a wider American and international public. Recent visits to the Villa Giulia in Rome, where the Euphronioskrater and other restituted objects from American museums are now on view, reveal them displayed amid thousands of other similar works in galleries largely empty of visitors. Thus they are somewhat lost and unappreciated by all but the most expert viewer. In the Museo Archeologico in Naples, an entire room is currently dedicated to 'restituzioni'—objects returned by American museums and collectors, which are clearly, and proudly, labelled as such. One gets the sense, at least with the current installation, that the fact of their restitution is more important than the importance of placing these objects in 'context'; that is, the archaeological argument for their return. Once an object has been illegally or improperly excavated, its archaeological context is gone, and we are not able to get it back, even by placing objects alongside those from similar contexts. They are still in the display cases of a museum.

Thus this brings up another ethical dilemma, articulated by James Cuno, former director of the Art Institute of Chicago who was recently, and controversially, appointed head of the Getty Trust. In his book *Who Owns Antiquity?*, Cuno points out the difficult question that arises when a museum is faced with an unprovenanced antiquity—already its archeological context has been lost, so then the ethical dilemma becomes whether or not the museum should bring that object into the public trust or let it stay unknown in private hands.[21] The acquisitions policies adopted by the Met, AAMD, and AAM are broad enough to encompass this notion of benefit for public trust as an ethical value, and, I would argue, one that seems distinctly American.

Thus the question for us is how effective are the new ethical standards at accomplishing the goal of removing museums from their complicit participation in looting antiquities? When releasing the AAM's new standards for acquisition of archaeological material in 2008, the organization's President, Ford W. Bell, stated:

> The American people rely on museums to preserve and interpret the world's cultural heritage. In recent years, however, the public has come to expect that museums, through

[20] Metro. Museum of Art, 'Policy for Acquisitions and Collections Management' (2008), <http://www.metmuseum.org/works_of_art/collection_database/collection_management_policy.aspx#acquisitions> (last accessed 4 February 2013).

[21] Cuno, *see earlier* note 9, at 7.

their collecting activities, do not contribute to the illicit trade in cultural property. Abiding by these standards will ensure that museums are acting legally, ethically and morally.[22]

But is he right? Will these standards 'ensure that museums are acting legally, ethically, and morally'? It seems to me, that although these new standards reflect a long-needed new conscientiousness on the part of museums to the problem of looting, museums like the Met have much latitude in acquiring an object without full provenance, provided it is not proven to be illegal and if there is a strong enough case for its importance. Thus, I am not sure it will prevent looters from doing what they do. Now, the stakes are effectively higher, which might encourage a different, and perhaps even more dangerous, kind of trafficking via new networks that will establish false provenances for looted objects. Even in this era of stricter standards, museums continue to buy objects from the same dealers, albeit with a stricter eye towards provenance. As curator Karol Wight, who replaced Marion True as head of antiquities at the Getty, explained, almost every prominent dealer in antiquities has come under some criticism in recent years. The museum can't boycott any dealer specifically, for that would limit them to buying works from auction houses or acquiring them from private collectors (both sources that have had their share of provenance issues as well).[23] The new ethical standards are therefore not enough to stop the illicit trade in antiquities and absolve museums of their secondary guilt in that trade.

III. From Ethics to Action: What Else Can Museums Do?

What are some other solutions to the problem of museums, collecting, and illicit trade in antiquities? A number of recent publications have offered ideas. James Cuno, in *Who Owns Antiquity?*, published in 2008, offers a multifaceted approach to defending cultural heritage. He writes:

> [T]he best way to preserve the archeological record and unprovenanced or 'alienated' antiquities is to encourage scientific investigation of the archeological record, protect archeological sites, broaden access to their finds though the restoration of partage, allow for the reasonable acquisition of unprovenanced antiquities, strengthen and establish new encyclopedic museums, and develop programs for sharing and exchanging collections and scholarly and professional expertise broadly.[24]

As Cuno defines it, partage would allow for museums and universities from outside a host country to conduct excavations in that country and then share their finds with local museums. This, according to Cuno, is how many archeological

[22] Am. Ass'n of Museums, *AAM Announces New Standards on Cultural Property* (2008), <http://www.aam-us.org/> (last accessed 4 February 2013).

[23] Randy Kennedy, 'Collecting Antiquities, Cautiously, at the Getty', *N.Y. Times*, 26 June 2007.

[24] Cuno, *see earlier* note 9, at xxxiv.

collections were built in the past. The problem with this idea, of course, is that current cultural heritage legislation mandates that any finds unearthed belong to the country of origin, so the museums in question could not legally build their collections this way now. Countries such as Italy, having fought so hard for the return of antiquities, would be loath to allow more of them to become permanent parts of foreign museums. In a sense this kind of partage could signal a return to the colonialist era of archaeology.

In a *New York Times* article published in December of 2010, Bernard Frischer proposed a modified version of this partage system. In his view, separating ownership from possession is the key to creating a system that would allow foreign institutions to pay for digs and share in subsequent discoveries with the host country. He states:

> If only ownership could be separated from possession, then museums might strike a deal with countries like Greece and Italy. Here's how it would work: The countries of origin would own anything that was excavated there and keep most of the finds on display in local partnering museums. But the museum that sponsored the dig would be allowed to borrow a percentage of the finds and exhibit them in America. Eventually, all the finds from a site would be exchanged on a rotating basis between the country of origin and the museum, which would pay the expenses and insurance.

Frischer also offers an alternative for collectors in this scenario: 'Even individual collectors could invest and participate in the exchanges, if they were trained to care for the finds on temporary loan to them. Someday, investors or their heirs could sell these shares at auctions and galleries, just like works of art. In this way, all the stakeholders in today's antiquities market could be part of the new deal'.[25] Frischer's suggestion also reflects the idea of long-term loans between museums and host countries, an idea also seen in the Met's agreement with Italy. This sounds like an ideal solution to the current tension between rich museums and private collectors eager to collect and live with beautiful objects. From a scholarly point of view, long-term loans would also be beneficial, allowing the objects to be seen and studied both in the context in which they were excavated, displayed in local museums where they can be seen along other items unearthed with them, and also in the context of larger, more global collections where they can be seen in a different but no less instructive light.

Of course, there are also many problems inherent in this proposed solution. In contrast to a museum or collector choosing an object offered on the market, an archeological dig involves a great deal of uncertainty and also demands not only great monetary resources but patience. Museums might not be willing to front large sums of money for digs when no-one knows exactly what will be found and whether it will be deemed beautiful or important enough. A partnership based on the prospect of loans also involves a certain amount of risk for not only the

[25] Bernard Frischer, 'Museums Should Dig In', *N.Y. Times*, 22 December 2010.

institutions concerned but also the objects. Shipping objects across the globe is not only costly but potentially dangerous for them; they are much more vulnerable to theft or damage. Certain types of objects, depending on their condition, size, fragility, etc., simply cannot travel.

And, host countries have to be willing to let their objects go, even temporarily. The biggest obstacle to implementing this kind of archaeological cooperation is therefore not practical but ideological. The tension between nationalism and globalism, which I believe is at the heart of all of these current controversies, will need to be resolved in some way. Writers such as *New York Times* international art critic Michael Kimmelman see cultural heritage as something that cannot be ascribed to a single nation but instead is the inheritance of all mankind. In an article written in 2010 titled 'Who Draws the Borders of Culture', he wrote: 'But the general question, looting and tourist dollars aside, is why should any objects necessarily reside in the modern nation-state controlling the plot of land where, at one time, perhaps thousands of years earlier, they came from? The question goes to the heart of how culture operates in a global age'.[26] Kimmelman is of course thinking most obviously of the debate over the Greek Government's continued call for the Parthenon Sculptures, also known as the Elgin Marbles, to be returned by the British Museum. The opening of the spectacular new Acropolis Museum in 2009 is perhaps their strongest argument yet, as Kimmelman pointed out in his review of it. But it is the nationalist ideal that foregrounds the demand for the sculptures' return that is also the stumbling block to the idea of a truly shared cultural heritage.[27] The British Museum has offered to lend the sculptures to the new museum if Greece will officially recognize the British Museum's ownership of them. The director of the Acropolis Museum's response to the idea was 'No Greek can sign up for that'.[28]

This notion of a right to one's own national cultural heritage is one that rings loudly especially in Italy, where the outrage against looting and the possible participation in it by American collectors and museums is palpable. And it is also to a large degree justified. Countries such as Italy and Greece as we know them today are relatively new, and are thus still, I think, seeking a national identity and finding it in their cultural heritage. These nations thus feel violated when what they claim as cultural heritage is removed, legally or not. It is only natural, then, that many in these countries see big, rich, encyclopedic museums as their enemies. But at some point museums and these nations need to find common ground and learn to share the artworks so valued by both.

[26] Michael Kimmelman, 'Who Draws the Borders of Culture?', *N.Y. Times*, 5 May 2010.

[27] Jeanette Greenfield, *The Return of Cultural Treasures* (Cambridge: Cambridge University Press, 1995), at 312.

[28] Michael Kimmelman, 'Elgin Marble Argument in a New Light', *N.Y. Times*, 24 June 2009.

12

Enforcing Import Restrictions of China's Cultural Objects

The Sino–US Memorandum of Understanding

Wang Yunxia[*]

I. Introduction

The illicit traffic of cultural objects is a significant international problem, representing a primary reason for their loss. To win the struggle against illicit traffic of cultural objects calls for a rigorously regulated export control from source countries, strengthened supervision, and all-round international cooperation. After a lengthy period of negotiations lasting eleven years, on 14 January 2009, the Chinese and American governments formally signed a Memorandum of Understanding (MOU) in relation to import restrictions for cultural objects.[1] The MOU signifies a joint agreement by both governments to enacting the 1970 UNESCO Convention on the Means of Prohibiting and Preventing the Illicit Import, Export and Transfer of Ownership of Cultural Property,[2] to which both nations are signatories. The MOU serves as a commitment by both countries to ensure the illicit traffic of cultural objects is halted. This chapter is designed to analyse the legal basis for the MOU—to make an interpretation of its main contents and an assessment of its effects since it was implemented over a year ago.

* Professor in Law School, Director of the Institute of Cultural Heritage Law, Renmin University of China, E-mail:wangyunxia1988@msn.com.

[1] The full title of the bilateral agreement is '*The Memorandum of Understanding between the Government of the People's Republic of China and the Government of the United States of America on Implementation of Import Restrictions of Categorized Archaeological Objects between the Paleolithic Era to Tang Dynasty and Historic-Site Sculptures and Mural Art Works of over 250 Years Old*' (hereinafter referred to as the MOU).

[2] Hereinafter referred to as the 1970 Convention.

II. Legal Basis for the MOU

A. The Serious Situation of Cultural Objects Stolen and Illegally Trafficked in China

China is proud of its long history which has left a legacy of rich and abundant cultural heritage. There are serious concerns surrounding how much will survive to be passed down to the descendants of future generations. Ever since the middle of the 19th century, Chinese cultural objects were a main target of the Western countries, who grabbed the historical artefacts as prized objects and for museum collections. Military turmoil in modern China along with the absence of a system of heritage management aggravated indiscriminate stealing, plundering, illicit excavation, and illicit traffic of antiquities. During the thirty years following the founding of the People's Republic of China in 1949, in which contact with the external world was severely limited and the desire for material wealth reduced as a result of the planned economy, criminal activities surrounding the looting and smuggling of Chinese antiquities dwindled. In the early 1980s, when mainland China opened up again to the outside world, the black-market trade and trafficking of cultural objects was reignited. During this time, there was a popular saying among peasants in poverty-stricken areas of West China: 'to get wealthy, go excavating tombs and in one night you may become a person with ten thousand Yuan'. Illicit excavation for a time was even a special industry in those areas. Since the late 1990s, as the Chinese government has invested more in protecting objects of cultural significance and cracked down on crimes against cultural objects, open illicit excavation and trafficking of cultural objects has disappeared underground as a black-market activity. As the sale of stolen cultural objects is driven by high profits and a lucrative market, the rate of incidences remains high, and criminal operations are increasingly organized and sophisticated. The illicit cultural objects trade is causing serious and often irreparable damage to China's national heritage. Among various types of crimes against cultural objects, 50 per cent involve illicit excavation of ancient burial sites. Most excavations lead to the smuggling of stolen cultural objects, the majority of which go to overseas countries (including the US) via Hong Kong and Macao.

To halt the stealing, plundering, excavation, and illicit traffic of cultural objects in China, it is essential to reform Chinese domestic policy frameworks through: 1) tightening existing cultural heritage laws, 2) strengthening the management of security around cultural heritage sites, 3) rigorously regulating importation and exportation, and 4) ensuring thorough investigation and prosecution of criminal operations involving the looting and trafficking of cultural artefacts. In addition to this, it is necessary to develop close cooperation with the international community. Only by intercepting objects at overseas channels for illicit traffic and smuggling of cultural objects, and returning recovered stolen cultural objects to their country of origin, can the problem ever be addressed. In recognition of this need, China became signatories to two international policy frameworks: the 1970 UNESCO Convention in November 1989, and the Convention on Stolen or Illegally Exported Cultural Objects in May 1997. Within the framework of the 1970 Convention, China has actively sought bilateral or multi-lateral cooperation with relevant countries to this end.

B. The Basis for International Cooperation Laid Down by the 1970 Convention

The 1970 Convention is aimed at prohibiting the illegal import, export, and trade of cultural property to provide an effective international legal mechanism to protect national treasures from being plundered and transferred. The way in which the1970 Convention is able to function as a protective instrument is detailed in this part of the chapter.

First, at the national level, the 1970 Convention requires all member states to protect and manage their cultural properties by effective measures, which includes:1) establishing and improving their national management institutions to protect and manage their cultural properties, 2) formulating laws and regulations regarding prevention of illicit import and export and illegal transfer of important cultural properties, 3) documenting and updating continuously detailed lists of protected cultural properties of great importance, 4) exercising a control system of issuing permits for exportation of cultural objects of great importance, and 5) imposing penalties or administrative sanctions on illicit exportation.[3]

Second, at the international level, the Convention requires every state party: 1) to take necessary measures to prevent museums and similar institutions within their territories from acquiring cultural property originating in another state party which has been illegally exported after entry into force of the Convention, 2) to prohibit the import of cultural property stolen from museums, public monuments or similar institutions in another state party, 3) to impose penalties or administrative sanctions on law offenders, and 4) to take appropriate steps to recover and return any such cultural property imported under the condition that the requesting state pay just compensation to an innocent purchaser or to a person who has valid title to that property.[4]

Furthermore, the Convention has established a fundamental framework for further cooperation among state parties. Any state party whose cultural patrimony is in jeopardy from pillage of archaeological or ethnological materials may call upon other related state parties to participate in a concerted international effort to carry out necessary concrete measures, including the control of exports and imports and international commerce in the specific materials concerned. Each

[3] *See* 1970 Convention arts. 5–6, 8.
[4] *See* 1970 Convention arts. 7–8.

state concerned shall take provisional measures to prevent irremediable injury to the cultural heritage of the requesting state.[5]

In summary, as state parties to the 1970 Convention, both China and the United States are expected to adhere to the stipulations of the Convention. They both have obligations to adopt necessary measures to prevent and check illegal importation and exportation and illicit transfer of cultural objects, measures including close cooperation among state parties and assisting other state parties in enforcing restricted importation and exportation and trade related to specific cultural properties.

C. The Basis of American Law

The United States is one of the largest market countries of cultural objects in the world. It has long practised a policy of laissez-faire towards cultural objects. With growing recognition of the importance of safeguarding cultural heritage for the people of that culture and as the common heritage of humankind, the United States actively participated in the drafting of the 1970 Convention and became the first and, for some years, the only, major antiquities market to support the Convention.[6] However, in 1972 when the Senate approved the Convention, it held that the Convention was 'not executory in nature'. 'This meant that for the Convention to have domestic legal effect, Congress would have to enact legislation by which the Convention would be implemented into domestic law'.[7] In 1983 the US Congress passed the Convention on Cultural Property Implementation Act (CPIA) and the American President ratified the 1970 Convention.

The Act authorized the President to impose import restrictions on categories of archaeological and ethnological materials that are vulnerable to pillage following a request made by another state party to the Convention. A request is made on the basis that pillage of cultural property is placing state cultural heritage in jeopardy. The requests from other state parties will be examined by the Cultural Property Advisory Committee to see if the implementation of import restriction complies with the following four standards: 1) the cultural heritage of the requesting state is in jeopardy from the pillage of archaeological materials, 2) the requesting state has taken measures to protect its cultural heritage, 3) the US import restrictions, either alone or in concert with actions taken by other market countries, would be of substantial benefit in deterring the serious situation of pillage, and 4) import restrictions would promote the interchange of cultural

[5] *See* 1970 Convention art. 9.

[6] Feldman, 'The UNESCO Convention on Cultural Property: A Drafter's Perspective', *Art and Cultural Heritage Law Newsletter*, Summer 2010, Vol.II, Issue No.1, *available at* <http://www.ings.abanet.org/webupload/commupload/IC936000/sitesofinterest_files/Art_&_Cultural_Heritage_Law_Committee_Summer_2010_Newsletter.pdf> (last accessed 4 February 2013).

[7] Gerstenblith, 'United States Implementation of the 1970 UNESCO Convention', *Art and Cultural Heritage Law Newsletter*, Summer 2010, Vol.II, Issue No.1.

property among states for scientific, cultural, and educational purposes.[8] If the Committee confirms the request complies with the standards, the US will sign a bilateral agreement (MOU) to impose import restriction of specific cultural objects from that country. To date, the US has signed such bilateral agreements with thirteen resource countries of cultural objects, including China.[9]

III. The Signing of the MOU and its Main Contents

The motion of import restriction of cultural objects from China was put forward as early as 1998. In 1999, approved by the State Council, the State Administration of Cultural Heritage of the People's Republic of China via diplomatic channel formally presented to the US requests for import restriction on cultural objects; the relevant negotiations formally commenced. On 13 November 2002, the Chinese government submitted to the US government the Application for the Imposition of Import Restriction of Cultural Objects for the Purpose of Protecting Its Cultural Heritages according to the 1970 Convention attached with 'a list of essential cultural objects'. Unfortunately, due to strong opposition against the restriction by some American museums and dealers of art and antiques, the US State Department made a decision to postpone the examination of China's application. The decision came under strong criticism from a circle of American archaeologists and legal institutes. It also triggered broad public concern over protection of cultural heritage.[10] The Chinese government made a strenuous effort to strengthen communication with relevant American museum curators, culture and history experts, and other professionals engaged in exhibitions of Chinese art and artefacts. In accordance with requirements of the 1970 Convention, China also adjusted the scope of cultural objects for import restriction and improved the conditions for protection of cultural heritage. On 14 January 2009, representatives of the Chinese and American governments finally authorized the Memorandum of Understanding on Import Restrictions of Cultural Objects from China.

The core content of the MOU is embodied in Article I:

> The Government of the United States of America, in accordance with its legislation entitled the Convention on Cultural Property Implementation Act, shall restrict the importation into the United States of archaeological material originating in China and representing China's cultural heritage from the Paleolithic Period through the end of the Tang Dynasty (A.D. 907), and of monumental sculpture and wall art at least 250 years old; including categories of metal, ceramic, stone, textiles, other organic material, glass, and painting identified on a list to be promulgated by the United States Government (hereinafter

[8] 19 U.S.C. § 2602(a)(1).

[9] These countries are El Salvador, Guatemala, Nicaragua, Honduras, Peru, Bolivia, Mali, Italy, Canada, Cambodia, Colombia, Cyprus, and China. Gerstenblith, *see earlier* note 7.

[10] Zhang Mulin, 'The Controversy of American Public Opinion over Restrictions of Importation of Chinese Cultural Objects', 3 *Chinese Cultural Heritage* (2005), at 107–8.

known as the 'Designated List'), unless the Government of the People's Republic of China issues a license or other documentation which certifies that such exportation was not in violation of its laws. For the purposes of this Memorandum of Understanding, the restricted Paleolithic objects date from approximately 75,000 BC.[11]

That is to say, not all cultural objects protected by Chinese law and prohibited or restricted for international export were included in the adjustment scope of the MOU.[12] The restriction range of the MOU was formulated on the basis of definitions laid down in the CPIA. According to its provisions the bilateral agreements signed with requesting nations solely restrict the import of archaeological and ethnological objects. What is more, the archaeological objects must be of cultural significance and at least as old as 250 years and they must be normally discovered as a result of scientific excavation, clandestine or accidental digging, or exploration on land or underwater; the ethnological objects refer to those created by tribes or non-industrial societies and important because of their distinctive characteristics, comparative rarity, or their contribution to the knowledge of the origins, development, or history of a people.[13] Obviously, the scope and category of Chinese cultural objects that comply with these conditions are narrow; therefore the 'Designated List' recognized by the US government only covers limited categories of Chinese cultural objects, such as metal objects, ceramics, stone blocks, textiles, other organic matters, glass, and paintings. Furthermore, according to Article I(C) and Article II(J), the MOU has no retroactive force. It only restricts the designated cultural objects illicitly exported from China after the MOU went into effect.

What merits attention is that the MOU by no means simply concerns import restriction; it includes reduction and deterring of pillage and illicit traffic of cultural objects in a more effective way and a series of measures for promoting exchange of legal cultural objects.

A. China is to Strengthen its Protection of Cultural Heritage

The MOU stipulates that the Chinese government will: 1) exert more efforts in education and publicity, helping people enhance their awareness of importance of cultural heritage; 2) strengthen general surveys of cultural objects and

[11] MOU art. I(A).

[12] According to the Management Regulation for Examination and Approval for Cultural Objects to Import and Export of the Ministry of Culture and the Standards for Examination and Approval for Cultural Objects to Import and Export of the State Administration of Cultural Heritage revised in 2007, examination and approval shall be conducted for art works, handicrafts, manuscripts, books, objects related to production and livelihood that existed prior to 1949 (or in 1949) before they export from China. Among them, those cultural objects of historic, artistic, and scientific value are basically forbidden to export from China. All cultural objects that existed prior to 1911 and in 1911 and cultural objects of ethnic minorities that existed prior to 1966 and in 1966 are forbidden to export from China.

[13] *See* 19 U.S.C. § 2601(2).

archaeological sites, intensify archaeological research to make the public awareness of its importance; 3) increase investment in protection of cultural heritage and professional resources so as to bring cultural heritage in every place under good protection; 4) strengthen training for customs staff members so that their ability to identify the value of archaeological objects be improved and illicit export of cultural objects be deterred; 5) make utmost efforts to prevent cultural objects looted or illegally exported from China from entering into the Hong Kong and Macao Special Administrative Areas and deterring the illicit traffic between the mainland and the two areas; and 6) refrain Chinese museums from purchasing restricted cultural objects looted or illegally exported from mainland China to destinations abroad, unless they are provided with legal export permits or proved to have left China prior to the imposition of US import restrictions.[14]

B. The US Provides Necessary Assistance for Protection of Chinese Cultural Heritage

The MOU states that the US government will do its best to improve the ability of its customs officers to identify Chinese archaeological objects and also provide help to China in training its customs staff, and the US government will also facilitate technical assistance in 'creating a national preservation strategy, stabilizing and restoring sites/buildings, enhancing the capacity of museums to preserve and exhibit collections, and strengthening regulation of the cultural relics market'.[15]

C. China will Facilitate Easier Access by the American Public and Museums to Chinese Cultural Heritage

The MOU states that the Chinese government will make utmost efforts in promoting long-term loans of archaeological objects of significant interest to American museums for public exhibition, education, and research purposes, promoting the exchange of students and professionals in such fields as archaeology, art history, conservation, museum curatorial practices, and cultural heritage management between appropriate Chinese and US institutions, as well as facilitating the granting of permits for Americans to conduct archaeological research in China.[16]

As we see, the measures adopted by the MOU aim at specifying the basic framework provided by the 1970 Convention. There are more requirements for the US as a principal market nation to provide various assistances to China in the field of protection of cultural heritage. In return, Chinese cultural heritage is required to be more accessible to the American public, museums, and archaeological institutions.

14 *See* MOU arts. II(B)–(F), (J).
15 MOU arts. II(E), (H).
16 *See* MOU art. II(G).

IV. Positive Impact on Protection of Chinese Cultural Heritage by the MOU

People of all walks of life in China have praised the signing of the MOU. The prevailing views are reflected in the following comments from a leading newspaper column: 'The U.S.A. will help China keep a watchful eye on its cultural objects that would illegally export from China'; 'It will be the end of smuggling undercurrent of cultural objects'.[17] On 11 March 2011, the US Immigration and Customs Enforcement (ICE) officials returned over fourteen pieces of invaluable ancient artefacts to China, which were seized by law enforcement officers from illicit traffickers according to the MOU. This was warmly received by the Chinese people. Indeed, the MOU has already exerted a positive impact on the protection of Chinese cultural heritage, especially in preventing illicit excavation and traffic of cultural objects in China.

A. Promote the Improvement of Chinese Laws and Regulations on Cultural Heritage

In the course of negotiations with the US, China improved its domestic legal environment for protection of cultural heritage, revised and improved its current laws and regulations to live up to the four standards required by the USCPIA. In 2006, the State Council and the Ministry of Culture successively promulgated the Regulation for Protection of the Great Wall and the Management Regulation for Protection of World Cultural Heritage, thus strengthening the protection of large cultural heritage sites and world cultural heritage. In 2007 the Ministry of Culture and the State Administration of Cultural Heritage successively revised the Management Regulation for Examination and Approval for Cultural Objects to Import and Export and the Standards for Examination and Approval for Cultural Objects to Import and Export, both of which considerably revised the 'age' restriction on export of Chinese cultural objects. The previous date used to determine antiquities prohibited for export was older than 1795 (the 60th year of the reign of Emperor Qianlong). Now the new cut-off date is any item older than 1911.[18] This revised guideline has significantly enhanced the protection of cultural objects. In August 2009 the Ministry of Culture promulgated the Interim Management Regulation for Confirmation of Cultural Relics, which standardizes the procedure, public participation, and means of confirmation of cultural relics. The universally applied recording system for cultural objects was also introduced. In this way protection of cultural heritage became more open

[17] Li Yun, 'The United States of America Will Help China "Keep a Watchful Eye" on Cultural Objects that Would Illegally Export from China', *Guangming Daily*, 19 Jan. 2009.

[18] *See earlier* note 11.

and more transparent. Although the development and improvement of cultural heritage law itself is imperative on the part of Chinese society and not solely the requirement of the US, the negotiations and signing of the MOU objectively plays a role in giving great impetus to the improvement of China's relevant legal environment.

B. Promote the Reform in China's Management System of Cultural Heritage

Management of cultural heritage in China mainly counts on its administrative departments related to cultural heritage and governmental protection and collecting agencies of cultural heritage. As the national competent administration on cultural heritage, the State Administration of Cultural Heritage only has the authority of giving guidance over protection, collection, and management affairs of cultural heritage to local administrative organs of cultural heritage and corresponding agencies. Their personnel, financial affairs, and daily management are under the leadership of local governments. That is why there is obvious difference in the management and protection of cultural heritage between localities. As localities have different understandings of the relationship between protection of cultural heritage and social development, there is a great difference in how much protection they attach to cultural heritage. Owing to stupidity and corruption of some local leaders, a large number of important cultural objects have been seriously damaged. However, since the signing of the MOU, the situation has substantially improved.

First of all, vertical management of cultural heritage has been strengthened. A direct example of this is that a notable change has taken place in the position of examination and approval agencies for cultural objects to import and export. There used to be seventeen identification stations in seventeen provinces (or municipalities directly under the central government). While their fundamental function was to identify cultural objects to export from China authorized by the State Administration of Cultural Heritage, these institutions remained attached to local administrative organs of cultural objects. There was no guarantee for the proper personnel, budget for expenditure, nor even specification of responsibility. With the revision of the Law for Protection of Cultural Relics in 2002, in accordance with the requirements of the 1970 Convention, the examination and approval system of cultural objects was introduced for their import to and export from China. There are clear stipulations in the Management Regulation for Examination and Approval for Cultural Objects to Import and Export (2007) for the position, qualification, and responsibilities of examining and approving agencies for cultural objects. Thereafter, the original identifying stations changed into independent state agencies for cultural objects to import and export. Jointly founded by the State Administration of Cultural Heritage and provincial governments, they examine and approve cultural objects applied for export from China according to law and issue permits to cultural objects that are qualified for leaving China. Going from 'identification' to 'examination and approval' is in fact a transition from the function of technological management to that of administrative management.[19] The original stations only had the function of identification of cultural objects. Now identification, examination, and approval functions are combined. The agencies now perform administrative roles of law enforcement on cultural objects, which is more instrumental to the management and security of cultural objects. There are two other examples of embodying the reform to achieve vertical management. One is the State Protection Bases for Underwater Cultural Heritage jointly established by the State Administration of Cultural Heritage and local governments in Ningbo, Qingdao and Wuhan City. The other is the National Information Center on Combating Crimes against Cultural Objects jointly set up in Xian City by the State Administration of Cultural Heritage and the Ministry of Public Security.

Furthermore, cooperation and coordination with other governmental departments pertaining to the guarantee of security of cultural heritage have been strengthened. Management and protection of cultural heritage require sophisticated professional skills and strong comprehensive coordination. All-round and effective protection cannot be achieved by only relying on cultural heritage-related organs or protection institutions. To achieve security of national cultural heritage under a unified and coordinated plan and give a fast and effective blow to crimes against cultural objects, in May 2010 the State Council approved the establishment of a system of Inter-Ministry Joint Conference for Security of National Cultural Objects, which involves nine ministries and committees including the Ministry of Public Security, the Ministry of Land and Resources, the Ministry of Environmental Protection, the Ministry of Housing and Urban-Rural Development, the General Administration of Customs, the State Administration for Industry and Commerce, the National Tourism Administration, the State Administration of Religious Affairs, and the State Administration of Cultural Heritage. They have a clear division of responsibility[20] and together combat criminal activities of stealing, excavations, reselling, and smuggling of cultural objects so as to achieve better security of cultural objects.

[19] *See* Shan Jixiang (Director-General of the State Administration of Cultural Heritage), 'The Replies to Journalists about the Promulgation of Management Regulation for Examination and Approval for Cultural Objects to Import and Export and the Standards for Examination and Approval for Cultural Objects to Import and Export', 8 *The World of Cultural Objects* (2007), at 1.

[20] Responsibility of Member Units of National Inter-Ministry Joint Conference for Security of Cultural Objects, *available at* the Website of the State Administration of Cultural Heritage, <http://www.sach.gov.cn/tabid/294/InfoID/29119/Default.aspx> (last accessed 25 December 2011).

C. Promote China's Progress in Combating Crimes against Cultural Objects

The criminal law of China has always imposed severe penalties on crimes of stealing, robbing, smuggling, and illegally transferring cultural objects and illicit excavations of ancient cultural sites and tombs. The death penalty could be imposed on three crimes before the 8th Amendment to the Criminal Law went into effect.[21] Even though penalties are severe enough, as offenders are profit-driven and there is lack of good management in quite a number of localities and absence of strict law enforcement, crimes of stealing, illicit excavation, smuggling, and illicit trafficking of cultural objects have occurred time and again. In recent years, the tendency in that direction has been worsening; criminal offenders are more professional, more violent, and have access to more intelligence.

In order to control the spread of crimes against cultural objects, from December 2009 to June 2010 the Ministry of Public Security and the State Administration of Cultural Heritage jointly conducted a 'Special Campaign to Combat Crimes against Cultural Objects in Key Areas' in nine Provinces in mid-west China, where crimes of illicit excavation were most rampant. Combat measures with a focus on crimes against cultural objects in key areas, crimes of stealing and illicit excavation of cultural objects in particular, acquired remarkable results. The high rate of crimes against cultural objects was effectively reduced and the chaotic situation of management over cultural objects rectified. The rate of crimes against cultural objects in 2010 dropped considerably as against 2009. According to the statistics of the Ministry of Public Security, there were 973 criminal cases on cultural objects of various types throughout the country in 2010, of which there were 387 cases of theft of cultural objects, and 451 cases of illicit excavations of ancient tombs. Compared with results from 2009, the rates dropped by 12 per cent, 21 per cent, and 18 per cent, respectively.[22]

However, the situation of security of cultural objects remains grim, especially after the 8th Amendment to the Criminal Law became effective with abolition of the death penalty for crimes against cultural objects. The undertaking of protection

[21] According to the criminal law of 1997, the criminals committing smuggling of cultural objects, illicit excavations of ancient cultural sites and ancient tombs, illicit excavations of ancient human fossils and ancient vertebrate fossils could be put to death. Although stealing of cultural objects is not an independent crime, if it were serious enough, the death penalty could be applied to it. Therefore, actually there were four crimes related to cultural objects that deserved capital punishment; the 8th Amendment to the Criminal Law which became effective on 1 May 2011 changes the sternest death punishment on these crimes to life imprisonment.

[22] Li Yun, '2011 Special Campaign against Cultural Objects Crimes Starts in May', *available at* the website of the State Cultural Objects, <http://www.sach.gov.cn/tabid/294/InfoID/29119/Default.aspx> (last accessed 25 December 2011).

of cultural objects is faced with a serious challenge. A number of experts are worried about the impact on security of cultural objects.[23] In order to consolidate the fruits of the first combat campaign and alleviate the impact of abolition of capital punishment for crimes against cultural objects, in May 2011 the Ministry of Public Security and the State Administration of Cultural Heritage jointly launched the 'Special Campaign of 2011 to Combat Crimes against Cultural Objects'. Compared with the first special campaign, the second covered more areas, which occupy half of the land area of China.

In addition, the mechanism for preventing and controlling crimes against cultural objects has gradually improved. On 13 May 2011, the National Information Center on Combating Crimes against Cultural Objects was set up in Xi'an City. The main tasks of the center are collecting, pooling, sorting out, analysing, and studying nation-wide information pertaining to crimes against cultural objects. Thereafter, it submits regular reports regarding the situation, providing support of information and technology to nationwide combat of crimes against cultural objects.[24]

Concentrated combat of crimes against cultural objects is a necessary measure adopted by China, because it is determined to curb serious cases of theft, illicit excavation, and smuggling of cultural objects, but a venture of such magnitude was interrelated with the Sino–US MOU. After it was signed, two highly placed Chinese leaders gave instructions immediately that more bilateral agreements should be signed in a planned way to preserve cultural objects and to deter the illegal export of cultural objects that led to the permament loss of them to China. To implement the instruction of top leaders, in April of 2009, eight relevant ministries and committees including the State Administration of Cultural Heritage, Ministry of Foreign Affairs, Ministry of Finance, and General Administration of Customs held a coordination meeting to implement the Sino–US MOU. As the leader of Ministry of Public Security said:

> [F]or the purpose of further guarding against and combating crimes of theft and illicit excavation, promoting the signing of bilateral agreements with more countries and demonstrating the firm confidence of China in preserving cultural heritage of mankind, the Ministry of Public Security and the State Administration of Cultural Heritage decided

[23] About fifty representatives from archaeological research institutes throughout the country who attended the '2010 Academic Seminar for Archaeology and Protection of Large-Size Sites' organized by the Chinese Society of Archaeology jointly put forward a Letter of Appeal to Put Off Rescinding the Capital Punishment on Excavation of Ancient Cultural Sites and Ancient Tombs. Experts claimed that in less than one month after the 8th Amendment to Criminal Law (Draft) was promulgated, crimes against cultural relics were generally on the rise. The serious criminal cases of grave robbers in Suizhou, Hubei Province, frenziedly attacked staff members for preservation of cultural objects and those in Chencheng, Shanxi Province, broke into a police substation. *Available at* <http://www.ieshu.com/News/deital/4afa2aea8aa76eddf65a3b2c12a8f5f6.html> (last accessed 25 December 2011).

[24] Xinhua News, 'The National Information Center on Combating Crimes against Cultural Objects was Set up in Xi'an City', *available at* <http://www.sach.gov.cn/tabid/294/InfoID/29105/Default.aspx> (last accessed 29 December 2011).

that from December this year to the end of June next year public-security organs and cultural-relics management organs will jointly launch a special campaign to combat crimes against cultural objects in key areas.[25]

It can be seen that to a great extent the signing of the MOU has fortified China's confidence in combating crimes of illicit excavation and smuggling of cultural objects and directly promoted the launch of special campaigns for two consecutive years combating crimes against cultural objects in key areas throughout China.

D. Put an End to the Channel of Purchasing Looted Cultural Objects to Chinese Museums

Quite a number of well-known museums in the world have had the inglorious experience of purchasing cultural objects of unknown origins. With the development of international human rights law, the international community gradually became aware of the importance of cultural heritage to the community's cultural confirmation of its creators and their descendants. Not to purchase cultural objects of unknown origins or that were illegally transferred has become a basic moral standard for professionals of museums all over the world,[26] while preventing domestic museums or other similar institutions from purchasing illicitly exported cultural properties from another state party to the 1970 Convention became one of the basic obligations of the state parties.[27] However, there are frequent occurrences of purchasing cultural objects of unknown origin by museums or similar public collecting institutions. For this purpose, the MOU requires American museums not to acquire restricted archaeological objects of this kind originally 'looted and illegally exported from mainland China to destinations abroad, unless the seller or donor provides evidence of legal export from China or verifiable documentation that the item left Mainland China prior to the imposition of U.S. import restrictions'.[28] Museums and other public collecting institutions in mainland China are also required not to purchase cultural objects of this kind.[29]

In China, public collecting institutions once took purchasing cultural objects looted and illegally exported from China as an important means to achieving their recovery, and they even directly attended auctions to buy them back at high cost, which was regarded as a 'patriotic act'. In the last two years, people of all walks of life in China have had the opportunity to reflect on this so-called 'patriotic act'. Many of them have become aware that at international auctions, the prices of

[25] *See* the website of the State Administration of Cultural Heritage, <http://zfdc.sach.gov.cn/Html/39/485_1.html> (last accessed 10 July 2011, no longer available).

[26] ICOM Code of Ethics for Museums arts. 2.1–2.4 (2004).

[27] 1970 Convention art. 7(a).

[28] MOU art. II(J).

[29] MOU art. II(J).

Chinese cultural objects are rocketing simply because international speculators are utilizing Chinese people's patriotic zeal. Purchasing cultural objects looted and illegally exported from China is equal to 'being robbed for the second time'. In particular, when the negotiation for the Sino–US MOU entered the final stage in October 2008, Christie's in France decided to put on auction two bronzed animal heads plundered from Yuanmingyuan (the Old Summer Palace) in the second Opium War. In response to this, the Chinese government expressed its intense disapproval of the purchase of Chinese cultural objects that have been looted from China. This changed the orientation of Chinese media covering such purchases. After the MOU was concluded, the Chinese government's view became clearer. Asked by a journalist about the significance of the MOU, the director of the State Administration of Cultural Heritage gave a definite reply that purchasing stolen cultural objects and those that have been illicitly taken from China is an act that gives the nod to unlawful excavations and smuggling. He emphasized that museums in mainland China are not allowed to purchase Chinese cultural objects that have been illegally obtained.[30]

E. Promote the Further Development of International Cooperation

The signing of the MOU means that the largest market country in the world is willing to act in concert in deterring the channeling of illicit traffic of cultural objects. Nevertheless, this is far from enough, because the US is simply one of the numerous markets. As required by the MOU:

> [I]n order for United States import restrictions to be most successful in thwarting pillage, the Government of the People's Republic of China shall endeavor to strengthen regional cooperation within Asia for the protection of cultural patrimony; and, in the effort to deter further pillage in China, shall seek increased cooperation from other importing nations to restrict the import of looted archaeological material originating in China.[31]

The state leaders of China have more than once proposed to continue to urge other nations and regions to sign this kind of memorandum. According to the MOU and the requirements of Chinese leaders, China sped up bilateral negotiations with relevant countries on the prevention of theft and illicit exportation of cultural objects. After the signing of the Sino–US MOU, China had signed bilateral agreements or MOUs with governments of Turkey, Ethiopia, Australia, and Egypt.[32]

[30] Luo Haolin, 'The State Administration of Cultural Heritage Is Against Buying Back Bronze Animal Heads Plundered from Yuanmingyuan', *Beijing Youth*, 6 Feb. 2009.

[31] MOU art. II(L).

[32] Up to the end of 2010, China has signed bilateral agreements or MOUs on preventing illicit traffic of Cultural objects with Peru, Italy, India, Philippines, Greece, Chile, Cyprus, Venezuela, the US, Turkey, Ethiopia, Australia, and Egypt.

In order to prevent and deter more effectively the illicit traffic of cultural objects, apart from active cooperation with relevant countries, it is essential to cooperate closely with the International Council of Museums (ICOM), the International Criminal Police Organization (INTERPOL), and other relevant organizations. On 9 November 2010, ICOM formally made known to the world the *Red List of Chinese Objects at Risk* both in Chinese and English. The list covers thirteen categories of the cultural objects protected by Chinese law. Cultural objects of each category are illustrated with typical textures, forms, craftsmanship and photos or pictures. This list is not a list of lost cultural objects and it does not cover all cultural objects under protection by Chinese law; it is simply a list of categories of cultural objects that are typically vulnerable to threats of illicit traffic. It aims at helping staff members of customs, police offices, museums, management departments of cultural heritage, and collectors of cultural objects identify cultural objects that are protected by international laws and Chinese law and are vulnerable to being stolen, illicitly excavated, and smuggled.

V. Conclusion

As there are quite a number of clauses that support and urge China to protect cultural heritage and prevent illicit traffic of cultural objects in the MOU itself, China is ready to take the MOU as a chance to improve the mechanism for preservation of cultural objects, strengthen combating crimes against cultural objects and present to the world an active image of a country with an open-door policy. In the past year, the MOU has had a positive and deep impact on China's protection of cultural heritage. However, the effects of the MOU in China are far from satisfactory. For example, both Japan and South Korea, which are close neighbors of China, are destinations and transfer stations of cultural objects stolen and illegally exported from China. Signing bilateral agreements with Japan and South Korea on preventing the stealing and illicit traffic of cultural objects should be one of the important tasks. Unfortunately, so far the task has not been fulfilled. Besides, Article II(F)of the MOU clearly requires the Chinese government to make every effort to stop archaeological material looted or stolen from the Inland from entering Hong Kong and Macao Special Administrative Regions with the goal of eliminating the illicit trade in these regions. However, owing to the basic policy of '*One Country, Two Systems*', it is difficult to achieve compatibility of the stern examination and approval regulations of mainland China and the policy for free trade practised by Hong Kong and Macao. The central government also finds it difficult to produce an essential impact on changing its free-trade policy towards cultural objects. Furthermore, special campaigns of combating crimes against cultural objects may reduce the crime rate for a short period of time, but if they cannot become a conscious act of governments of all levels and the society as a whole, 'dying embers may flare up again'. The theft that happened at the Palace Museum on 8 May 2011[33] illustrated the poor security measures taken by Chinese museums. In addition, another basic requirement in the MOU refers to straightening out the management order of cultural objects markets, which is of great importance in the attempt to stop the easy disposal of stolen cultural objects, but there are still loopholes in the management of markets. Authentic and fake cultural objects of various kinds can be seen in antiquity markets and second-hand markets without any means of control or regulation. All this is to a certain extent the outcome of the complex environment of cultural heritage preservation in China. It also has to do with the poor awareness of cultural heritage protection of the relevant government sectors and their staff members, and weak law enforcement as well.

Of course, in the eyes of some Chinese experts, the Sino–US MOU is not perfect. Some of them pointed out that the import restricted Chinese cultural objects to those within the scope of the 'designated list' of the American government and with a history of over 250 years as a prerequisite, which is apparently too limited compared to the scope of cultural objects under Chinese law. The fact that the MOU must be renewed every five years affects the stability of long-term implementation and that it has no retroactive force is detrimental to the return of Chinese cultural objects that have left China unlawfully.[34] There is indeed much room for improvement. However, the MOU is a result of all-round consideration and balance of two countries' own national interests. We cannot expect the US to protect Chinese cultural objects despite its own interests and legal basis. It is by 'keeping a watchful eye on one's own door' that will protect China's enormous cultural heritage, and will curb the stealing and illicit traffic of Chinese cultural objects.

[33] On the evening of 8 May 2011, an inexperienced thief slipped into the Palace Museum and easily stole nine pieces on exhibit in a Hong Kong Private Treasures Display that was exhibited temporarily at the museum. This caused a great deal of public concern about the museum's security, or rather lack thereof.

[34] Gao Sheng, 'New Development of Sino-U.S. Bilateral Cooperation in Protection of Cultural Objects—From the Angle of U.S. Restrictions on Importation of Chinese Cultural Objects', 12 *Rev. of Int'l L. of Wuhan Univ.* (2010) at 85–6.

Index

Act of State doctrine, 79, 84, 85
Admiralty law, 3, 126, 129, 140, 146, 147, 149, 212
African Commission on Human and Peoples' Rights, 62
American Association of Museum Directors (AAMD), 152, 208, 211, 215, 232, 235, 236
American Association of Museums (AAM), 204, 211, 215, 228, 231, 232, 233, 235, 236
***Amicus curiae*,** 137, 139, 146
Armed conflict, 13, 20, 22, 26, 27, 38, 40, 41, 43, 47, 48, 56, 58, 60, 63, 68–73, 80, 92, 108, 181, 184

Belligerent occupation, 38, 181

Carabinieri Tutela Patrimonio Culturale, 3, 69, 70, 74–76, 217
Collectors, 11, 21, 65, 67, 74, 91, 112, 119, 120, 151, 162, 163, 164, 187, 188, 196, 207, 208, 209, 210, 225, 229–239, 254
Common good, 2, 125, 135
Common heritage, 16, 20, 27, 57, 135, 143, 212, 243
Compensation, 14, 19, 26, 30, 88, 98, 107, 143, 146, 147, 182, 212, 242
Cooperation, international, 5, 9, 15, 148, 183, 218, 234, 239, 240, 241, 242–243, 249, 253–254
Council of Europe, 11, 29, 45, 46, 204
Crimes against cultural heritage, 40–44, 58, 59, 241, 249, 250–252, 254
Crimes against humanity/war crimes/ international crimes, 13, 14, 17, 29, 41, 42, 43, 50, 51, 59, 62, 63, 92, *see also*; International criminal law
Cultural
  destruction, 2, 3, 13, 29, 40, 41–63, 181, 213
  diversity, 16, 28, 58
  expressions, 2, 10, 11, 21
  heritage, 1–5, 9–13, 16–25, 27, 28, 29, 31, 32, 33, 35, 39, 40–64, 79. 80, 81, 85, 86, 93, 94, 96, 97, 98, 99, 102, 108, 117, 118, 119–121, 124, 125–149, 164, 173, 177–205, 206–214, 226, 227, 228, 229, 237, 239, 242, 243, 245–249, 251–255
  identity, 3, 54, 57, 132
  intangible heritage, 1, 12, 16
  outstanding universal value, 15, 56
  patrimony, 2, 3, 11, 18, 25, 27, 32, 33, 35, 69, 81, 229, 242, 253
  property, 1, 2, 3, 4, 9, 10–12, 13, 14, 17, 18, 20, 21, 24, 29, 30, 31, 32, 33, 35, 37, 38, 41, 43, 44, 47, 48, 49, 51, 55, 68, 70, 72, 73, 74, 75, 79–108, 117, 126, 127, 132, 136, 165, 167, 168, 181, 182, 185, 192, 213, 220, 231, 237, 242, 243
  rights, 3, 12, 18, 23, 28, 31, 39, 64, 108, 131, 141
  underwater, 16, 94, 125–149, 183, 245, 249
Culture, 16, 20, 22, 32, 39, 40, 44, 50, 53, 55, 56, 57, 59, 64, 93, 108, 125, 137, 177, 178, 195, 196, 203, 204, 210, 222, 224, 226, 239, 243, 244
Customary/custom/general international law, 3, 29, 47, 48, 55, 56, 80, 81, 86, 92, 94, 95, 97, 99, 100, 125, 129, 134, 142, 143, 147, 140, 157, 184, 197, 212, *see also* Immunity, Restitution/return/ repatriation

Dispute settlement/resolution, 2, 17, 18, 20, 21, 90, 177–205
  alternative means of, 2, 90, 109, 177, 178, 187, 191, 205
  arbitration, 2, 4, 5, 18, 20, 34, 38, 95, 98, 109, 185, 186, 187, 192–194, 195, 196, 204
  conciliation, 185, 186, 192
  litigation, 4, 5, 88, 101, 102, 103, 104, 105, 109, 119, 160, 167, 168, 169, 177, 178, 180, 186, 187–188, 189, 194, 195, 196, 220, 221, 231
  mediation, 4, 185, 186, 190–192, 195, 196
  negotiation, 2, 4, 20, 186, 188–190, 192, 195, 196, 212, 218, 241, 244, 247, 248, 253
Draft Code of Crimes against the Peace and Security of Mankind, 54
Draft International Convention on the Repatriation of Objects of Artistic, Historical or Scientific Interest which Have Been Lost or Stolen or Unlawfully Alienated or Exported, 38

Ethical codes/guidelines/standards, 5, 75, 151, 204, 228, 230–237
European Court of Human Rights (ECtHR), 18, 104
European Union (EU), 38, 160
Exhaustion of domestic remedies, 89, 90
Expropriation, 3, 19, 37, 83, 86–92, 100, 103–108, 119, 120, 198
Extraordinary Chambers in the Courts of Cambodia, 43, 58, 59

Federal Bureau of Investigation (FBI) Art Crime Team, 173, 219, 224, 225
Forfeiture, 111, 112, 150, 156, 158, 159, 165–166, 167, 168, 169, 170, 171, 174, 189, 212, 218, 219, 220

Genocide, 17, 53, 54, 55, 57, 59
Good faith (*bonne foi*), 4, 25, 35, 91, 132, 147, 153, 160, 161, 180, 182, 194, 202

Holocaust, 15, 168, 188, 191, 193, 198, 204
Human remains, 67, 69, 73, 155, 191
Human rights, 1, 12, 13, 16, 17, 23, 24, 29, 31, 38, 53, 62, 81, 100–103, 104, 108, 109, 117, 252, *see also* European Court of Human Rights (ECtHR)

Illicit trade/traffic, 2, 5, 14, 65–76, 94, 102, 103, 110, 118, 120, 121, 129, 131, 150, 151, 157–160, 162, 163, 175, 177, 179, 180, 181, 182, 187, 194, 199, 206–227, 237, 240–255
Immunity, 3, 4, 20, 80, 109, 129, 130, 137, 138, 139, 180, 194, 198, 199, 201
  from execution/seizure, 3, 79, 80, 81, 89, 92–108, 180
  from jurisdiction, 70, 80, 81–92
Indigenous peoples/communities, 12, 16, 17, 18, 20, 22, 185, 186, 221, 222
Inter-American Court of Human Rights, 18
International Centre for Settlement of Investment Disputes (ICSID), 19
International community, 15, 16, 28, 29, 31, 32, 37, 38, 41, 52, 55, 56, 57, 58, 59, 61, 62, 125, 135, 178, 203, 241, 252
International Council of Museums (ICOM), 204, 205, 232, 233, 235, 254
International Court of Justice (ICJ), 17, 38, 55, 57, 80, 90, 92, 93, 100, 185, 187
International Criminal Court (ICC), 13, 41, 43, 56, 58, 59, 62, 63
International criminal law, 2, 13, 47
International Criminal Tribunal for the Former Yugoslavia (ICTY), 41, 43, 44–59, 63
International humanitarian law, 13, 23, 24, 38, 52, 53, 62, 100
International Institute for the Unification of Private Law (UNIDROIT), 182
International Law Commission (ILC), 50, 54
International organizations, 41, 205
INTERPOL, 219, 254
Investments, 1, 17, 19, 98, 122, 246

Jus cogens, 100

Lex rei sitae rule, 180
Local community, 68, 69, 70, 71, 72, 74, 226
Looting/pillage/plunder, 3, 4, 5, 15, 20, 25, 29, 42, 48, 49, 67, 68–75, 87, 102, 119, 131, 148, 150–153, 174, 177, 180, 181, 183, 184, 189, 198, 206, 207, 210, 211, 212, 214, 216, 220, 221, 222–227, 231, 233, 236, 237, 239, 241–243, 245, 253

Memorandum of Understanding (MOU), 5, 20, 158, 240–255
Military necessity, 3, 43, 48, 50
Mixed criminal courts, 2, 40–64
Museum(s), 2, 5, 11, 12, 20, 21, 32, 66, 68, 69, 70, 73–75, 79, 81, 83, 84, 85, 88, 89, 91, 93, 98, 101, 102, 104, 105, 117, 119, 121, 127, 129, 132, 134, 151, 152, 163, 169, 182, 187, 188, 189, 190, 193, 195, 204, 207, 208–220, 228–239, 241, 242, 244, 246–253, 254, 255
  encyclopedic, 229, 237, 239

Non-governmental organizations, 74, 142, 204
North American Free Trade Agreement (NAFTA), 19

Ownership, 3, 4, 14, 37, 58, 82, 85, 86, 103, 119, 120, 122, 123, 124, 126, 132, 152, 153, 154, 155, 160, 161, 162, 167, 168, 170, 171, 174, 179, 180, 181, 191, 198, 199, 200, 209, 211, 215, 221, 229, 233, 234, 235, 238, 239

Peace treaties, 2, 23–39
Permanent Court of International Justice (PCIJ), 38
Persecution, 20, 29, 49, 50, 51, 56, 59, 64, 87
Possession, 3, 18, 32, 34, 35, 82, 108, 110, 119, 124, 133, 138, 139, 153, 154, 186, 188, 192, 199, 200, 202, 209, 211, 212, 238
Pre-emption, right of, 18, 127

Private international law/choice-of-law/conflict of laws, 2, 13, 113–115, 146, 180, 197
Property rights, 4, 12, 18, 67, 88, 119–124, 125, 126, 131–133, 135, 141, 144, 145, 146, 148, 225
Public goods/interest/policy, 2, 11, 14, 18, 104, 113, 116, 117, 123, 145, 146, 178, 200, 203–205

Remedies, 24, 26, 29–31, 38, 89, 90, 159, 187, 220
Reparation, 23–27, 33, 38, 104, 181, 184
Replevin action, 156, 160–162, 167, 168, 169, 174, 218
Responsibility, 21, 42, 61, 72, 76, 104, 208, 212, 223, 248, *see also* State
  individual criminal, 2, 13, 42, 181
Restitution/return/repatriation, 2, 3, 4, 5, 11, 14, 15, 17, 20, 23–39, 71, 72, 73, 74, 75, 79, 80, 81, 83, 84, 85, 86, 87, 89, 91, 94, 99, 103, 104, 105, 107, 108, 109, 110, 111, 112, 113, 117, 119–124, 131, 134, 147, 151, 157, 159, 160, 161, 165, 167, 168, 171, 173, 174, 177, 178, 181, 182, 184, 185, 186, 187, 188, 190, 191, 192, 194, 197, 198, 202, 203, 205, 207, 209, 210, 211, 212, 216–222, 226, 228, 229, 230, 231, 233, 235, 236, 238, 239, 242, 246, 247, 255
  restitution in kind, 25, 26

Salvage, law of, 201
Sea, law of the, 126, 129, 130, 134, 136, 140, 144, 147, 149
  Area, 135, 143, 144
  contiguous zone, 133, 134
  continental shelf, 3, 133, 134
  Exclusive Economic Zone (EEZ), 133
  flag State, 129–130
  international deep seabed, 135, 140, 143
  international waters, 138, 200, 201
  territorial waters, 136, 138, 141, 201
Seizure, 47, 56, 80, 81, 94, 98, 99, 104, 107, 112, 120, 127, 134, 180
Soft-law, 1, 9
State,
  immunity, 3, 4, 79–109, 137, 138, 139, 194, 199
  jurisdiction, 17, 43, 47, 113, 114, 129, 133, 135, 138, 140, 141, 142, 173, 180, 183, 193, 198, 211
  of origin, 3, 126–131, 136, 137, 139, 141, 142, 144, 145, 193, 203
  property, 55–57, 120, 138
  responsibility, 13, 25, 91
  sovereignty, 3, 15, 16, 114, 115, 116, 124, 129, 133, 134, 135, 138, 139, 141, 146, 148, 193
  succession, 2, 10, 32–37, 38, 82

Theft, 4, 14, 42, 48, 65, 67, 68, 70, 74, 75, 150, 153–157, 167, 168, 169, 179, 181, 182, 187, 194, 198, 199, 206, 207, 209, 210, 212, 217, 220, 222, 224, 226, 227, 239, 250, 251, 253, 254

United Nations (UN), 17, 28, 31, 38, 43, 64, 217
  General Assembly, 213
  Secretary-General, 22
  Security Council, 46, 56, 62, 213
United Nations Educational, Scientific and Cultural Organization (UNESCO), 2, 12, 17, 61, 62, 65, 72, 75, 148, 181, 182, 183, 184, 185, 192, 203, 204, 212, 231
  Intergovernmental Committee for Promoting the Return of Cultural Property to its Countries of Origin or its Restitution in Case of Illicit Appropriation (ICPRCP), 2, 17, 192, 212
  World Heritage List, 15, 18, 52, 57, 60

Warship, 94, 129, 130, 136, 137, 139
World Intellectual Property Organization (WIPO), 1, 204, 205
World Trade Organization (WTO), 1